From Handel to Hendrix

The Composer in the Public Sphere

MICHAEL CHANAN

VERSO

London • New York

First published by Verso 1999
© Michael Chanan 1999
All rights reserved

The moral rights of the author have been asserted

Verso
UK: 6 Meard Street, London W1V 3HR
USA: 180 Varick Street, New York, NY 10014–4606

Verso is the imprint of New Left Books

ISBN 1–85984–706–4

British Library Cataloguing in Publication Data
A catalogue record for this book is available from the British Library

Library of Congress Cataloging-in-Publication Data
A catalog record for this book is available from the Library of Congress

Typeset by SetSystems Ltd, Saffron Walden, Essex
Printed by Biddles Ltd, Guildford and King's Lynn

In memory of
Judith Bromberg

b. Vienna, 1906
d. Tel Aviv, 1998

Contents

Author's Note

This book is the culmination of a project which I began many years ago and which has already seen the publication of two previous volumes, *Musica Practica*, with the subtitle The Social Practice of Western Music from Gregorian Chant to Postmodernism, and *Repeated Takes*, or A Short History of Recording and its Effects on Music. The second of these was a 'spin-off' from the first, intended to plug a gap in the literature on both music and the media in the twentieth century. As such, it provides an essential background to the last three chapters of the present volume, which in general plan, however, is a companion to the first, retelling from a different angle the same history as the latter part of the earlier book. This is reflected in the fact that from time to time I have borrowed sentences or occasionally a paragraph or two from the other two books, where the paths of history join up or cross.

I am grateful to the Media School, LCP, for support while writing the present volume. Thanks also to Glyn Perrin for preparing the music examples, and to him and other friends for encouragement, and, as ever, to P.K.

Michael Chanan
London, June 1999

Prologue

Hendrix Joins the Handel Blue Plaque Band: A First for Guitar Hero

Stuart Millar

Almost unnoticed, the elderly man in the Jimi Hendrix baseball cap, squeezed uncomfortably against the crash bars, wept and smiled. Across the street, the world's media pointed their lenses at the pop stars who turned out to pay tribute to the guitar hero. For the elderly man, it was different: James Al Hendrix was here to remember his son.

Almost three decades after his death, Jimi Hendrix yesterday became the first rock star to be commemorated with a blue heritage plaque. On the wall of his former home at 23 Brook Street, in the heart of Mayfair, the earthenware plaque unveiled by another guitar legend, Pete Townshend, declares: JIMI HENDRIX, 1942–1970, GUITARIST AND SONGWRITER, LIVED HERE 1968–1969.

He may have lived in the house for only a year, but for his father, now seventy-eight, and his stepsister Janie, the occasion marked something of a homecoming. 'We always hoped that they would recognize Jimi and to have that happen in London is very special,' said Ms Hendrix, who manages his estate. 'He loved it here; this is where he was discovered and he had the best times here.'

Hendrix's enduring appeal was underlined by the fans, who turned out in their hundreds. Twenty-something clubbers squeezed against Italian tourists clutching camcorders, while ageing rockers in headbands argued over great guitar solos.

When Hendrix moved into Brook Street with Kathy Etchingham, he was at the height of his fame, about to release his classic third album, *Electric Ladyland*. Thirty years on, he was still causing controversy. Many of the fans were outraged to hear that their hero's father and sister had not been invited to the unveiling, but had merely heard about it while in London to promote a new Hendrix album. 'It's a disgrace,' said Pat Salisbury, who had got there at 12.30 to be sure of a good spot, only to be penned back to make way for the cameras. 'It should be them that are over there posing for pictures beside Jimi's memorial.'

There have also been rumblings of discontent from the occupants of number 25, which carries a blue plaque in remembrance of another great composer who loved to crank up the volume, George Frederick Handel. The Handel Society is reported to be annoyed, claiming that the Hendrix plaque marks a 'dumbing down'. But Townshend was dismissive of such claims. 'Not all performers in pop and rock do deserve this honour, but Jimi does . . . he was so special, so extraordinary, he's up there for me with Miles Davis and Charlie Parker as somebody who was a virtuoso, an innovator. He was different, extraordinary and new.'

The Guardian, 15 September 1997

1

Composer and Public:
Shaping the Question

The origins of bourgeois musical life in the birth of the public sphere

In the twentieth century the figure of the composer in the Western musical tradition has become a problematic and paradoxical one. Endowed with a mysterious gift, the composer is supposed to be the linchpin of living musical culture, the fount of new music; but at the same time, the more dedicated to the mysteries of the art, the more the composer is marginalized from the apparatus of the music industry, and dependent for survival on grants and subsidies of various kinds. As a result, there are very few composers nowadays who devote themselves solely to the exclusive traditions of the opera house, the concert-hall and the recital room. To earn a living as a composer today, you either have to write for films and television, or spend a large part of your time performing or teaching or broadcasting, or even becoming a functionary. But then, of course, the idea that the composer was ever exempt from other activities of these kinds is a historical aberration of rather recent times. Until the nineteenth century the composer was always first and foremost a performing musician, who owed his or her job to an aptitude for providing the right type of music for the right occasion. In the capacity of composer, they usually took charge of musical ensembles as leader or conductor, and often owed their reputation as much to their ability to extemporize as to their written scores; this, of course, sounds much more like the jazz composer of the twentieth century than the so-called classical composer. The loss of these practices as public functions belongs to the nineteenth century. Even then, it has probably never been true except for a small number of composers over the last two centuries.

One of them, Giuseppe Verdi, is described by Isaiah Berlin as 'the last of the great naive masters of western music'[1] – naive, that is, in Schiller's sense, in his essay 'On Naive and Sentimental Poetry' (1795), where he distinguishes two types of artist. Those who are not conscious of any rift between themselves and their milieu, who are happily married to their muse, Schiller calls the naive; while those whose relationship to their muse is turbulent, who no longer experience harmony between their sensibility and its expression because in them the artist has become self-conscious and self-estranged – these he calls the sentimental. Perhaps this once celebrated essay has gone out of currency because both 'naive' and 'sentimental' now have radically different meanings, but the distinction remains present, and nowhere more so than in music, where it has become enshrined in the folklore about the great composers. It is found, for example, in the contrast between two of Schiller's younger contemporaries, Beethoven and Schubert. Clearly Schubert is not naive in any ordinary sense, and in fact he is seen by many as the very epitome of the sentimental, while Beethoven is the forceful, the masculine and the quite unsentimental; but in Schiller's terms it is precisely the other way round: Beethoven, as we know from his composing notebooks, struggled with the notes, drafting and redrafting bar after bar, and indeed pushed constantly at the frontiers of musical language (especially after he found himself going deaf); while Schubert composed with the greatest facility, as eyewitnesses attest, as if the music simply flowed through his pen on to the page; and, famously, if the work was interrupted, he simply abandoned the piece unfinished (and not only in the case of the Eighth Symphony). We shall return to the comparison between Beethoven and Schubert.

Whether Verdi is indeed the last such composer or not, of equal interest is the inversion of the question: the interrogation of the preceding tradition in which he might be said to occupy such a position. For while Schiller's distinction is clearly the product of emergent Romantic sensibilities, what he describes is a difference which, applied retrospectively, defines for us the dimensions of a tradition in which such a distinction becomes meaningful in the first place. The figure of the composer as a named individual who stamps their personality on their music finds its origins in the passage from the late Middle Ages to the early Renaissance. While the general historical factors contributing to this development are shared by other art forms, and a similar question can be asked about the emergence of the painter and the author, in terms of musical history there is an additional element: the emergence of the composer in this period is in certain respects a product of the development of notation in the eleventh and twelfth centuries, which for the first time allows the preservation of a score with a signature on it.

We first encounter the composer on the eve of the Renaissance, in the figure of the supremely gifted instinctive musician like the blind Landini – famed during his lifetime in fourteenth-century Italy for his virtuosity on the portative organ and skill in improvisation, as well as his highly innovatory compositions – for whom notation provided a means of communicating what he heard inside his head. But this is only the beginning of the story. For the sociologist Max Weber, in a study in musicology called *The Rational and Social Foundations of Music*, notation becomes the decisive catalyst in the evolution of European music. Through notation, composition becomes a calculable procedure based on comprehensible principles by which large-scale musical forces in various combinations can be organized in harmonious co-operation, an achievement accomplished precisely through the agency of the composer and the score. Moreover, it is no accident, in Weber's view, that the culture which perfected notation also developed a unique musical idiom, a rational harmonic language in which the fundamental structural unit is the triad – the common chord – and the system of diatonic scales which replaced the medieval modes. Both features – notation and diatonic harmony – are paradigms of the same process of rationalization which Weber finds at the root of modern social development. In short, for Weber there is a certain homology between the evolution of music and that of society, a relationship which is also one of our main interests here.[2]

The type of composer represented by Landini has exemplars in every age – in the twentieth century one might think of Duke Ellington – but in the heat of the Renaissance another kind of consciousness begins to appear. The evolution of the composer into the source of a new sense of subjectivity in music follows the spread of music printing, in a process which changed the social relations of the composer in much the same way as the character of the literary author was changed by general printing. Before the advent of printing, only the fewest copies were made of even the most renowned pieces – not enough to create a commercial trade. Nor could the conditions of formal and professional music-making provide sufficient business for the music printer. When Petrucci became the first person to offer printed sheet music for sale in Venice in the early 1500s, the market which he tapped consisted primarily in non-professional music-lovers: the principal customer was the educated amateur performer. The growth of music publishing thereupon followed the growth of this domestic musical practice, and became its barometer – it is obviously related to the spread of musical literacy – until, in the late eighteenth century, an expanding market, improved music printing technology, and the decline of traditional forms of patronage all promoted the music publisher to a new prominence – with corresponding effects on the composer's sources of income.

If printed music was a new means of reaching an audience, then we discover here the beginnings of a new type of musical public, a public made up of musically active listeners who purchased sheet music in order to perform themselves. This public was increasingly bourgeois. Printing favoured the music for which there was a market, and the market was to be found primarily in the growth in popularity of secular music among the emerging bourgeoisie; the music they purchased was destined for domestic consumption, to be played in locations where performance was free: at home and at social gatherings of various sorts.[3] It was this public, both as domestic consumers and as paying listeners in the concert-hall and opera house, which would nurture the development of the composer as the principal agent in the evolution of musical style, the growing complexity of musical language, and its deepening subjectivity; although the composer would not become fully dependent on this public for a long while yet, and often resented its impersonal demands.

An early paradigm of the new type of composer was Monteverdi, who in 1616 declined to set a short dramatic scene suggested by a patron because, he told him, 'I do not feel that it moves me at all . . . nor do I feel that it carries me in a natural manner.'[4] This expressed desire to be moved in a natural manner makes him, in Schiller's terms, perhaps the first sentimental composer. At any rate, Monteverdi anticipated the entry of music into the public sphere of emergent bourgeois society, as one of the first to demonstrate the possibilities of a transition from the court (in Mantua) to the public (in Venice). The innovations Monteverdi began to introduce in his Fourth Book of Madrigals when he was still at Mantua had provoked the criticism of those who considered themselves – in the phrase of the Italian musicologist Lorenzo Bianconi – guardians of public decency in matters polyphonic. Monteverdi replied in the preface to his Fifth Book where, instead of the *prima pratica* or primary practice defined by the theorist Zarlino, in which the harmony is 'mistress of the words', he advocated a new *seconda pratica*, where 'the words are the mistress of the harmony'. Appointed *maestro di capella* at the Ducal Chapel in Venice, where there was a large musical public beyond the court, Monteverdi could now afford the luxury of printing his Sixth Book of Madrigals (1614) without dedication – without, that is, either patronage or subsidy save the outlay of the publisher, who could be certain of excellent financial returns – and here the change in style – which represents, says Bianconi, 'a breach in the monopoly of the polyphonic madrigal and its esoteric destination' – is indicative of a cultural milieu that was decidedly more modern in outlook than that of the Mantuan court.[5]

With the emergence of a new public, there are corresponding changes in the forms of both musical consumption and musical composition. But as Bianconi observes, 'public' in this context (and from now on) means different things. For a start, it is not homogeneous; it consists, for example, in both private gatherings and – by the end of the seventeenth century – the first paying audiences, entities which involve different patterns of expenditure and entail different relationships with the composer. The former are dispersed, and include both patrons and purchasers of scores; the latter gather in one place to listen to professional musicians *en masse*. These different but overlapping publics encourage different but related forms of music. The courts and cities of the seventeenth century, says Bianconi, saw the abundant use of music for demonstrative purposes on a scale hitherto unknown. On the other hand, 'no less "public", though quite different in kind, is the late-seventeenth-century market – particularly expansive in the northern capitals of London, Paris and Amsterdam – for instrumental chamber music': music for private consumption yet necessarily sustained by a socially conditioned collective taste.[6] In London, for example, Purcell was both the leading musical functionary at court and the arbiter of public preferences: where Purcell led, the market followed. In 1683, he invited subscriptions in the *London Gazette* for an edition of his own trio sonatas, of which he himself was both editor and distributor. The same journal carried announcements of a new series of public musical concerts. The growing market was fertile ground for a variety of entrepreneurial endeavours which clearly prefigured more modern patterns of musical consumption, albeit in embryonic form. As the process develops, opera will move into the public theatre, a new form of concert-giving will appear, and eventually the music publisher replaces the patron of the *ancien régime*. (Soon afterwards, the impresario and the agent will appear on the scene, middlemen who organize the market and function as mediators of musical taste.) This shift, says Jürgen Habermas in his classic study of the public sphere, not only produced a change in the make-up of the public but amounted to the very creation of the public as such, in its modern bourgeois form, and it is seen more clearly in the case of the concert-going public than in that of the reading or even the theatre-going public.

Until the final years of the eighteenth century, the composer was still largely bound to the provision of functional and 'occasional' music, the composition of works for various purposes and occasions, including diversion, which served especially 'to enhance the sanctity and dignity of worship, the glamour of the festivities at court, and the overall splendour of ceremony. Composers were appointed as court, church, or council musicians, and they worked on what was commissioned,' just like writers in the service of patrons and actors in the service of princes.[7] But the new public created new opportunities, first prefigured in the form of the musical clubs established in England, at Oxford and Cambridge, in the 1650s, and the gatherings in the London taverns chronicled by Anthony Wood, Roger North and, of course, Pepys. Such groups were originally made up of gentleman amateurs; North records how 'the masters of music entered and filled the consort, which they carried on directly for mony collected as at other publik enterteinements'.[8]

The credit for the first regular series of public commercial concerts is often given to the London violinist John Banister, who launched them after being dismissed as leader of the King's band for remarking, in the King's hearing, that he thought English violinists better than French. The concerts were held in his own house in Whitefriars in 1672 and advertised in the *London Gazette*, thus drawing on the same coffee-house audience which formed the core of the emergent public sphere, and the readership of the early newspapers. The ensemble at these meetings was the same as the consort favoured by amateurs; some of the players also sang, and much of the music was vocal. When Banister died at the end of the decade, his mantle fell on a music-loving coal merchant. Thomas Britton, known as 'the musical small-coal man', had started a similar weekly music meeting in 1678 in a room above his shop, where Banister's son was one of the players. Initially Britton's meetings were free, but after Banister's death he began to charge a yearly subscription; cash, however, was not yet exchanged at the door. Those who played at Britton's concerts over the years included Thomas Arne, Pepusch (musical arranger of John Gay's *Beggar's Opera*), and, in Britton's last years, Handel. For composers these meetings were an important alternative site of activity, not initially for their earning power but for their unassuming character: their informality and conviviality held a promise not to be found in the decorum of the aristocratic home or the demands of the opera house, and encouraged a new style which, in due course, led to new forms. One could scarcely wish for more striking evidence of the intimate link between aesthetics and the social – in this case, a certain musical style and the emergent bourgeois public sphere – than the lives of Banister and Britton, in whom the origins of the paying concert as the characteristic form of bourgeois musical life are so clearly symbolized: a professional musician booted from the court, and a coal merchant. These new forms of gathering for the purpose of music-making do not mark a sharp break with the aristocratic milieu – on the contrary, in England and elsewhere they are supported by scions of the aristocracy – but, rather, a shift in sensibilities, the emergence of a new attitude towards music as to other art forms, which, in the mid-eighteenth century, will be called by the German philosopher Alexander Gottlieb Baumgarten the domain of aesthetics.

On the Continent, the new institutions of bourgeois musical life took slightly longer to appear. In Italy, music clubs known as Academies became widespread, the first dating from 1690; in Germany the same thing was known as the Collegium Musicum, and was often connected to a university. The first regular concert series in Hamburg was mounted in 1722 and in Paris in 1725. Here, in the public concert, admission for payment turns the musical performance into a commodity (which, like all aesthetic commodities, has certain peculiarities: what is consumed is not a material object but an action, an activity with a symbolic content). Simultaneously there arose a kind of music released from external purpose. As Habermas puts it:

> For the first time an audience gathered to listen to music as such – a public of music lovers to which anyone who was propertied and educated was admitted. Released from its [previous] functions in the service of social representation, art became an object of free choice and of changing preference.[9]

The result, of course, will be that through the evolution of these preferences, music will evolve new forms of social representation – especially, as we shall see, the representation of several new-fashioned varieties of subjectivity, both individual and collective.

On the genesis of music criticism in the age of Handel

The public sphere, according to Habermas, is the social space where public opinion is born out of a process of rational debate. It is a primarily political zone which mediates between society and state, where private individuals come together, independently of existing authorities, to engage in public discussion, to exercise common powers of reasoning over public issues, precisely in order to influence the state, 'to compel public authority to legitimate itself before public opinion'.[10] This process, whose history is different in different countries, is identified with the demand for representative government, a liberal constitution (or, in Britain, constitutional monarchy), civil freedoms before the law. The public sphere thus embodies a potential for participation and emancipation which negated the structures of the absolutist state – although this potential, once the institutions of bourgeois democracy were established, would become a problematic ideal in the face of pressure to extend the rights of citizenship to all.

The public sphere is embedded within the wider public domain, a heterotopic or multidimensional space where the individual, in the course of everyday life and in pursuit of various activities, encounters diverse unknown others, strangers belonging to different social groups and classes whose paths cross more or less at random. The expansion of the public domain, like the growth of the public sphere in Habermas's sense, is a function of urbanization, especially that of capital cities like London and Paris. The growth of the city brings the development of new forms of public sociability: the provision of relaxing urban spaces, often open-air, where social distinctions tended to be disregarded at least enough for the ranks to mingle, ranging from the large urban parks and pleasure gardens, with their tree-lined walks, refreshment booths and bandstands, to the first attempts to make the streets fit for pedestrian strolling as a form of relaxation. According to Richard Sennett in his study of the public domain, these urban amenities were enjoyed by the broadest spectrum of society, 'so that even the labouring classes began to adopt some of the habits of sociability, like promenades in parks, which were formerly the exclusive province of the elite'.[11] Foreign visitors to London were often impressed by the mingling of the ranks in these public spaces. A letter home by Leopold Mozart in the 1760s speaks of walking in St James's Park in London with his children when the King and Queen, for whom Wolfgang had just played in private, came driving by and greeted them. Oddly, Sennett fails to mention the pleasure gardens, which were musically very important sites of activity, especially in broadening access to the most up-to-date styles. Vauxhall in London had been a place of public entertainment since 1660, praised by Evelyn, Pepys and Boswell, where music was particularly prominent, and a shilling admission was low enough for throngs of thousands at a time when a new Handel oratorio was priced at a guinea. For the final open rehearsal of Handel's *Music for the Royal Fireworks* at Vauxhall in 1749, twelve thousand people paid 2s.6d. each. The English were proud of these pleasure gardens. The musical traveller Burney considered an imitation he visited in Paris decidedly inferior.

The political public sphere would sometimes spill out into the parks and larger urban open spaces, above all at moments of social crisis and mass demonstration, but it was not born there. It originates in locations where individuals gather in their capacity as private citizens – not for idle recreation but to inform themselves and take part in open discussion. It took shape, says Habermas, in the coffee houses, clubs, reading and language societies, lending libraries and meeting-houses, which grew up in the course of the eighteenth century along with concert rooms, theatres and opera houses, and where those who gathered provided the readership of the emergent press, for the new public was from the outset a reading public, and the evolution of the public sphere cannot be separated from the growth of the press and its functions; in this sense, we can think of the press as the first instance of a new kind of virtual space which provides a zone of social communication and repository of knowledge and memory. These spaces developed new forms of discourse to facilitate their purposes. Sennett describes the coffee house as a place where speech flourished, and:

> the talk was governed by a cardinal rule: in order for information to be as full as possible, distinctions of rank were temporarily suspended; anyone sitting in the coffee house had a right to talk to anyone else, to enter into any conversation, whether he knew the other people or not, whether he was bidden to speak or not. It was bad form even to touch on the social origins of other persons when talking to them . . . because the free flow of talk might then be impeded.[12]

Outside the coffee house, social rank was of paramount importance. In order, therefore, to gain reliable knowledge and information through talk, the coffee house created the fiction that social distinctions did not exist. If a gentleman sat down here, he was subject to the free, unbidden talk of his social inferior. This situation produced its own speech patterns, reflected in the reports of coffee-house talk by writers like Addison and Steele. In England, says Habermas, quoting a government proclamation from the 1670s, the coffee houses were early considered to be seedbeds of political unrest: 'Men have assumed to themselves a liberty, not only in coffee-houses, but in other places and meetings, both public and private, to censure and defame the proceedings of the State, by speaking evil of things they understand not, and endeavouring to create and nourish an universal jealousie and dissatisfaction in the minds of all His Majesties good subjects.'[13] But the government could not resist the growing pressure of this new kind of public opinion, and censorship in Britain effectively came to an end in 1695, when Parliament declined to renew the Licensing Act which controlled the print trade. In France, the same freedom would not be attained until the Revolution (and was then cancelled by Napoleon); in Germany, it took until the middle of the nineteenth century.

If the primary impetus in the formation of the bourgeois public sphere was political, it had profound implications for the pursuit of art. From the depths of benighted late feudal autocracy, writes Terry Eagleton, arose a vision of a universal order of free, equal, autonomous human subjects, obeying no laws but those they ordained for themselves. With this conception, the emergent bourgeois public sphere breaks decisively with the *ancien régime*, installing the middle classes in image if not yet in reality: 'What is at stake here is nothing less than the production of an entirely new kind of human subject – one which, like the work of art itself, discovers the law in the depths of its own free identity, rather than in some oppressive external power.'[14] Like the work of art as defined by the discourse of aesthetics, the bourgeois subject is autonomous and self-determining, and indeed aesthetics provides a crucial link in the scheme of things, a site where fractured and unequal moieties can be reunited – at least in the writings of thinkers like Kant and Schiller in Germany, or Shaftesbury and Coleridge in England.

The political public sphere is premised on the norms of reasoned debate – the idea, says Habermas, of continuous controversy carried out publicly between arguments and counter-arguments in conditions of equal access without regard (in principle) to social differences or privileges. The same norms were applied to literary and cultural concerns; thus the issues of aesthetic taste came to be mediated by the institution of criticism, which emerged towards the end of the seventeenth century, soon after the appearance of the early press. Here, says Habermas, 'the judgement of a public that had come of age, or at least thought it had, became organised', and a new occupation appeared, that of the literary, art and music critic, who assumed the dual task of serving as both the public's spokesman and their educator.[15] According to a leading music encyclopaedia, music criticism was a haphazard growth, carried on for long periods 'either by musical amateurs . . . or by musicians who were amateurs in all else'; and it ranges 'from press notices and reviews to the elaborate productions of scholarship and the remoter speculations of aesthetic criticism'.[16] What escapes the encyclopædia's attention is the correspondence between the emergence of music criticism, the press in which it appears, and the concert life which succours it, which are all produced in the same movement, the same passage of society from the *ancien régime* to bourgeois democracy – in short, the emergence of the bourgeois public sphere.

In fact it was opera, not concerts, that attracted the first published music criticism – in England, in the pages of *The Spectator* in 1711, when Addison and Steele launched an attack on the Italian *opera seria* presented by the Royal Academy of Music (the opera company, not the music college, which dates from the nineteenth century) at the Haymarket Theatre, where the success of the season was Handel's first work for London, *Rinaldo*. This was not only because opera attracted attention as a more prominent form of public performance than the embryonic concert, but because it belonged to the theatre, to which it had rapidly migrated in the course of displacing the courtly entertainments from which it evolved. Its criticism thus became a province of the literati, who in Hanoverian England formed the cultural vanguard of the Whig supremacy, and were offended by the activities of the Royal Academy in the first place because of the foreign irrelevance of Italian opera. *Rinaldo*, a typical example, was based on an episode in Tasso's *Gerusalemne Liberata* in which the hero is freed from the amorous snares of a sorceress. Four years earlier, Addison, a leading member of the Whig propaganda machine, had written the libretto for an opera in English composed by Thomas Clayton: *Rosamund*, based on the life of Henry II's wretched mistress. His embitterment at its failure lent vehemence to his attack on Handel. A composer, he declares, 'should fit his Musick to the Genius of the People, and consider that the Delicacy of Hearing, and the Taste of Harmony, has been founded upon those Sounds which every Country abounds with: in short, that Musick is of a relative Nature'.[17] Here the ideological subtext of opera is that of an incipient nationalism, which is in no way a fixed and traditional category but, like the public sphere itself, a field of contestation on which the bourgeois nation-state will be built.

It was precisely the exoticism of Italian opera which appealed to the aristocracy, Whig and Tory alike, who constituted its patrons – the same aristocracy who took the Grand Tour to Italy, commissioned their architects to build their houses in the Palladian style, and brought adornments back from the Continent to fill them; several of these gentlemen were Handel's patrons. The kind of opera they wanted was strictly apolitical – although the new middle classes regarded it as foreign popery, and flocked instead to hear it satirized in *The Beggar's Opera* and a host of ballad operas like it. Handel, universally recognized as the most outstanding composer working in London since the death of Purcell, was caught up in this political rivalry as a German and a former court musician to the Hanoverian King, and the Tories preferred to espouse the cause of his rival, Bononcini, as an affront to the dynasty and its chief political agent, Walpole; whereupon the Whigs came to Handel's defence – while the Prince of Wales joined the Bononcini camp out of hatred for his father. One searches in vain, however, for any reflection of these intrigues of the time in the subtexts of Handelian opera, which is designed in the first place, like the Italian model, to satisfy a nostalgia for a bygone age, and therefore employs a quasi-mythological genre far removed from the contemporary political world.

There is, however, another kind of politics associated with the English adoption of Italian opera, the question of what is really hidden behind accusations such as popery; for the term was one of the code-words of the day that served, like 'celibate' and even 'priest', as a pejorative synonym for homosexuality or, in the language of the time, sodomy, 'that utterly confused category', as Foucault called it. What has been suppressed in the conventional reading of Handelian opera is the nexus which linked *opera seria* with the Grand Tour of Italy and the homoerotic appeal of both, which recent scholarship has brought back to light. The cultural historian George Rousseau cites a contemporary account dating from 1729 and entitled 'Reasons for the Growth of Sodomy in England', in which Italy is seen as 'the mother and nurse of sodomy; the place where men kissed each other, where Englishmen first learned the unnatural vices that permitted them to become catamites and pathics (i.e. objects of sport for older and usually richer men); the place where every man could easily procure a sex partner, where every churchman and politician ... could find his Gany-mede ...'. To offer evidence, the author of this diatribe 'pointed to the success in England of Italian opera and the theatre's decline into pantomime'.[18] Handel's life, both public and private, took place, as Gary Thomas puts it, within three milieux which can be identified as the most important private and public spaces occupied by homoerotic men of status and privilege: the urban theatre, the Italian sojourn, and the country retreat of the English nobleman.[19] This association makes the story rather more complicated; the critical question is not whether Handel was homosexual, which cannot be answered, but what kind of significance, if any, this might have for the kind of music he wrote, to which I shall return in a moment.

The Royal Academy was not so much a court opera on the continental model, though the King was the chief patron and contributed a thousand pounds a year, but – as Paul Henry Láng puts it in his monumental study of Handel – like the Metropolitan Opera House in New York before the First World War and income taxes, a plaything for the leaders of society: 'Neither showed the least interest in native art, each wanted the best singers procurable from abroad, and the directors of each felt that since they were footing the bill they had the right to dictate the policies and run the show.'[20] But the expense of mounting a lavish operatic spectacle made its funding highly problematic. In Germany only the richest courts could afford to keep it up. Attempts on the part of commercial cities like Hamburg and Leipzig to establish permanent opera houses similar to the court operas of Dresden or Mannheim broke down before the 1740s, and eager audiences were served for the most part by travelling Italian opera troupes which reached as far as Moscow (where their influence on musical taste was considerable). In Italy itself, opera houses were often run by committees of leading patrons who offloaded the risk on to the impresario. In England, with financial confidence restored by the economic policies of the Whigs, it seemed the obvious thing to do to turn the opera into a business undertaking on commercial principles, with shares divided among a number of patrons; the truth is that the investors were more like the first theatrical angels. When the Royal Academy was launched, in the years of easy money and hazardous financial gambling before the South Sea Bubble, the issue of stock was heavily oversubscribed – and heavily satirized: a journal edited by Richard Steele, *The Theatre*, 'quoted' Royal Academy stocks, sarcastically distorting famous names in the modern-day style of *Private Eye*: 'At the rehearsal on Friday last, Signior Nihilini Beneditti [Nicolini] rose half a Note above his Pitch formerly known. Opera stock from 83 and a half, when he began; at 90 when he ended.'[21]

The problem with opera production is pinpointed by John Rosselli in his study of the Italian opera industry. Limited liability companies in opera management, he says, are a historical freak, because while shareholders were protected from having to pay out losses beyond the amount of their stake, there was precious little hope of attracting dividends.[22] In the eighteenth and nineteenth centuries, a canny, careful and hard-working impresario could make a fair success of it, but only on condition that there was some form of subsidy, endowment or privilege to keep him afloat. A number of leading Italian impresarios depended on the profits from the gambling that went on in their opera houses. In 1805 Domenico Barbaja, a former café waiter and billiards player, made his fortune by introducing a new French invention, the roulette wheel, to the foyers of Milan's La Scala. As the French armies took over Northern Italy after Napoleon's victory at Austerlitz, Barbaja put together a gambling syndicate covering some twenty towns; by the 1820s he was running an opera circuit which included Vienna, where he introduced Rossini. Nothing reveals more clearly than the Italian gambling connection the extent to which opera is the sumptuary art *par excellence*.

When the South Sea Bubble burst in 1720, the Academy's stocks fell with the rest, though the company limped on, with new operas by Handel and others every season, until 1728. Nine years later the famous venture which Handel himself undertook to follow it went bankrupt, and the great composer turned from opera to oratorio. He was able by this means to get round the ban on theatrical entertainment during Lent, and thus to draw a ready audience without fear of competition. Musically, the transformation was a relatively easy one: the oratorio was a sacred drama composed of *tableaux vivants* and the dividing line between the genres was slight, especially when the oratorio was staged. Baroque opera was already static, and its principal components – recitative, aria and ensemble – were basically the same, whether in opera, oratorio, or even the German Passion. Moreover – according to Edward J. Dent, one of the doyens of English music criticism – the dramatic use of the oratorio chorus, which was Handel's special métier, came not from the English Church but from the English lyric theatre.[23] It also belongs to the ethos of the odes and pastorals, and to the sacred and stately anthems which form the bulk of occasional pieces that Handel composed to texts by the leading poets of the day, including Pope and Dryden. Hence the ease with which Handel borrowed musical numbers from his own compositions and inserted them into new contexts. Financially, oratorio made Handel's fortune – at his death in 1759 he left the considerable sum of £20,000 to friends and charities.

The transition from Italian opera to English oratorio also enabled Handel's music to find a broader audience, and it was only then, with the oratorios, years after his naturalization, that he began to become the national composer whom the Victorians venerated above all others a century later. Switching from classical mythology and the heroics of ancient history to heroic stories from the Old Testament like *Saul*, *Solomon*, *Jephtha* and *Judas Maccabaeus* also turned out to be ideologically canny. *Solomon*, for example, with a libretto carefully tailored to eighteenth-century sensibilities, appealed equally to establishment royalists, Christian Nonconformists, and even middle-class Jews. With the price of admission raised to a guinea, the morning after its first performance Handel took £300 in profits to the Bank of England, where he held a personal account. But if Handel's image as an upright English gentleman was nourished by the oratorios, not the operas, which ceased to be performed until the Handel revival of the twentieth century, the question that emerges, especially in the light of the new scholarship about the homoerotic associations of Italian opera, is what and whose ideological interests are served by constructing this image of Handel, and what is suppressed in order to achieve it?

Handel's private life has long been acknowledged by scholars to be something of a mystery. The common view of modern biographers is that although he was a lifelong bachelor, there is no evidence that he was homosexual. Some speculate about secret amours with female opera singers. On the other hand, there is an obscure anecdote in which Handel replies, in answer to a question from the King about 'his love of women' (or, rather, lack of it): 'I have no time for anything but music'. According to one recent scholar, this evasive response is reflected by different modern biographers in various ways through locutions such as 'Handel firmly barred the doors on the subject'; 'as an individual he remains hidden'; he maintained 'an enigmatic aloofness in matters of sex, politics and religion', and so on. On the other hand, says Gary Thomas, the early biographies, published by contemporaries in the years after Handel's death, contain a sprinkling of remarks which allude not to chaste bachelorhood but to homosexuality; in particular, Sir John Hawkins's comment that Handel's 'social affectations were not very strong; and to this it may be imputed that he spent his whole life in a state of celibacy; that he had no female attachments of another kind may be ascribed to a better reason'. This Thomas calls 'a masterpiece of innuendo .... The language certainly indicates that Hawkins "knows something" and wants to communicate that he knows it, but ... he shrinks from naming [it] openly because it cannot be named.'[24]

Thomas establishes that both the milieu of Handel's sojourn in Italy, and the later milieu of his life in London, were constructed around the idea of the Arcadian academy, 'that mythic-pastoral *locus amoenus* (pleasant place) populated by shepherds and shepherdesses [which] has a long and richly established history of homosexual appropriation'.[25] In Rome, where Handel arrived in 1706 at the age of twenty-one, he is linked with the names of the composer Corelli and his patron, Cardinal Ottoboni, with whom the former lived virtually his whole life. Ottoboni ran an establishment which was a smaller and more private version of the original Academy, founded in 1690 for the purpose of cultivating the arts of music and poetry, which had an international membership of men and women of prestige and influence belonging to both the nobility and the Church. Burlington House, Piccadilly, the palatial residence of the young Earl of Burlington, Richard Boyle, where Handel took up residence for three years in 1713, provided a similar milieu, where other residents and visitors included Alexander Pope and John Gay, both of them ' "homosocial" if not homoerotic', as well as the artist William Kent, 'about whom there can be no doubt'.[26] (Pope wrote in a letter to a female confidante of the prospect of a visit to Burlington's country retreat: 'I am to pass three or four days in high luxury, with some company, at my Lord Burlington's. We are to walk, ride, ramble, dine, drink, and lie together. His gardens are delightful, his music ravishing.')[27]

In the light of the composer's extensive and intimate association with demonstrably homosexual men and milieux, Thomas finds it telling that even the most scholarly biographers remain neutral at best about the possibility, let alone likelihood, that Handel too was homosexual. But the critical question, he says, is not 'Was Handel gay?', but 'What is so threatening about a homosexual Handel?' This is to shift the issue away from a question about an individual composer's biography to a problem about the nature of musical expression. If music drama is a plaything of deviant erotic desires and the perversity of polymorphous sexuality, albeit wrapped up in narratives contained by orthodox and uplifting morals, how can its emotional expressivity be trusted?

Handel scholarship, observes Thomas, has both suppressed the historical evidence of a homoerotic Handel and, at the same time, used the very eroticism of opera to deny the possibility that Handel could have expressed a different sexuality. 'We may have no positive proof of Handel's love affairs,' writes Láng, 'but how could a man unacquainted with love compose the wondrous idyll known as the "Nightingale Chorus" from *Solomon*?' Thomas counters that this same logic might have led Láng to wonder how a man unacquainted with the love of men could possibly have composed David's moving lament over Jonathan in *Saul*, or the chorus 'He saw the lovely youth' from *Theodora*. All three examples, by the way, come from oratorios, not operas, thus demonstrating once again the essential continuity between the two.

From this perspective, Handel becomes 'a site of dialectical tensions and relations in culture, with contradictions and connections, consonances and dissonances' around the minefield of sexuality – in short, a 'homotext' called 'Handel'.[28] In this homotextual Handel, the world of *opera seria* becomes something more than the evocation of a nostalgic ideal; it is also a symbolic space where narratives about tragic love provide a vicarious means of expression of forbidden sexual desires. In fact this is not exactly a new perception; the eroticism of opera has always been apparent, and in the eighteenth century the role of the castrato carried inevitable connotations of a third sex, a receptacle for the projection of the secret desires of both the other two. Indeed, on the opera stage all sorts of transvestism is licensed: a woman acting the part of a man disguised as a woman, or a man playing a woman alongside a woman playing a male youth, and so forth.[29] However, to acknowledge the thrill of sexual ambiguity violated the norms of the patriarchal order, thus relegating the vicarious pleasure which its representation provides to the spectator to the same realm of private and secret desire as sexuality itself, thereby reinforcing it; an arrangement which, in accordance with the Freudian economy of the psyche, serves to guard and preserve its potency.

In the present context, the issue of Handel's sexuality also raises a critical question about the nature of the emergent bourgeois cultural sphere, its universal claims and rational norms, and the capacity of these norms to contain divergence – as long as it remains hidden below the surface. Handel's homoeroticism is a pointer to a wider process, namely the advent of homosexuality – though not yet named as such – not as a private aberration but as a profoundly problematic social category. Handel's English career, observes Thomas, coincided with a crucial development in the practice and conception of homosexuality which went beyond the cultivation of a homoerotic subculture among the nobility: the emergence of a new urban phenomenon, that of the molly and the molly house, which provided a certain kind of homoerotic man with a new social identity. Facilitated by the social uprootedness attendant on urbanization, the molly house – which, in this context, we can perceive as a kind of errant relative to the institutions of the public sphere – provided a convivial and anonymous location for homoerotic men to congregate, drink, dress up, and in the back rooms, have sex. This subculture spilled out into the public domain: witness the case of a certain Queen Seraphina, a transvestite who caused a scandal in the Vauxhall Pleasure Gardens in 1732. In short, the molly houses helped to give shape to a subculture which, a hundred and fifty years later, would be categorized and castigated in clinical discourse as 'homosexual' and 'deviant'. If music, seen through this prism, becomes one of the signal sites for the secret expression of homoeroticism, we are bound to ask what this tells us about the kinds of meaning that music carries, and to regard with suspicion any theory of musical expression which is too abstract, too narrow or too normative. But this is a question I shall return to in a later chapter.

Of J.S. Bach and J.A. Scheibe

If criticism of opera originated with the English literati, it is in Germany that we find the first stirrings of something more scholarly – and more strictly musical. There is a curious connection. Addison and *The Spectator* go down in history not only for their enunciation of a protomodern anti-mythological sensibility, but also for their influence on the German musical polymath Johann Mattheson, friend and possibly lover of the young Handel when he first arrived in Hamburg in 1703 at the age of eighteen. Did Handel perhaps send his friend copies of the new journal from London a few years later, with its attacks on his own work? At any rate, Mattheson started bringing out a literary magazine called *Der Vernünftler* ('The Reasoner') in Hamburg in 1713, and he followed it nine years later with the first musical journal proper, *Critica Musica*, devoted partly to translations of general historical and aesthetic items, partly to more local questions of musical taste. During the following decades Germany saw a great burgeoning of musical journals, most of them with a limited life of a season or two, or at most a few years. One writer estimates their number during the course of the century at 500.

These journals are predominantly theoretical, directed by composers and theorists at each other – another magazine publisher was Telemann, a composer who once boasted that he could write in any style – and they belonged to a movement of renovation in musical art much influenced by Handel's melodiousness. In this modern style, the polyphony of J.S. Bach seemed anachronistic – his own son, Carl Philipp Emanuel, called him 'an old bigwig'. The journals reflect the preoccupations of their target audience, a large and active class of modern professional musicians. Indeed, they have a modern equivalent in the publications of the twentieth-century postwar avant-garde, *Die Reihe* ('The Row'), which began in 1955 with an issue on electronic music, and *Perspectives of New Music*, which the music department of Princeton University started seven years later. The philosopher Stanley Cavell has commented about these journals, in which the writers are mainly composers, that the theories and analyses they contain are addressed not to a general audience but, as has been suggested about their music itself, to one another. They are very short on ordinary criticism, and 'sometimes they sound like the dispassionate analyses and reports assembled in professional scientific and academic journals'.[30] Something similar is true – except for the greater dose of rhetoric in their language – of many of the musical journals in eighteenth-century Germany. Their spirit is that of the century's leading theorists, for whom Berlin served as the publishing centre: J.J. Quantz, C.P.E. Bach, F.W. Marpurg and others. Later, however, as amateur music-making in Germany began to spread beyond aristocratic and court circles, the growth of a middle-class audience with its own developing taste created a demand for a less specialized, though still practical kind of publication, and the first more popular, non-technical musical journal, that of J.A. Hiller, made its debut in 1766.

Given the alignment of these journals with stylistically progressive music, perhaps it was only to be expected when Johann Adolf Scheibe launched an attack on Johann Sebastian Bach in the Hamburg journal *Der Critische Musikus* in 1737. Scheibe – writing, as many did in those days, anonymously – did not deny Bach's artistry, especially as an organist; but the tone of his remarks seems to echo the sneering attitude of the critic in the modern, pejorative sense of the word:

> I have heard [him] play on several occasions. One is amazed at his agility . . . This great man would be admired by the whole nation if he had more amenity, if he did not keep naturalness away from his compositions by making them turgid and confused, darkening their beauty by an excess of art . . .[31]

Scheibe had been a pupil of Bach, whom the master had passed over in favour of another when he applied for a post for which Bach was one of the judges, and it has been suggested that in this attack he was giving voice to resentment. But the substance of his complaint – that Johann Sebastian's music was lacking in clarity and naturalness, and overladen with laborious effort that failed to conform with reason – was also expressed by others. Bach had once been reproved by his employers in Arnstadt in 1706 'for having hitherto made many curious *variationes* in the chorale, and mingled many strange tones in it, and for the fact that the Congregation has been confused by it'.[32]

Scheibe's criticism cannot be dismissed as the incomprehension of mediocrity. Like most eighteenth-century critics, Scheibe was strongly partisan to the new homophonic style of the Baroque, known as *le style galant* in France and *Empfindsamkeit* (the sentimental style) in Germany; one of its practitioners was Carl Philipp Emanuel Bach. The father retained an attachment to polyphony; his music was generally regarded as conservative. Indeed, he was appointed to the post of Kantor at Leipzig only after the municipal and church authorities, with their progressive burgher elements, found that their first choices, Telemann and Graupner, were not available. Now, in the old-fashioned High Church polyphony of Palestrina, Lassus, Byrd and Tallis, the fabric of the music is contrapuntal, composed of a complex interplay of melodies moving independently against each other, with a fullness of harmonic sound. The new homophony represses this horizontal complexity: here the parts move together, and present the profile of a dominant melody over an accompaniment of chords: a unidimensional harmonic progression is impressed upon the texture of the music.

This stylistic shift is critical. To begin with, the interaction between horizontal and vertical is one of the fundamental semiological features of Western music. The two dimensions are symbiotic: it is not as if a simple distinction can be drawn between melody, which is continuous, and harmony, which moves in blocks; and the horizontal must not be thought of as homogeneous and unilinear either, although the new style came perilously close. Secondly, a paradox: from another perspective, the modern style of Johann Sebastian's sons contains strong conservative tendencies, while Johann Sebastian's conservatism turns out to have certain progressive effects. T.W. Adorno speaks of the revolutionary force with which Bach's music thrust beyond the immediate limits of social perception. But the conflict, he says, between modern and conservative styles which caught J.S. Bach in its web is not as simple as it seems at first sight. Warning us that 'the controversy whether Bach belongs to the Middle Ages or already to the Modern Age is undialectical', Adorno considers the presence in Bach of a medieval tradition which, like the absolutist state, does not bow unprotestingly to the demands of the rising bourgeoisie.[33] The stronghold of this tradition was the very style of sacred music which Johann Sebastian made his own, and his problem – according to Thomas Mann's fictional composer Adrian Leverkühn in *Dr Faustus* (whose discourse he partly modelled on Adorno) – was not how to write harmonically in the form of polyphony, but how to write polyphonically in a harmonic language. And the result, in works like the great set of preludes and fugues known as 'The 48', was a paradigmatic demonstration of the rationality of the whole system.

In fact, Johann Sebastian was quite capable of writing the most stylish music. The Leipzig critic Mizler, defending the master against Scheibe, spoke of works of his composed 'perfectly in accordance with the newest taste'.[34] Indeed, the cantatas – more than two hundred of them, probably composed at intervals throughout his career – parade before us the gamut of genres and devices of the Baroque era: religious pastoral, dramatic scena, sinfonia; aria, recitative and arioso; trumpet fanfares, multiple choirs and the typical chromatic bass; as well as the *obbligato* oboe and viola d'amore of Italian opera, and the rhythms of French *danse*. Similarly, the instrumental variety, originality and virtuosity of the Brandenburg Concertos extends the concerto grosso far beyond Vivaldi; and the Passions, the Mass in B minor and the *Christmas Oratorio* all systematically juxtapose sets of movements written in deliberately contrasting styles, including the modern – though these religious works are, of course, always dominated by the Lutheran chorale, 'the Ariadne's thread' of Bach's music, as Láng puts it.[35] Then there is the keyboard music, where the wealth of preludes, inventions, suites and partitas include the widest range of genre pieces in the different national styles of the day, French, Italian and English. In the German Suites, for example, Bach employs the latest Italian keyboard style of Scarlatti. Johann Sebastian's mastery of all these different styles sends Láng into ecstasies:

> It is a sheer wonder to see the grave Lutheran cantor, the epitome of German baroque massiveness, clad in the impeccable silk stockings, lace-trimmed jacket and powdered wig of the French rococo, and moving about in this circle with the assuredness of the very masters whose style he attempted to imitate. The imitations turned out, however, to be works such as no rococo composer could ever approach, for over the feathery touch, the agreeable pointed rhythm, and the sweet melancholy of the *style galant*, the German master pours the poetic warmth of a lyricist inspired to meditation where his French colleagues are seeking *divertissement*.[36]

This, however, is the privileged judgement of the music historian. Practically none of this music was widely known to Bach's contemporaries, except in Leipzig, where he joined the Collegium Musicum and contributed orchestral suites, harpsichord concertos, and secular cantatas – including the *Coffee Cantata*, a tribute to the owner of the coffee house where the Collegium met. But he wrote no operas (though his command of operatic style is perfectly evident in the Passions and the cantatas), published very little, and remained a figure marginal to the nascent market for domestic music, where music dealers mediated the taste of the bourgeois public, and the *style galant* took root. When the second edition of the *Art of Fugue* appeared two years after his death, no more than thirty people over the next five years were interested enough to buy it. (Mozart, some years later, found a copy in the library of one of his patrons, Baron Swieten, and the discovery had a strong influence on his own music.)

In short, beyond his membership of the Leipzig Collegium Musicum, Bach had little connection with the cosmopolitan and progressive society which Scheibe represented, which is of course none other than that of the emergent bourgeois public sphere. To a man of Scheibe's instincts, those of a bourgeois intent upon the demolition of extravagant pretensions, Bach had little to say, and was even anathema. The irony is that musically speaking, Scheibe thus becomes a cipher for the blinkers of history, unable – unlike later generations – to perceive the music composed by the Kantor in Leipzig as a great practical demonstration of the rationality of the harmonic system, a demonstration which becomes the very foundations for musical progress. Adorno is right: what raised Johann Sebastian above the standards of his time was the manner in which, absorbing every current of the emergent bourgeois music, his very medievalism discovered in them the means of construction of the modern harmonic language.

Rousseau and the '*Querelle des bouffons*'

The first opera critics complained about bad libretti, the ridiculous acting of the singers, the imperfections of the staging, the way high society courted the castrati. They thus vented their frustration at both the perversion of an artistic medium of such seductive power, and the stillborn ambition for opera in English. Yet across the Channel, where nationalist aspirations were satisfied by royal encouragement for French lyric tragedy, opera remained recalcitrant and in the middle of the eighteenth century, became the subject of attack in a vicious pamphlet war, a war between opera companies known as the *querelle des bouffons*.

The *querelle* produced something like sixty contributions in the space of two or three years. The affair began in 1752, the year after the first volume of the *Encyclopédie* appeared, when one of its contributors, Baron Grimm, used a mediocre opera by Destouches as an excuse to praise the Italian opera he had seen in Dresden. Grimm complained that in the Frenchman's opera there was no connection between the words and the music, the singing failed to express the sentiments of the protagonists, the composition was altogether too complicated. A few months later an Italian opera company led by one Eustachio Bambini arrived in the French capital, bringing with it an extensive repertory of works by Pergolesi, Scarlatti, Jommelli, and others. They had been there before without much success, but this time their visit became the subject of an extraordinary controversy which divided Parisian society into two camps. According to Rousseau's account in his *Confessions*: 'The most powerful and most numerous party, composed of the highly placed, the rich and the ladies, supported French music; while the other, more lively, bolder, and more enthusiastic, was composed of the true connoisseurs, the people of talent and men of genius.'[37]

Indeed, the *querelle* was as much ideological as aesthetic. French opera, devoted to the Bourbon myth of *gloire*, was traditional and academic, the heroes of classical mythology and ancient history inhabiting a world of allegory designed to flatter princes. As progressive and cosmopolitan critics of conservative and chauvinistic forces in all departments of science and art, the *philosophes* – Holbach, Diderot and d'Alembert all joined in along with Grimm and Rousseau – opposed this authoritarian tradition and, instead, championed the new Italian *opera buffa* (hence the term 'bouffon'), whose popular melodic character they considered more 'natural' and 'agreeable' than the heavy declamatory style associated with Versailles, the Frenchified Italian Lully (sixty-five years dead), and to some extent even Rameau, his heir, now nearing seventy. Moreover, not only did the tunefulness of *opera buffa* give it a more democratic and popular quality, but so did the plots. *Opera buffa* brought a new contemporaneity into the opera house. Instead of gods and kings and the fables of mythology, the characters on stage were ordinary modern mortals. The new genre, especially as exemplified in the libretti of Carlo Goldoni, reflected the emerging order of the bourgeois world. Goldoni's Venice was a city in which, as one writer describes it, an environment of middle-class merchants and continual monetary metaphors served as a reminder that beneath all the military and chivalrous pretences beat the true heart of modern society, the real war that the people of Europe waged with trade.[38] Take Pergolesi's *La serva padrona*, one of the most successful of the operas presented by Bambini. Here the heroine is a servant and the hero a bourgeois bachelor who ends up marrying her. A plot like this, with the moral that a maid is as good as her mistress, would be highly likely to alarm conservative circles in a city like Paris – or as d'Alembert ironically put it:

> I am astonished in a century where so many authors busy themselves writing about freedom of trade, freedom of marriage, freedom of the press and freedom in art, that nobody has so far written about freedom in music ... for freedom in music implies freedom to feel, and freedom to feel implies freedom to act, and freedom to act means the ruin of states; so let us keep the French opera as it is if we wish to preserve the kingdom – and let us put a brake on singing if we do not not wish to have liberty in speaking to follow soon afterwards.[39]

The most powerful proponent of freedom to feel – and the most intransigent critic of French opera – was Rousseau, the enemy of all artifice. As representative in music as in philosophy of the pre-Romantic valorization of the simple and the natural, Rousseau held that harmony was not born of the same natural proclivity as melody. It is, rather, an invention of European sophistication, and can exercise significance only as accompaniment to melody and commentary upon it. Entering the fray with a reply to a reply to Grimm, he drew on material he was preparing for the *Encyclopédie* to illustrate the merits of Italian opera, with which, from his sojourns in Italy, he was thoroughly familiar. Moreover, he was himself the composer of a French pastiche of Italian *opera buffa*, a piece called *Le devin du village* which had recently been performed both at Versailles and in Paris itself with great success. According to his biographer, Maurice Cranston, this work was

> designed to avoid the over-elaborate theatricality, which, in Rousseau's opinion, was the bane of the Paris opera . . . In the *Discours sur les arts et les sciences* Rousseau condemned the false values of a sophisticated culture: in *Le devin du village* he demonstrated the aesthetic, and indeed the moral, qualities of a less sophisticated culture – close to nature, to the heart and to the purity of uncorrupted man. The ironical outcome was that the most sophisticated public in the world adored it.[40]

The greatest irony was that the republican philosopher had written an opera which particularly pleased the King. But this, as Cranston observes, is not entirely surprising: at any rate, where the moral of *La serva padrona* is egalitarian, Rousseau's opera depicts a shepherdess distressed because her sweetheart has gone off with a lady aristocrat, but in the end they are reunited and the proper order of things prevails; moreover, since the King was not a great musical connoisseur, Rousseau's unpretentious tunes appealed to him.

Rousseau's talent as a composer was only moderate. A few years earlier he had come unstuck with a previous operatic essay, *Les Muses galantes*, of which Rameau remarked that some of its numbers showed the hand of a master and others the ignorance of a schoolboy. None the less, Rousseau's participation in the *querelle* transformed it from a journalistic dispute into a confrontation between himself and Rameau, with serious aesthetic and philosophical consequences. The other *encyclopédistes* had at first hesitated to criticize Rameau, who was not only the most popular French composer of his day but had broken the heavy formalist mould of Lully and was therefore to some extent a progressive force. Rameau as a composer had a great gift for melody and a deep harmonic understanding, and sometimes seems the most Mozartian of composers before Mozart. He had also contributed to some of the same ideological currents espoused by Rousseau – for example, in his dramatic ballet *Les Indes galantes* (1735), which Rousseau had tried to emulate, where, in order to portray a tableau of noble savages, he uses a North American Indian melody as transcribed by a returning explorer. The result is thoroughly invigorating, even though the transcription squeezes the Indian tune into European diatonic shape, and Rameau rounds it out with Apollonian harmony.

But Rameau was also an intellectual and the most outstanding theorist of his day, with a permanent influence on harmonic thinking. Music, he says in the Preface to his *Treatise on Harmony*, 'is a science which should have definite rules; these rules should be drawn from an evident principle; and this principle cannot be known to us without the aid of mathematics'.[41] His method was perfectly Cartesian – 'the exposition of an evident principle, from which we can then draw just and certain conclusions'[42] – and he frequently refers to Descartes while revising the details of Descartes's own musical theories. Moreover, the insistence on mathematical precision separates the reasoning of the mind from the sensual experience of the ear, demanding obeisance to the former. The metaphysical conclusions that he drew from acoustics were thus completely inimical to Rousseau, with his emphasis on experience and natural feeling, and of scant appeal to the pragmatic and anti-metaphysical approach of the *encyclopédistes* as a whole. If Rousseau challenged his claims that melody derived from harmonic structure, d'Alembert protested that it was ridiculous to confuse the rules that govern geometry with the features that give pleasure in music, an attitude shared by Diderot.

Rousseau's principal contribution to the polemic, entitled 'Lettre sur la musique française', is infamous for the unsustainable thesis that French opera was impossible because the French language was unsingable, while the superiority of Italian opera derived from the much more song-like qualities of the Italian language (its rounded open vowels, as opposed to the closed and nasal sounds of French). He argued that because of the qualities of their language, the Italians had a livelier and more precise sense of rhythm. He also upheld the bolder modulations of the Italian composers over the pedantic transitions of the French, criticizing the latter for so filling out their harmonies that in the end they 'make a great deal of noise but have very little expression'.[43] The actors and musicians of the Opéra were so incensed by this that they responded by hanging and burning its author in effigy.

Yet in the end, Rousseau's influence on the course of European music was at least equal to that of Rameau, and generally more progressive. In the first place, *Le devin du village* had an immediate effect on musical taste at a moment when Rameau, as Diderot put it, had outlived his reputation. Within a few years, the philosopher's modest effort had been translated into Dutch, English and German, and performed throughout Europe; in 1790 it even reached New York. In France itself it helped to establish a new model for the genre of *opéra comique*, which in turn stimulated German *Singspiel*. The process began when the librettist Charles-Simon Favart, an expert in vaudeville and pastiche somewhat in the style of English ballad opera, mounted a parody, *Les Amours de Bastien et Bastienne*, which in certain respects went even further than Rousseau, both in imitating peasant speech and in bringing to the stage real peasant dress rather than its stylization. Fifteen years later, in 1768, the twelve-year-old Mozart composed his own *Bastien und Bastienne* to a German version of Favart's text (first performed in Vienna in the garden of Dr Anton Mesmer, ten years before he became famous in Paris for the technique of mesmerism, which Mozart himself later satirized in *Cosi fan tutte*). A trifle, perhaps, but there is no better indication of the way in which, by highlighting certain qualities of *opera buffa*, Rousseau focused for the whole of Europe a growing rejection of cultural absolutism. As Cranston sums up:

> Historians of music, in talking of romanticism and classicism, commonly contrast the romanticism of Weber and his successors with the classicism of Mozart, but in a more general sense of romanticism, as something to be contrasted with rationalism, romanticism as the lyrical expression of feeling, transcending the constraints of formal categories, this quality . . . dates from the success of *Le devin du village*.[44]

Even then, the influence of his little opera is only part of the story, for in his later writings, even without making explicit reference to music, Rousseau develops the same bent even further. And when he speaks of music in *La nouvelle Héloïse*, it seems indeed that here, for the first time, we encounter what Isaiah Berlin has called 'fully-fledged Romanticism', in a form that goes even beyond Mozart:

> . . . when, after a series of agreeable arias, they came to those great expressive pieces that can arouse and describe the disorder of violent passions, I forgot at every moment the notion of music, singing, and imitation; I seemed to hear the voice of grief, wrath, and despair; I seemed to see mothers in tears, deceived lovers, enraged tyrants; and in the emotions I was compelled to experience, I had difficulty in remaining in my chair. I understood then why this same music that had formerly bored me now excited me till I was quite carried away; for I had begun to understand it, and as soon as it could affect me at all, it affected me with all its force. No, Julie, one is not half-receptive to such impressions: they are excessive or non-existent, never weak or mediocre; one must remain insensible or allow oneself to be moved beyond measure; either it is the empty noise of a language one does not understand, or it is an impetuosity of feeling that carries one away, and that the soul cannot resist.

2

Subjectivity and the Space of Music

Feeling

The issue of feeling which emerges in eighteenth-century critical debates is related to the question of music's deepening subjectivity: its extension – indeed, redirection – into an intense inner-directed space of sentience. According to Alejo Carpentier, the Cuban novelist who was also a historian and connoisseur of music, the concept of emotional expression as it is understood by music-lovers in the twentieth century did not exist for either composers or listeners of the Renaissance or the Baroque. In 1895, he says, when Proust studied the audience at a concert listening to Beethoven's Fifth Symphony, he thought they seemed like 'people sunk in a state close to that of hypnosis [or] hashish smokers who had become intoxicated together'. Proust himself, listening to a sonata, 'lies in wait for that moment when a brief phrase on the violin "addresses itself to him"; and when he finds it, "it tells him everything it had to tell him", to him and him alone, associating itself with the memory of a love, a musical phrase made specially for him which only he could hear, without other listeners knowing. . . .' But when Bach was writing his Brandenburg Concertos, says Carpentier: 'I do not believe that [he] ever thought of arousing similar reactions in his audience.' And if – to go back even further – a piece like Monteverdi's *Lamento d'Arianna* was a bestseller for its day, this was not because its composer had poured his own emotions out in the music, but 'by virtue of a certain mimesis of the spirit', and according to the requirements of the text. In short, emotional response happens 'by contagion, by a process of sentimental ecology, let's say, [in which] certain intimate, eternal and universal human fibres vibrate together'.[1]

The question of how this sentimental ecology functions, its internal logic, is the subject of a later chapter on the questions of musical semiotics. The question here is not semiotic – *how* music expresses whatever it expresses – but historical: how these expressive capacities take on different historical forms. What is clear – and agreed by many writers of different disciplines – is that music enjoys a special relationship with the inner world of emotions, which it seems able to evoke without recourse to language or referentiality. Music, says Umberto Eco, presents the problem of a semiotic system apparently without a semantic plane – in other words, without articulate content; Roland Barthes sees it slightly differently: music, he says, is a field of signification but not a system of signs. Either way, music circumvents the world of language and objects, and allows the direct expression of the inner world of the body and its emotional states. Exactly how this happens is theorized by a number of psychoanalysts, among others,[2] but the quality of access to the deepest psychosomatic levels was already evoked by Schopenhauer:

> The unutterable depth of all music by virtue of which it floats through our consciousness as the vision of a paradise firmly believed in yet ever distant from us, and by which also it is so fully understood and yet so inexplicable, rests on the fact that it restores to us all the emotions of our inmost nature, but entirely without reality and far removed from their pain.[3]

Yet this is music as Schopenhauer knew it, in the early nineteenth century. It was not always experienced in this way, as essentially inner-directed; in the Christian West, for one thing, it was seen rather more as an emanation of the Godhead. The historical issue is how music turned inward, and became associated with a subjectivity which was in itself a new and historically produced phenomenon.

In the Middle Ages, according to Carpentier's argument, the personally expressive content of music played a very minor and subsidiary role; other functions, relating to communal purpose and use, were far more significant. This is not to say that music at that time was lacking in expression, but that the voice of the composer as the individual responsible for such expression was of little import. Even the Renaissance introduced emotive expression not as the voice of the composer but, rather, as that of the dramatic subject of the madrigal or the dramatis personae of the opera, though this allows the composer to speak more personally through the selection of texts and the manner of their treatment. Only in the nineteenth century, however – the heroic age of the composer as the very paradigm of bourgeois individualism, from Beethoven to Mahler – does emotive subjectivity expand to become the very *raison d'être* of the music. Even if emotive subjectivity

is not an invention of the bourgeois public sphere, nevertheless it is
here that it takes on new and intense expression.

The construction of the subject before the rise of bourgeois society
was bound up with the individual's location within a social hierarchy
determined, to a greater or lesser degree, by the rights and obligations
of the feudal system. Once the bourgeois social order begins to
reconstruct the subject as a monadic unity logically prior to its entry
into social relations, this traditional fixedness is cast into crisis (here
we ought to speak of the rise of Protestantism as an expression of this
crisis). In Eagleton's account, once the bourgeoisie had dismantled the
unifying political apparatus of absolutism, either in fantasy or in reality,
it found itself facing the loss of the institutions through which social
life was organized. This is one of the reasons why the aesthetic realm,
that of sentiment, affection and the body, comes to assume its modern
significance. It is necessary to construct a new kind of human subject,
'sensitive, passionate and individualist'. And the problem only intensifies in proportion to the success of the political and economic project
of the bourgeoisie, as the individual is economically isolated and thrust
into the antagonistic relations of the market, and politically the subject
is redefined in terms of universal abstract rights. For the same process,
by releasing the individual into lonely autonomy, abandons the subject
to its own private space, which can be reached only by the imagination;
that is to say, the symbolic exchange of identities by aesthetic means
(although this alone will never be enough to guarantee social harmony). 'In the sphere of aesthetic culture ... we can experience our
shared humanity with all the immediacy of our response to a fine
painting or a magnificent symphony.'[4] The aesthetic therefore offers
the middle class a model for their political aspirations, 'exemplifying
new forms of autonomy and self-determination, transforming the relations between law and desire, morality and knowledge, recasting the
links between individual and totality'.[5]

Music – for the reasons put forward in their various ways by thinkers
like Eco, Barthes and, before them, Schopenhauer – is particularly fit
for the process Eagleton calls 'refashioning the human subject from
the inside' – the discovery of what the philosopher Ernst Cassirer, as
Eagleton reminds us, called 'the law governing the structure of the
inward personal world'.[6] Music speaks through feeling, which Rousseau
held was prior to (cognitive) knowledge, and the body, which is prior
to rationality. Herein, however, lies great danger for social authority,
for when the expression of emotion and sensuous pleasure develops its
own dynamic, there is always a risk that it will escape ideological control
and domination. The figure of the composer, in whom the mysterious

powers of music are personified, therefore also comes to represent a danger, an ideological challenge to the ruling order, precisely because new music is given to elaborating new dimensions of feeling which go beyond the narrow requirements of maintaining social order (not that this would have been news to Plato).

The salon

If the danger of deep subjectivity is no accident, the process which brings it forward is the function of definite historical conditions, a certain social formation found in particular social locations, mediated by the characteristic social relations to be found there. The location of music in social space means that it can also be understood in terms of what Henri Lefebvre has called a spatial practice: an activity, involving certain patterns, codes and forms of behaviour, by which spaces of different types are constituted, and in which the forms of society reproduce themselves.[7] In Lefebvre's view, space is not a neutral substratum or background to human activity, but is directly shaped in and through such activity. Indeed, because space in this way enters actively into the activity in question, the activity itself should also be seen as a form of production of space, the lived space of the lifeworld in which these activities are literally embodied. In this light, because the medium of music is organized and focused sound, which thereby takes possession in a special way of the space where it is heard, it can be considered a particularly plastic and vivid form of spatial practice – or, better, a family of spatial practices, depending on the space and the purpose of the gathering.[8]

The bourgeois public sphere takes shape, beginning in the second half of the seventeenth century, in the general public domain where private citizens come together as a public, for both political and cultural aims. It is a public consisting of private individuals from families of good social standing whose autonomy is based on the ownership of private property and privileged education. It takes shape in places where the private individual enters into public assembly, where men go to participate in free discussion, and in the columns of the emergent press; in short, those spaces where the principles of behaviour and the norms of self-expression are collectively produced to serve the purposes of social intercourse by means of a generalized decorum. Many of these gatherings make room for music, and in some, music-making is one of the primary purposes, fulfilling what Adorno called the anthropological property of bringing together communities.

The public sphere is idealized as universal, but in fact it is socially restricted. In principle, says Habermas, the bourgeois public's critical debate took place without regard for social rank, and according to universal rules. These rules secured a space for the individuated person, but at the same time, while claiming universality, the private individual who thus takes their place in public is not, of course, the 'common man'; male, yes, but propertied, educated and patriarchal. The cultural public sphere, however, even in its early literary form, is wider. It extends to those who are formally or legally excluded from the political public sphere, but not from participation in the market for cultural commodities and activities: those without property and without the vote, both men (many of them) and women (all of them). Moreover, in the extension of the literary realm into the salon, wherein the bourgeoisie emulated the aristocracy, women often took a more active part than the owners of private property and family heads themselves; their presence alone would be enough to imply a different orientation. For us it is critical that the salon was not just a literary institution but also a musical one, and here perhaps the influence of women was particularly strong, not only as animators of discussion but also as performers. (Numerous contemporary testimonies inform us, for example, that girls made up the majority of piano pupils, and women were far and away the primary consumers of keyboard music in the eighteenth and nineteenth centuries. The leading historian of the piano Arthur Loesser calculates that in Paris is 1845 there were some 60,000 pianos, and something like one in five of the city's women had some degree of ability to play them.)[9]

Nevertheless, it is still a mediated presence, in which the individual is already gendered. As feminist commentaries on Habermas point out, the new category of the 'public man' was constructed through a series of oppositions to 'femininity', which mobilized older conceptions of domesticity and the woman's place in support of a new concept of women's 'nature'. In the rhetoric of the 1780s and 1790s, the male domain of reason was conventionally counterposed to a femininity characterized by pleasure, play, artifice, style, *politesse* and eroticism.[10] But here music creates a special and unique space in which these constructed categories can be mixed, to some extent suspended, perhaps even dissolved in its fluid and fluctuating evocation of sentiment. As a symbolic domain of imaginary psychic scenarios, all the more potent for remaining unnamed, music is outwardly governed by expressive conventions, while inwardly it becomes a space of sentient and emotional resonance in which the individual can project private meanings and desires, often even without recognizing them for what they are, or might become.

The salon, the most imposing room in the distinguished bourgeois home, was the public face of the private sphere, the sphere of the family, with its internal core of intimacy. Here the private individual stepped out of the seclusion of their living-rooms into a space where those who gathered formed a small public; but still a protected space – because it was domestic – where the family presented itself to society: not 'society' in the former sense of the higher echelons, but the circle of acquaintances of appropriate social standing to lend status and respectability to the hosts (and suitable partners for their children). This domestic space, says Habermas, was the scene of a psychological emancipation that was the counterpart of the political and economic emancipation which was the object of the political public sphere; it represented a space of individuated autonomy separated from its economic origins – that is, wherein its economic origins were suppressed – which provided the bourgeois family with its consciousness of itself. Here, questions of subjectivity counted: the self-image of the family and the relations between its members, the representation of its domain of intimacy, its organization of gender relations, these form a principal current of the literature which it consumed, a literature which also – Jane Austen is a prime example – depicted the very musical life which concerns us. It is striking, for example, how in Jane Austen's novels men are typically listeners, albeit discriminating ones, while women are practitioners, albeit concerned about not performing in the wrong company – not, that is, to 'strangers', which is what professional musicians and the lower classes do.

In other words, this is a space where women can demonstrate command – if only in a domestic setting – without threatening their menfolk; and men, as long they remain solidly heterosexual, can display interest in feminine concerns without immediately impugning their masculinity. Indeed as Eagleton reminds us, the well-tempered display of affect and good taste, and the judicious expression of opinion, served as eloquent testimony to a person's participation in universal common sense and a community of sensibility.[11] Music in such a setting is strongly hemmed in by questions of etiquette, and one of its principal functions is to educate the sentiments which occur in such an environment and channel them into appropriate forms of polite expression. At its most conformable, music thus becomes the very model of the regulation of subjectivity in the interests of social decorum. (The situation of women as professional musicians, on the other hand, at that time strongly centred on the opera house, was extremely delicately balanced – not because it threatened masculinity, but because women could not always shake off associations with the singer as courtesan, mistress, or loose woman.)

On the other hand, music also acquires another, more vicarious aspect, in becoming a site for the self-preoccupation of the private individual. Here, precisely because of its profound subjectivity, music becomes a medium of negotiation of the often confused feelings which accompany, at the deepest level, the new conceptual framework of individual identity. The dynamic of the modern subject is a process of differentiation and demarcation of feelings and instincts, a response to the changing locations of the 'self' over the course of the eighteenth century as the public sphere redefines the private sphere and the regime of the bourgeois family becomes the norm. The process is different for men and for women, because the two genders have quite distinct personal and social futures mapped out for them, but for both of them the sense of self, and the subjectivity associated with it, is both a lived experience and at the same time a mental construct, a product of literature and philosophy embodied in an intellectual vernacular which was derived from the Enlightenment. By the early nineteenth century, as a recent commentator puts it, 'one had learned to speak familiarly of cleavages between head and heart, classic and romantic, reason and imagination, nature and freedom, public and private, depth and surface. The subject who did so, who was in large part formed by doing so, took on a markedly high degree of intensity and dynamism.'[12]

The salon where these processes were played out came in various shapes and sizes. The most famous were those of the rich and famous, where the leading virtuosi of the day performed: high-society salons where the musicians were professionals, though not usually supposed to mix with the guests. Very different was another type, supported by disinterested patrons and by musicians and artists themselves, like the salon celebrating 'humanitarian art' which met in Paris at the Hôtel de France in 1836, where Liszt, his mistress, the Comtesse d'Agoult, and the novelist George Sand, who were living there, were the leading lights; Sainte-Beuve described its atmosphere as 'a mass of affectations, vanities, pretentiousness, bombast and uproar of every kind', but it attracted figures such as Lamennais, Heine, Mickiewicz, Meyerbeer, Berlioz and Chopin.[13] Here we find the gestation of a more bohemian world. Different again was the bourgeois salon simple of the kind portrayed by Jane Austen, where the primary interests of the hosts were to cash in on the social exchange, and music became a commodity which could be swapped for social status. Here indeed the daughter of the house went on display with the purpose of attracting suitors. As

one woman wrote to a London music magazine, she had taken up
singing on the advice of her friends for the sole purpose of marrying
into a wealthy family, and had accomplished her goal in a short time.
At the same time, a correspondent in a Leipzig publication wrote that
in Vienna young men took up chamber music in order to gain access
to the salons of highly placed families through whom they might get
good jobs. Unmusical parents would therefore indulge in these activities for social reasons, but there was also a strong belief that musical
pursuits provided a valuable means for the socialization of children.
'The watchword of middle class values', says William Weber, who quotes
these examples, 'was discipline, and musical training helped instil it in
young people. For girls especially, learning the piano was virtually a
puberty rite, since it was conceived not as a hobby but rather as a social
obligation integral to their upbringing.'[14] The same idea of the benefits
of music subsequently became the rationale for the activities of philan-
thropic mill and mine owners who promoted brass bands and choruses
among their workers.

'Sonate, que me veux tu?'

The literary public sphere in which bourgeois musical life was embedded gave essential support to the political domain. Indeed, one of
Habermas's commentators suggests that since the category of the
public was the consequence of the growth of urban culture in its new-
found forms, to that extent the origins of independent political life –
the public sphere in Habermas's sense – must be sought in this wider
domain of social and cultural activity from which a self-confident
middle class began to emerge.[15]

   The cultural sphere provided not only a terrain for self-expression
but a setting for the articulation of the experience of the novel forms
of privacy and intimacy within (and around) the bourgeois family. In
creating this space, it succoured the intensification of individualism in
a private, psychological sense, but because it takes shape in public, the
subjectivity which emerges is always orientated towards an audience.[16]
This is partly because the subject constantly requires the recognition of
others in order to feel legitimated, but the process is also shaped by
the economic form in which the public sphere inevitably operates. In
other words, the expression of subjectivity is inexorably drawn towards
a commodity form, which is governed by the shape of the market for
printed matter, which includes music as well as literature. In fact the
literary public sphere served to convert culture into a commodity twice

over: as a product on the market and then as an object of discussion, preferably in the form of an object which is itself a commodity, like the printed page, which the private individual must consume in order to enter into the discussion; this includes music criticism. 'Inasmuch as culture became a commodity,' writes Habermas, 'and thus finally evolved into "culture" in the specific sense (as something that pretends to exist merely for its own sake), it was claimed as the ready topic of a discussion through which an audience-oriented subjectivity communicated with itself.'[17]

Even when the activity is outside the cash nexus, like the private performance of music, it is still drawn towards this commodity form. For the composer and the professional musician, the salon was a crucial feature of the private sphere in this other aspect, as the point of entry into the market. Not directly, perhaps; Mozart complained of the habit of giving the musician a gift – a watch, an initialled snuff-box – instead of cash. But it rewarded the effort because this was where the musician found pupils and the composer a public to buy his music. The German composer Flotow described in his memoirs how the system worked during the heyday of the salons in Paris in the 1840s:

> ... one makes several appearances in the course of the winter, and then, at the beginning of Lent, one announces a concert and sends a dozen high-priced tickets ... to the hostess of every salon at which one has played. That is the usual practice ... The cost of such a concert is negligible. It is given on a profit-sharing basis, takes place in daylight, which saves the expense of lighting, and no heating is necessary, because the audience turn up in their outdoor clothes. Placards at street-corners are unnecessary, and in any case would serve no purpose. Nor is there any need for a box-office, and there is hardly even any need to have an attendant on duty at the door to collect the tickets ... The audience consist of habitués of the various salons and always give the virtuosos, whom they have already met, and the music they play, most of which they already know, the warmest possible reception. Any artist who is ambitious can easily maintain himself in Paris in this agreeable fashion, without wasting much time or trouble over it.[18]

So professional salon life provided a network of social obligations to be exploited; it diversified patronage, and constituted an up-market focus for commercial activity. Indeed, the growth industries of concert-giving, music publishing and musical journalism all fed off the social prestige of the salon, which continued to provide a focus down to the last great salons of Paris and London in the 1920s, where Russian émigrés like Igor Stravinsky and *enfants terribles* like William Walton were popular –

although by this time decorum was no longer on the agenda, and the professional musician's earning capacity was in the hands of impresarios, managers and agents.

But if the entry of music into the bourgeois public sphere brought a new emphasis on music's subjectivity, it also involved the expansion of music into wider social spaces and social functions, where this commodity character is further extended. There is a move into new performance spaces, from the enclosed rooms of the princely palace to a new public setting, to the assembly rooms built by private subscription where the social elite could meet for balls, music, lectures and theatre, and thence to the dedicated concert-hall, the purpose-built space of musical representation, where the right of entry is embodied in the price of the ticket, and the emphasis is not on convivial participation but on dramatic display, virtuosity and spectacle. But music is not indifferent to the space in which it is performed; therefore this is a combination which in turn produces new musical genres: the courtly masque is transformed into opera, the concert-hall nourishes the symphony and the concerto. Thus the concert-hall will elicit symphonies by Bruckner and Mahler which call on the audience's concentrated attention for a stretch of as much as ninety minutes and a form of aristocratic diversion which lasted for a segment of an evening will finally become Wagner's gargantuan *Ring* cycle, which requires the audience's exclusive devotion for four whole evenings. These forms are very different from those intended for domestic consumption, in every way more demanding of the listener than the small-scale genres – like the lied, the nocturne and the prelude – popularized by the salon.

The nineteenth century claimed the symphony (and the string quartet and the sonata) as the highest model for the exercise of musical art, calling it 'absolute' and 'pure' in order to express the sense that this was music proper, in and of itself, as Thomas Mann's Adrian Leverkühn would say – music fully developed, made by instruments alone, without the need for any kind of text. The precondition for the symphony, whose development parallels that of the instrumental sonata, is in the expansion of the instrumental ensemble in the setting of the concert room in 1780s and 1790s. This is when Salomon brings Haydn to London, where the ageing composer finds a new relationship with the bourgeois concert audience which elicits those last twelve of his symphonies which, together with Mozart's last half-dozen, are the first mature paradigms of how to handle large ensemble instrumental music. As Carl Dahlhaus records in his historical study of musical aesthetics, at the time of Scheibe, before the triumphs of the Mannheim orchestra in Paris, instrumental music had been disparaged, and: 'unless provided by a programme-note with some intelligible meaning, was regarded not as eloquent but simply as having nothing to say'.[19] In Fontanelle's famous words, 'Sonata, what do you want of me?' ['*Sonate, que me veux tu?*']. We shall have to come back to the significance of this major shift in public taste; here we merely register how radically attitudes have changed by the time the symphonies of Cannabich are praised in 1791 by one Daniel Schubart, in words – says Dahlhaus – that anticipate E.T.A. Hoffmann's celebration of Beethoven: 'This is no mere babble of voices ... it is a musical whole whose parts, like spiritual emanations ... form a whole.'[20] If this is the language of Romanticism, the phenomenon was also observed by the sober Scottish economist Adam Smith, when he wrote in 1795 (in a curious anticipation of semiotic thinking): 'instrumental Music does not imitate, as vocal music, as Painting, or as Dancing would imitate, a gay ... or a melancholy person; ... it becomes itself a gay ... or a melancholy object'; the musical subject is therefore 'altogether different from what is called the subject of a poem or a picture, which is always something which is not either in the poem or in the picture'. Or – as the German philosopher Herder baldly declared five years later – 'Music has developed into a self-sufficient art, *sui generis*, dispensing with words.'[21] All of which means, of course, that in this way music also asserts its autonomy in relation to the literary public sphere in which bourgeois musical life has taken shape.

The critical figure here is Beethoven. It is no accident that Beethoven becomes the paradigm of the social emancipation of the composer within the public sphere who flagrantly and defiantly positions himself in the world according to his newly won, independent and individual conscience. Mozart still believed that music must never be uncouth. Writing to his father while he was composing *Die Entführung aus dem Serail*, he describes the moment when, as Osmin's rage increases, he suddenly breaks into an *allegro assai* which

> is bound to be very effective. For just as a man in such a towering rage oversteps all the bounds of order, moderation and propriety, and completely forgets himself, so must the music too forget itself. But as passions, whether violent or not, must never be expressed in such a way as to excite disgust, and as music, even in the most terrible situations, must never offend the ear, but must please the hearer, or in other words must never cease to be music, I have gone from F (the key in which the aria is written), not into a remote key, but into a related one, not, however, into its nearest relative D minor, but into the more remote A minor.[22]

(One would never suspect from the Peter Shaffer/Milos Forman film *Amadeus* that Mozart was such a cool and rational self-analyst.)

With Beethoven, however, music begins to make its own autonomous demands, and the composer passes beyond the well-behaved expression of a subjectivity formed by extra-musical factors, to which music was required to conform. It is ironic that it was aristocratic patrons who supported him, embracing his individuality as a sign of their disinterested demonstration of discernment and educated taste at a moment when the bourgeois public still found him too difficult. Nevertheless, Beethoven is the first composer who is able to determine his own conditions: when the King of Westphalia proposed to employ him in 1809 it was on the understanding, as his Viennese patrons acknowledge, that 'the aspiration and the aim of every true artist [was] to place himself in a position in which he can occupy himself exclusively with the composition of larger works and will not be prevented from doing to by other duties or by economical considerations'.[23] With Beethoven's self-assertion, the composer's personality acquires a new dimension and, at the same time, makes demands on the listener as a silent partner in a secret dialogue; thus music begins to teach its public not just how to objectify their feelings and place them under the guidance and control of an acceptable intersubjectivity, but how to develop their emotional capacities, how to feel new emotions. In short, music now asserts itself as a problem for the public sphere, at the very moment when the composer takes up the mantle of the expression of revolutionary heroism and Romantic longing. In this moment of self-possession, music challenges the ideological hegemony of the literariness of the literary public sphere. It would be better to recast the idea of the literary public sphere as a cultural one, which at first operates under literary hegemony but in which, in due course, other forms of utterance and discourse will claim their own space.

Genre and the chronotope

It is not as if there was no purely instrumental music before the late eighteenth century. What has happened is that new instrumental genres have appeared which make new demands on the listener – in a process of innovation that tests our concept of genre. Musicologists – says Jeffrey Kallberg, one of them – tend to operate with a concept of genre which is self-enclosed, and drawn in terms of the formal characteristics which define a certain class of works. One of the problems with this type of static construct is that it makes it very difficult to understand how genres change, and new ones appear. Kallberg himself seeks a more open concept in which genres do not exist in isolation from each other, where they can be mixed and combined in various different ways, where generic expectations may be broken, and marginal and hybrid examples point to new conventions.[24]

The function of genre, according to Kallberg, is to provide a common framework for the act of aesthetic communication, a kind of contract between composer and listener: the composer adopts certain conventions, patterns and gestures; the listener consents to interpret them in the appropriate manner. The contract may be indicated to the listener in a number of ways, including title, metre, tempo, a characteristic opening gesture, a theme with a certain morphology. Here, musical terms double up as instructions (like allegro and andante) and descriptors of genre (movements headed Allegro or Andante). Such contracts, however, are made to be broken, certainly to be played with and composed against, and departures from the norm, the frustration of expectations and the rejection of generic prescription can become major forces in the process of change. The paradox is that a genre may change utterly and yet remain an example of the same genre if that is what people decide to call it; and this, of course, is exactly what has happened in the case of genres like the symphony and the sonata.

This account broadly agrees with Wittgenstein's concept of family resemblance, introduced in the *Philosophical Investigations* and then applied to aesthetics by a number of different writers. Here the genre is approached not as a class but as a family, in which there is no particular defining feature which is shared by everyone. Any two members of a family may share features with a third, without looking anything like each other. What makes them members of the same family is their common genealogy. Similarly, there is no particular defining characteristic of an artistic genre, which is, rather, composed of a cluster of features which are variously shared in different examples. What links them is, again, their genealogy. To employ a certain genre is to follow a model which belongs to a tradition – even though the earliest and latest examples of the tradition may turn out to be utterly different.

This is also close to the model of genre to be found in the work of the Russian thinker Mikhail Bakhtin, who perceives the work of art first and foremost as a social phenomenon. In Bakhtin's view, all artistic works belong to one genre or another, or combine the features of different genres, but genre has a double orientation. On the one hand, each work possesses certain principles of selection, certain forms of perception and of conceptualization. On the other, it presupposes a certain audience, certain types of reaction, certain ideological values. In short, each genre is orientated in a particular way: on the one hand, towards its content, the themes and events and characters that are portrayed within it; on the other, towards the audience and the conditions in which it is perceived. This gives us a different and much more subtle way of looking at genre: it means, first, that the genre has a certain relationship to social reality; and second, since social reality undergoes historical changes, so the orientation of a genre can also change – indeed, if it does not, it risks becoming outmoded. In this way, genres develop and evolve, and new genres appear, although almost invariably a new genre is made from the elements of existing ones subjected to novel recombinations, sometimes with new elements added in.[25]

All this is to place the genre within a social setting, and open it up to a historical analysis geared to the recognition of external influences. Bakhtin, however, is also concerned with the question of the historical form of the artistic genre as an internal quality of the genre itself, which he indicates in his concept of the chronotope: loosely, the spatio–temporal character of the work, or the mode in which it combines the representation of time and space. The term, which simply means 'time–space', is borrowed from Einstein's Theory of Relativity, he says, and adopted for literary criticism 'almost as a metaphor (almost, but not entirely). What counts for us is the fact that it expresses the inseparability of space and time (time as the fourth dimension of space).' The chronotope constitutes the organizing structure of the narrative where 'the knots of the narrative are tied and untied'. It identifies the distinctive ways in which the treatments of time and space are combined, the manner in which 'time, as it were, thickens, takes on flesh, becomes artistically visible', while 'space becomes charged and responsive to the movements of time, plot and history'.[26] In adopting the term for music, there are two provisos. First, perhaps we should want to say that here time is the dominant dimension; secondly, that narrative should be understood metaphorically. In regular terms, the closest parallels to the literary chronotope to be found in music obviously occur in opera, oratorio, song cycle, and various forms of programme music, all of which incorporate explicit narrative elements. But 'absolute' music – non-programmatic instrumental music – may well present a semblance of narrative, a kind of X-ray of its form, its movement, its climaxes and tensions, which is not, however, tied to diegetic content – that is to say, the elements and events which comprise the story, since there isn't one. (But it is it no accident that certain types of listener try to invent such stories; I shall return to this question.)

The chronotope, then, is hardly a property limited to the representational genres of music – it can also be considered as a formal matrix which is present in music of all kinds. In the first place, all types of music give structure to time and create their own sense of space and volume. Musical time is not to be measured by the clock, says the aesthetician Suzanne Langer. It is

> radically different from the time in which our public and practical life proceeds . . . Musical duration is an image of what might be termed 'lived' or 'experienced' time . . . Such passage is measurable only in terms of sensibilities, tensions, and emotions; and it has not merely a different measure, but an altogether different structure from practical or scientific time.[27]

Likewise music creates its own peculiar sense of space – what Langer calls volume, or virtual space, a space filled by its own characteristic forms, which expand and contract as it unfolds. This is widely recognized: what Langer calls virtual space another writer calls kinetic space; a third calls it plastic space; and yet another calls it the staggered planes of musical depth. In short, the virtual space of music is a property of the musical language and forms employed. A solo violin partita by Bach occupies a totally different virtual space to the symphony by Mahler, yet in both of them, time and space are polyvalent and multidimensional (which, on the other hand, cannot be said for Mantovani or Andrew Lloyd Webber, where everything is reduced to a narrow corridor of entirely predictable sentiment).

Secondly, there is also a formal correspondence between narrative and the musical treatment of time, which Thomas Mann touches on in *The Magic Mountain* at the point where the narrator ponders the temporal nature of narrative:

> For narration resembles music in this, that it fills up the time . . . Similarly, time is the medium of music; music divides, measures, articulates time, and can shorten it, yet enhance its value, both at once. Thus music and narration are alike, in that they can only present themselves as a flowing, as a succession in time, as one thing after another; and both differ from the plastic arts, which are complete in the present, and unrelated to time save as all bodies are, whereas narration – like music – even if it should try to be completely present at any given moment, would need time to do it in.[28]

However, the time music occupies has a special quality. As the character Joachim in the same novel puts it:

> You see an unpretentious concert number lasts perhaps seven minutes, and those seven minutes amount to something; they have a beginning and an

end, they stand out, they don't so easily slip into the regular humdrum round and get lost. Besides they are again divided up by the figures of the piece that is being played, and these again into beats, so there is always something going on, and every moment has a certain meaning, something you can get hold of . . .[29]

As well as the way in which the unfolding stream of notes is constantly infused with subtle differences and interactions between rhythm, beat and pulse, music always comprises different time spans that overlay each other in the passing moment: the phrase, the passage to which the phrase belongs, the section in which the passage is embedded, the movement in which the section occurs, and the time span of the whole work.

Bakhtin, however, is concerned less with the various formal temporal and spatial devices employed in different genres than with the relationship which these characteristics bear to the historical culture in which they arise. While Bakhtin was no Marxist, what comes to mind in this connection is Marx's famous passage on the historical character of the imagination. How, he asks, could the conceptions of nature and social relations that underlie Greek imagination and art still be possible when there are railways, locomotives and electric telegraphs? 'What is a Vulcan compared with Roberts and Co., Jupiter compared with a lightning conductor, and Hermes compared with Crédit mobilier?'[30] Or, one may add, the Bacchae compared with Beatlemania? In short, the chronotope is more than the simple combination of certain characteristics in the treatment of time and space: it is a culturally and historically specific amalgam.

In music, different chronotopes arise in various ways, including different schemes for linking a succession of pieces or movements. The very word 'movement' implies the development of an architectonic sense in which the individual piece becomes part of a larger pattern of contrasts and echoes of expression and mood. In this way, for example, dance music came to play a role of enormous historical importance in the development of instrumental forms from the seventeenth century onwards. When the simple forms of dance are borrowed by instrumental music and elaborated, the post-Renaissance composer is able to play upon the listener's predilections in a variety of ways. Since all these forms carry with them varying expectations of length, repetition, periodic structure and conclusion, a composer may constantly stretch, expand, vary and confound the listener's expectations, relying on the underlying tonal relations to provide the performer with signposts to the macrostructure. The combination of different dances into suites is therefore a procedure by no means as simple and arbitrary as it first seems. The original dance form is stylized and becomes what Bianconi calls 'a diffuse and evocative melodic and sonorous gesture'. In the hands of a J.S. Bach, this architecture achieves an emotional and intellectual sweep of monumental quality. Such osmosis of instrumental music and dance leads to a 're-organisation of the principles of composition and the very concept of musical "time" (increasingly dynamic and accentual in orientation) and space (increasingly anchored to the fundamental cornerstones of tonality)' which leads to sonata form.[31] In the development of the sonata, symphony and concerto which supersede the dance suite, there appears within each movement an internal differentiation of sections where thematic and tonal contrasts develop a new plasticity and intensity, and a new, quite different chronotope emerges, that of sonata form, which is able to subsume dance forms old and new – indeed, all types of musical form – into a radical musical discourse which takes on new subjective functions.

Harmony in perspective

These musical transformations are not only similar to chronotopic alterations in other art forms (though the parallels between them should not be drawn too closely). They are also broadly homologous to shifts in what we can call the social chronotope, in other words, the chronotope as a historical form of perception: the implicit but altering spatio–temporal construction of experience in different historical periods, which is so deeply embedded in the lifeworld that it carries the force of second nature. But second nature is malleable, and subject to historical change. The differing configurations of time and space have been studied by the geographer David Harvey.[32] In the world-picture of European feudalism, distance in both time and space was weakly grasped; it merged into a mysterious cosmology populated by external authority, heavenly hosts or the sinister figures of myth and imagination. Social space consisted in an intricate territory of interdependence, obligation and control, with different rules at different levels. Artistic space was tactile, plastic, permitting many different simultaneous points of view. The Renaissance reconstructed all three types or levels of space. The world-picture was transformed by the voyages of discovery and the new cartography; social space was unified by the growing domain of chronometrical time, and artistic space by the invention of perspective.

The art of perspective redefines the subject by conceiving the world from the standpoint of the seeing eye and projecting into it the unifying principle of the viewpoint of the individual. In the process it underpins the Cartesian principles of rationality which became integrated into the ideology of the Enlightenment, Descartes's famous 'cogito ergo sum', for perspective is how the subject of the cogito sees when he opens his eyes (the gender in Descartes being the normative male). This eye, however – or, to echo Terry Eagleton, this 'I' – denotes not a substance but a formal framework of perception, with the subject paradoxically squeezed out of the very system of which it is the linchpin. (Here Eagleton echoes Wittgenstein's formula by which the eye is not within its own field of vision, but at the edge of it.)[33] This, in turn, creates a problem for the apperception of the subject, which now has to be reconstructed. At the same time, the perspectival order combines with the new rule of chronometrical time measurement to separate the analytic and rational construction of time and space from their subjective experience, and thus supports the development of the new science. (And not only science, for as Marx put it: 'The clock was the first automatic device applied to practical purposes; the whole theory of the production of regular motion was developed through it', and it is therefore one of the prerequisites of industrialization.)[34] Through the adoption of analogous principles in other spheres of activity, especially financial ones like banking and book-keeping, the economic, social and cultural environments were recast, and subjectivity was reshaped as an unfathomable extra which falls outside its own reality, and in which knower and known no longer occupy the same field.

Musically, the tonal harmonic system which emerged in the Renaissance to replace the modal system of medieval music created a new and overarching chronotope in conformity with these same rational principles.[35] But it also transcended them, for the space it occupies is both inside and outside the subject at the same time – hence its privileged powers. Unlike the modes, which lie parallel to each other but separate, the new language is not only unified but also open and dynamic; paradoxically, therefore, it is also very difficult to pin down, as every harmonic theorist knows in their heart. If the chronotope is identified with the properties of the dominant musical language, then it is no longer a fixed and static scheme but an interacting multiplicity of codes. These codes are variously manifest in different genres, where their reading depends partly on other codes employed; the same codes may therefore function differently in different spheres and at different levels. This is not really a single chronotope but a family, which occupies the same historical territory.

The laws of perspective were first elaborated in mid-fifteenth-century Florence by Brunelleschi and Alberti, and came to govern the forms of visual representation for over four centuries, until modernism transcended them. It is probably no coincidence that the trajectory of the tonal harmonic system is very similar. But until these systems explode from within under pressure of radical sociohistorical change at the turn of the nineteenth century, they are both perfectly capable of adjusting to historical shifts of style. Indeed, the harmonic system is particularly good at it. Thus, if the internal scheme of tonal relations gave rise to new dynamic structures, the process inevitably came to imply a sense of direction. A sense of direction produced a sense of development, and harmonic language began to represent a linear path with the appearance of a causal relationship between successive moments. To the optimism of the nineteenth century, this was tantamount to the idea of progress, even history itself. This is not a theory born of hindsight but a power in the music that was felt at the time, and not only by those well-versed in the art. Charles Rosen quotes a remarkable passage by Coleridge, written in 1809, ostensibly describing 'a simphony of Cimarosa':

> Each present movement bringing back as it were, and embodying the Spirit of some melody that had gone before, anticipates and seems trying to overtake something that is to come: and the Musician has reached the summit of his art, when having thus modified the Present by the Past, he at the same time weds the Past *in* the present to some prepared and corresponsive future . . . A similar effect the Reader may produce for himself in the pages of History . . .

Cimarosa, says Rosen, does not seem the right composer here, which suggests that Coleridge's observations come to him second-hand, and he is repeating what he has learned about music from informed amateurs – in other words, he is reporting not his own experience but a matter of informed public opinion.[36]

As a modern commentator puts it: 'The music does not exist purely in the present tense, taking each moment as it comes, but leads the listener forward to coming events, often through passages which are themselves of no great intrinsic interest.' The result, says Christopher Small, is that large-scale harmonic forms become 'in essence psychodramas, the spiritual voyage of an individual',[37] which is not an image of history so much as the composer's role as historical subject. This, then, is the characteristic chronotope of nineteenth-century symphonism, from Beethoven to Mahler, regarded by many as the peak of musical art. By the time of Brahms and Bruckner, writes Edward Said, the musical idiom has a 'more solid, more assured, less strident texture than in Beethoven himself. Duration is much less frenetic and rushed, there is a greater sense of the composer's egotistical privilege.' There is also a greater sense of abstract introspection, because this music is becoming socially contained, confined within the safe space of the concert-hall (or the protective domestic interior). 'The world of patronage is now separately capitalised, as represented by the concert occasion and the publisher, [not to mention the impresario and the agent,] and the place of music in the social narrative has become largely meditative, self-referential, and decorative.'[38] This, of course, is the very period when the great nineteenth-century concert-halls are being built, designed as status symbols of nationalist bourgeois ascendancy, in which the arrangement of orchestra and audience produces a more attentive relationship to the music, which reinforces the tendency of symphonic music to develop a more and more abstract and complex idiom. The silence and outward passivity of the concert audience, as Christopher Small points out in a highly original study of the concert-hall called *Musicking*, is a historically recent practice. When Canaletto portrayed the Rotunda in the Ranelagh Pleasure Gardens in the 1740s, he showed the audience 'standing or walking about, talking in pairs and in groups, or just coming and going', with a knot of people gathered round the orchestra platform. This building, the grandest music room in eighteenth-century London, was very different from a modern concert-hall: 'a big circular space three stories high', with no seats, except in the dining alcoves round the outside. 'It appears', says Small, 'that the building has not caused socialising and enjoying music to be divided into separate activities as does a modern concert hall,' which, with its different arrangement of space, emphasizizes the individual's internal privacy.[39]

A similar changed occurred in the theatre, which also saw a growth of self-discipline in the audience. In the 1850s, says Sennett, a Parisian or London theatregoer had no compunction about talking to a neighbour in the midst of a play. By 1870 the audience was policing itself; a new reign of silence focused its attention, allied with the practice of dimming the house lights. The role of the audience is being redefined: they are no longer there to participate in a social event but to witness a spectacle. The distillation of the new attitude is found in the opera house Wagner built at Bayreuth, with its perfect sightlines, hidden orchestra, and electric lighting. In the concert-hall – which Walter Benjamin will call a school of asocial behaviour – those who were to witness the magnetism of the performer first prepared themselves by an act of self-suppression: 'The performer aroused them, but to be aroused they have first to make themselves passive.'[40] A most peculiar position in which to find yourself caught: you are required to restrain the display of feeling in order to experience it all the more fully. This is the period when the figure of the composer is first overtaken by that of the conductor, whom Adorno called a special type of public personality with 'a propagandistic and demagogical touch';[41] a figure of charisma and command, who becomes both the receptacle of the audience's bottled-up intensity of feeling and the composer's surrogate on the public stage.

Thus we return to the question of music as a spatial practice. The musical language is also a function of the real space in which the music is generated. The relationship between the virtual space of the music and the physical space of performance and audition is not one of indifference, it is complementary, and music has always directly exploited the acoustic space of performance in order to render the virtual space of the music in a particularly plastic form. The virtual space of music, however, is always physically embodied (until the invention of the gramophone), represented in the figure and role of the performing musician engaged in a social activity. If this serves to remind us that music is frequently composed not only for particular performers but also to fit particular kinds of acoustic space, then the truth is that acoustic spaces, as the spaces of representation of the musical lifeworld, have their own histories, and create their own expectations. Polyphony was for the cathedral, the madrigal and the masque were for the palazzo, the lied and the sonata for the salon, the symphony and the concerto for the concert-hall. Each type of space implies a twofold set of social relations – on the one hand among performers, on the other between performers and listeners – which corresponds to the social, cultural, sometimes religious and always ideological values that the space represents, and which often the very architecture was designed to express. These relations run the gamut from the formal and hierarchical to the informal and convivial, depending on the particular combination of forces employed, and the physical properties of the space of performance; hence the social conventions and values embodied in the musical language concerned. In short, music is always, whatever else it is, an expression of actual or ideal social relations. Moreover, as part of the immediate lifeworld of musical society, these relations formed an element in every composer's practical knowledge of what music was for, just as they evoked an intuitive response in every musician and every listener, all according to the genre in question.

A full account of music as a spatial practice in the public sphere would become an account of musical forms in terms of the different acoustic spaces for which they are designed. It would also be an account of the social relations of performance and audition. It would constitute a taxonomy of musical genres, in which the chronotope is constituted by the values implied in the particular combination of forces and the musical language employed, which in turn is a function of the type of performance space, with its particular physical, social and historical characteristics, for which the music is fitted. We shall often find, in the pages that follow, that what we discover, whether we remark on it or not, is a complex interrelationship between changes in social time–space in the cultural public sphere and the artistic chronotopes of developing musical forms.

The musical situation

All told, to follow Habermas and consider music and the composer within the public sphere is to embark on an inquiry which leads to a reconsideration of the nature of the public sphere itself, and in particular that part which Habermas calls the literary public sphere. Neither today, when it has become radically transformed by the expansion of the media – with effects both positive and negative, as we shall see – nor in its earlier historical phases, is the public sphere a singular space; it is not a uniform and homogeneous space, or even a dual space – political and literary – but quickly becomes several and multiple: political, literary, artistic, scientific; institutionally organized in parties, associations and societies, both locally and nationally; and also informally, in places of public gathering, where it merges into the wider public domain of commodified and commercialized cultural consumption. The more organized these various domains become, the more institutionalized and normative; after all, the public sphere is an arena where collective understanding is negotiated and established in the ambiguous but compelling form of public opinion. But public opinion itself is also multiple, shifting, constantly changing; and since the private person passes through many of these spaces, individual identity and allegiance dance back and forth in a flux of interpretations which sometimes reinforce and sometimes contradict each other.

The process is encouraged in several ways. For one thing, since the primary function of the public sphere is political debate, and since discussion within such a public, says Habermas, involves the problematization of areas which had previously not been questioned – indeed, its very purpose is the detection, identification and interpretation of social issues and dilemmas – the public sphere necessarily becomes an arena of differentiation of views and a space of conflict. Politically this finds expression in the creation of parties and pressure groups. But such conflict is also often played out vicariously in the aesthetic domain in the form of arguments and confrontations of taste between different social fractions which constitute themselves around different objects of approval – certain books and certain writers, paintings and painters, musical works and composers.

William Weber, for example, investigating mid-nineteenth-century concert life, describes the battles which arose in England for control of the elite concerts of the day as an expression of political battles over the issue of reform; and as one reviewer of the time put it: 'Lords spiritual and temporal are useful in their proper places, but they are sorry managers of a concert.'[42] Behind the question of control lay serious matters of taste. While wholesalers, dramatizing their affluence, emulated the nobility with a gregarious salon life and vigorous support for virtuosi and the Italian opera, lawyers, artists and civil servants capitalized on their learning and intellectual skills with intensive involvement in symphonic and chamber music concerts – in other words, they deemed a taste for the formal discipline of these composers appropriate to their own superior levels of education.[43] Disputes between musical camps provided the opportunity for social rivalry, which spread to other classes. The 1830s, for example, saw the emergence of large choral societies among the lower middle classes, especially in London, where they had strong roots among religious Dissenters. Since these societies dramatized mass involvement in social and political life, their social status became a politically volatile issue. In 1834, when the Crown mounted a festival of Handel oratorios in Westminster Abbey to commemorate the seventy-fifth anniversary of the composer's death, it had the obvious purpose, says Weber, 'of dramatising royal leadership after the bitter dispute of electoral reform. Its administrators not only restricted admission to a carefully chosen list, but also excluded local church choirs from the chorus, inviting only singers from Anglican churches and predominantly upper-middle-class provincial choruses.'[44] This policy of discrimination caused a bitter outcry among London's new choral societies; they responded by presenting their own amateur festival of Handel oratorios, and then setting up the important Sacred Harmonic Society. Symbolically, this society became in due course the proud owner of the bust of Handel which used to stand in Vauxhall Gardens. Ironically – and as if to demonstrate the ultimate victory of the commercialization of art over political or social pride – this bust now adorns the offices of the music publisher

Novello's, which some years ago joined television and motorway cafés to became part of the Granada group.

But if the cultural public sphere is succoured by the market, then the commercial process also produces differentiation. As it develops and expands, the market likes to divide up into sectors, a trend which intensifies in the twentieth century with the mass production of cultural commodities, but can already be seen in the development of the market for printed music in an earlier period. When the Leipzig printer Breitkopf introduced a new form of musical type in the 1750s, and again at the end of the century with the invention of lithography, new forms of music printing did not displace the older but extended the range of music publishing, with each technology becoming adapted to different musical markets. Engraving remained the primary form for orchestral scores, moveable type for keyboard music, while lithography proved the ideal medium for songs with illustrations on the front cover, which led the popular market during the nineteenth century. Although it was invented by a musician (one Aloysius Senenfelder), lithography was especially well suited to the production of graphic art, which – as Walter Benjamin remarks – was enabled 'for the first time to put its products on the market, not only in large numbers as hitherto, but also in daily changing forms'.[45] The lithographic stone offered comparable advantages for music in the attempt not just to keep up with changes of taste but to exploit passing fashions as well, especially in music for domestic use. So the leading music publishers, in the age when they acquired financial dominance in musical life, relied on no single method of printing exclusively, but employed each in accordance with its suitability for a particular sector of the market. As commercial concerts expanded, as opera flourished and operetta became increasingly popular, the publishers could only create a supply of music to exploit a demand which followed its own laws of progression. They could hardly do otherwise and remain in business, since musical taste was highly volatile, and the publisher was a long way from the ability to manipulate it easily.

But here again, the individual participates in different sectors, which are therefore permeable to influences developing in other sectors. As Habermas puts it, boundaries within the public sphere are always porous, and each sector is open to others; while at the same time, all partial public spheres point to the idea of a comprehensive public sphere which putatively includes them all. This is also a very good description of the musical world, which always consists of porous relationships between different types of activity and practices. No one, neither publisher nor musician nor members of the audience, ever meets with only one type of music, but encounters different musics in different situations which are all recognized as music (except for music which comes from outside or below, and may be felt to represent a threatening and irreducible Otherness). Indeed, in the late seventeenth century, a composer like Purcell wrote music in every genre of the day with equal ease: music for sacred and ceremonial use, for domestic use, a huge amount of incidental music for the theatre, and in *Dido and Aeneas*, the greatest of early English operas; and, says one of his biographers, 'he would as soon make a song to be sung about the streets as . . . an anthem'.[46] The public which heard such musics was the same general public, largely but not exclusively bourgeois, which assembled in different fractions and fragments with overlapping membership. Two centuries later, in Victorian times, the same individual, whatever their class, would participate in the audition of a similar diversity of musics. Naturally there were variations in the forms of musical activity in the different social classes, and each class had its own characteristic repertoire, but there was also plenty of overlap. Paganini was guyed in a working-class song from north-east England, 'Baggynanny', about a group of drunken miners who go to hear him play and are more impressed by his diabolism than by his musicianship[47] – a song which attests that the new commercial concerts of the era were not quite out of reach of the working-class pocket, at least occasionally. Generally, the upper classes cultivated opera and the salon, the orchestral academy and the singing club, and the men went to the music hall; while the middle echelons went in for domestic music-making, orchestral and choral societies, and the more sedate type of music theatre. Below stairs and among the working classes, parlour songs, music hall, choral societies and brass bands all flourished, as well as the informality of the tavern. And for all ranks of society there was also the music of the fairs and of public events, not to mention the church, which would be heard by auditors of every social class in the same space. Moreover, in many of these situations, much of this music would consist in arrangements of pieces from other repertoires.

As for today's acousmatic lifeworld, it is very difficult not to hear an extraordinary range of musical genres without even trying; you would have to stop watching television, listening to the radio, going to the cinema, and eating out – you would have to walk around with earplugs. The musical lifeworld is inescapably heterogeneous – or, in Bakhtin's word, heteroglot. It is made up of the proliferation of competing and intersecting acts of musical communication which coexist within any given historical space: these include the dominant traditions and divergent dialects, each with its own repertoire of genres, as well as the idioms of different generations, classes, genders, races and localities, each contributing its own utterances to the cultural polyphony of the times. The changing composition of these voices and the balance between them is the history of the musical sphere, which is denuded and distorted when it is recounted too narrowly and conventionally. Part of the necessary corrective is to reconceive the figure of the composer as a personality in the public sphere, a site where different forces meet: cultural and economic, historical, aesthetic and political, social and psychological – to conceive the composer in the public sphere as a subject located in a body of music and, rather than dissolving the subject into the music, to place history inside the subject, and thereby reinsert music into history. Let me therefore now turn to three exemplary figures who belong to what music history knows as the First Viennese School: Mozart, Beethoven, and – the only one who was born in Vienna – Schubert.

3

The First Viennese School

Mozart, pianos and women

When Count Arco, chamberlain to Archbishop Colloredo, threw Mozart out of the room with a kick on his backside in June 1781, expelling the rebellious young composer from the security of his position as a retained musician into the uncertain existence of what we nowadays call the freelance sector, his father, who had the highest opinion of his son's genius and hated his own servile position, was highly sceptical of his chances. In the event, says the twentieth-century music publisher Ernst Roth, it was not quite as bad as Mozart's heartbreaking letters and romantic biographers make out:

> Anyone who takes the trouble to find out what Mozart earned, even in the dark years of 1789–91, will discover that, while it was no princely income, it was by no means desperately little. If he and Constanze had not had the fatal habit of always spending more than they had there should have been no misery. Joseph Haydn died a wealthy man; Gluck had money to spare for speculating in stocks and is said to have left a fortune of 600,000 florins, thereby rivalling any composer or publisher who ever made money with music.[1]

Mozart derived his income from several sources: fees from piano lessons, commissions for new works, payments from publishers, ticket sales from concerts, and from 1787, his salary as the imperial *Kammerkompositeur*, a sinecure granted by the Emperor to help keep him in Vienna. One of the principal sources for this kind of analysis is Mozart's letters, a mine of information about the problems of making a living as a composer, which richly document the balancing act involved between these different activities. For example, writing to his father from Mannheim in December 1777, where he would have liked to stay but there wasn't a post, he paints a rosy picture of the prospects that surely await him in Paris:

> Wendling assures me that I shall never regret it . . . Once a man has written a couple of operas in Paris, he is sure of a settled yearly income. Then there is the *Concert Spirituel* and the *Académie des Amateurs*, which pay five *louis d'or* for a symphony. If you take pupils, the usual fee is three *louis d'or* for twelve lessons. Further you can get sonatas, trios and quartets engraved *par souscription*. Cannabich and Toeschi send a great deal of their music to Paris.[2]

Three months later, however, he is still in Mannheim – living off private lessons and commissions, but without publishing. 'I still have two of the six clavier sonatas to compose,' he tells his father at the end of February 1778:

> but there's no hurry, for I can't have them engraved here. Nothing is done in this place by subscription; it is a miserly spot, and the engraver will not do them at his own expense, but wants to go halves with me in the sale. So I prefer to have them engraved in Paris, where the engravers are delighted to get something new and pay handsomely and where it is easier to get a thing done by subscription.[3]

These remarks reflect the degree of risk which attached to music publishing, and remind us that the rights accorded to composers of music lagged behind those accorded to the written word; and, as Mozart was well aware, the lack of musical copyright necessitated great caution on the composer's part.

In October, after leaving Paris, he tries a different kind of venture. He writes to his father from Strasbourg of giving concerts, 'an even worse undertaking than in Salzburg'. The first was a solo performance: 'I played quite alone and I engaged no musicians, so that at least I might lose nothing. Briefly, I took in three *louis d'or* in all.' He was immediately encouraged to give

> a grand concert in the theatre. I did so and to the surprise, indignation and disgrace of all the people of Strassburg, my receipts were exactly the same . . . I took in a little more money certainly, but the cost of the orchestra (who are very bad but demand to be paid handsomely), the lighting, the guard, the printing, the crowds of attendants at the entrances and so forth made up a considerable sum.[4]

In short, Mozart's tour advanced his experience and his reputation, but he ended up back at Salzburg in the service of the Archbishop, who made precious few concessions to him.

The circumstances which led to the definitive break with the

Archbishop a couple of years later began with an important operatic commission for Munich, *Idomeneo*. The opera's success increased Mozart's faith in himself, and persuaded him, when he was summoned to rejoin the Archbishop's retinue for a period in Vienna, to stand up to his employer in more determined fashion than before. Frustrated that Colloredo failed to recognize his genius as a composer, complaining that at the dinner table he was placed between the valets and the cooks, he declared that the most intolerable insult was the veto imposed on the free, direct control of his musical finances. When the Archbishop ordered his retinue back to Salzburg, Mozart declined to go. There were arguments and noisy scenes, and finally Count Arco kicked him out. A recent biographer believes that the notorious kick in the pants has obscured the main point: Mozart was not dismissed, says Braunbehrens; he resigned.[5] The Italian musicologist Giorgio Pestelli thinks his actions do not quite have the romantic aura of Schiller, who ran away from the Duke of Würtemberg's castle the following year; none the less, he believes that whether Mozart forced the circumstances or the circumstances forced him, the break was highly symbolic, not only because he was a figure of such stature 'but also because of the violent friction of the time at which it happened, a few years before the French Revolution'; Mozart's rebellion was thus 'to assume the significance of a declaration of war between the new bourgeois world and the old regime of artistic production'.[6]

This needs some qualification. First, it would be a mistake to cast the Archbishop as an unreconstructed representative of the old regime. Politically, he was a reformist in the same mould as Joseph II (whose ten-year reign as Emperor, 1780–90, coincided almost exactly with Mozart's time in Vienna), an enlightened despot with portraits of Rousseau and Voltaire hanging in his study. Though he was unquestionably more radical than his employer, Mozart's conflict with the Archbishop was personal and financial, not political. Secondly, the break becomes all the more symbolic because of its effect on the style and content of Mozart's music, of which more in a moment. Thirdly, it also has a more private dimension. It was, on Mozart's part, an act of Oedipal revolt: by outward rebellion against the Archbishop, Mozart was able to break loose from both the Archbishop and his own father.

The only suitable base for a composer with Mozart's abilities and ambitions at that time was Vienna. No other city had so many musicians and such a pronounced love of music. The aristocrats who maintained their winter quarters in the city, like Colloredo, brought their orchestras with them; there were probably as many as a dozen such orchestras in residence at the height of the season. Those who did not maintain permanent orchestras had no difficulty hiring suitable musicians on an occasional basis. Moreover, in the liberal atmosphere brought about by Joseph II's reforms, concert-giving was not a special privilege of the nobility but a pursuit in which the bourgeoisie also engaged; this helped to attract musicians and ensure their plentiful supply. Furthermore, neither the aristocracy nor the bourgeoisie were passive consumers but, rather, enthusiastic amateur musicians themselves – an enthusiasm which found expression in the institution of the salon, which was supported by aristocracy and bourgeoisie alike.

This extensive music-making had several important effects for a composer like Mozart. First, it meant that there was a constant supply of pupils anxious to find the most renowned teachers. Secondly, it created a constant demand for new compositions for the private orchestras of the nobility and the public concerts of the bourgeoisie, both of which demanded almost exclusively new music, as well as the domestic milieux, which consumed keyboard music and chamber works in great quantity. The result was not only a booming market for sheet music, but most music, including Mozart's, was written on request or with a specific performance in mind. Thirdly, it meant that there was a large and eager audience ready to pay good money for public concerts. The result? Mozart's annual salary at Salzburg was 400 florins. Braunbehrens calculates that his income in Vienna from documented sources alone was never less than 756 florins (in reality it must have been somewhat larger); in only two years out of the ten he spent there did it fall below four figures; and in the best year it was as much as 3,216 florins. In fact, his average income corresponded to that of a court secretary – a rather lofty position.[7]

No one was better equipped for the life of a freelance composer than Mozart. His experience as a child prodigy, his early career as an international virtuoso performing concertos, his first-hand acquaintance with opera in all the major capitals of Europe, are all experiences that Haydn, for instance, missed. His problem was that he needed a manager or an agent, but such roles did not yet exist. His survival strategy rested on his assimilation and command of the widest range of styles of the day: both the extrovert and introvert sides of the *style galant*; both sacred and secular counterpoint; the 'heroic' styles of Italian *opera seria* and of Gluck; Italian *opera buffa* and the vernacular German *Singspiel*; the thematic clarity of popular dance and song forms on the one hand, the principle of thematic transformation on the other. He was capable of *tours de force* of classical counterpoint, like the finale of the *Jupiter* Symphony or the ball scene in *Don Giovanni*, and all these resources he treated, compared to Haydn, with a greater wealth of chromatic and dissonant effects, unusual tonalities and unexpected modulations, like the dynamic and almost brutal modulations in the finale of the Fortieth Symphony or the last piano concerto, not to mention his use of orchestral and harmonic colour to increasingly telling and penetrating effect. Freed from the emotional limitations of the Salzburg salons, he embraces the same language of passion which erupted in the new German literaure of the decade: Goethe's *Werther*, Wieland's *Oberon* (on which Weber based his last opera, written for London in 1826), and Klinger's *Sturm und Drang*, the play which gave the movement its name. If Mozart read Goethe's novel, he would have identified not with Werther the unhappy lover so much as Werther 'the burgher whose pride is wounded battering at the barriers of class', as Walter Benjamin puts it, 'who demands recognition for himself in the name of the rights of man'.[8] For this was precisely the spirit of the youthful challenge he threw down to the Archbishop.

After he settled in Vienna – which he loved, he said, for its pianos – Mozart resumed the composition of piano concertos. A few were designed for pupils, but most were for his own use in the many private and semi-public subscription concerts of the day. He became associated with a certain Martin, who organized amateur concerts at an inn called the Mehlgrube and then presented a subscription series in the Augarten, a public park in one of the suburbs, where Mozart appeared as composer-performer. A letter to his father shows how he tackled the task of writing music for a more popular audience than that of the salons:

> These concertos are a happy medium between what is too easy and too difficult; they are very brilliant, pleasing to the ear, and natural, without being vapid. There are passages here and there from which connoisseurs alone can derive satisfaction, but these passages are written in such a way that the less learned cannot fail to be pleased, though without knowing why.[9]

Mozart found great success in Vienna as a composer-performer. In the three years 1784–86 he produced no fewer than twelve new piano concertos, and at one stage he reported twenty-two concert appearances in less than six weeks: 'Well, as you may imagine, I must play some new works, and therefore I must compose.' These concertos become broader in their dimensions and bigger in their orchestral forces. There is more precision, delicacy and, above all, sonority in the orchestral writing; greater virtuosity but also darker harmonies, a more alert and subtle sense of key change, more uncertainty of mood. There is more blending of piano and winds but also more chromatic colouring, agitation and drama. In a word, these concertos are increasingly operatic. Treating the concerto as a dramatic form, Mozart made the soloist of his concertos more like a character in an opera than ever before. In every concerto by Mozart from 1776 on, says Charles Rosen, the entrance of the soloist is an event, like the arrival of a new character on stage.[10] You could add a text to one of these movements, said Kurt Weill, and it would become a dramatic aria.[11]

Opera was Mozart's supreme métier. In addition to everything else, he had already written a dozen operas and dramatic pieces in different styles before *Idomeneo*, which was followed by another nine in the space of ten years. One of these is a small but curious item, *Der Schauspieldirektor*, written for a private performance as an excuse to show off the actors and singers. The piece portrays the rivalry between two quarrelling prima donnas and the vain attempts of the impresario, a tenor, to pacify them. In the mid-nineteenth century, this vaudeville was turned into a full-scale opera with Mozart, Aloysia Langer and the singer-manager Schikaneder (the impresario and librettist of *The Magic Flute* and the first Papageno) as the principal characters. Mozart's nineteenth-century biographer Otto Jahn criticized this pastiche for the dishonour showed to Mozart's memory by presenting him in this not very creditable light; and as Edward J. Dent remarked, it could only confirm a view of opera as a concert of agreeable music with a more-or-less foolish play going on in the background.[12]

Nothing, in the case of Mozart, could be further from the truth. For as Braunbchrens puts it, almost every one of the operas of Mozart's Vienna period:

> reflect contemporary social phenomena and conflicts to an unusual degree. Mozart drew such parallels more resolutely and consistently than any other opera composer of the time, to the point of courting intervention by the censor. He demonstrated again and again his ability to detect cracks in the social structure, and he was not afraid to provoke his audience. His operas offer a commentary on contemporary issues and in doing so lay the groundwork for a new type of opera.[13]

In short, he becomes not just a public figure but a notable voice in the public sphere. We shall leave out of account only the last opera, *La clemenza di Tito*, commissioned for the coronation of Leopold II as King of Bohemia. A conventional *opera seria* adapted from an old libretto by Metastasio which hardly corresponded to Mozart's radical ideas about the medium, it is full of splendid music but dramaturgically weak.

*

The very first work which Mozart wrote for the Viennese stage, *Die Entführung aus dem Serail* (1782), already reveals both the originality of his approach and his political sympathies. Turkish subject matter was not just popular but, at a moment when the Russian–Austrian alliance against Turkey was being strengthened, timely, and Mozart's approach to it was far from conventional, either dramatically or musically. Dramatically, instead of following the general practice of the day, and setting a finished libretto, he required a collaborator – in this case the playwright Gottlieb Stephanie – receptive to his own theatrical ideas, prepared to rewrite and allow him to imprint his own concerns on the dramatic substance. *Die Entführung* is thus a revised version of a piece which Stephanie modelled on a libretto by a certain Bretzner, who took it from an English comic opera, *The Captive* (1769), which in turn had been adapted from Dryden's *Don Sebastian*. If this means that in certain respects the evolution of the libretto follows a familiar dialogical pattern, the music is a wonderful jumble of styles, freely mixing Italian *opera buffa*, popular song, French *vaudeville* and the grand tragic aria, in a manner which, according to contemporary accounts, brilliantly exploited the varied characteristics of a cast of highly accomplished singers. It seems that no mean part of Mozart's genius was his acute ear for the singers he wrote for, but the result is also a *Singspiel* of a quite novel kind, where a seemingly conventional scenario is turned on its head.

The story concerns Belmonte, a Spanish nobleman, trying to rescue his lover Constanze, her maid Blonde, and his servant Pedrillo from the clutches of the Turkish Pasha Selim, who has fallen in love with Constanze. The rescue is foiled by Osmin, overseer of the seraglio, despite an attempt to drug him with a sleeping potion. But instead of punishing his prisoners, the Pasha, recognizing Belmonte as the son of his enemy, magnanimously releases them with the words (spoken, not sung):

> 'It must be very natural for your family to do wrong, since you assume that I am the same. But you deceive yourself. I despise your father far too much ever to behave as he did. Have your freedom, take Constanze, sail home, and tell your father you were in my power and I set you free so you could tell him it is a far greater pleasure to repay injustice with good deeds than evil with evil.'

The effect is neatly described by Braunbehrens. The subject of Mozart's opera was the clash of opposing cultures, but in an altered perspective. A group of Europeans, representatives of the 'civilized' maritime nations, are detained against their will at the court of a Turkish ruler: 'after a rescue attempt from outside fails, they are shown magnanimity of a higher moral order than they ever knew in their European homelands'.[14] The treatment is farcical, in accordance with the format of the *Singspiel*, but the constituent elements are carefully calculated to raise unsettling questions about ethical standards. Blonde, for example, resisting the approaches of Osmin, to whom the Pasha has given her as a slave, cries out: 'Pasha this, Pasha that! Girls are not goods to be given away! I'm an Englishwoman, born to freedom, and I defy anyone who would force me to do his will!' The fact that Blonde is English (says Braunbehrens) is no coincidence. 'In the literature of the period, England regularly features as an example of a nation whose citizens enjoy full personal and civil rights, in deliberate contrast to conditions under an aristocratic despotism.'[15] Indeed, Mozart once referred to himself in a letter as an 'arch-Englishman'.

Die Entführung belongs to a literary tradition which originates with Montesquieu's *Persian Letters* (1721), in which, through the medium of an imaginary Persian visitor, the author criticized French institutions; the opera represents a variant of this genre, where the adventures of a European traveller in foreign lands provides a context which again illuminates the social situation at home. As Braunbehrens puts it: 'It was a sign of the times that such a cultural comparison could only be presented in the form of an adventure story.'[16]

Not yet present in *Die Entführung* is the realist portrayal of social interaction which marks out the three operas which Mozart wrote to libretti by Lorenzo da Ponte: *The Marriage of Figaro*, *Don Giovanni* and *Così fan tutte*. According to a biographer of da Ponte, the two of them were men of totally opposed characters and tastes who had little in common.[17] Da Ponte was a lesser version of his friend Casanova. As a young man in Venice in the 1770s, he acquired, like Casanova, a name as both a promising poet of advanced ideas – a radical with Rousseauist sympathies – and a libertine; in later years – he lived to the age of eighty-nine – he became a staunch conservative, and at times, in London and then New York, an opera impresario, a grocer, a schoolmaster, first Professor of Italian at Columbia College, and finally an impresario again. But da Ponte provided what Mozart needed: an able poet of his own generation and sympathies, willing to subordinate himself to the composer, who knew how to write about contemporary subjects in a contemporary idiom. This includes a breakthrough in ensemble writing, so that the contrapuntal style in which Mozart expressed his personal moment of liberation in the Haydn quartets here became the means for what the sociologist Alfred Schutz, in an essay on Mozart's operas, called a representation of the basic structure of the social world.[18]

Furthermore, in response to da Ponte's ability to fashion and concentrate the dramatic situation, Mozart turns his sense of style to new uses: it becomes a commentary upon the emotional state of the character rather than simply its supposed externalization; in this way, style itself becomes iconic and, therefore, socially significant and representative. George Bernard Shaw was to complain in the 1890s that the musical world failed to understand the portrayal of social reality in Mozart. 'I have heard public meetings', he said, 'addressed successively by an agricultural labourer's delegate, a representative of the skilled artisans and a university man: and they have taught me what all the treatises on singing in the world could not about the Mozartian differentiation between Masetto, Leporello and Don Giovanni.'[19] In fact, Mozart's characters frequently adopt a style of singing appropriate not simply to their class but to their self-perception, which is not necessarily the same thing, with the result that all three operas are stylistic novelties which conform to no single genre.

Among the most perceptive accounts of the trilogy is that of Christopher Ballantine. They richly demonstrate, he says, how 'the way social reality seems to be is not the way it "really" is', and the conventional arrangements men and women find themselves in and to which they seem bound frequently belie their deeper motivations and relationships. The external forms of their behaviour, hardened by social approval and custom, constitute a kind of *mask*. In their daily activity, men and women tend not to see behind these masks, their own and each other's, which screen their true relations and motivations: 'Mozart's major comic operas are scrupulously critical of these masks: they discover them in the manifold varieties and situations in which they occur, and then strip them away.'[20]

There is more. All three operas involve a Shakespearean play of confused identity and the sexual and erotic ambiguities that result, to which Mozart responded with music of such an unprecedentedly erotic character – especially in *Così* – that Kierkegaard considered him the most sinful of composers. At the same time, all of them are critically penetrating about the concupiscence of men and the subservient condition of women, and the frequent empathy of these male-authored works towards their female characters is unusual not only in their own time. In *Così*, the canny bachelor Don Alfonso induces a pair of suitors to play a trick on the two sisters they are courting, but it is the women, and especially the sisters' maid, Despina, who provide the superior example of intelligence in sentimental matters. (This is not the only case in Mozart where a woman of lower social status is the more canny: the same is true of Blonde in *Die Entführung* and Susanna in *Figaro*.) In

Don Giovanni, women are the victims of the diabolical seducer, and the supernatural ending, where the Commendatore's statue carries him off to hell, is not only a punishment exacted for the Commendatore's murder but also an appropriate due for his merciless use of women for the purposes of his own pleasure. It is in *Figaro*, however, that the women play the strongest role of all: it is they who propel the action forwards at every point. And at the end, Susanna and the Countess, by disguising themselves in each other's clothes, bring about the total discomfiture of the Count which Figaro had boasted he would achieve himself, thus giving Figaro something to think about too.

According to Charles Rosen, the sense of intrigue in these operas is indissoluble from their musical form. Mozart's historical opportunity lay in the new-found capacity of the symphonic style to fuse with a dramatic conception as no previous style had done. It is no accident that the finale of every opera from *Die Entführung* on ends in the key in which the opera started, and the complex tonal relations which are possible in sonata style lend themselves to dramatic complexity. So does motif development, which feeds the rich counterpoint of the ensemble and lends the arias a dynamic dimension. 'The changing forms of a motif not only give a logical coherence to the music, but allow it to express not a fixed sentiment, but an emotion that changes before our eyes . . .'[21] This is said of the aria '*Se vuol ballare*' in *Figaro*, but the same is true of other numbers like the great sextet of recognition in the third act, which is cast like a slow movement sonata form. Does the listener hear these relationships? It doesn't matter. There is at least one person, says Rosen, who is sure to recognize the reappearance of the tonic even without thematic reference: the performer, who thereby shapes the performance and, in the case of opera, translates this knowledge into plastic dramatic credibility.

In the case of *The Marriage of Figaro*, the political content is impossible to hide, but the circumstances which brought it to the stage have frequently been misconstrued. According to the familiar version, it was Mozart's idea to make an opera out of Beaumarchais's play *Le Mariage de Figaro*, a work of great scandal when it was staged in Paris in 1784. There were already two operas of the play to which it was a sequel, *Le Barbier de Séville*, by Paisiello and Benda. Mozart probably thought – and rightly – that the Viennese public would not be interested in *Figaro* only because it had been banned, but also because it was *The Barber*'s sequel. Composer and librettist therefore conspired together against the ban which had been placed on the performance of Beaumarchais's play by the Austrian censor, with the not-always-diplomatic Mozart relying on da Ponte, an urbane Christianized Italian Jew who was in favour at court, to pacify the Emperor and allow its performance. Thereupon, da Ponte provided a libretto which pithily abbreviates the play – not so much toning down the political rhetoric as refashioning the action to fit the demands of the operatic format.

As Braunbehrens shows, this version is only partly correct. The idea of the opera was Mozart's – da Ponte himself says so – but the truth is that Joseph II had a special interest in bringing the work to the stage – for the right audience. Since it was well known that the Emperor wished to abolish the legal privileges of the nobility and make its members subject to the same laws as the common man, a performance at the Burgtheater, before a broad public, would have seemed like official approbation of universal equality. This was not his intention, for the Emperor was not a revolutionary but an autocratic monarch, whose reforms were concerned with promoting the centralization of the state and modernizing its economy; his interest in equality was purely theological. A performance by the Italian company of the Hofoper (the imperial opera house), on the other hand, would send an entirely different message. The high admission prices and the use of the Italian language, which ordinary audiences did not understand, ensured a different class of patron. At the Burgtheater, in German, the public would have seen a degenerate and unsympathetic nobility through Figaro's eyes; while at the Hofoper, the nobility would be confronted with a representative of their own class, and with servants who would not silently tolerate whatever befell them. In short, the Emperor's command for the opera to be performed at the Hofoper was not a concession or an accommodation, but a political calculation. The opera advocated a basic element of Josephine policy, the elimination of aristocratic privilege, and was therefore a singularly effective means of propaganda among the nobility itself – they evidently did not find it much to their liking, for it initially ran for comparatively few performances.

Figaro is more than that, of course, as an examination of the circumstances again reveals. Writing for the Hofoper, Mozart had the advantage of what the Irish tenor Michael Kelly, who sang in its first performance, considered the best operatic cast that had ever been assembled. Since Mozart always wrote for the voices available – which here included four high sopranos evidently at the top of their form – *Figaro* is not the easiest opera to cast. This has left an ironic legacy. One of the sopranos, Marcellina, is nowadays often transmuted into a mezzo-soprano. The result is the loss of what is perhaps the opera's most outspoken political statement, which goes far beyond Josephine propaganda: her aria in the fourth act, where she calls upon women to defend themselves against the concupiscence of men. This omission is not, one feels, accidental. The corresponding passage in the original play was cut from its first production at the demand of the actors, to be restored by Beaumarchais in the published text. 'When the heart is free from personal interest,' Marcellina sings, 'every woman is forced to the defence of her poor sex against these ungrateful men with their oppressive wrong-doing.'

Don Giovanni and *Così* are further explorations of the nature of this wrong-doing. In the case of *Don Giovanni*, the idea came from da Ponte. Don Juan was already a proven and popular subject. Its origins go back to a Spanish play of 1630 by Tirso de Molina incorporating the old popular tale of the statue that came back to life. The story was then taken up by major dramatists like Molière, Corneille and Goldoni, but circulated even more widely in popular theatrical forms, including *commedia dell'arte*, puppet shows, farce and vaudeville. Molière's version dates from 1665; ten years later came Thomas Shadwell's *The Libertine*, for which Purcell subsequently wrote music; Goldoni's play dates from 1736; Gluck's ballet from 1761; operas by Vincenzo Righini from 1777, and Giuseppe Gazzaniga from 1782. It was the last, with a libretto by Giovanni Bertati, which da Ponte took as a model for his own version for Mozart. The libretto – and the score as well – was written in a hurry to a commission for an opera for Prague after *Figaro*'s great success there. It is something of a hotchpotch. Casanova was in Prague at the time, and it appears that when da Ponte was recalled to Vienna by the Emperor a few days before the premiere, he asked his old friend to make any last-minute alterations to the libretto which Mozart might require. According to da Ponte's biographer, there is no knowing how much he may have contributed, but 'that he may have done so has great fascination'. Indeed, historical sources show that Leporello in the opera bears a certain resemblance to Casanova's servant Costa. Whether Casanova himself provided a model for Don Juan is a different matter – after all, he owed his own renown to his fulfilment of a popular image.

The successive versions are marked by a rich dialogical interplay of revisions – with attempts to salvage the story for the formal theatre – and reversions to type. Goldoni, for example, the author of rational bourgeois comedies, removed the supernatural devices of the walking, talking stone statue and the descent into hell; in his version, Don Giovanni's fate is naturalistic: he is struck by lightning. Gluck's ballet removes all comic elements and places it in the tradition of *opera seria*.

If the statue and descent into hell are restored in da Ponte's libretto for Mozart, this is doubtless in order to satisfy the operatic hunger for theatrical spectacle. Yet in large part the immediate appeal of Bertati's version to Mozart and da Ponte was that here the Don is neither a romantic figure nor a licentious demon but an ordinary aristocrat who takes and never pays, and who is rightly condemned at the end because of his offences against natural social justice. It is crucial, in other words, that Mozart's *Don Giovanni* is presented as a contemporary story. Nevertheless, Mozart obviously enjoys the elements of popular fable – the Punch-and-Judy elements, as Rosen calls them – which, together with Leporello's clowning, have 'the greatest share in the imaginative and philosophical depth of the opera'.[22] This brings Mozart's version closer to the anti-rationalist world of the fable to be found in Carlo Gozzi, whose allegiance lay in the traditions of popular theatre and *commedia dell'arte*. In fact Mozart clearly felt a certain affinity for this type of theatre, for *Don Giovanni* is not the only example in his output. Indeed, Gozzi, the author of other dramatic fables to inspire composers (Puccini's *Turandot*; *The Love for Three Oranges* by Prokofiev, based on an adaptation by Meyerhold), was also the source for *The Magic Flute*, which, in the hands of Mozart and Schikaneder, became an expression of liberalism, and a covert attack on the government full of satire against the Austrian Catholic patriarchy, as well as a splendid piece of propaganda for the Freemasons – but more of this in a moment.

Partly as result of its stylistic mélange, this new *Don Giovanni* was decidedly indecorous. But if a critic of the first Berlin production wrote that the ear was enchanted while virtue was trampled underfoot, then, as Rosen says, 'the scandalous side of *Don Giovanni* has political as well as artistic overtones'. In the 1780s political and sexual liberalism had become intimately connected; for respectable citizens, 'the idea took the shape of a governing fear that republicanism implied ... sexual license. The Marquis de Sade ... did, indeed, claim the most extravagant sexual freedom as a logical corrollary of political liberty; his ideas were current everywhere in a milder form ...'[23] Mozart's intention is clearly not to advocate such ideas himself, but to play upon them. When Giovanni welcomes his guests with 'Viva la libertà', the dramatic context does not imply political liberty so much as freedom from convention. But this is to reckon without the music, which suddenly shifts from E flat major back to the tonic C major, with the entry of trumpets and drums *maestoso* in exhilarating martial rhythm.[24] When the Don mockingly echoes the revolutionary cries of liberty and fraternity, the dialectic of the historical context only reaffirms them, for no one in 1787, says Rosen, the year when the meeting of the Estates-General echoed over all of Europe, could have missed its significance. The overall effect is an unsettling ambiguity. On the one hand, Giovanni is a corrupt aristocrat; on the other he is a social rebel defying the rigid strictures of society. Mozart constructs the iconic interplay of his music accordingly. Donna Elvira and Don Ottavio, for example, as representatives of a dying aristocracy, must sing in the style of *opera seria*, difficult high-voiced parts riddled with artifice; by contrast, the *buffo* style of Giovanni and Leporello is more modern, more natural, and even, in Giovanni's case, more seductive. Once again, the result in terms of genre is unclassifiable, neither *Singspiel* nor *opera buffa*. Moreover, the ensembles and large-scale finales represent a new musical idiom, which Braunbehrens describes as 'through-composed sequences that lend a totally new temporal structure to the stage action'.[25] In short, for those who cannot avoid the desire to idealize the author's intentions, *Don Giovanni* can be seen only as a flawed masterpiece. From another point of view, however, its ambiguities are evidence of its dialogical character and the built-in contradictions of its intertextual tensions.

In *Così fan tutte*, it is not for nothing that Fiordiligi and Dorabella begin by singing in *opera seria* style. Here, says Ballantine:

> Mozart uses the archaic musical gestures of *opera seria* to symbolize situations in which people construe themselves or their world in antiquated ways . . . In the earlier part of *Così*, the sisters are less in touch with . . . their feelings than with somewhat outmoded notions such as honour, dignity, status and duty . . . Their real possibilities, and hence the truth about their present condition, are masked . . .

When they decide to succumb to the flatteries of their new suitors in the duet '*Prendero quel brunettino*' ('I'll take the dark one'), 'their words confirm this view: it will be mere sport, a joke. But the music tells us something quite different: exquisitely sensuous, graceful and lovely, what it really reveals is the rapturous frisson of a burgeoning erotic involvement.'[26]

In part, *Così* acquires its effect by becoming a parody of operatic conventions, though without ceasing to be operatic, without itself violating those conventions – though frequently contradicting them, which is not quite the same thing. What Mozart does is not just to use the music to contradict what the words imply, but also sometimes to treat the words in such a way that the seemingly appropriate musical setting is undermined. The opera's alleged amorality is therefore a misunderstanding, for by these means it becomes an anatomy of the social conventions which are preserved within those of opera, above all in the matter of the sexual mores and the relations between the sexes which we now call sexual politics. With his notable empathy for his women characters, Mozart is also able to look at his men with acute and unflattering objectivity; thus Alfonso is able to tell the sisters at the end: 'I deceived you, but my deception undeceived your lovers, who will henceforth be the wiser.' The only one he has neither deceived nor undeceived is Despina, the maid, who, as Ballantine says, inhabits with Alfonso the most socially progressive position in the opera. Significantly, she is also the lowliest person in it. Her other attitudes follow suit: she has subversive feelings towards men (she talks of women ruling the earth), she lacks servility, she is disinclined to acquiesce in archaic, superstitious attitudes. As a result, when Alfonso invites the two suitors to agree that women all behave the same – 'così fan tutte' – we may hear Despina's silent voice replying: 'and the same goes for men', echoing back at him the sentiments he has just expressed: that women are like that *because of the way men treat them*. In short, Despina, even more than Alfonso, assumes a 'creatively negative' posture towards the received social order, including Alfonso himself. This is crucial: it is what Mozart himself is doing with this opera, more consistently than in any other.

So *Così* is even more problematic than *Don Giovanni*. It might be possible to deal with *Figaro* by excising the offending passage, just like Beaumarchais's actors, leaving a brilliant and witty social comedy which apparently flattered bourgeois pretensions. *Don Giovanni*, with its proto-romantic mystery, presented no great problems, for all its contradictions, since justice is clearly seen to be done in the end. *Così*, however, despite the obligatory concluding moral, caused acute discomfort. That is why, beginning with Beethoven, the nineteenth century much preferred *The Magic Flute*, where Mozart, they thought, redeemed himself. For this very reason, *The Magic Flute* becomes a far more moralistic and, for the twentieth century, less interesting opera, redeemed not by its philosophy, imbued with the symbolism of Freemasonry, but by the sublimity of its music, combined with the innocent pleasure which is always to be found in the inspired combination of fairy tale and farce. However, if Braunbehrens is correct, this is to miss the original significance of *The Magic Flute* completely.

In the first place, Freemasonry in the years before the French Revolution had a uniquely emancipatory character, and in Vienna in the 1780s the movement acquired a very high profile, the result of a wide following among the intelligentsia. Despite the Josephine reforms, the Emperor remained an autocrat, and in these conditions

Freemasonry provided a forum among followers of Enlightenment thinking in different fields working to extend the spirit of reform – scientists, artists, writers, even senior government officials, including members of the nobility; one of the Viennese lodges even claimed that 'Freemasonry is constitutionally democratic'. Indeed, Freemasonry flourished precisely because the reforms had helped to create a liberal atmosphere. In these circumstances, in which so many of Mozart's friends and even patrons were members, it would have been surprising if he had not joined a lodge himself.

Joseph attempted to control the Freemasons not by banning them but by passing an edict placing them under state supervision. This had the desired effect of making the secret society less attractive, and as the political heat increased with the Revolution in France, membership became more dangerous. However, not only is there no evidence that Mozart ever thought of giving up his membership, but it seems that he aligned himself with the progressive faction within the movement which declined to countenance any retreat from progressive politics. *The Magic Flute* should therefore be seen as Mozart's contribution to the debate about Freemasonry, an apologia in defence of its liberal character. According to Braunbehrens, however, it is also a contribution to the debate within it, on an aspect particularly dear to Mozart's heart: the role of women.

The periodical literature of the time, he says, shows that the character of Freemasonry as a men's club was often discussed and called into question, especially in the liberal salons which Mozart frequented, like that of Countess Thun, where women played a leading role. A reading of *The Magic Flute* in proper historical context therefore suggests that the conventional notion of the story, in which Sarastro is the embodiment of Good and the Queen of the Night the embodiment of Evil, is superficial. Against the background of Viennese Freemasonry the characters and incidents in the opera are frequently self-contradictory. For example, the priests' duet ('Beware the wiles of women . . .') 'is set to such parodistic music that it is unclear whether the priests are making fun (of Sarastro, for example) or Mozart is caricaturing the priests'.[27] Then again, one of Tamino's trials requires Tamino to abjure Pamina's company. Yet Sarastro's order is countermanded by the priests, who admit Pamina to the Temple because she too has remained steadfast in the face of death. Moreover, Sarastro's power over the priests is also limited because they represent a democratic fraternity – and in that case it is also significant that the Chorus of Priests includes women's voices. In fact Sarastro is a misogynistic, slave-owning despot who, far from being a model of virtue and wisdom, urgently needs to apply his teachings to himself. It is hardly surprising that the Queen of the Night is his sworn enemy. In short, 'it is as if Mozart and Schikaneder wrote a private memorandum to the Freemasons, admonishing them to replace self-righteousness with modesty, fight authoritarianism in their own ranks, pursue freedom, equality and brotherhood, and maintain their goal of "enlightenment", which brings with it reason, justice and humanity'.[28] Except that it wasn't a private message at all, but a contribution to the wider public debate.

Beethoven, Goethe, Schiller, Hegel

Beethoven was born in 1770 in Bonn, where his father was a tenor in the service of the Elector Maximilian, who favoured the same progressive ideas as his brother, the reform-minded Joseph II, benevolent despot of Austria, follower of Voltaire and the Encyclopaedists. Ludwig thus grew up in a climate of enlarged intellectual freedom and the free circulation of ideas, a cultural environment furnished with a progressive reading club (to which he belonged) under the aegis of the Court which became a forum for radical thinking, and a university (which he attended) where Kantian philosophy was taught. Although he was not a prodigy like Mozart, Beethoven's talent flowered early, and he was appointed court organist at the age of fourteen. Three years later he also occupied a viola desk in the court orchestra, playing in several Mozart operas; this orchestral experience was a powerful influence.

The biographical data reveal that as a youth Beethoven got on well with people and made friends outside the circle of court musicians, especially in the university and the reading club. From a musical point of view, there is nothing especially radical about the pieces he was composing, only a penchant for surprises: clashing discords, unexpected rhythms, an echo of Haydnesque *Sturm und Drang*. Ideologically, however, Beethoven was to return repeatedly to this period. Several times in important later works he used material from vocal pieces written in Bonn. It is not just that he never let a good tune go to waste, but that the themes concerned became musical symbols for certain ideas from his schooling among the Bonn intelligentsia at the moment when the French Revolution took place. The first few bars of his setting from this period of Goethe's *Der Freie Mann* became the opening of the finale of the Fifth Symphony, then reappeared in another guise at the beginning of the Fifth Piano Concerto. A motif from the *Cantata for the Funeral of the Emperor Joseph* turns up in *Fidelio* – the words of the original passage are 'Then all mankind rose up into daylight'. A poem by

Bürger about mutual love provides the theme for the *Choral Fantasia*, to a run-of-the-mill poem by Kufner in praise of music and its powers; later it becomes the choral theme of the Ninth Symphony, where it is joined to Schiller's *Ode to Joy*, which Beethoven had first thought of setting as early as 1793 (and which Schiller had originally entitled 'Ode to Freedom': the change was to oblige the censors).

In 1793 Beethoven was freshly arrived in Vienna, a protégé of Count Waldstein, through whom he had access to the highest social circles. He was rapidly adopted by the aristocracy, which was liberal, enlightened and music-loving. For the sake of his commanding musical presence, they were quite prepared to tolerate his eccentricity and his bluntness; for his part, he made friends among them, and considered himself their equal. Meanwhile, the political conditions of Mozart's day had altered. Joseph II's successor Franz developed a pathological dread of the very word democracy, and political repression replaced Joseph's benevolence. Beethoven was perfectly aware of what was going on. 'You must not speak too loud here or the Police will give you lodgings for the night,' he writes to his publisher Simrock back in Bonn.[29] The depth of his sympathy with those who ended up as political prisoners is publicly expressed ten years later in *Fidelio*: the prisoners' chorus, the noble captive, and the reactionary governor are all taken from the oppression of the 1790s, and the genre, that of the 'redemption opera' [*Rettungsoper*], is associated with progressive ideas about natural justice.

But as the poet Grillparzer wrote in the deaf man's notebook a long time afterwards, 'at least the Censor can't touch music', and for Beethoven these were years of growing success, as yet untroubled by the deafness which first manifested itself around the end of the decade. This is the period of his early classical masterpieces. The recognition he was winning as both composer and pianist was unusual for a man still in his twenties. To a friend he wrote that he could sell everything he wrote five times over; years later, faced with financial problems, this is just what he tried to do – on account of which Berio once called him the first modern composer. Needless to say, he is devastated to discover the trouble in his ears, and in the same year he writes from Bonn to his old friend Wegeler: 'My ears hum and buzz all the time, day and night. I can truly say my life is miserable, for two years I have avoided almost all social gatherings because I can't possibly say to people "I am deaf" . . . Heaven knows what will become of me . . . Already I have often cursed my Creator and my existence. If possible I will defy my fate . . .'.[30] It is not until much later that his deafness becomes noticeable to other people, and not for several more years after that did it force him to withdraw from performance. The pianist Czerny recorded that 'although he had pains in his ears and the like ever since 1800 he still heard speech and music perfectly well until 1812'.

This is only apparently contradictory. What musician would not be terrified by signs of deterioration in the ears? And who can doubt that the threat of deafness, the buzzing, humming and ringing of tinnitus in the ear, can drive a composer mad: Schumann and Smetana both ended up in the asylum. (It is bad enough for a mere amateur who suffers from a milder version of the complaint, like the present writer.) But if Beethoven had gone deaf overnight he would have been done for, like a painter struck with blindness. He would not have become the representative figure in German music of the new bourgeois spirit, the equal of Goethe or Schiller in literature. He would probably be remembered as a lesser composer than Haydn or Mozart, and the history of music would have been different.

What seems to have happened is that his personality underwent a transformation. This is what Goethe perceived when he met him in 1812:

> I made the acquaintance of Beethoven in Teplitz. His talent amazed me. However, unfortunately, he is an utterly untamed personality, not at all in the wrong if he finds the world detestable, but he thereby does not make it more enjoyable either for himself or for others. He is very much to be excused, on the other hand, and very much to be pitied, as his hearing is leaving him, which, perhaps, injures the musical part of his nature less than his social. He, by nature laconic, becomes doubly so because of this lack.[31]

He was forced back upon himself, certain traits in his character became accentuated, but the process was gradual, and the first years of his deafness were years of growing maturity; work of great originality poured out of him unabated. He was sure of himself, established, surrounded by loyal friends whose admiration he returned with affection and respect. Ideologically and morally at peace, his only anxiety was money, which we learn about especially from his correspondence with publishers; we begin to detect that in business matters he has double standards. But he solves his problems by securing for himself an annuity to which a group of leading patrons subscribe, including Archduke Rudolph, Prince Lobkowitz and Prince Ferdinand Kinsky.

Beethoven's meeting with Goethe had taken place two years after he wrote the music for a production of Goethe's play *Egmont*. The Overture, already performed in his later years as a concert piece, is a concentrated example of the same musical dramaturgy as the *Eroica* and Fifth Symphonies. The play, according to Walter Benjamin:

is no political drama, but a character study . . . The only trouble with it is that this portrait of the fearless man of the people is all too idealized and this in turn lends greater force to the political realities uttered by Alba and William of Orange. The [ending] unmasks the supposedly political ideas of Count Egmont and reveals them as the poetic inspiration they fundamentally are. Goethe . . . had a very limited view of the revolutionary freedom movement which broke out in the Netherlands in 1566 under the leadership of Count Egmont.[32]

But this was not a problem for Beethoven, who saw no contradiction between poetry and politics, and was also both more naive and more radical than the poet. Goethe, says Benjamin, 'found the enlightened despotism of the eighteenth century problematic in the extreme. Nevertheless, he proved unable to reconcile himself with the Revolution.' Beethoven became a republican and stayed a republican, with the strongest of populist leanings – which partly explains why he was later so readily taken up by the nineteenth-century French socialists. At the same time he resolutely believed in the man of destiny, like Napoleon – or himself. What he hated was tyranny, and those who betrayed their principles, as did Bonaparte. *Egmont* was a perfect vehicle for these sentiments.

Early in 1805, England, Russia and Austria had formed a coalition against France, and national spending on preparations for defence was increased. In Austria the prices of consumer goods rose, and there was a serious shortage of food. Discontent ensued, and there were riots in Vienna. Beethoven was at his summer countryside retreat at the time, deep in the composition of *Fidelio*. Vienna grew increasingly nervous as the French advanced into Austria, taking Salzburg and marching down the Danube. The preparations were too little and too late. Nobles, bankers and merchants fled. The Emperor commanded the personnel of his theatres to remain, but the fate of the staging of *Fidelio* hung in doubt.

On 13 November, the French arrived, and entered the city without a fight. A few days later, after a tussle with the censor, *Fidelio* received its premiere, but in the absence of Beethoven's leading supporters – the cream of the city's aristocracy – the opera was not a success. This is somewhat ironic, for Beethoven, unlike his patrons, was not in fear of the French. He took the events in his stride – he had already lived through similar occurrences in 1792 as a twenty-one-year-old pianist-composer in Bonn, when the French, provoked by counter-revolutionaries on their border, sent their forces into Germany, and the Elector of Bonn, Beethoven's employer, packed up and left the city. It was then that Beethoven obtained leave of absence and set out for Vienna, never to return. (The French army was advancing fast, and the Hessian troops were rushing to intercept them. An entry in the composer's notebook reads: 'Tip to the coachman, because he went like the devil right through the Hessian armies, one thaler.')

By the time the French came to Vienna thirteen years later, Beethoven had already voiced his disappointments in Napoleon, but continued to support the French Republicans for the liberation from obscurantism and clerical rule which they brought to the territories they occupied. But now his attitude changed, as he began to see in Napoleon the rapacious desire for imperialist conquest. He wrote to Camille Pleyel in Paris: 'Dear Camillus – that was the name of the Roman who chased the wicked Gauls out of Rome: I too should like to . . . chase them away from all the places where they don't belong!'[33] When Napoleon marched on Austria once more four years later, and again the aristocracy left, including most of Beethoven's friends in the Court and the administration, Beethoven lamented the departure of Archduke Rudolph with a sonata of the greatest poignancy called *Les Adieux*, inscribed: 'The Farewell, Vienna, 4th May 1809'. When the French opened fire on the city a week later with a battery of howitzers, Beethoven, like others, sought refuge; he found a niche in the cellar of his brother's house, where he covered his head with pillows 'so as not to hear the cannons' and protect his hearing. Within hours the city capitulated and found itself once again suffering the miseries of a two-month occupation. Food shortages were worse than in 1805, and again there were riots. The worst effects were financial, for the shortages led to a steep rise in the interest rate. Beethoven, who was not so badly off at the time, none the less felt the pressure severely; he was unable to work, and soon grew short of money.

It was not until 1813 that Europe combined against Napoleon and began to drive him back to Paris. With the allied victory in 1814 cultural life began to return to normal, and Beethoven's music was freshly acclaimed. Vienna hosted an international peace congress, and Beethoven was heard and applauded by the assembled potentates. *Fidelio*, now considerably revised and tightened up, was chosen as the first opera to be presented to the Congress celebrities – another irony in view of what was to come. To begin with, Beethoven found it increasingly difficult to compose. At the same time the effects of the war on the Viennese nobility proved grim. Even so solid a noble as Count Waldstein sank into debt, and many went bankrupt.

Moneylenders and bankers came to their assistance, thereby

accelerating the process of middle-class takeover from the aristocracy; artistic and musical patronage became the prerogative of the bourgeoisie. Beethoven lost a considerable portion of his income through the effects of devaluation on his patrons, including the bankruptcy of Prince Lobkowitz. And in spite of the esteem in which he was held, demand for his music decreased, for it was no longer performed and commissioned on the same scale. Since the Congress the rage was for dance music, Italian *opera buffa* and *Singspiele* of the most frivolous type. Talleyrand had joked: '*Le Congrès danse mais il ne marche pas*'. The government, Stendhal commented, encouraged 'music, suitable to the taste of the age, which diverted the mind from politics', and 'pleasures of a more sensual kind which are less troublesome to a government'.[34] Beethoven complained: 'since the Italians have taken hold here the best art is in jeopardy. The nobility has no eyes for anything but ballet, no feeling for anything but race-horses and dancing-girls.' He added: 'Rossini is a talented and melodious composer; his music suits the frivolous and sensuous spirit of the time and his productivity is so great that he writes an opera in weeks where Germans take years.'[35]

Political prospects, far from improving, grew bleaker. The princes went home to take up the thrones designated for them by Metternich, the Austrian Chancellor; in Germany, the French autocracy was replaced by the local aristocracy: despotism, in Marx's words, 'was given naturalisation papers. The Germans thus exchanged one Napoleon for 36 Metternichs, and the Congress had ensured reaction for 33 years.'[36] In Vienna Franz II resumed the crown of the Holy Roman Empire. Political demonstrations took place and, as Frida Knight puts it, older citizens of radical opinions who remembered the difficult days of the 1790s were shocked at the revival of repression.[37] That Beethoven was one of them we learn from his friend and first biographer Anton Schindler, who himself was arrested in Brunn (Brno) merely because his papers were not in order.

Schindler first met Beethoven soon after his release from jail. The composer had heard of his misadventure from a mutual friend and asked to make his acquaintance, 'to hear from my own lips the events that had taken place in Brunn'. They began to meet regularly in a tavern where Beethoven went to read the newspapers, which was frequented by a group of 'Josephinists' – admirers of Franz's reformist predecessor Joseph II. Beethoven was not out of place in this company, though not because he had forgotten his republicanism; he consorted with Josephinists, says Knight, because they were partisans against the rigid police state imposed by Metternich. Beethoven's political sympathies were well known – he never hid them. He kept himself well

informed of everything that was going on, especially through his friend
J.K. Bernard, who in 1819 became editor of the *Wiener Zeitung*. He tells
him, for example, of student uprisings in 1817, and a couple of years
later reports: 'The banker Rothschild from Franfurt has arrived . . . He
went to see Prince Metternich immediately . . . These big bankers have
all the ministers of Europe under their thumb and can make trouble
for the governments whenever they please. There can be no political
solutions now without their help.'[38] The composer was constantly
warned by his friends as they sat in the Viennese cafés please not to
talk so loud, and preferably to leave off saying certain things altogether.
Beethoven, however, disdained the government spies, and may well
have been protected by his many patrons in high places. Ironically, he
was once arrested none the less. One day, in the summer of 1821, he
went roaming in the countryside, as he had always been used to do.
But on this occasion he wandered far and got lost, and with his
dishevelled appearance, he was arrested as a vagrant. Nobody would
believe him when this strange deaf madman kept yelling he was
Beethoven, until someone was called to identify him.[39]

Schindler, on the other hand, was a nervous fellow who, outwardly at
least, respected the establishment, and therefore disapproved of the
Master's insulting remarks about it, which he later excised from the
conversation books before they were published. The flavour of these
remarks, however, is preserved in the letters – for example, in the jokes
which Beethoven exchanged with the publisher Steiner, to whom he
affectionately referred as 'the Adjutant': 'Since the Adjutant by recently
indulging in tittle-tattle has again disclosed his treacherous and seditious opinions, his right ear must be sharply seized and pulled . . . so
that fear and dread of committing any crimes in future may be instilled
into him.'[40] It is these circumstances which explain the nature of the
late works: on the one hand, the intense introspective exploration of
the piano music and string quartets; on the other, the two huge final
defiant public statements of liberal humanistic faith, the *Missa Solemnis*
and the Choral Symphony.

The middle-period works are not only flush with heroic virility, they
also contain music of immense tenderness, like the Violin Concerto
and the Fourth Piano Concerto. It is the range and contrast of moods
that is growing all the time, and with Beethoven's mastery of orchestral
writing the tenderness is all the greater, because the degree of violence
he unleashes is also the more unprecedented. There is already untold
power in the Fifth Symphony, and when the composor Louis Spohr

heard the Seventh he declared that Beethoven was fit for the madhouse (Carl Maria von Weber had thought the same after hearing the Third). Popular biographies link this battering music with his deafness, but it has nothing to do with it. (They say that his deafness made him pound his piano till he broke the strings, but the strings broke because the pianos of the time were still mechanically deficient. Liszt also used to break them.) The crux of the matter is this: Mozart's late music already contains much oscillation of mood, but never such extremities. He too rings the most exploratory harmonic changes, only everything is contained within a decided elegance: he always maintains (in Wilfred Mellers's phrase) a civilized equilibrium between lyrical grace and tonal drama. Above all, there is none of the breakages of the thread, the disruptions, which become so forceful in Beethoven's last period.

The late works of Beethoven are full of the most terrifically uncouth features: ruptures, dislocations, violent altercations of loud and soft, melodic leaps, startling harmonic switches, disruptive rhythmical shifts, along with constant experiments in the formal arrangement of the movements. But these are not the incoherent ravings of a mad-man at the end of his tether, and Beethoven is far from being the only artist of his period who seeks to break the frame of artistic illusion, to shatter the smooth surface which Schiller called *Schein*, and in this way anticipate the stance we more readily associate with modernism a hundred years later. There are several artists among the Romantics who already possess this impulse: Hoffman in his novel *Katur Murr*, which purports to be written by a cat; and Tieck in his play *Puss in Boots*. Both employ devices in which the audience is addressed directly, from behind the façade of the polished artifice, as if the artist himself were speaking through the veil of art, or trying to break out from behind a one-way mirror. In Mann's *Doctor Faustus*, Wendell Kretzschmar, the music teacher, lecturing on Beethoven's last piano sonata, shouts out over the music, at the point where it dissolves into a sea of trills, that here the appearance of art is thrown aside:

> 'These chains of trills!' he yelled. 'These flourishes and cadenzas! Do you hear the conventions that are left in? Here – the language – is no longer – purified of the flourishes – but the flourishes – of the appearance – of their subjective – domination – the appearance – of art is thrown off – at last – art always throws off the appearance of art. Dim-dada! Do listen.' . . .[41]

The musical experience of the late Beethoven, says Adorno, shows a definite mistrust of the classical unities: 'the unity of subjectivity and objectivity, the roundness of symphonic successes, the totality emerging from the movement of all the parts'. In short, 'he exposed the classical as classicising'. He is no longer satisfied with conflicts so obviously contrived, with manipulated antitheses and the illusory appearance of unity. He seems to seek transcendence in the fragmentation of the surface: 'In the last quartets this takes place by means of the rough, unmediated juxtaposition of callow aphoristic motifs and polyphonic complexes. The gap between both becomes obvious and makes the impossibility of aesthetic harmony into the aesthetic content of the work; makes failure in a higher sense a measure of success.'[42]

If Beethoven's music stages a heroic confrontation with hope, the musical arena for this confrontation is sonata form. Beethoven treats sonata form as a point of summation for the entire preceding history of musical forms, all of which, he demonstrates, it is possible to encompass within its own formal principles. According to the text-books, sonata form is at the same time a certain type of thematic construction and a certain arrangement of movements, both of which achieve a sense of formal balance and symmetry by their observation of certain key relations – those governed by the hierarchical system of triadic harmony. The form demonstrates and dramatizes the logic of tonal contrast. But on a symbolic level, even the music theorist Hein-rich Schenker admits that the 'fundamental purpose' of the form was 'to represent destiny', in the shape of the 'personal fate' of the motifs employed: 'The sonata represents the motifs in ever changing situations in which their characters are revealed, just as human beings are represented in a drama . . .'[43]

Sonata thinking contains a series of divergent principles within the general framework of a closed and rational structure. The decisive factor is containment. It became a system, a principle of composition rather than just another musical form, which thereby constituted unity in variety, fusing together on the one hand the ideal, the rational, the abstract concept of necessary formal truth, and on the other the sensuous, the subjective and the emotional. A number of writers have observed a correspondence between the sonata principle and the systems of metaphysical thought which culminated in Hegelian dialec-tics. Among them is the musicologist Philip Barford, who sees in both the same mediation between the sensuous and the ideal, the subjective and the universal, and the same fusion of passion and principle. The question has been debated in the pages of the journal *Telos* by two Solomons, Maynard and Robert C. The former argues that this resemblance stems only from the general applicability of Hegelian dialectics to the analysis of musical form, and the true vocation of the sonata is to embody a purely utopian notion of universal order, in which tragedy is resolved into harmony and serves 'to relieve us of guilt and responsibility'.[44] For the latter, sonata form – at least in Beethoven – does not end with resolution, but sets up new tensions and a renewed struggle, and 'one would have to be more than stone-deaf not to hear in Beethoven's music a progression of struggles, victories, and destinies that exactly characterise the human spirit of the times in which he composed'. There is not the slightest evidence that Beethoven knew anything of Hegel (or that Hegel cared anything for Beethoven), but the composer is an apt manifestation of Hegel's 'world-spirit' [*Weltgeist*], the 'heroic archetype' of revolutionary national aspirations.[45]

Wilfred Mellers goes so far as to see Beethoven's three periods as the three stages of the Hegelian triad, but then his whole interpretation of Beethoven tends towards metaphysical psychologism. Nevertheless, the metaphysical element is definitely present. Evidence: Bettina Brentano's famous report of her conversations with the composer, which, even if the words are hers and not his, still has the ring of authenticity: 'Speak to Goethe about this, tell him to listen to my symphonies, for then he will admit that music is the only entrance to the higher world of knowledge which, though it embrace someone, a man cannot grasp.'[46] This is the famous passage where Beethoven compares music and himself to electricity – at that time, still a novel phenomenon, and the youngest of the branches of science, its future accomplishments as yet undreamt of. As Goethe recounted in *Poetry and Truth*, those were years in which electrical machines appeared in the fairgrounds among the curiosities and magical tricks. Music, says Brentano's Beethoven:

> is the electrical soil in which the spirit thinks, lives and invents ... Music relates the spirit to harmony. An isolated thought yet feels related to all things that are of the mind: likewise every thought in music is intimately, indivisibly related to the whole of harmony, which is oneness. All that is electrical stimulates the mind to flowing, surging, musical creation. I am electrical by nature.[47]

(Is that why the Central Electricity Generating Board took to using the *Eroica* in its television advertisements?)

Everyone seems to agree that there is something utopian about sonata. There is disagreement whether this is the illusory utopia of an aristocracy bolstered by doctrines of enlightened despotism and political liberalism, or – the more general opinion – the revolutionary utopianism of the new bourgeois world order. But there is no question that the idea of sonata as a Hegelian phenomenon is highly suggestive. First of all, it is a way of musical thinking which generates contradictions between oppositions of tonality, themes and rhythmic figures. These extend over the course not only of the individual movement but of a whole multi-movement structure. Behind the surface dissimilarities generated by these oppositions is a latent identity which we feel but do not always comprehend. This identity is disclosed by analysis, which reveals that the themes consist, as Ballantine puts it, in partial and contradictory 'appearances' of a Hegelian kind. Hegelian Reason then goes to work on them in the development section. The recapitulation which follows is no mere reprise or repetition, but restatement *on a new level*. The sonata, like the Hegelian unification of opposites, ends only when reason has organized things so that 'every part exists only in relation to the whole', and 'every individual entity has meaning and significance only in its relation to the totality'.[48]

The preceding musical ideal of fugue assumes a harmonious, balanced and ordered totality. Sonata 'wants nothing to do with this assumption. It negates it with the experience of contradiction'. The internal contradictions of the sonata replace the symmetry of the Baroque. Stable themes are replaced with increasingly unstable subjects and groups of motifs; thematic transformation replaces imitation and variation, both of which, at the same time, it eagerly encompasses. Sonata dramatizes the principle whereby something may become something else under the driving force of contradiction; it is the highest musical articulation of the idea of forward movement through conflict. Indeed, Beethoven seems to be testing this thesis in his penchant for rude, commonsensical clichés – the currency of the obvious which, according to Hegel, offers only a deceptive security – which are then subjected to a heroic ordeal before they emerge transformed and triumphant. Ballantine quotes a passage from Hegel which sounds like a description of a passage in a late Beethoven string quartet:

> the spirit . . . matures slowly and quietly towards the new form, dissolving one particle of the edifice of its previous world after the other, while its tottering is suggested only by some symptoms here and there . . . the indeterminate apprehension of something unknown . . . harbinger of a forthcoming change. This gradual crumbling which did not alter the physiognomy of the whole is interrupted by the break of day that, like lightning, all at once reveals the edifice of the new world.[49]

We are in the realms of the *Phenomenology of the Spirit*.

Beethoven was born in the same year as Hegel, and becomes the most Hegelian of the classical composers. He was eighteen years old at the time of the French Revolution. Mozart was fourteen years older, but died only three years later. History therefore sees the difference between them in Beethoven's assimilation of the experience of the Revolution. Beethoven is like Hegel's 'world-historical individual' standing at the head of the modern era which he helped to inaugurate. He is the first modern composer, says Ballantine, because he is the first to confront a universe whose order he could neither believe in nor accept. Chaos is real or immanent, and in the task of facing it Church and State are no longer able to offer any succour, because the chasm has opened up under their very feet.[50] Indeed, Beethoven was as anticlerical as he was republican. It is no accident that in 1825, when he presented the Choral Symphony and three movements from the *Missa Solemnis* in what turned out to be his last concerts, Schindler was afraid that the latter might be prohibited because of objections by the Archbishop. The ruling that forbade the performance of the sacred text in Latin in a theatre was lifted only on condition that the pieces were presented in German and billed as 'Three Grand Hymns'. Once more this is ironic, for the *Missa Solemnis* is not a church service anyway, but a dramatic and poetic interpretation of the words of the Mass. It is no coincidence, says Adorno, 'that the transcendental moment of the *Missa Solemnis* does not refer to the mystical content of transubstantiation but to the hope of eternal life for humanity'.[51]

But if this is the transformation of liturgy into spiritual autobiography, it is not the same interior world isolated from public experience embodied in the late sonatas and string quartets. The *Missa Solemnis* and the Choral Symphony appealed directly to the living memory of the city itself in the course of the Napoleonic Wars. As the music critic Ernest Newman somewhere described it, when Beethoven, in the final 'Agnus Dei' of the Mass, calls his audience back with warlike trumpet fanfares and drum rolls from the rapturous vision of the divine to the harsh realities of life, there is a terrifying immediacy in the cry of the soloists and the anguish of the chorus in the final prayer for peace. It is dangerously close to a travesty that the song of human brotherhood from the symphony in the same concert should be adopted by the European Community as their anthem, but entirely appropriate that it has become the hymn of the followers of liberation theology in Latin America.

The Schubertiade

When the Czech composer Tomaschek played Goethe his now forgotten setting of Mignon's song '*Kennst du das Land*', Goethe was pleased with it and told him:

> I cannot understand how Beethoven and Spohr could have so completely misunderstood the song as to set each verse to a different melody. I should

have thought that the same distinctive features in the identical place in each stanza would be sufficient indication to the composer that what I expect is a song pure and simple. By her very nature, Mignon can only sing a song, not an aria.[52]

Goethe made a similar complaint when he first heard Schubert's setting of *Erlkönig*, which – thanks to one of the composer's most loyal friends, Joseph von Spaun – is the subject of a famous anecdote. 'We found Schubert in a state of great excitement, reading *Erlkönig* aloud from a book,' wrote Spaun in a reminiscence:

> He walked up and down several times with the book in his hand. Then suddenly he sat down and in an incredibly short time – no longer than it took him simply to write it down – the glorious ballad was put on paper. As Schubert had no piano, we rushed to the Convict with it, and there, that very same evening, *Erlkönig* was sung and received with rapturous applause.[53]

The year was 1815; Schubert was eighteen years old. Here, of course, is that image of Schubert with which we began: a naive artist in Schiller's sense, from whom the music simply flowed. Whether or not this particular tale is quite true, and not perhaps exaggerated – it is, after all, the fond memory of one of the composer's closest friends – it lends itself to a distortion; it suppresses too easily the headwork which precedes the activity of putting to pen to paper. Schubert retains his claim to naivety *à la* Schiller in the evident rapidity of this headwork, a facility he shared with composers like Handel and Mozart, in contradistinction to a Mahler, say, or a Boulez; but this hardly signifies an uncritical attitude to composition. In fact, in the case of *Erlkönig*, he revised the song three times before 1821, when it became – on the initiative of his friends, who took care of the expenses – Schubert's first published work, and the first to begin to spread his fame abroad. These are the details dug up by scholarly biographers; the popular accounts ignore such indicators, or mention them only as incidentals, thus helping to suppress any deeper understanding of the composer's art. We shall find it to be only one of various acts of suppression on the image of Schubert, in the interests of rendering as innocuous as possible a composer whose music was in a crucial sense a disturbing deviation from the social norms of bourgeois society.

Nevertheless, both the story and the song may strike us as the epitome of Romanticism, above all for the sense of possession in both composer and poem, plus the fact that it was a masterpiece of precocious youth. Indeed, no single example could be better chosen to exemplify the process of aesthetic transformation which separates the nineteenth century from the eighteenth. What we know of the song's genealogy and the responses it evoked in those it touched directly constitutes a vivid demonstration of the dialogical process in action, so to speak, a historical instance of the metamorphosis of a text through translation, imitation and musical interpretation.

To begin with, there is the question of the *Urtext*. The poem originates in the stylized recovery of folk art which preceded Romanticism proper, and helped to prepare the ground for it. Goethe's source was a free translation into German by his mentor Herder of an ancient Danish ballad, *Sir Olaf*. In Herder's version, the ballad tells of a bridegroom riding to meet his bride; the Erlking's daughter bewitches him, and he is found dead in the morning. In refashioning Herder's reading and giving it the *Sturm und Drang* treatment, the poem comes to exemplify both the personification of the forces of nature and the theme of childhood innocence and vulnerability which are prime Romantic traits. In Goethe's poem the bridegroom becomes a father riding with his child in his arms; the Erlking himself is the bewitcher, and the father is a helpless spectator of a drama which he cannot fathom. According to another well-known anecdote – this time about Goethe – the transformation of Herder's ballad was the result of an incident witnessed by the poet one autumn evening, when he saw from his garden a rider galloping past his gate. He wrote the poem when he subsequently discovered that the man was a farmer taking his sick child to the doctor.

But if Goethe transforms Herder's ballad, Schubert transforms the poem. He ignores the strophic form and applies the method known as *Durchcomponierung* – straight-through composition. We are therefore not surprised to discover that Goethe did not think much of Schubert's setting when he first heard it. Years later, however, when he heard it sung by Wilhelmina Schroeder-Devrient, he is recorded as saying: 'Had music, instead of words, been my instrument of thought, it is thus that I should have framed the legend. I once heard this composition in my earlier life, and did not think it agreed with my views of the subject. But executed as you execute it, the whole becomes a complete picture.'[54]

According to one of Schubert's friends, writing in the *Wiener Zeitschrift für Kunst* in 1822, the 'organic unity' of his setting of *Das Erlkönig* comes from 'the harmonic expression, the tone imparted to it by the accompaniment':

This is the foundation on which the tone picture is laid ... the melodic expression characterises the inner meaning of the action, the changing emotions of the father, the child and the erlking, while its outward aspects, such as the galloping horse and the intermittent howling of the gale, are outlined by the most appropriate figures of accompaniment.

Such a treatment was the only one possible if the 'romance-like tone of the poem' was to be sustained without sacrificing the differences in speech of the characters within it, for in this way differences in vocal expression are unified by the accompaniment, which also provides a musical painting of the atmosphere.[55]

The song, then, is a dramatization of the poem in the form of a dialogue of alternating voices. Not the least of Schubert's accomplishments is to distribute these voices within the singer's tessitura in such a way that the singer never need stoop to a forced difference in vocalization in order to catch the contrasts – the lay of the melody does it for them. (Here I say 'them', because it is a significant fact about the *lied* that the gender of the singer is in a special sense indeterminate: unlike the operatic aria, it is not specific to the voice of a particular sex.) Despite Goethe's evaluation of such settings, this is truly song, a musical form close to the amateur, not an operatic aria, which, contrariwise, exploits the virtuosity of the trained voice.

If Schubert's method is a means of shifting point of view within the narrative, then it pivots around the treatment of the piano when the Erlking speaks. For the rest of the song, the narrative point of view is external. As one account puts it: 'we watch the ride, we hear the child's voice and the father's reassuring answers. But only the child hears the Erlking . . .'.[56] That is, the child and the music, for the piano transports us into the child's position with its rocking, almost lulling movement: the voice which the boy hears turns out to be soft and enticing, 'a kind of elfin fairy music, in stark contrast to the pounding, harmonically restless accompaniment that otherwise pervades the song', as Lawrence Kramer describes it.[57] The song has even been criticized on the grounds that the Erlking 'addresses the child in too sweet and caressing tones. [But] there is a horrible menace in that sweetness.'[58] This, of course, is exactly the point. What Schubert expresses here – and in similar ways in so many other songs – is an attraction for death and a sweet escape from the troubles of the world that makes its peculiarly intense beauty of expression both suspect and disreputable. This is not a sentiment which is present in the poem. It is the gift of the music, which gives the words a kind of double-voicing. And it is present in Schubert long before he knew he had contracted syphilis, and had to face the prospect of his own death.

And if it isn't death, then it's sexuality, another field of suppression.

It is truly remarkable how most of the voluminous writing on Schubert's lieder avoids any comment on their poetic texts, and thereby fails to mention the most obvious fact about some of his most popular songs, like *Die Forelle* and *Heidenröslein* – that they are sexual allegories. And not at all subtle ones, but full of blatantly Freudian imagery, like the fisherman's rod and the rose with its thorn. One commentator mentions in passing: 'When Ferdinand Schubert [the composer's brother], in 1845, produced a set of song-books for use in the Viennese schools, he included "Heidenröslein"; the education authorities of the city objected to the inclusion of such a song, because of its "lascivious text".' The writer adds: 'Fortunately the song can be sung without awareness of such undesirable symbolism.'[59] This is where late-twentieth-century sensibilities turn Schubert as we shall see into a very different composer from the image which prevailed from the time of his 'rediscovery' in the mid-nineteenth century until very recently.

Schubert lived in the same city as Beethoven, and died there only a year after him. It was not a large city – quite a bit smaller than London and Paris, the other major musical capitals of the day – but it almost seems as if he lived in a separate world. In the popular biographies, at any rate, Schubert regarded Beethoven as a distant god, to whom he eventually sent some of his songs with a certain trepidation; although at least one account suggests that they were personally acquainted. Nevertheless, there is a certain truth here. The two composers clearly belonged to different milieux. This is not a question of class; a system of class divisions – whether Marxist or, for that matter, the kind applied by market researchers – fails here. It is not, for example, about Beethoven's association with the Viennese aristocracy, which never impeded the wider social intercourse of professional musicians among themselves; but it is to do with the limits of Schubert's social sphere, the self-containment of a clique, a brotherhood of alienated youth – we must remember that Schubert was only thirty-one when he died – combined with a personal peculiarity rather odd in a musician, to which a recent biographer, Elizabeth Norman McKay, has drawn attention. Throughout his life, she says, 'he seems to have been remarkably uninterested in attending performances of his music . . . and singularly unconcerned about their reception, placing little value on the reactions of audiences'. There is a note in his diary in 1816 to the effect that whether a performer 'receives applause or not will depend on a public subject to a thousand moods'.[60] From this one can only conclude that Schubert perceived a distinction between the public, which was impersonal, and the audience comprised by his friends and acquaintances, from which he drew the most intense succour.

McKay discusses the likelihood that Schubert suffered from cyclothymia; perhaps someone will come along and tell us that he had Asperger's Syndrome, and that this explains his professional unreliability and at times boorish behaviour. For us, what is most noteworthy in this oddity is that it suggests the need to reconceptualize further our understanding of the bourgeois musical sphere. Indeed, it leads us to the discovery of an intermediate, transitory or interstitial space, a masculine space outside the family but only semi-public, typically the domain of youth and the young tyro, based within a circle of close friends which often creates an intimacy greater than that of the family, and therefore preserves a privacy in which a composer like Schubert can reject the public world and its materialist and conformist values. Such rejection is, of course, the expression of a form of alienation which also leaves its mark in the music – in this case in Schubert's preference for lieder and chamber music, and his special appeal to intimacy and inwardness. This much was enough for the generations who rediscovered his music later in the century (little was published in his lifetime, and many of his bigger scores remained stored away in his brother Ferdinand's drawers until twenty or thirty years later). But Lawrence Kramer goes further, and suggests that Schubert represents an 'errant' subjectivity, with an attitude of insubordination to the norm, which expresses itself especially by placing the norm of virile masculinity in question. The protagonist of *Die schöne Müllerin*, the song cycle which is one of his greatest achievements, is a miller's journeyman who 'defaults on all the requirements of manliness'. He has no capacity for masculine rivalry, he cannot win the woman he loves, and at critical moments he breaks down.[61]

And then there are songs – to well-known poems by Goethe, like *An den Mond* and *Ganymed* – which evoke the theme of erotic friendship between young men in classical Greece. (Ganymede, notes Kramer, regularly embodied the object of homosexual desire in the art and literature of early modern Europe, from Michelangelo to Shelley, who retraced Winckelmann's steps through Rome discovering sculpted Ganymedes, 'those sweet and gentle figures of adolescent youths in which the Greeks delighted'; one of which made it 'difficult to conceive anything more delicately beautiful'.)[62] There has recently been scholarly argument that homosexuality figured prominently in the lives of Schubert and his circle, and that Schubert himself was homosexual, or at least bisexual – it is generally accepted that he died of syphilis (with complications), first diagnosed in 1822 or 1823, which he probably contracted from one of Vienna's prostitutes. Whether he was homosexual is a question which remains unanswerable, as Kramer agrees, but he makes a very strong case that Schubert's music sings, among other things, of homoeroticism.

The Convict, where Schubert and Spaun became friends, was the familiar name for the Imperial Seminary where Schubert had been a pupil when he became a choirboy in the court chapel. The son of a suburban schoolmaster, Schubert was the first great Viennese composer to be born in Vienna. At the time of the first French occupation of the city, when Napolon installed himself in the Schönbrunn palace, the child was learning violin and piano from his father and elder brother. At the age of ten he was placed under the tuition of the parish organist, who said of him: 'If I wished to instruct him in anything fresh, he already knew it. Consequently I gave him no actual tuition but merely talked to him, and watched him with silent astonishment.'[63] A year later he joined the court chapel, went to school, and soon became leader of the orchestra. Back home in the school holidays, the family now formed a string quartet, and thus surrounded by music, exuding it through every pore, the boy began to compose. An extraordinary output of overtures, symphonies, string quartets, sonatas, choral music and, above all, songs began to stream from his pen.

By the time he left the Convict and went to train as a schoolteacher, Schubert had entered a male milieu of friends and admirers who mostly came, like himself, from the growing lower middle class of the imperial capital (or cities like Linz), sons of the servants of the state and civil society, serious-minded but boisterous, emotional, rebellious. Here his music was quickly and readily appreciated; a few years later, when they would assemble specifically to hear his music, these evening parties, replete with punch and merriment – and dancing if women were present – would acquire a name which has entered musical history: the Schubertiade.

The Schubertiade has acquired an image of innocence and purity of heart which, historically speaking, is only a half-truth (and, like all half-truths, tells the wrong half). Schubert was still in his teens when older friends of his from the Convict, including Spaun, drew him into a self-education circle that had originated in 1811 in Linz, where it centred on a group of former students of the grammar school. A brotherhood in the style of the day devoted to the cultivation of friendship and idealistic philosophies, modelled on the late-eighteenth-century ideals of *Bildung*, or self-improvement and education, the Linz group was apparently particularly zealous to convert like-minded young men to its creed, and Schubert joined the Viennese branch of this circle, of which

Spaun and the poet Mayrhofer, with whom Schubert would later share lodgings and whose poems he would set, were leading members.

According to Elizabeth Norman McKay, new members of the circle were expected to make written contributions for discussion at their meetings. It is hard to imagine Schubert writing essays, says McKay, who intelligently suggests that the questions posed could be answered through the setting of a poem to music (and there were several budding poets in the group): 'As the only composer in the circle, his contributions of new songs, the texts of which reflected the circle's interests and ideals, and which he would sing (accompanying himself) at their meetings, were especially valued.'[64] The appreciative response of his friends gave encouragement, and in the spirit of self-education encouraged by the circle, he used the experience to teach himself his craft; in the process, he turned a popular form of domestic music-making, the German lied, into a high art form. On this reading there is no better example of how closely tied a musical genre can be to a particular social space.

A *Bildung* circle of this kind was not politically focused, but it came under political pressure none the less. In the renewed wave of repression launched by Metternich as the Congress of Vienna ended, a system of police intelligence, aided by a host of paid informers, directed its attention particularly towards students and young people, whose ranks were likely to harbour those with 'revolutionary' tendencies, radical and dangerous opinions, and freethinkers (like Schubert's brother Ignaz). In the summer of 1815, the circle around Schubert were shocked and alarmed to discover that someone had denounced them to the police. Their friends in Linz approached their mentor, a respected man of the Church, to write a testimonial for the authorities; the Vienna branch was permitted to continue its activities. Two years later they started a short-lived yearbook entitled *Beyträge aus Bildung für Jünglinge* ('Contributions towards the Education of Young Men') which expressed the conviction that the ideal world could exist only in art and that its appreciation contributed to the individual's development into a productive and active member of society. The yearbook was banned after the second issue in 1818. Ironically, its editor, Mayrhofer, was later to be employed as a state censor – despite the incongruity, as McKay puts it, of the appointment to such a position of a poet obsessed with literary freedom.[65]

The assassination in Mannheim in 1819 by a radical student of the highly popular dramatist Kotzebue, an apologist of absolutism, unleashed a new wave of repression throughout the Austro-German Empire in the form of the infamous Karlsbad decrees. The following

year, Schubert himself was in trouble with the police, arrested in the
company of another friend from his Convict days, the poet Johann
Senn, who seems to have been the most politicized of the group. Senn
was a leading light in a student association which now came under
surveillance. In March 1820 the police took action, swooping on the
members' homes. They arrived at Senn's lodgings to find not only
Senn but four of his friends, including Schubert. According to the
official reports, when the police demanded to search the premises,
Senn replied angrily that he 'did not care a hang about the police',
and 'the government was too stupid to be able to penetrate his secrets'.
The others all 'chimed in against the authorised official in the same
tone, inveighing against him with insulting and opprobrious
language'.[66] Senn was held for fourteen months and then banished
from Vienna, his career ruined. Schubert got off with a black eye and a
severe reprimand. (Remarkably, the idea of Schubert as a young
firebrand is found in a 1930s 'biopic' in which Richard Tauber plays
the composer – the silliest of all musical film biographies but one
where Schubert, in the middle of a fanciful tale of unrequited love,
finds an opportunity to sing anti-government ditties.) Nor did the
repression diminish. In 1826, Schubert was accepted as a member of
the important Ludlams Höhle, an artists', writers' and composers' club
frequented by both Viennese and foreigners; its hundred members
included figures like Salieri, Weber, Moscheles, Rellstab, Rückert and
Grillparzer – several were already friends of his; an informal meeting-
place where respected figures, distinguished in their field, would let
their hair down and indulge in a certain amount of buffoonery, but
nothing particularly subversive. Schubert had not yet been inducted as
a member when the premises were raided by Metternich's police, after
a tip-off from a disaffected unsuccessful applicant for membership.[67]

   In a word, the Schubertiade belonged to a quite specific milieu that
can be called proto-bohemian – not yet fully so, because not yet fully
self-conscious of its separation from the norms of the bourgeois lifeworld. It was constituted originally as an intermediate space, a masculine zone beyond the family but still self-enclosed, which shifted
between the privacy of the home and the semi-public location of the
tavern or the coffee-house; a transitory space, from which members
would withdraw when they got married – until the gathering adapted
to the presence of women. But by this time the atmosphere of political
repression had taken its toll, and the *Bildung* group had broken up,
although some of the friends now met under the aegis of a reading
circle led by that other friend of Schubert, Franz Schober, whom some
of them blamed for leading Schubert into bad ways. Now the musical

gathering refocuses around Schubert himself; we discover that the first reference to a Schubertiade as such, a gathering devoted to Schubert's music, dates from 1821. In this evolving milieu, the 'restless longing' and 'aching heart' so often evoked in the songs Schubert composed to the poems of friends like Mayrhofer are not airy nothings, but at least in part the reaction of a generation of intense and passionate youth to the repressive conditions of daily life under the rule of Metternich. But by the same token, such emotions were also directed against the deliberate placidity of life in the domestic interior cultivated by the respectable bourgeois, of the kind later lampooned under the name of Biedermeier. The character of Biedermeier was born in the pages of a popular German humorous journal in the 1850s; the poems attributed to him purported to represent the views of a Swabian schoolmaster, but the term came to be applied retrospectively to an attitude first manifested in the years immediately after the Congress of Vienna, and especially in the imperial capital itself. Like the English Colonel Blimp of a later period, the name became a byword for everything old-fashioned, narrow-minded, politically timorous and aesthetically philistine – clearly everything that Schubert was not.

The peculiar quality of this type of gathering is described by Roland Barthes. Who listens to the lied? he asks. Its place is not the bourgeois salon, but a space which is 'scarcely socialized': 'a few friends – those of the Schubertiades; but its true listening space is, so to speak, the interior of the head'.[68] Hence what Kramer calls the sense of 'a receding interior that becomes more secret and more authentic the further, the deeper, it recedes'.[69] The choice of song for this milieu, which allows a peculiar form of privacy to be shared in close company, is no accident. The Schubert lied is a report on the interior state of the subject. Listening to the lied, says Barthes, 'I sing the lied with myself ... I address myself, within myself'. The world of the lied consists in turn of a memory, a landscape, a movement, a mood – of anything which may be the starting point of a wound, of a nostalgia, of a felicity; but it exists only in the subject's head, imprisoned in deepest intimacy; where 'I struggle with an image which is both the image of the desired, lost other, and my own image, desiring and abandoned ... In short, the lied's interlocutor is the Double – my Double, which is Narcissus: a corrupt double, caught in the dreadful scene of the cracked mirror, as Schubert's unforgettable *Doppelgänger* puts it.'[70] What makes this song so terrifying, of course, is that the speaker of the poem is engulfed by the music of his double.

The image of the *Doppelgänger* is especially apt. If a picture of Schubert is now emerging in which a sense of rebelliousness with political implications is linked to a personality entirely at odds with Biedermeier values and mentality, then the essential quality of the Schubert lied, which expresses this, is its double-voicedness – indeed, triple-voicedness, for the lied is subtended between the voice of the poet, the voice of the composer, and the voice of the singer. Schubert makes it a theatre of subjectivity which plays on the alternate fusing and separation of these identities. The singer enters into an expressive dialogue with the authorial subject, but finds a double subjectivity. If – as frequently occurs – the gender of the authorial subject, normally assumed to be male, is suspended, then the undecidability of the speaker's identity may become part of what the song is about. With Schubert's songs, as Kramer puts it, the sexual predicate can freely follow the sex of the singer – but the song may carry a different import as a result.[71] This, of course, is another matter suppressed by musicology, which rarely considers the musical text from a performative point of view – and from the point of view of the construction of subjectivity, the lied is perhaps the most performative of all musical forms. For the song is said to reveal the inner truth of its poem, but in order to do so it requires the singer to put their own subjectivity on the line.

Kramer finds examples among Schubert's most popular songs, including *Der Tod und das Mädchen* ('Death and the Maiden'):

> The design of this celebrated song is exquisitely simple. There is a D-minor piano prelude in the manner of a funeral march; a plea by the maiden for Death to pass her by; a reassurance by Death that he has come to bring rest, not punishment; and a D-major postlude in which the funeral march is recast as a lullaby or hymn.

The vocal part is a dialogue between characters of two sexes performed by a singer who has only one. That is to say, the vocal part, regardless of the singer's sex, has two genders: the maiden's part in the upper register, Death's in the lower. Consequently: 'a woman who sings this song shifts vocally from her own to the other sex, from a persona to an impersonation, and a man does the reverse'. The alternation of persona and impersonation is an effect of double-voicedness. The effect – if we let it be heard, says Kramer – can be virtually two different songs.

In *Die Forelle* ('The Trout'), in which an innocent creature is cruelly deceived by a man with a long pole, the effect of the song depends not just on the pleasures of sexual innuendo but on the triangular relationship between the narrator, the fisherman, and the trout. When a man sings it, it is about masculine rivalry and phallic triumph. When a woman sings it, then she is the trout, and may well evince a different attitude to the dénouement.

In *Heidenröslein* ('Meadow Rose'), in which a 'wild boy' is attracted by the wild rose of femininity and plucks it despite the rose's resistance, the speaker, observes Kramer, broaches the question of virility as a simple narrator with the assumed gender of the male. Much of the effect of the song in performance depends on how the singer renders the refrain, 'Röslein, Röslein, Röslein rot', particularly the third and last time. If they draw out the lingering at the close, as many singers do, the effect is to create a momentary doubt over the narrator's casual acceptance of the rose's fate, through a narrative slippage from the boy's point of view to the girl's. 'When the singer is a man,' says Kramer, 'the passage sung this way suggests a regret that is real, not pro forma; when the singer is a woman, the regret may take on overtones of fellow-feeling, protest, even suppressed anger.'

One last example. One of the most explicitly erotic texts Schubert ever set is *Heimliches Lieben* ('Heavenly Loves'), a poem by a woman, Caroline von Klenke, apparently addressed by a woman to her secret lover. 'O would that the lips that burn with yearning must part, that my being were not dissolved when it clasps itself so firmly on your mouth.' On the level of the composer's empathy with the lyric ego of the poet, Schubert's setting is a celebration of a woman's sexuality. On the other hand, what does it feel like when it is sung by a man? We are back in the territory of *Ganymed*.

The dramatis personae of Schubert's songs, Kramer remarks, 'are men and women who take emotion as law and desire as logic. Most of them, the wanderers included, are internal exiles from the normality of middle-class life and love. Virtually all of them claim their exile as their authenticity and value their authenticity more than happiness.'[72] What has always been recognized is Schubert's extraordinary depth of empathy with the Other; less so that he uses the double-voicedness of the song also to explore sexuality. Many of the sexual ambiguities in Schubert's songs arise in the space between the supposed gender of the poet and the gender of the singer; they play on the slippage of gender, its suspension and reversal, which occurs when a voice, assumed to be male, is discovered to be female, and vice versa. The result is frequently homoerotic, but may also express a power of empathy with femininity.

This reading only confirms the impression made by Schubert's music when it was rediscovered after his death – an impression of effeminacy, especially compared with the music of Beethoven. This view was first perpetrated by Schumann, who befriended Ferdinand Schubert and retrieved many of his brother's scores from his drawers: operas, masses, and the great C major symphony which he sent to Mendelssohn, who conducted its first performance in 1839, and which Schumann famously extolled for its 'heavenly length'. But as he also wrote: 'Schubert is a maidenly character compared to that one [Beethoven]; by far more loquacious, softer, broader'; certainly he is capable of powerful sonorous moments, but 'he still always behaves like a woman to a man, who commands where she pleads and persuades'.[73]

The impression of difference here is not at all false. As Kramer puts it, Schubert, whatever his sexuality, was constructing models of masculinity that went against the grain of the age, a hedonistic alternative to the heroic, goal-directed masculinity ascribed to Beethoven. Furthermore, in his lifetime, Schubert was known and celebrated only for his small-scale music, his songs and dances – an intimate and retiring personality quite the opposite of Beethoven's. When his large-scale music became known, it challenged the paradigms of the higher genres which Beethoven had created, with his structural integrity, mastery of organic form, and, above all, his virile drive and momentum (though his later music, with its ruptures and interruptions, was frequently criticized). The critical commonplaces about Schubert's stylistic faults: Schubert is a wonderful melodist but structurally weak; he repeats himself too much; he substitutes sensuousness for momentum; he loses himself in the pleasure of the moment and neglects the discipline of the whole – these are always contrasted with Beethoven. Subsequent commentators sometimes reduce the dichotomy to a simple question of formal mastery, which Schubert allegedly lacks, or cannot properly control. None the less, composers like Bruckner and Mahler will combine the formal principles of the Beethovenian symphony with those of Schubert, and produce symphonies of even heavenlier length (for which they in their turn would be criticized).

From the point of view of the late twentieth century – for example, in the view of the feminist musicologist Susan McClary – what has long been heard as effeminacy is the result of an imperative, a compulsion to define an acceptable masculinity, with profound effects on our whole approach to music. 'In Western culture,' McClary argues, 'music itself is always in danger of being regarded as the feminine Other that circumvents reason and arouses desire.'[74] Thus, for Schumann, 'Music is the feminine friend who can best communicate everything that we feel internally.'[75] As feminist critics of Habermas have argued, the public sphere did not just exclude women from the political domain and relegate them to the cultural, but the definition of gender and sexual roles was a structural and constitutive element in the public sphere, with far-reaching consequences. But this is not a question of simple opposition; it involves the regulation of alternative subjective constructions of self and identity which might disrupt the primary roles. The problem with the idea of effeminacy is that it is part of this complex; it constitutes an ambiguous construction of an errant – contrary, dissenting, anomalous – masculinity, which arises within a binary opposition that imprisons it. In fact it is impossible to pin Schubert's sensibility down to either the effeminate or the homoerotic. To do so would be to imprison again a music which is always essentially open, double-voiced, internally dialogical – in brief, unfinalized.

4

The Romantic Ascendancy

Of Philistines and invective

In 1820, a maxim of Immanuel Kant's found its way into Beethoven's conversation book. A well-known sentence from the *Critique of Practical Reason*, 'Two things fill the mind with ever new and increasing wonder and reverence the oftener the mind dwells upon them – the starry sky above me and the moral law within me', becomes 'The moral law in us, and the starry sky above us – Kant!!!'. Maynard Solomon observes about this jotting that like 'most of his generation, Beethoven understood Kant in a sloganised and simplified form'.[1] Lawrence Kramer, on the other hand, finds special significance in Beethoven's 'presumably unconscious editing'. For Kant, the sky above precedes the law within, in a rhetorical sequence that cannot plausibly be reversed. Beethoven's paraphrase sweeps the two terms into an unqualified polarity between inner and outer, self and nature. 'It is no doubt simplistic to remark that this reversal of hierarchies spells the difference between Enlightenment and Romanticism, but the temptation to say so is too great to resist.'[2] For us, what is also interesting is the observation – which Kramer mentions in passing – that Beethoven picked up Kant's famous sentence from a newspaper article. It indicates the circulation of ideas in an intellectual vernacular set in motion within the public sphere by the press.

Music, through the practice of criticism, becomes part of the same process. Ideas about music are set in motion through the press beyond the circle of those who have already heard the music, and the critic therefore enters into dialogue with a double public. In other words, the practice of criticism acquires a double orientation: on the one hand towards the music and its listeners, on the other towards the echoes and traces which it creates in a more general cultural awareness

– towards the space of music within the wider public sphere, its claims on the attention of civil society in the name of its truth-telling capacity and civilizing influence.

This influence was subject to intense disaccord occasioned by composers who broke the rules – which they became increasingly inclined to do – and whose disrespect for formal prescription offended traditionalists, and aligned Romantic music – albeit ambiguously – with various progressive social and political trends. In the 1840s, in the throes of Romanticism, a composer like Berlioz was both celebrated and reviled. According to a reviewer in London:

> Berlioz is fantastic in the structure of his movements – unmeaningly so – and this (to say nothing of his crude and baseless method of harmonization, and his defiance of rule and common sense in part writing), renders his music necessarily tiresome and unattractive to a polite ear.[3]

While the very same formlessness had quite the opposite effect on the Russian critic Vladimir Stasov:

> Although we fail to see a Byron in Berlioz, as some of his well-wishers have called him . . . we leave each of his concerts in a most extraordinary mood, a mood entirely different from that produced by the usual concert. We feel shaken, uplifted, as if we had been in the presence of something great, yet we cannot account for this greatness. We recall that for a moment we caught a glimpse of beauty in all its splendour, something wonderful indeed – and then everything dissolved in a mist of vague yet lofty aspiration. This vagueness endows each work with a sense of incompleteness, of uneasiness, a sense of reaching out for something, of futile seeking after form. It is as though you saw before you shades wandering disconsolately along the banks of the Lethe, finding no repose. Who can deny Berlioz's poetic feeling, his poetic nature? Yet all musical forms elude him; he always remains himself, leaving others with an unquenched thirst, and unfilled desire.[4]

In other words, the very quality of music which most excited the Romantic imagination – and repelled the conservatives – was its inexplicit surging, its vagueness, its sense of transcending the articulate, the contingent and the limited. These were all among the traits which the extraordinary writer-poet-painter-musician E.T.A. Hoffmann had so exultantly praised in Beethoven as early as in 1810.

Hoffmann's writings on Beethoven were a turning point in musical criticism not merely because of his effusiveness, but because he linked the metaphysics of the sublime in Beethoven's music with a technical analysis of its source. In his essay on the Fifth Symphony, he dismisses complaints about lack of coherence in Beethoven's music as akin to complaints of lack of organic unity in Shakespeare's plays, and proceeds to analyse 'the inner structure' of the music, in which there is a demonstrable affinity between themes and motifs in different sections and movements of the work. It is a seminal enunciation of crucial internal structural principles – known to modern musicology as thematicism – that will operate with growing effect for more than a century, unifying the musical discourse of symphony, sonata, and a host of related forms around the multiple and contrasting transformations of themes and motifs.[5]

Hoffmann's music criticism is also significant for another reason. Where Scheibe had criticized Bach for being behind the times, the relationship between critic and composer had now become inverted, with the free composer as progressive and the institutional critic as conservative. But Hoffmann was also a composer himself, and in this context his aggressive defence of Beethoven was like an act of solidarity; here the composer of bourgeois ideology had come into existence: the embattled genius. The struggle against popular misunderstanding dates from the same moment. When the publisher replaces the patron and begins to mediate the composer's relation to the growing middle-class audience, increasingly supported by a whole industry of middlemen, then the modern sense of artistic alienation, loss of contact with the public, begins to set in. With the increasing anonymity of the audience and the growing number of musical magazines to cater for them, the source of misunderstanding becomes concentrated in the figure of the uncomprehending and hostile critic, who thereby exchanges his pedagogic function for that of the demagogue. The composer is forced to enter the fray in self-defence. Schumann fights for Chopin, Berlioz and Mendelssohn; Berlioz comes to the defence of Liszt; Liszt attacks the critics and hails Wagner. They all enjoyed the support of the radical German poet Heine, resident in Paris since the early 1830s, praising Liszt and Berlioz and hailing the genius of Chopin (though they also sometimes felt attacked by his frankness).

Schumann, a fiery young man of twenty-four when he founded a new musical journal, the *Neue Leipziger Zeitschrift für Musik*, in 1834, and probably better known in his lifetime as a music critic than as a composer, is perhaps the most significant of these figures for his influence on the climate of public musical debate. With his passionate advocacy of musical innovation, and reports from paid correspondents in Berlin, Paris, Vienna and elsewhere, the journal was read throughout Germany and even abroad. To fight the progressive fight, Schumann created in his writing a fictional company of comrades, the *Davids-bündler*, or League of Davidites against the Philistines, whom he then provided with piano music in the closing march of *Carnaval* ('March of the Davidsbündler against the Philistines') and in the *Davidsbündler-tänze*. The *Davidsbündler* – which, in Schumann's words, alluding to Goethe's autobiography, 'wound itself like a red thread through the journal, humorously blending "Truth and Poetry" '[6] – is a synthesis of several currents. Its members were friends and acquaintances dubbed with pseudonyms – Mendelssohn, for example, became Felix Meritis. This penchant for pseudonyms was characteristic of the *Bildung* circles of Schubert's generation, including musical associations like Carl Maria von Weber's *Harmonische Verein*, which met until about 1813, where all the members took pseudonyms and Weber called himself 'Melos'; in some cases these societies of male companions had homoerotic overtones. For himself, Schumann adopted a dual personality, inspired by the double personalities of his near-contemporary Jean Paul, whose novels he devoured; he signed himself either Florestan or Eusebius, to represent the fiery and poetic sides respectively of his own creative personality. Florestan is the hero of Beethoven's *Fidelio*, imprisoned for political opposition; Eusebius is the name of an obscure fourth-century Christian saint, with connotations of martyrdom and suffering. Florestan was also the Davidites' leader, rallying musical progressives against their reactionary and uncultivated Philistine enemies.

In view of Schumann's nervous disposition and his later mental collapse, his biographers make much of the psychological symptomology of the split personality. It is not unusual for children or even adolescents to create imaginary companions, says one of them, but for an adult to do so – Schumann was twenty-one when he invented Florestan and Eusebius – is the sign of a psychotic tendency.[7] From Schumann's voluminous writings we learn that his inventions spoke to him, gave him ideas for literary and musical projects, and supported him in times of emotional stress, like good inner voices. Some draw attention to the possibility that the opposition between them is an expression of a split in Schumann's sexuality, a reading based on explicit references to homosexuality and 'pederasty' in his early diaries.[8] All this may well be true; of most interest to us here is the fact that the private meanings matter less than the public nature of their expression. If Schumann's criticism – as Sennett puts it – has the tone of a friend talking to other friends in print about common enthusiasms,[9] then it also represents a new type of claim upon public attention, the demand that the voice of a radical subjectivist fervour prevail over the timidity of consensus. To psychologize this discourse is to ignore its implications for the public sphere. For this is not the same kind of subjectivism as that of, say, the feuilleton writer, whose object is to report an experience and render a state of feeling for the benefit of a duly appreciative reader. Schumann's is a militant and aggressive subjectivity. 'Assembled Davidsbündler,' he writes in the journal, 'youths and men, you must kill the Philistines, musical and otherwise.'[10] Indeed, Schumann saw the condition of music expressly in political terms. 'Like the political present,' he wrote, 'one can divide the musical into liberals, centrists and reactionaries, or romanticists, moderns and classicists.' If modern did not quite yet mean to Schumann what it means to us, the arraignment of forces already takes on the modern appearance derived from the French Revolution, and there is also a modern sense of embattled generations: 'On the right sit the elderly – the contrapuntists, the anti-chromaticists; on the left the youthful – the revolutionaries in their Phrygian caps, the anti-formalists, the genially impudent, among whom the Beethovenians stand out . . .'. The centre, the *juste milieu* – this is the mediocre mainstream. H.F. Chorley, music critic of *The Athenaeum*, an English literary review, appointing himself arch-enemy on the Right, described Schumann's music as a 'display of unattractive cacophony', with harmonies 'so obtusively crude that no number of wrong notes would be detected by the subtlest listener'. Not just Schumann. To Chorley's stuffy ears, Chopin was peculiar and Berlioz, Babel.[11]

This, of course, is to become an increasingly familiar type of complaint. Every time the critics, assailed by innovation, became accustomed to a new stylistic paradigm – say, to radical harmonies – along came another bunch of newer radicals to upset them with noisy orchestral effects or caterwauling instead of singing. In this sense, the violent rejection of the modernist revolution in the early years of the twentieth century is not a new phenomenon but only another act in a long-drawn-out tragicomedy which has been documented by Nicolas Slonimsky in his remarkable and delightful *Lexicon of Musical Invective*, a dictionary of 'critical assaults on composers since Beethoven's time'. Here Slonimsky catalogues the terms of abuse employed by the critics: from 'Aberration' (Wagner, Prokofiev, Stravinsky), 'Anarchy' (Moussorgsky, Wagner, Debussy, Schoenberg) and 'Antichrist, tonal' (Wagner and Bruckner); through 'Decadent' (Debussy, Schoenberg, Richard Strauss and even Verdi!), 'Howling' (Liszt, Saint-Saëns, Mahler, Richard Strauss, Bartók, Milhaud, Stravinsky, Varèse), and 'Nihilist' (Tchaikovsky as well as Schoenberg!); to 'Squeaking' and 'Squealing' (the usual bunch plus Rachmaninov), and 'Zoo noises, feeding-time' (Schoenberg and Varèse).[12]

This is not just a battle between conservative and progressive, but something more sinister. With the rise of the piano, the growth of the amateur, and the huge output of salon music during the course of the nineteenth century came the equivalent of the kind of music nowadays to be found in the record stores under 'Easy listening'. Nietzsche would later sum up what had happened: 'As the critic gained ascendancy in theatre and concert, the journalist in the schoolroom, and the newspaper in society, art degenerated into the lowest kind of amusement, and aesthetic criticism into the cement of a social group that was vain, distracted, egotistic, and totally unoriginal.'[13] It is hardly surprising if composers sometimes used music as well as words to fight back. Wagner pilloried the Viennese critic Hanslick in *The Mastersingers* in the figure of Beckmesser. Mahler, in his satirical song *Lob des hohes Verstands* ('In Praise of Lofty Understanding'), likened the critic to the Donkey who chooses Cuckoo as a better singer than Nightingale because Cuckoo sings a proper chorale and keeps good time. When the century turned, Schoenberg was driven to remark ironically that beauty exists only from the moment when the uncreative begin to miss it. One of his oil paintings is a vision of a critic with grotesque Expressionist daubs of colour all over his ugly mug.

It was in Italy that the intimate relationship between music journalism and the market first emerged most starkly. When Italy saw an explosion of musical magazines in the 1820s, most were almost wholly taken up with opera, and nearly all belonged to publishing houses or agencies, and were trade journals rather than consumer fare. They depended largely on subscriptions from members of the opera industry itself: impresarios, composers, dancers – above all, singers. Agent and journalist was often one person, each activity lending the other support, and the journals were the agents' mouthpieces. This raises problems, observes John Rosselli in his book on the Italian opera industry, for anyone trying to use them as evidence for the history of opera or music criticism. Many of them, he says, were 'venal in the most literal sense: they printed what they were paid to print'.[14] Some would openly inform the reader on the masthead that 'Articles for insertion must be paid for in advance', along with the request 'Kindly indicate contracts already concluded, seasons available and repertoire of operas'. To the doyen of English musical journals, *The Musical Times*, this practice was contemptible; it once announced self-righteously that it was donating to charity the sum of £20 with which someone had attempted to bribe one of its correspondents. But at least it makes quite plain for us the close relation between the functions of opinion-making and advertising which, in Habermas's account, belong to the transformation of the public sphere produced by the growth of nineteenth-century capitalism: a change wrought, among other factors, by the growth of the mass media, in which the press became ever more intertwined with commercial interests and the public presentation of private interests.

Here, however, we discover a curious and significant phenomenon, whereby the musical press not only confirms the emphasis Habermas places on advertising and its expanding function in accounting for the transformation of the public sphere, but anticipates the emergence of a new practice, that of public relations. Modern journalism was created through formally separating editorial matter from advertising, so that the critical content presented itself as free and disinterested comment (it goes without saying that the primary purpose remains that of market intervention, and without advertising the press would never survive). The essence of public relations as a branch of advertising, a practice which originated in the United States and spread to Europe only after the end of the Second World War, is to bypass the advertisement and invade the editorial space of the press – without being seen to do so. The distinction between advertising and editorial content evaporates. Public relations fuses both, on condition that the advertisement is not recognizable as the self-presentation of a private interest. Where advertising is characterized by the sales pitch, the technique of opinion management employed by public relations 'invades the process of "public opinion" by systematically creating news events, or exploiting events that attract attention'.[15]

But the music market had already learned to operate in this way during the course of the nineteenth century. At a time before the invention of recording turned the performance itself into a saleable commodity, the natural and necessary focus of all publicity was the musical event and its capacity to attract attention, and especially the drawing power of the performer's personality. In the mainstream musical press, music becomes a culture of harmony which on the one hand invites its public to an exchange of opinion about articles of consumption, and on the other subjects it to the soft sell of a multiplicity of attractions controlled by specific operators (impresarios, concert-halls, orchestras, etc.) offering brand-name products – the virtuoso performer, and the composer-conductor. The interpenetration of information, editorial comment and advertising thus reflected the peculiar nature of music as commodity, and the consequent nature of the musical market, which became increasingly orientated towards these symbolic personalities. Like any similar situation, for a particular firm to capture the market and establish a clientele depended, as everyone knows nowadays, on two steps: brand recognition, and brand differentiation. But if the job of musical impresarios, publishers, agents and managers was to massage the representatives of the press to these ends, they could not have succeeded without the musical personalities to trade upon.

The Romantic personality: especially Liszt and Chopin

When personality enters the public sphere as the special aura of the performing artist, the public appearance of individual character undergoes a transformation, becoming not only a matter of individual bearing but an expressive factor in its own right. A culture of personality develops which serves, in Richard Sennett's phrase, as a 'school of serious egoism', and we enter the age of the Romantic virtuoso.[16] A new relationship develops with the public, in the form of the audience held in collective awe by the performing artist's charisma, a paradoxical scene in which the individual is given special licence to emote in public, while the audience become passive spectators of a new kind of visual musical display. In the classical music culture of the twentieth century, the term 'virtuoso' spells the cool technical wizardry of the performer who so completely dominates their instrument that they are capable of playing anything written by anybody; in the Romantic era, the figure was performer and composer combined, and the process generated a new intensity of style. No one exemplified this more than Franz Liszt, who once famously remarked: 'The concert is – myself'. Indeed, Liszt is the figure in whom the whole question of the public role of the nineteenth-century composer is seen at its most emblematic.

As a German-speaking Hungarian who spent his youth in Vienna and Paris, toured for many years from one end of Europe to the other, settled in Germany and retired to Rome, there is first the matter of Liszt's internationalism. There is a good case, says one of his biographers, for considering Liszt not just the first musical internationalist but the first pan-European composer: 'The case is two-fold: his influence upon, and his absorption of, the cultures with which he came into contact.'[17] If this is true, it should be seen in the present context in terms of a life which recapitulated the movement from absolutism to bourgeois ascendancy in a few brief years, in the course of the transition from a prodigious childhood to international fame as a young virtuoso, catapulting the musical subject from infancy under absolutism to youthful maturity in the public sphere in the radicalizing atmosphere of Paris in the 1830s. Although Liszt always thought of himself as a

Hungarian, and supported Hungarian causes, he did not speak the language (which didn't stop the Hungarians later putting his name to their new Conservatory of Music). He was born in 1811 near Eisenstadt, then part of Hungary; his father Adam worked for the Esterházy estate, and played the cello in the court orchestra at Eisenstadt under Haydn. This was a Court in which music was enjoyed and encouraged among its employees, but when the young Franz revealed phenomenal musical gifts, the reigning Prince declined to let his father take him to Vienna, where Czerny, probably the finest teacher of his day, was ready to accept him as a pupil. If the Prince would not respond to the father's petitions, Adam Liszt would have to attract support for the young genius from other sources, through public concerts. The boy made his first public appearances, in local towns at the age of nine, in 1820, and thereby secured a stipend from a group of Hungarian magnates which enabled his father to take him to the capital, where he made his debut in 1822.

Adam Liszt clearly had a keen sense of publicity, for when father and son set out the following year, with Adam as his son's concert manager, he deliberately planned a tour which would follow in the footsteps of Leopold Mozart escorting the young Wolfgang through Germany to Paris and then to London; the significance was obvious to all. Biographers note that at a concert in Pest at the beginning of this tour, the boy played an astounding improvisation on the Rákóczi March. This is a tune of unknown origin, named for Prince Ferencz Rákóczi, leader of the Hungarian Revolt against Austria of 1703–11, and already therefore an icon of nationalist aspiration; but also, to Liszt, of rebellious sentiments directed against stubborn aristocrats. (He later introduced the Rákóczi March to Berlioz, who used it in his *Damnation of Faust* as an icon of the revolutionary spirit.)

Within weeks of the young prodigy's arrival in Paris, the Parisian journals begin to rival each other in a chorus of eulogy, he is lionized by society ladies, attends three dozen of the most elegant *soirées* in the space of three months – his patrons include the future King Louis Philippe; a year or two later come the first references in the press to his magnetic attraction for female members of the audience. One must picture, then, a handsome youngster of amazing talent and voracious intellect, whose education has been interrupted by the need to earn a living for himself and his parents as a budding virtuoso, who is not yet sixteen when he loses his father to illness on their way back to Paris from his third tour of England. He withdraws from society in order to educate himself, reading Chateaubriand and Byron, Montaigne, Voltaire and Lamartine. Looking back on this period later, he would write of the 'bitter aversion' he developed to that environment in which art was 'more or less debased to the level of trade for profit [and] labelled as a source of amusement for fashionable society'.[18] Moreover, he also understands what the profit motive does to those it subjugates. In 1829 he is excited by the Paris premiere of Rossini's *William Tell*, with its theme of patriotism, liberty, and deliverance of the oppressed. Already a public figure, fêted as pianist and handsome young dandy, he now takes up with a new generation of writers, artists and musicians, stirred by the spirit of the Revolution of July 1830. Liszt himself is sufficiently touched by the July events to sketch (though not actually write) a Revolutionary Symphony. By the end of the year, we find him attending meetings of the foremost group of religious humanitarians, followers of the Comte de Saint-Simon, where he attracts attention at *soirées* by abandoning himself to fantastical improvisation at the keyboard; he is regarded by the Saint-Simonians as quite a catch. The precocious young virtuoso, barely twenty, was drawn to the movement not only by its early idealistic socialism but also by its doctrine of the artist as the priest of a radical regime of brotherly love. One account speaks of jottings made by Liszt in 1832 which demonstrate how much he had absorbed the Saint-Simonian conception of the modern artist as an inspired being who is unappreciated, even mistreated, by the 'critical' society in which he lives.[19]

The movement which developed after Saint-Simon's death in 1825 was a bizarre mixture of proto-socialism and religiosity which, building on the founder's critique of the bloodletting of the French Revolution and the militarism of Napoleon, came to regard private property as incompatible with the industrialization through which science and technology would solve humanity's problems. (The movement's influence on later generations of socialists is indubitable, while Saint-Simon himself may even be considered the great-granddaddy of Euro-socialism, in his demand for a united Europe to supersede the warring nation-states, with a European Parliament and the joint development of industry and communication.) Bending the founder's doctrines in a more definitely socialist direction, the Saint-Simonians also extended Saint-Simon's belief that scientists and engineers should take on the spiritual direction of society also to encompass the artist. This remarkable vision, in which for the first time (apart from the writings of Schiller) the artist acquires a central political role, attracted – in the jargon of a later age – fellow-travellers like the radical poet Heinrich Heine, freshly arrived from Germany, and the proto-feminist novelist George Sand, as well as composers like Fromental Halévy, Berlioz, and especially Félicien David, who became a member and the movement's principal composer. Indeed, music formed a prominent part of the movement's activities, especially as it moved from speculation about the principle of a *musique sociale* into practice, with a success, says Ralph Locke, that exceeded expectations.

Even as the movement took on the garb and organization of a church, the Saint-Simonians remained deeply subversive. A proclamation by the movement during the July Revolution called for the common ownership of goods, the abolition of the right of inheritance, and the enfranchisement of women. If it is true, as most biographies suggest – if they mention the connection at all – that Liszt's direct connection with them was short-lived, broken off before 1832, when their leaders were arraigned on trumped-up charges of immorality and imprisoned, nevertheless, he was no renegade, and by no means abandoned the principle of the artist's sympathy for social struggle against injustice. In an essay dating from 1835, 'On the Position of Artists and Their Place in Society', which appeared in instalments in a leading French music journal, Liszt, says Ralph Locke, emulates a number of Saint-Simonian writers in his argument about the artist's unhealthy isolation, and in the priestly image of the artist as a bringer of fire; in one passage he acknowledges that his ideas on the social and religious power of art had first been voiced by a certain 'society of men' who preached 'the new trinity of science, industry and art', and had been persecuted and subjected to 'calumny, ridicule and petty legality' – a bold confession, says Locke, of indebtedness to a movement then in disrepute.[20] Indeed, this is not just an egotistical argument for a more elevated status for the artist; in an example of the Saint-Simonian penchant for social planning, Liszt advances projects for bringing music to the broad audience of working people by combining the public employment of composers with community orchestras, choirs, and the publication of cheap editions of good music. He calls for the introduction of musical education in primary schools, the establishment of philharmonic societies and independent academies of music. If such ideas were not unique – they can also be found, though less vehemently expressed, in the writings of Berlioz, Balzac and others, as well as various professed Saint-Simonians – they mark an entirely new departure in music's relation to the expanding public sphere in which it finds itself situated. If the Saint-Simonian appeal to music is based in a thoroughly Romantic conception of its emotive and harmonizing powers, the wish to take the grandest music to the people is not only an echo of the French Revolutionary tradition of musical ceremonial but a programme for the democratization of music, which would break the traditional bonds between high musical culture and its high-placed patrons – an idea which is no less radical and utopian today. In this vision, music is no longer merely a product and concomitant of social and public life, but demands of the public sphere proper recognition as both a force in society and an end in itself.

Two years later Liszt's political sympathies found expression in a visit to Lyon, where the weavers were in rebellion and he gave a benefit concert for the unemployed with the fashionable opera singer Adolphe Nourrit (another Saint-Simonian, who also trained vast choirs of working men in Paris). The experience resulted in a piano piece called *Lyon*, a heroic march in the spirit of the 'Marseillaise', inscribed at the head with the weavers' slogan, 'Vivre en travaillant ou mourir en combattant' ('Live working or die fighting'). The piece is dedicated to Liszt's spiritual mentor Lamennais, the Catholic poet, politician and radical whose concern for the plight of the poor led him to propose the alignment of the Church with progressive social trends, and the condemnation of his liberalism by a papal encyclical. Indeed, throughout the 1830s and 1840s, until his withdrawal from virtuoso concertgiving, Liszt performed at and sometimes organized major benefit concerts and festivals for needy groups and worthy causes like refugees and flood victims. On the one hand he contributed music for the cause, writing a number of male-voice choruses which advocate the dignity of labour and the struggle of the working class, some with texts by Lamennais. (An *Arbeiter-Chor*, 'Workers' Chorus', written just before the Revolution of 1848, was turned down by a Viennese publisher; it surfaced in 1930 when Anton Webern, of all people, made an arrangement for performance in Vienna by a workers' movement chorus which he conducted.) On the other hand, Liszt would attack the hypocrisy of the liberal government of Louis Philippe, which sounds suspiciously like the neo-liberalism of more recent times: 'Nothing is more commonplace', he wrote in in 1835:

> than to glorify the pretended sovereignty of art in hollow and sonorous phrases, as true and as false as the pretended sovereignty of the people . . . Practically no politician ever makes a speech about the budget without expressing his solicitude for the fine arts . . . Everyone admits the social necessity of art . . . If, however, one wished to take the trouble to consider the facts . . .[21]

The facts were that the citizen king had dismissed the musicians of the Royal Chapel and closed the Royal Music School.

Heine, himself attracted to the Saint-Simonians, wrote of Liszt's support for the movement in his chronicles of music in Paris in the 1840s:

For long he was an ardent upholder of the beautiful Saint-Simonian idea of the world. Later the spiritualistic or rather vaporous thoughts of Balanche enveloped him in their mist; now he is enthusiastic over the Republican-Catholic dogmas of a Lamennais who has hoisted his Jacobin cap on the cross . . . That so restless a brain, driven distracted by all the sufferings and all the doctrines of the day, impelled to concern itself with all the needs of mankind . . . cannot be a placid player of the piano to peaceable citizens in comfortable nightcaps, is easily understood. When he sits down at the piano [and] begins to improvise, it often happens that he storms all too madly over the ivory keys, and there resounds a chaos of heaven-high thoughts whence here and there the sweetest flowers breathe out their perfume; so that the hearer is at once agonised and enchanted, yet none the less agonised.

The extraordinary following which Liszt commanded Heine dubbed Lisztomania. What most hurt Liszt was Heine's suggestion that this 'frenzy unparalleled in the history of frenzy' was not a spontaneous response to genius but artfully manufactured:

It sometimes seems to me that the whole enchantment is to be traced to the fact that no one in the world knows how to organise 'successes' as well as Franz Liszt or, better, how to stage them. In that art he is a genius. The most eminent persons are his high accomplices and his hired enthusiasts [– the claque, as it's called in the opera house –] are admirably trained.[22]

In this art of musical performance as spectacle, Liszt went far beyond his role model, the Italian violinist Paganini, whose fiendish virtuosity was reputed to arouse feminine hysteria and even accusations of devilry, but who started touring abroad only in 1828, at the age of forty-five; his international career lasted barely half a dozen years, then died from the whiff of scandal. Here, too, Liszt's role is emblematic of the transformation of the musical public sphere in yet another direction, for where Paganini was still his own manager, Liszt had a far more modern outlook, doubtless fostered by a Saint-Simonian comprehension of economic reality but devoted to very different ends. His experiences of touring the Continent during the 1830s – culminating in the financial disaster of his gruelling 1840 tour of England, when he had to contend with untuned pianos, advertisements torn down and tickets unsold – left him highly critical of a condition in which, outside the capital cities, the conduct of musical life was left to local musicians and musician-impresarios with good intentions but limited vision and little business acumen. In 1841 he found what he needed in the self-effacing figure of an Italian music copyist by the name of Gaetano Belloni, whom he employed as his secretary – there was not yet any other name for what he did. The author of a popular history of the music business calls him a shadowy figure, the only one of Liszt's circle who left not a single letter or diary leaf unburned, the soul of discretion.[23] While very little is known about how he operated, it is clear that he effectively invented a new type of job, becoming the prototype of the promoter. One correspondent, chronicling one of these tours, reported how Liszt would travel between concerts both day and night, and Belloni 'was always ahead of him, seeing to and arranging everything', and Norman Lebrecht speculates on what he was doing: the work of the publicist, priming the local press in advance. He also managed the business side, cashed the takings, paid for the halls, negotiated with piano manufacturers. There is a memoir of him standing in the wings at one of Liszt's recitals, counting the heads of the paying public and calculating the box-office receipts – an anecdote which spoke so eloquently from one entertainment industry to another 'that it earned Belloni a cameo appearance in Charles Vidor's Hollywood biopic of Liszt's life'.[24] The tribute was thoroughly appropriate: after six years' touring, Liszt had a quarter of a million francs on deposit with Rothschild's.

When Lebrecht concludes, in his populist manner, that Liszt can be regarded as the first concert-hall star, and Belloni as the inventor of the star system, what he points to can be understood in the present context as both an enlargement of the commanding musical personality and the beginnings of a transgression of musical values by those of publicity and spectacle – also a transgression of the Saint-Simonian ideals of a social music of community and participation. Liszt, in the end, is a critical figure in public musical life in the mid-nineteenth century because he embodies so acutely the clash and contradiction, and the growing conflict, between the ideals and the reality of the bourgeois cultural public sphere. To complete the picture, after the mid-century and the failure of the liberal revolution of 1848, he progressively withdraws from international public exposure – first to return to the life of *Kapellmeister* in Weimar, then to retirement in Rome, where he takes minor religious orders. But he never ceases to compose, and after several years he is tempted back to public life by celebrations of his jubilee in Budapest and a series of charity concerts in Vienna. It is a trajectory which is musically rich and fecund, replete with prophetic explorations of musical language, like the late *Bagatelle without Tonality*; but it is also a retreat reminiscent of Marx's description in 'The Eighteenth Brumaire of Louis Bonaparte' of the fate of bourgeois revolutions, which storm quickly from success to success, attaining ecstasy in their everyday spirit, but soon reach their zenith, when a 'long crapulent depression' then sets in.[25]

Heine is the most succinct guide we could wish for to the tenor of music in Paris at the moment when it takes over the role of Vienna and becomes the European musical capital *par excellence.* He clearly perceived, for example, the difference between Rossini and Meyerbeer: 'Meyerbeer's music is social rather than personal . . . Rossini's music was better adapted to the spirit of the Restoration.' Meyerbeer's moment came with the July Revolution. In *Robert le Diable*: 'which had germinated in his mind during the horrors of that period . . . the hero who does not exactly know what he wants, and is perpetually at strife with himself, is a faithful picture of the moral fluctuations of that time'. And when the opera's grand choruses 'burst forth in harmonies of anger, of jubilation, of sobs', people 'listened and wept, rejoiced and groaned in enthusiastic accord'. The French Grand Opera now took on a new importance:

> It has effected a reconciliation with the enemies of Music . . . the well-to-do bourgeoisie . . . while the more distinguished 'Society' has quit the field. The fine aristocracy, that elite distinguished by rank, education, birth, fashion, and leisure, has taken refuge at the Italian Opera, the musical oasis where the renowned nightingales of art still trill their fioritura, where the enchanted rills of melody still flow . . .[25]

Among those who seek in music the highest spiritual enjoyment, meanwhile, the favourite is Chopin. Born in Poland of French descent, Heine noted, Chopin received part of his education in Germany:

> The influences of the three nationalities affect his personality to an extent that is very remarkable . . . Poland has bequeathed to him chivalrous tendencies, her historical sorrows; France, her delicate grace, her charm; Germany, her profound romanticism . . . [but] when he sits down at the piano and improvises, then he is neither Polish, nor French, nor German . . . his true fatherland is the dream kingdom of Poetry.[26]

Of Berlioz, Heine records hearing the *Symphonie Fantastique,* 'a bizarre nocturne' in which the best thing is 'a Witches' Sabbath wherein the devil reads the mass, and church music is parodied with the most terrible and savage buffoonery'.[27] Berlioz, too, became passionately – if briefly – involved with the Saint-Simonian movement in the early 1830s. A young liberal with leftist leanings, he had taken part in the July Revolution, and spoken proudly of the battle for the conquest of liberties. A letter he wrote in 1831 to Charles Duveyrier (who later wrote the libretto, with Scribe, for Verdi's *Sicilian Vespers*) was intercepted by the Austrian censor, who made a copy and labelled it 'letter of a Saint-Simonian', as a result of which Metternich's ambassador in Rome was advised not to let this dangerous musician enter Austria. Nothing ever came of plans to write a work for the movement, but where Mendelssohn, a Jewish aristocrat who also encountered the Saint-Simonians at about the same time, was repelled by their radical politics, it seems that it was their burgeoning metaphysical mysticism which Berlioz found distasteful, and once the movement degenerated into a sect he had no more time for it. His politics now veered closer to that of the establishment which he never quite belonged to, and his operatic magnum opus, *The Trojans*, celebrates French imperialist deams and the conquest of North Africa more effectively than the work of any other composer. It is ironic that in writing the *Requiem* to a government commission in 1837, and three years later the *Symphonie Funèbre et Triomphale* for the official commemoration of the tenth anniversary of the July Revolution, Berlioz should have produced, in these huge public paeans to revolutionary idealism, the very music of which the Saint-Simonians hardly dared to dream.

In the Parisian musical world depicted by Heine, the composer – except, perhaps, for Chopin – is not yet wholly reduced to the new model of the Romantic musical genius which Schindler contemporaneously produced in his biography of Beethoven, published in Vienna at the beginning of the 1840s, an otherworldly figure immersed in the inner mystery of his art, detached from everyday life and practical concerns. In bowdlerizing Beethoven, evacuating both his problematic sexuality and his politics, Schindler is shoring up defences against a double onslaught which the public sphere now wreaks upon the master's followers, for at the very moment when Liszt and others take on a new political dimension of a kind never previously available, the public image of the composer is further embellished in quite a different direction by what we might call the revenge of the literary public sphere on the musical – the transformation of Chopin, Liszt and their mistresses into characters in novels, written by Balzac and the two women themselves, under their masculine noms de plume George Sand and Daniel Stern. Chopin's lover George Sand, a serial lover of male geniuses, adopted her pseudonym in 1832 for her novel *Indiana*, which brought her immediate fame for its passionate protest against the social conventions that bind a wife to her husband against her will. Daniel Stern was the pseudonym of Liszt's mistress, the Countess Marie d'Agoult, the subject of her own social scandal when she left her husband and family to live with Liszt in 1835; their second daughter, Cosima, became Wagner's second wife, also in scandalous circumstances.

The first of these *romans à clef* was Balzac's *Béatrix* (1839), where the novelist, already a dab hand at satirizing high-society cuckoldry and the psychology of young women in conflict with parental authority, drew on George Sand's private indiscretions to produce a portrait of Marie as the eponymous heroine who leaves her titled husband to become the protective muse of a composer-singer, a portrait that one biographer of Liszt calls 'coldly and cleverly accurate in physical detail and in character portrayal'. Or betrayal: Liszt is portrayed as vain and pretentious, prophetic, demonic, angelic, exuberant, but inwardly cold, who apes and trifles with other men's work, and Sand herself as an authoress with a sexually ambiguous name 'who, with venomously feline sharpness, introduces us to the failings and flaws of Béatrix'.[28] Sand followed suit with her novel *Horace* (1841–42), where Marie becomes a society lady of 'artificial' intelligence with ambitions as a patroness of the arts. In reality, Marie conducted a salon where prominent writers and thinkers debated the ideas that resulted in the 1848 Revolution; her own writings included letters in advocacy of republicanism and a history of that Revolution. But she also made her own contribution to the genre of the *roman à clef* in *Nelida*, serialized in 1846, where Liszt is portrayed as an antihero, an artist of inferior social rank who elopes to Switzerland with the eponymous heroine (Nelida is an anagram of Daniel) – as Marie and Liszt had done – only to abandon her for the dazzle of society and the lure of great commissions. The publication of this particularly spiteful version of the story, with its quite unsubtle name-play, inevitably sealed the split between Liszt and his former lover, but if this account hardly does justice to these two remarkable women, it indicates clearly enough how the enlargement of the public personality of the Romantic artist overflows the separations marked out for more ordinary members of society, to overrun the private domain of the intimate life and drag it into public view; and, even more remarkably, how this transgression of the protective skins of bourgeois decorum is accomplished by the subjects themselves – partly in self-irony and partly in public pursuit of their own claims to special status as social visionaries. (I am reminded of Adorno's comment that it is intellectuals themselves who are wont to give intellectuals a bad name.) In short, here is the gestation of the bohemianism of later generations, the ideological refraction of the contradictory social position of artistic creation in the bourgeois public sphere, where the artist on the one hand is encouraged to claim the individualism promoted by bourgeois ascendancy, and on the other derided and penalized for departing, as a result, from the decorum and bounds which public opinion deems permissible and in accordance with good polity.

To counter the sloganized and simplified envelopment of public opinion, the Romantic movement elevated the principle of ambiguity, in which received opinion dissolved in the face of the enigmatic text. In music, for example, from chords that could be interpreted as belonging to different keys came entire passages that were harmonically ambiguous. According to Charles Rosen in *The Classical Style*, this effect could be accomplished in one of two ways. One, already found in Bach and Mozart, was to pass so rapidly through a series of keys that none of them achieves stability. The other was to use a succession of chords in such a way that their key allegiance is difficult to interpret. This produces a kind of floating or wandering tonality characteristic of the music of Chopin and Liszt, and belongs especially to the piano. Because wandering tonality undermines the clear and balanced alternation of tonal centres, this music comes to seem, as a result, both more 'irrational' and more 'subjective'; we readily think of it as the very hallmark of Romanticism. At the same time, because the architectonic use of harmony is diminished, the accent falls on harmonic details: unusual progressions or even single chords. Since all this is difficult to sustain over large-scale forms, it explains, from a technical point of view, the predilection for miniature forms in composers like Chopin and Schumann. Chopin's *Preludes*, for example, or the individual songs of Schumann's *Dichterliebe*, are the most condensed musical utterances before Schoenberg and Webern, and they break all sorts of rules.

Chopin's Romanticism, however, is in certain respects deceptive. It is a surface beneath which there plays a capricious timidity that is the very antithesis of the extrovert grandeur Romanticism inherited from Beethoven. The evidence that this was the expression of a physical limitation is summarized in a description of the contrast between Chopin and Liszt by the music critic Harold Schonberg. Liszt was:

the thunderer, the matinee idol ... the lady-killer, the Paganini of the keyboard. Chopin envied him his strength ... the eighteen-year-old Chopin, all set to conquer the world at the keyboard, knew he would have to do it by finesse rather than power. When he played in Vienna he was prepared for the critical remarks about his lack of sonority ... 'It is being said everywhere [he wrote] that I played too softly, or rather, too delicately for people used to the piano-pounding of the artists here.' In Warsaw . . . those who could hear him were ravished; 'on the other hand the gallery complained that I played too softly' . . . In Paris he confined his playing almost exclusively to the salons, where everybody could hear him without difficulty.[29]

It is hardly accidental, on this reading, that Chopin cocooned himself in the world of the Parisian salon. There he remained indifferent to the political struggles of the 1830s in which friends of his, like Liszt, Berlioz and the painter Delacroix, were energetically involved, and he felt equally distant from their aesthetics. Of Liszt, whom he admired so immensely as a pianist, he commented: 'One of these days he'll be a member of parliament or perhaps even the King of Abyssinia or the Congo – but as regards the themes from his compositions, well, they will be buried in the newspapers.'[30]

But Chopin could be an enigma even to his own friends. Delacroix wrote in his journal how, in spite of his sweet temper, the composer would become angry when his music was praised for its sonority. Delacroix was somewhat puzzled and added apologetically that Chopin spoke, of course, only as a pianist, not as a composer. According to the psychoanalyst Anton Ehrenzweig, the reverse is more likely. Chopin was uneasy that sheer sonority (like Liszt's) could only drown out the subtle and complex inner structure of the music. For Chopin, the piano, with its newly perfected mechanics, was supremely a singing instrument, of the most delicate colour and nuance. To project these qualities required new techniques of fingering, touch and the use of the pedals, a new freedom with rhythm, changes of tempo and rubato; these, however, were to be the means to an ever more internal form of musical exploration, through which Chopin becomes, in musical terms, perhaps the most radical composer of his generation.

For an anonymous reviewer of his Opus 15 *Nocturnes* in 1833, the pieces are charming but bedevilled by an affectation: the tentative, languid wavering of rubato, 'the terror of girls, the bogeyman of fumblers', which no known arrangement of note values on paper can properly express. He criticizes the composer for not performing more in public so that others could learn to imitate the technique, and it was a common response during Chopin's lifetime, says Jeffrey Kallberg, 'that the composer's own rhythmically inflected manner of performing was unique, and nearly impossible to reproduce – perhaps even completely impossible if one had not heard him play'[31] (a problem which is alleviated in modern times by recording, which allows composers to provide definitive documentation of their own interpretation). This difficulty is connected with another highly elusive quality in Chopin's piano writing, which even today relatively few pianists are able to master: the rhythmic independence of what is conventionally called the accompaniment, the 'support' of the right hand by the left. It is not support, but a strange kind of counterpoint. Chopin's left hand never merely accompanies by producing a lush vertical sound: it has an independent rhythmical structure which often contains a thematic and harmonic significance of its own. The specific Chopin sound, says Ehrenzweig, results from the recalcitrant fusion between the two superimposed rhythms; pianists would be wise to forgo the conventional lush and sweet sonority, and emphasize instead the harshness of the rhythmical clash.[32] (But not, one could add, to make it sound brash and macho, like certain young virtuosi of the 1980s.) In short, Chopin is first the source and then the victim of a critical stylistic shift, much imitated and betrayed through imitation. The sonorous swooning Romantic style of Chopin performance which sounds so heart-on-sleeve to the late twentieth century is nothing but the corruption of what started as a highly individual style, a fetishization of critical nuances which, in Chopin himself, were much more poised and delicate. In his own day, Chopin was way ahead of Schumann or Mendelssohn in the matter of keyboard technique; and even Liszt, until he met Chopin, relied primarily on sheer bravura. In taking over Chopin's innovations he gave them a more extrovert and orchestral dimension, but it was Chopin who created the basic figurations of a style that dominated pianistic art until Debussy and Ravel, Bartók and Prokofiev.

Chopin's nationalism, too, is deceptive. The adolescent had imbibed the ardent patriotism of the Warsaw intelligentsia, and gave it musical expression in the use of Polish dance forms – the polonaise, the mazurka – which he heard at first hand from the peasants in the countryside. But he then absented himself when the time came for insurrection against the Russians, to seek success in the musical metropolis (curiously repeating in reverse the trajectory of his father, who had left France to seek his fortune in Poland in 1787 in order to escape conscription). Thus if Chopin's work seems to be one of the earliest intimations of the nationalism which is to dominate European music in the second half of the century, then this is paradoxical, for these traits appear in Chopin as a longing for a world on the wane. As Adorno put it: 'A listener must stop up his ears not to hear Chopin's F minor Fantasy as a kind of tragically decorative song of triumph to the effect that Poland was not lost forever ... But what triumphed over that triumph was an absolute musical quality that

could be no more nailed down than confined within national frontiers.'[33] This he calls a quality which cremates the national moment
that kindled it.

In one other area as well, the impression which Chopin's music
created was highly ambiguous – not, this time, the question of the
composer's actual sexual inclinations, which indeed were perfectly well
known, but his special appeal to women, which was widely noted, and
the representation of sexuality embedded in the very contours of the
notes. This, says Jeffrey Kallberg – author of a study of gender and
ideology in the Chopin nocturne – is a matter which musicology has
always shied away from, because it has not escaped the dogma of
formalist belief in music's autonomy.[34] But if genre is a social as well
as an aesthetic construct – and this is the domain of the public sphere
which concerns us here – then the feminine orientation of Chopin's
primary sphere of activities is of paramount significance. The question,
says Kallberg, is not so much how music 'speaks' sex, but how sex
'spoke' music: entering into the reception of music, metaphorically or
by allusion, capturing or inflecting its emotive charge. But this is a
complex and subtle problem.

Take the nocturne, one of Chopin's preferred genres, which –
according to the composer-pianist Czerny, writing in 1839 – 'is really
an imitation of those vocal pieces which are termed *Serenades*, and the
peculiar object of such works – that of being performed by night,
before the dwelling of an esteemed individual – must always exercise
an influence upon its character'.[35] If the gender in this pronounce-
ment is unambiguously masculine (for who is it that sings the serenade?), Chopin's treatment of the nocturne, on the other hand, with
his wafting fragments of melody and ambiguous tonalities carried on
a stream of rubato, seemingly irrational and subjective, is distinctly
double-voiced, a decentred figuration which transcends male identity
to become a mirror of the feminine, albeit highly stylized. The music
seems to don the garb of the feminine sensibility who listens to the
seranade, as if to flatter its audience by whispering their secrets. It
comes to evoke, in the language of the time, the soul of the recipient
– or, at least, it sustains a dialogue in which men aspire to listen to
women listening to men, and women listen to men listening to
women. But this is the problem: there is a certain slippage here, a
dangerous ambiguity in the way the feminine is constructed.

To draw from Kallberg's survey of the literature, this music, according to an anonymous review of the Opus 27 *Nocturnes* in 1836, will
'always be most attractive to all hearts inclined toward the feminine';
but for others, 'the representation of sentiment in the notturno runs

the danger of falling into the effeminate and languishing, which displeases stronger souls and altogether tires the listener'. This is an attitude of timid male conformism which leads only to the disparagement of Chopin, the nocturne and other typical genres of piano music. Fifty years after his death, an American writer is quite explicit – but still confused – about the issue: Chopin's nocturnes are often called feminine, says James Huneker: 'a term psychologically false. The poetic side of men of genius is feminine, and in Chopin the feminine note was over emphasized – at times it was almost hysterical – particularly in these nocturnes.'[36] For his contemporaries, however – in numerous testimonies by the likes of Berlioz, Théophile Gautier, the young Charles Hallé – Chopin is an elfin figure, a sylph, not man but angel; his music evokes small fairy voices, the keyboard is as if brushed by an angel's wing – in short, he is the Ariel of the piano. This trope is not so much effeminate as sexually ambiguous, androgynous, hermaphrodite – above all magical, supernatural. For Thomas Mann's fictional composer Adrian Leverkühn, the angelic in Chopin's figure reminds him of Shelley: 'the peculiarly and very mysteriously veiled, unapproachable, withdrawing, unadventurous flavour of his being, that not wanting to know, that rejection of material experience, the sublime incest of his fantastically delicate and seductive art'.[37] For George Sand, too, writing to friends about her lover, Chopin is 'this angel', 'poor angel', 'an angel of sweetness and kindness'. That for Sand this angelic quality is related to questions about gender we learn from her novel *Gabriel*, an experimental *roman dialogué*, which she drafted in 1839 in Marseille during Chopin's recovery from their distressing sojourn in Majorca: the tale of a youth of the nobility in the time of the Renaissance whose female sex has been disguised from her, for reasons of family intrigue, since birth. When the hero-cum-heroine discovers her biological sex, and is given the option of remaining male and living the life of a prince, or assuming a female identity and joining a convent, she/he rejects the deal and chooses to pose alternately as man and as woman. *Gabriel*, says Kallberg, is a critique of received notions of gender, by way of a metaphorical stylization which personifies the character and personality of Chopin and his music; although, given that 'George Sand' is also a fictive construction, the eponymous hero contains something of both Chopin and the author, whose identities are equally transgressive. Chopin's music seen through this prism, which was that of his contemporaries and not just some retrospective theoretical construct, challenges the social norms of gender identity in the powerful but inarticulate space of music, becoming both seductive and unsettling, threatening and compelling at the same time. We are left with the paradox of a kind of public secrecy, and a space for the healing of divisions – which is always one of music's gifts to the social weal.

The hubris of Richard Wagner

Wagner, on arriving in Paris at the end of the 1830s, resorted to hack work – choruses for the vaudeville, songs, arrangements of selections from popular operas – in order to survive. He also spent three weeks in prison for debt; the truth is, he was up to his neck in it. Throughout his apprentice years, as he moved from Würzburg to Magdeburg, Königsberg, Riga and finally Paris, he left debtors behind him. It is a consistent and central feature of Wagner's personality that he always wanted more and more money to satisfy his ambitions. To begin with he borrowed from friends and relatives, in order to travel or put on concerts. As for all composers of the time who were forced to act as their own impresarios, it was not Wagner's fault if the concerts lost money and even drove him deeper into debt, or if he had to finance the publication of his scores himself, with the same results. Yet rather than learning to be more pragmatic, he became more profligate, and in this one can see only a deliberate and megalomaniac flaunting of sense in the manner of the Hollywood mogul who follows a multi-million-dollar flop with an even more expensive project. Fortunately for Wagner, he found the ultimate patron in the mad King Ludwig of Bavaria and, when even his money ran out, in the gullibility of his own followers throughout Europe who formed themselves into Wagner Societies in order to subscribe their shekels for the construction of a temple at Bayreuth. One can hardly escape regarding this as a definitive trait in Wagner's character, since the psychology of gold is the central subject of his magnum opus. One writer who captures this well is Peter Conrad: the Rhinemaidens, he says, enjoy gold innocently, the dwarfs mine it industriously, the giants build with it, the leisured gods need it to maintain a political system in which they live off the profits of others' toil. If Nibelheim, as Shaw pointed out, is a manufacturing town, then, as Wagner's grandson Wieland perceived, Valhalla is Wall Street.[38]

As Pierre Boulez reminded the audience in the programme book when he conducted *The Ring* at Bayreuth in the centenary year 1976, one of the most radical elements in Wagner was that his operas were incompatible with normal performance routines. 'Opera houses are rather like cafés where, if you sit near enough to the counter, you can hear the waiters calling out their orders: "One *Carmen*! And one *Walküre*! And one *Rigoletto*!"' Wagner loathed this system and the relationship with the public which it presupposed, and therefore expunged from his work all elements of *divertissement* and the theatrical norms and conventions in which opera was then bogged down.[39] Hence also the innovations in the architectural design of the theatre at Bayreuth. Yet this, said Boulez on another occasion, is a field in which Wagner has proved to have almost completely failed: 'Architecturally speaking, the Bayreuth model has remained a dead letter and we still have Italian-style theatres', in which the orchestra pit has been disproportionately enlarged to accommodate bigger orchestras. 'From the other side of this giant swimming pool – where it is possible during a performance to watch the family life of the orchestra – singers do their best to get through the wall of sound ... and ... both visually and acoustically we witness the defeat of what is truly theatrical. ...'[40]

It was not only Wagner's frustration with the reactionary regimes of the provincial theatres where he worked – at Würzburg as *répétiteur*, and as a conductor thereafter – but also the influences of his youth that inclined him towards revolutionary sympathies. Leipzig, where he spent his teens and went to university, was a centre of liberal thought. As a child he had imbibed the bohemianism of the theatrical family into which he was born, and he felt his vocation first as a poet-dramatist, not a composer. German literature at this time, says that impeccable witness Friedrich Engels, laboured under the influence of political excitement:

> It became more and more the habit, particularly of the inferior sorts of *literati*, to make up for the want of cleverness in their productions by political allusions ... every literary production teemed with what was called 'tendency', that is, more or less timid exhibitions of anti-governmental spirit ... and misunderstood gleanings from French socialism, particularly Saint-Simonism.[41]

As a composer Wagner admired Meyerbeer, who overcame this timidity and, in expressing the ideology of the July Revolution, turned his back on Italian models and brought to opera a modern sense of universal struggle. (As Heine wrote, it was lucky for Meyerbeer that governments didn't understand music, 'otherwise they would discern more than a party struggle between Protestants and Catholics in *Les Huguenots*'.)[42] It is not surprising that Wagner is found on the barricades in Dresden in 1849, and forced to flee when the insurrection is rapidly put down. On the other hand, he is not to be awarded the revolutionary credentials of the able and cool-headed Russian refugee who commanded the Dresden insurgents, and was afterwards taken prisoner, Mikhail Bakunin (the description is Engels's).[43]

Did Wagner align himself with the socialists because there was no republican party to offer a centre between the Left and the constitutional monarchists? He seems not unlike the bourgeois politicians also described by Engels, of whom, towards the end of 1847, there was hardly one 'who did not proclaim himself a socialist in order to insure to himself the sympathy of the proletarian class'. Yet these gentlemen, when the barricades went up, watched nervously from the wings, while Wagner did not. His allotted task was to supervise the printing of pamphlets urging the Saxon troops to desert and join the 'popular front'. His own writings demonstrate a passionate devotion to the revolutionary ideal, which he takes it upon himself to personify:

> I will destroy the existing order of things, which parts this one mankind into hostile nations, into powerful and weak, privileged and outcast, rich and poor ... that turns millions to slaves of a few, and these few to slaves of their own might, own riches. I will destroy this order of things, that cuts enjoyment off from labour, makes labour a load, enjoyment a vice ... Down to its memory I will destroy each trace of this mad state of things, compact of violence, lies, care, hypocrisy, want, sorrow, suffering, tears, trickery and crime ...[44]

If the terms of social analysis in Wagner's revolutionary writings are sometimes reminiscent of Schiller, and if he displays a hatred of gold that puts us in mind of the vehemence of the young Marx on the same subject, on the other hand, only Wagner has the hubris to decide on a personal pact with socialism. Shortly before the Dresden insurrection, he declared unfounded the fear that socialistic doctrines represented a threat to the free development of art. On the contrary, he said, it was for art:

> to teach this social impulse its noblest meaning, and guide it toward its true direction. Only on the shoulders of this great social movement can true art lift itself from its present state of civilised barbarianism, and take its post of honour. Each has a common goal, and the twain can reach it only when they recognise it jointly.[45]

A decade and a half later he was required by his 'highly-prized young friend' Ludwig II to justify himself. 'Whoever has assigned me the role of a political revolutionary,' he wrote, 'with actual enrolment in the lists as such, manifestly knew nothing at all about me, and judged me by an outer semblance of events.' He had needed 'to try to make plain to myself the tendency of the state, in order to account for the disdain with which I found my earnest artistic ideal regarded everywhere in public life'. This did not lead him into politics proper, he said, which never really touched him. The political movements of the time attracted his attention when they 'appeared to offer prospects of the realization of my ideal premises'.[46]

This is only partly self-justification. For if Boulez is right when he says that the impression Wagner gives is 'primarily theatrical, that of a man who dramatised the conflicts of his day and used them to his own advantage as a means of nourishing his own work',[47] then it rings entirely true when, in the letter to Ludwig, he continues:

> The calculations of the ... Socialists ... lost my sympathy from the moment they seemed to end in systems that took ... the repellent aspect of an organisation of society for no purpose other than equally allotted toil ... I, too, was ... picturing to myself a world that I deemed possible, but the purer I imagined it, the more it parted company with the reality of the political tendencies of the day around me; so that I could say to myself, My world will never make its entry until the very moment when the present world has ceased – in other words, where Socialists and politicians came to end.

What is finally convincing about this remarkable document is the summary which the composer then delivers of the origins of his magnum opus and what he intended by it; no critic has ever been more succinct:

> The political relations of the beginning of the ... fifties kept everyone in a state of nervous tension ... precisely at that time I had already sketched, and finally completed, the poem of my *Ring des Nibelungen*. With this conception I had unconsciously admitted to myself the truth about things human. Here everything is tragic through and through, and the will, that fain would shape a world according to its wish, at last can reach no greater satisfaction than the breaking of itself in dignified annulment.

It is the character of harmonic language which entails that this annulment should have been expressed through a fatal weakening of the central role of the tonic, which Wagner achieves by expanding harmonic ambiguity to monumental proportions. His voyages up and down the self-proliferating sets of key sequences are monster-sized and extend over hours; chromaticism has become all-pervasive. 'It was the wealth and density of his music,' says Boulez:

> and its large-scale continuity, that most puzzled his contemporaries, more especially in the world of opera where listeners were not remarkable for

their acuteness. Add to this a harmonic inventiveness also springing from his need for continuity, his ideal of endless transition. The further he advanced, the more closely he approached regions in which for long stretches the musical language lost its clear direction; and this uncertainty, the instability of passing resolutions and the discovery of twilight areas in which outlines become blurred, began increasingly to preoccupy his mind at the deepest level.[48]

For Boulez, along with Lévi-Strauss, Wagner stands essentially for 'myth made effective by musical construction', which for the anthropologist is manifest in the special nature of their common relationship to time: 'as if music and mythology needed time only in order to deny it'.[49] And in order to accomplish this, Wagner was obliged to change the traditional structures of musical thinking, those of time most of all. It is here, says Boulez, in his researching and restructuring of time, that he finds Wagner's real subversive achievement.

This subversion of the dominant chronotope is intimately connected with another effect, which Boulez does not mention. When the orthodox ordering of time is suspended, other structures of repression are also loosened; and because tonality bore a certain analogical affinity to the bourgeois sense of individual identity, this loosening produced strange effects on the listening subject. It is no accident that the exploitation of harmonic ambiguity reaches its apex in the erotic transports of *Tristan and Isolde*. The upward leap and its chromatic fall with which the Prelude opens is repeated over and over again, urging the music forwards, falling and rising again, higher and more intense; technically, this is nothing more than a rising minor sixth that ends in a deceptive cadence, initially suggesting the key of A minor, which is then transformed into a major sixth, suggesting a different key, only for the process to be repeated again and again, the resolution of the ambiguity always itself ambiguous. Because of the effect of continual unresolved suspension, this is the music which is sometimes regarded as the source of atonality. At the same time, for Leonard Bernstein, expressing a long-standing thought, it is as if a fiercely unappeased sensual desire can no longer be contained in a tonal framework; while the whole opera, according to Wilfred Mellers, is like 'a protracted attempt at an orgasm which would resolve the dichotomy between spirit and flesh'.[50]

This is the place to mention Max Weber's remarks about the connection between the development of Western music and the Christian denigration of the body. His argument that the prohibition against the body's physical manifestation in religious ritual and music paved the way for music's rationalization can be interpreted as a continuing process of sublimation. But the act of sublimation takes on what Adorno calls a mimetic aspect, and creates, among other things, a musical schema with an ideological affinity to the body politic, both social and psychosocial. If in Wagner the early Romantic epithets of nature ('Italian', 'Rhenish', 'Scottish', 'Hebrides') are left behind, this is because the physical geography of the landscape has been replaced by an ideal fantasy space in which to suspend the ego. But this suspension also admits – indeed, invites – association with a roving libido, which sublimation, rationalization and the Protestant ethic have banished from sight. Even in opera, sexuality was sublimated through the various kinds of artifice employed (like the castrato). In Kierkegaard's view, only Mozart transcended this containment and avowed the true erotic content of opera, much to the discomfort of the nineteenth century. In this sense, *Tristan and Isolde* is not just a metaphorical rendering of Berlioz's *Romeo and Juliet*, as Bernstein suggested, but a huge musical icon for the impending dissolution of the bourgeois ego-ideal, projected through the portrayal of an irresistible and self-destructive narcissism.

This narcissism was Wagner's own, and the only thing that prevented it destroying him was his undoubted genius. Its most famous witness was Nietzsche. Nietzsche originally came under Wagner's spell as a sixteen-year-old schoolboy when he first encountered a piano score of *Tristan*. The two men first met eight years later, in 1868, shortly before Nietzsche became Professor of Classical Philology at the University of Basle. On Nietzsche's side, the product of what both men understood as a rare meeting of souls was the dedication to Wagner of *The Birth of Tragedy out of the Spirit of Music*, where he eulogizes *Tristan and Isolde*. Within a few years, however, he began to feel the oppression of Wagner's hubris. According to his sister: 'he was seized with a dread presentiment that in order to remain Wagner's friend he would be obliged to renounce his own path of future growth and development'.[51] He was driven to put the composer to the test:

In the spring [of 1874], we had heard a performance of Brahms' *Song of Triumph* . . . , a work that made a deep impression upon my brother. He bought the score and took it with him to Bayreuth, without having the faintest idea (as I then thought!) that this would be misinterpreted by Wagner. But later I came across this sentence in my brother's notebook: 'The tyrant admits no individuality other than his own and that of his most intimate friends. The danger is great for Wagner when he is unwilling to grant anything to Brahms or to the Jews.'[52]

(Here it should be said that her own anti-Semitism seems not to have caused her to repress her brother's objection to that of Wagner.)

In the wake of the Prussian victory over France in 1870, and Germany's unification, Wagner's nationalism spread rapidly among young German intellectuals; many of them, after the economic crash of 1873, found his idealization of the medieval German artisan community distinctly attractive, though one of its effects was to set back the plans to open the theatre at Bayreuth in 1875. In notes for his *Thoughts Out of Season: Richard Wagner in Bayreuth*, the reasons Nietzsche gives for this failure include:

> Influence of the money crisis.
> General uncertainty of the political situation.
> Doubts as to the wise leadership of Germany at present.
> Period of art agitation (Liszt etc.) now over.

The main thing, he says, is that 'the significance of an art such as Wagner represents does not fit into our present social and economic conditions'.[53] When the first Bayreuth Festival finally took place, a year later, it seemed to Nietzsche that Wagner's highest aspirations were submerged in a sea of rich idlers who paid their 900 marks for the twelve performances only in order to be seen and boast of having been present, and he was struck by 'the illusory character of Wagner's ideals'. Even worse, the hard core of Wagnerites, the members of the various branches of the Wagner Society who assembled every evening in the tap-room, were not, as Nietzsche's sister put it – for of course, she was there too –

> the most delectable type of visitors, as they beat upon the table with their fists, raised their beer glasses threateningly on high and were ready to engage in a hand to hand fight with anyone who presumed to express a thought that could be regarded as the slightest deflection from the strict Wagnerian code. Wagnerites of this kind seemed to my brother to be a parody on themselves.[54]

Half a century later this self-parody would become unremittingly evil and, ignoring Nietzsche's denunciations, would claim his subsequent philosophy for itself as well, making it worse, far worse, than parody.

This music, Nietzsche later wrote, 'is addressed to inartistic persons; all possible means are employed by which an *effect* can be created. It is not an *artistic effect* that is achieved, but one operating solely upon *the nerves*.'[55] Wagner, he continued, has no genuine confidence in music as it might be when detached from the drama, and therefore imposes upon it both a symbolic interpretation and all the industry and ingenuity of stage machinery he can muster; this only reveals the dangers of realism, the effort to employ effect for its own sake. The music itself turns into a sort of acquired language with only a limited vocabulary and a different syntax, inarticulate and terrifyingly distinct at the same time, 'as if it were trying to make itself heard by deaf people'. Nietzsche's assessment of Wagner's musical language is remarkably prescient: a new syntax which in Wagner himself is limited, but whose influence on the evolution of music, he says, is bound to be inescapable.

The final break came shortly afterwards when, by fateful coincidence, Nietzsche and Wagner met on holiday in Sorrento. Nietzsche later told his sister what happened. Wagner explained to Nietzsche his idea for an opera about Parsifal, speaking of it not as an artistic conception but as a religious experience:

> My brother ... considered it quite impossible that Wagner, the avowed atheist, should suddenly have become a naive and pious believer. He could only regard Wagner's alleged sudden change of heart as having been prompted by a desire to stand well with the Christian rulers of Germany and thus further the material success of the Bayreuth undertaking. My brother was confirmed in this belief by a remark Wagner made when referring to the unsatisfactory attendance at the first Festival [which had incurred a huge financial loss]; almost angrily, he exclaimed: 'The Germans do not wish to hear anything about gods and goddesses at present, they are only interested in something of a religious character.'[56]

This is the opera upon which Debussy later commented that it 'provides us with a rather striking image: Bach as the Holy Grail, with Wagner as Klingsor, trying to destroy the Grail and take its place'. (But Bach, he added, reigns supreme, and 'Wagner is fading out, a murky and disquieting shadow'.)[57]

The Mozart of the Champs-Élysées

When revolution triumphed in France in 1830, the French bourgeoisie marked the new regime by reforming the Opéra, which had languished during the Restoration. A plan was devised to relieve the state of the expense and turn it over to commercial management instead, and for once the project succeeded. Under the direction of Louis Véron, an excellent businessman and a true bourgeois with an instinctive under-standing of the susceptibilities of the new audience, it began to show a profit for the first time in 160 years. This success was partly due to the combination of the composer Meyerbeer, the playwright Scribe, and the expenditure of enormous sums on lavish productions. The result was to turn the Opéra into a factory for the production of epics, each one manufactured according to the same fixed formula, with the effect – as one writer has neatly put it – of punishing Wagner's *Tannhäuser* 'for breach of commercial practice by putting the ballet in the wrong place'.[58]

Meanwhile, the composers who wrote for the Opéra-Comique – Auber, Adam, Thomas, and others – had long forsaken its tradition of parody and social satire, and now turned out little grand operas that were also increasingly sentimental. 'The scores of many of our composers', wrote Jacques Offenbach in 1855, on the eve of his own success, 'resemble the most fashionable ladies on the Boulevards, in that their crinolines are excessively luxuriant. In suitable light they look substantial enough and show pretty colours, but looked at closely, in déshabillé or at the piano, as the case may be, they are phantoms; phantoms inflated with wind and noise.'[59]

Jacques Offenbach, originally Jakob Ebert (or Eberscht, or Wiener, or maybe Levy – the reference books disagree), was the son of an itinerant Jewish musician and synagogue cantor who had settled in Cologne but sent his progidiously gifted son to Paris, since this was apparently the only place – as the success of Meyerbeer and Halévy, Auber, Hérold and Adam demonstrated – where a Jewish musician could make a name without obstacle. Nevertheless, the Opéra-Comique, where for a time the young musician was a cellist in the orchestra, proved resistant to his ambitions as a composer, even when he made his name in the salons as a virtuoso, and the comic scenes he began composing proved their popularity both there and on the concert platform. Offenbach wanted to revive the light and graceful touch of the eighteenth-century Opéra-Comique with music that was gay, cheerful and, above all, witty. But the appropriate conditions for this endeavour were not yet all in place in the 1840s, when the basis for the economic prosperity of the 1850s and 1860s was only in process of formation, when utopian socialism flourished among the intelligentsia, and there was still a widespread Romantic belief in progress. The cynical society that was to acclaim the operettas of Offenbach (though he was not a cynic himself) did not blossom until the days of the Second Empire – that is to say, not until the failure of the revolutions of 1848 destroyed the unreconstructed Romanticism of a previous generation. It was also of considerable help that the new dictatorship forbade the expression of independent opinion, stifled political life, and encouraged the musical stage as a distraction from the real world which it none the less began to reflect, for as Siegfried Kracauer explains (in one of the few biographies of a composer to place its subject squarely in his social and political milieu), the new regime was based on a flight from reality, and there was a visible diminution in the capacity for distinguishing real values from fictitious ones.

Even Queen Victoria felt it. 'All so gay, the people cheering the Emperor as he walked up and down in the little garden,' she wrote in her diary on the occasion of a state visit. 'And yet how recently the blood has flowed, a whole dynasty been swept away, and how uncertain is everything still! All is so beautiful here, all seems now so prosperous, the Emperor seems so fit for his place, and yet how little security one feels for the future!'[60] Another royal personage, the Archduke Maximilian, later Emperor of Mexico, who was brought up in the courtly traditions of the Habsburgs, felt it too: 'There is something amateurish and theatrical about the whole thing,' he wrote home, 'and the various roles are played by officials who are not very sure of their parts.'[61] This was the Court which was the model for Offenbach's parodies of courtly life. At the same time, with the expansion of the credit system, the emphasis in matters economic lay more on speculation and finance than on solid industrial development, and if winning lottery tickets and sudden and dramatic changes of fortune are part of the stock in trade of Offenbach's early operettas', 'sudden changes of fortune were just as characteristic of the world about him, for members of the ruling caste speculated in the hope of strokes of fortune worthy of the operettas'.[62] In short, the Offenbachiade operetta 'would never have been born had the society of the time not itself been operetta-like; had it not been living in a dream-world, obstinately refusing to wake up and face reality'.[63] (If this sounds like Reaganomics or Thatcherism, one can only regret that we have no Offenbach of our own.)

Even after the revolutionary interlude of 1848, the *coup d'état* which brought Louis Napoleon to power at the end of 1851, and his coronation as Emperor a year later, the Opéra-Comique still resisted Offenbach's approaches. But in 1855 he seized his chance and applied for a licence – not forgetting to pull the necessary strings in order to get the permit granted – to reopen a small forgotten theatre on the Champs-Élysées near the Palace of Industry where the World Exhibition was due to be held, which he then called the Bouffes-Parisiens. There he presented, among other pieces, a musical farce which caught the mood of the moment: *Les deux Aveugles*, a burlesque on the beggars of Paris in which a pair of buskers pose as blind musicians and quarrel over a miserable sou. The two actors became famous practically overnight, and the waltz they play to unsuspecting passers-by became the rage.

Before the year was out, Offenbach had followed this skit with another rip-roaring success entitled *Ba-ta-clan*, a piece of *chinoiserie* in which the action takes place at the court of Fé-ni-han, the absolute ruler of a petty kingdom with only twenty-seven subjects. Fé-ni-han turns out to be a Parisian, and so do two of his entourage: one of them a ruined man of fashion, the other a one-time music-hall star, both of them pining for the Maison Dorée and the opéra. Here the chief ingredients of the true Offenbachiade, its carnivalesque sense of parody, are already in evidence. The piece 'dealt as unceremoniously with grand opera as it did with the glamour and pomp that sorround a tyrant . . . . The "Chinese" sung and spoken by the characters in *Ba-ta-clan* was a senseless Franco-Italian gibberish, and the effect was a complete parody of Italian opera.'[64] Meyerbeer was dealt with in a similar manner, for Offenbach brazenly worked in passages from *Les Huguenots*; there is even a parody of a grand-opera rebels' song.

In the first of his classic operettas, *Orpheus in the Underworld*, dating from 1858, the principal object of operatic parody is Gluck's opera on the same subject, but here the gods are 'in carnival costume, scattering jokes and witticisms in the jargon of the boulevards'.[65] Pluto, in order to escape punishment for the rape of Eurydice, incites the gods against Jupiter, who in no way shrinks from mean and dishonest devices to maintain his power, so that his reign corrupts Olympus just as the dictatorship corrupted the bourgeoisie; but when he takes the gods with him by omnibus to the underworld, they forget their complaints. The opera ends in the frenzy of the famous cancan, while among the strokes of brilliance which enliven the proceedings along the way, the chorus of classical tragedy is replaced by Public Opinion, whose manipulation by Jupiter makes it 'abundantly clear that Public Opinion can be manipulated with impunity by the powers that be'.[66]

Strangely, although it was easy to detect contemporary illusions, and the idea of a satire on antiquity as the scarcely veiled ridicule of the current regime was not original, it was not until the work was attacked by the critic Jules Janin that it really took off. The reasons for this hestitation were twofold: on the one hand it was dangerously close to the bone; on the other, the object of the satire was ambiguous. The references appeared to be contemporary, but could also be taken to refer to the time of Louis Philippe – hence the potency of the famous cancan at the end, whose heyday was the 1830s. But this ambiguity quickly turned into the source of the work's success. Earlier in the operetta, the rebellious and oversatiated Olympians threaten to break the make-believe, in a passage where, as Kracauer observes, Offenbach seems to have been calling upon his audience to awaken. 'You live in the azure of material prosperity,' the operetta seems to say:

Confess that you are just as bored as the gods, and follow the lead that they are giving. What was the lead the gods were giving? They were setting about making a revolution . . . And so that their anger might be given a thorough contemporary note, the orchestra [strikes] up the *Marseillaise*, which in the days of the Second Empire was very definitely a revolutionary song. The challenge was plain enough.[67]

Perhaps the only thing Kracauer misses is that this may also be read as a satire directed against those high-born revolutionaries of the 1830s and 1840s who confined their propaganda to their own class, since the workers – or so they believed – were unfortunately ignorant and backward. That is why the audience which flocked to the theatre after Janin denounced it mostly took it as a kind of hymn to the greater glory of the Second Empire; although one contemporary commentator perceived the finale 'as though the whole century, with its governments, institutions, customs, and laws, were plunged into the whirl of a tremendous, all-embracing saraband'.[68]

It is unnecessary to analyse in any detail Offenbach's subsequent successes, which included *La Belle Hélène* and *La Vie Parisienne*. Suffice it to say that in the former, which repeats the formula of the satire on antiquity, the intoxicating revels are again accompanied by a presentiment of doom; while the latter, which takes a contemporary setting, is aptly summed up in Karl Kraus's appreciative witticism that in this operetta, 'life is nearly as improbable as it really is'.[69] Nietzsche, on the rebound from Wagner, considered that Offenbach attained the supreme form of wit, and valued him highly as an antidote to the German moralist.[70] At the same time, burlesque apart, Offenbach's music remained an end in itself. As Kracauer notes: 'the emphasis lay less on the satire than on the gaiety which was the result of it and which had an independent existence of its own'.[71]

Kracauer also speaks of the curious relationship between Offenbach and Wagner:

Wagner used mythology and saga to create musical dramas which in spite of, or because of, their pessimism, in the last resort aggravated the political impotence of the German bourgeoisie, while Offenbach exploited the same or similar material to make satires in which he playfully put topsyturvy political conditions to rights.[72]

Perhaps this is why Offenbach's attempts to parody Wagner were unsuccessful; his entire *œuvre* was exposed as so much wind and noise. On one occasion, however, he ridiculed Wagner in person, in a skit called *The Musician of the Future*, composed for a review in 1860, in which Wagner, composer of the 'music of the future', arrives in

Elysium, meets up with Grétry, Weber, Mozart and Gluck, insults them and tells them it was time they were scrapped; whereupon the four masters turn upon him and expel him from the temple of art. Wagner's response to this attack was naturally pitiless, and he said of *Orpheus* that the warmth of its music was like 'a dung-heap on which all the swine of Europe wallowed'. Kracauer adds, however, that after Offenbach's death, in the clarity of his own old age, Wagner admitted that there was a certain resemblance between Offenbach and the divine Mozart, 'and thus the phrase coined by Rossini, who called Offenbach the "Mozart of the Champs-Élysées", received corroboration'.[73]

Several elements came together in Offenbach's success. One was the double incorporation not only of characters, situations and scenes from the Paris of his youth, but also its music, in such a way that their combination with the parody of grand opera became truly absurd; especially, for example, when a pathetic recitative suddenly gives way to a dance rhythm, or a finale explodes into a cancan. Another factor was Offenbach's incredible facility, in which he took great pride. On one occasion, in order to win a wager, he composed an entire operetta in just one week. This, says Kracauer, is veritably music as journalism. Indeed, Offenbach was even more a commodity producer than Meyerbeer, and once actually declared: 'one must have ideas and tunes that are as genuine as hard cash'.[74] At the same time he had the good sense to adopt an aesthetic in proportion with his talents, so that in expressing a preference for small-scale production he was not merely bowing to the circumstances which kept him out of the Opéra-Comique but turning to his advantage the fact that this was the opposite of the inflated pomposity which, he believed, had led the musical theatre astray. Not surprisingly, he expressed the greatest admiration for Mozart.

He was not unlike Mozart in his relationship to his librettists and his attitude towards the work in hand. Given his unerring sense of theatre, he would refrain from putting the finishing touches to a work until he saw it on stage, when he then removed anything that got in the way of dramatic continuity. For the same reasons, he not only worked in close collaboration with his librettists but did not shrink from making suggestions – it was his idea to introduce Homer into *La Belle Hélène* as a war correspondent – and giving them directives, which was also true of Mozart, not to mention Verdi. He was also – like Mozart with da Ponte or Verdi with Boito – supremely fortunate in his collaborators: the works by which he is mostly remembered (apart from *The Tales of Hoffmann*, his only successful attempt at grand opera) were authored by Ludovic Halévy (nephew of the composer, son of the playwright) in collaboration with either Hector Crémieux or Henri Meilhac. Halévy, says Kracauer, was a man who went through life observing everything and forgetting nothing, who imbibed his sense of theatre as a child from his father and his uncle, and then went into government service. His success in both fields led to the extraordinary situation, imaginable only in the world of the Second Empire, in which he collaborated in writing a libretto for Offenbach, *M. Choufleuri restera chez lui le . . .*, with his boss in the government, Count de Morny, half-brother of Louis Napoleon and stage manager of his *coup d'état*. Halévy is also remembered, of course, as the author, together with Meilhac, of the libretto for Bizet's *Carmen*.

Offenbach was fortunate, says Kracauer, in that the opening of the Bouffes coincided with the beginning of a new international era, and his genre appealed as much to the foreigners who came to visit the World Exhibition or to savour Parisian gaiety as to Parisians themselves. In fact the Offenbachiade was itself 'an *émigré* product', and its musical idiom was no more a local one than the humour of Charlie Chaplin in early cinema a couple of generations later. The result was that Offenbach's success abroad was rapid, and within two years of the opening of the Bouffes-Parisiens he undertook the first of many international tours with a visit to London. Vienna took to him most especially, and it was not long before Viennese operetta provided the Offenbachiade with serious competition. Viennese operetta, however, was a 'feeble, middle class caricature . . . of Offenbach, which substituted cosiness for gaiety, stupidity for nonsense, and idle prattle for wit'.[75] Musically – apart from Johann Strauss, and even then only really in *Die Fledermaus* – Viennese operetta served up nothing but hedonism and schmaltz. For Karl Kraus, the success of Lehár, a cynical crowd-pleaser, was a barometer of the moral degeneration of Viennese life, the very antithesis of Offenbach, entirely lacking the latter's element of critique; while in England, the Gilbert and Sullivan operettas are better-behaved than Offenbach's, but they use the same means: social and political satire with a good dose of the ridiculous, parody of grand opera, quick change from sentimentality to disarming merriment. The commercial success of Gilbert and Sullivan is a matter of record. It enabled their manager, Richard D'Oyly Carte, to build two of the finest theatres in London, the Savoy and the English Opera House (now the Palace Theatre), the first to be equipped with electric lighting. Sullivan, however, constantly thwarted in his attempt to make his name as a more serious artist, released his frustration in gambling, losing a quarter of a million pounds in the process.

5

Semiotics in Question

Semantic domination

The forms of artistic intercourse, as Bakhtin has noted, are extremely varied and differentiated, ranging from the intimate audience of the salon to the mass readership of the novel. The readers of a novel and the audience in the concert-hall are collective organizations of different types, and 'without these distinctive forms of social intercourse there are no poems, no odes, no symphonies'.[1] In the space between Bach and Offenbach, however, the collective organization of music underwent enormous change. Music not only acquired an enlarged public presence, but – as we have seen – experienced a radical transformation in the way it was publicly understood; it reconstructed subjectivity, acquired political resonance, and exerted an unsettling effect on social identities. While bourgeois musical taste was originally formed in the environment of the literary public sphere, music's growing autonomy leads to the assertion, through the agency of the composer, of its own special nature – sometimes in parallel to literary values, sometimes in contradistinction to them. The enlargement of musical meaning which takes place in the process not only alters the relationship between music and literary culture, but also poses the problem of how musical meaning is created and communicated.

Until roughly the time of the French Revolution, musical judgements were dominated largely by literary values. Not only was early music criticism, as we have seen, the province of literati, but a tendency like the doctrine of emotions, associated with the style of *Empfindsamkeit* exemplified by C.P.E. Bach, is the very model of a musical aesthetic under the thumb of a literary culture. Johann Mattheson, for example, represents music as a rhetorical art which is always directed towards the audience. He considers it essential for the composer to be conscious of the way the audience thought and felt, to be aware of their intellectual, emotional, and social predilections; the associated doctrine of affections provided a means of regulating the composer's imagination in the interests of the susceptibilities of the listener. What actually happens here, to put it crudely, is that music is labelled by stereotyped emotions ('happy', 'sad', 'hopeful', 'longing', etc.) through a process which the musicologist Richard Norton calls 'semantic domination', in which words, inevitably blunt and arbitrary compared to music itself, have the effect of pinning the music down. This doctrine is rejected by the Romantics. As Mendelssohn once put it: 'If you ask me to explain a piece of music, I can't do it, not because music is too vague, but because words are too vague.'

Norton discovers the process of semantic domination already at work in the sixteenth-century concept of Musica Reservata, associated with the name Adrianus Petit Coclico, a pupil of Josquin des Prés, from whom he claimed it derived. One of the more obscure doctrines in musical history, it defines a style which is not at all obscure, in which the composer's technique is placed at the service of the ideas and emotions to be found in the text, and thus reminding us that most music of the time was vocal. This is indeed the practice in the madrigals of Monteverdi and Gesualdo. It is through the text (or sometimes the title) that, in Norton's words, 'externalized human emotion makes its appearance in music ... To use a thoroughly capitalistic metaphor, words are the currency with which consciousness purchases meaning from the subjective sphere of public tonality and turns it into an object for itself.' He describes how this works, using the example of the Renaissance *caccia*, or hunting song:

> Without words, we are of course impressed with the vigorous melodic and rhythmic activity of the two upper 'hunting' voices, as they proceed apace in canon over a steadily moving bass line: some physical thing or event is being set forth in musical gesture. Without words, however, it is difficult to identify this activity with any precision. Is it a quail hunt, a sailing party, or a house on fire? All of these events are busy affairs, with a lot of running or moving about. But with the addition of the text ... we discover that a particular human behaviour is being imitated in music.[2]

The process operates not only with the representation of overt behaviour and action but also with internal states, because of their kinaesthetic shape: the emulation in music of the internal movements of the body – heartbeat, breathing, muscular tension and relaxation – entailed in the manifestation of feelings; the origin, perhaps, of the ancient doctrine of music as mimesis. Norton's example is the sorrowful

Lachrimae of John Dowland, seven 'passionate pavans for lute, viols, or violins, in five parts', where the reference to falling tears 'is tonally embodied in music of continually drooping melodic lines and moderate rhythms. The music is for instruments, but the title secures an affective state for the listener. . . .'[3]

A latter-day version of the doctrine of emotions is found in a book called *The Language of Music* by the English musicologist Deryck Cooke, who believes that music not only expresses feelings directly but possesses a veritable vocabulary of the emotions. This vocabulary is based on a systematic classification of the melodic units which semiologists like Nicolas Ruwet call melemes.[4] Meleme, however, is not a word you will find in Cooke's index. A resolute empiricist, Cooke interprets the rise and fall of intervals within the hierarchy of diatonic relations, major or minor, to explain the expression of emotion in music, cataloguing examples with blithe disregard not only for historical and social context, but also for poetic usage. Briefly, his argument is that European composers from the fourteenth century (if not earlier) to the present day have all used the same codifiable melodic patterns to express particular emotions, which cannot be just coincidence.* But this procedure is deeply problematic. In taking words that come attached to music in the form of either settings or titles to identify the

---

* For instance, the ascending phrase which includes a minor third, made up of the first five notes of the minor scale, as in this song by Schubert:

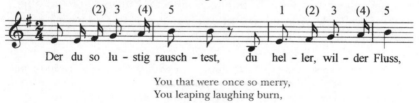

Der du so lu - stig rausch - test,   du   hel - ler, wil - der Fluss,

You that were once so merry,
You leaping laughing burn,

Schubert: *Winterreise* Opus 89
VII: 'Auf dem Flusse'

This phrase is expressive, says Cooke, of an outgoing feeling of pain, an assertion of sorrow, a complaint, a protest against misfortune. To support this he quotes: an anonymous fifteenth-century madrigal; an anthem by Robert Whyte *circa* 1565; a madrigal by Byrd, 1588; two madrigals by Morley, 1594 and 1595; a phrase from Schütz's *St Matthew Passion*, 1666; the opening chorus of Bach's *St John Passion*, 1722; a chorus from Mozart's *Requiem*, 1791; Tamino's first entry in Mozart's *The Magic Flute*, also 1791; three songs from Schubert's *Winterreise*, 1827; one of the songs from Mahler's *Lieder eines fahrenden Gesellen*, 1884; a setting of Baudelaire by Debussy, 1889; a phrase from Strauss's *Don Quixote*, 1897; a phrase from Walton's *Belshazzar's Feast*, 1930; another from Bartók's *Cantata Profana*, also 1930; and finally, a phrase from 'that pathetic and bitter popular song, "Brother can you spare a dime" – the protest of the out-of-work American war hero, (Deryck Cooke, *The Language of Music*, Oxford University Press, 1962, pp. 122–4).

emotional content to be ascribed to the meleme, it is indifferent to both the semiotic distinction between denotation and connotation, and to poetic ambiguity. And when purely instrumental pieces are cited, then – as David Osmond-Smith notes – they are well basted with adjectives – which Roland Barthes called 'the poorest linguistic category' – to reinforce the supposition that Cooke already has in mind.[5]

Cooke sees only a single vector in the relation between music and words. He gives no consideration of the different possible levels at which both music and words may communicate, even though his examples are generally cases of heightened speech, which belong to poetic or dramatic contexts, and are thus imbued with the multiple meanings of different types of aesthetic ambiguity. Whether one refers to traditional literary criticism – say, to William Empson's *Seven Types of Ambiguity* – or to semiology and the concept of polysemous signification (semiotically speaking, says Umberto Eco, ambiguity must be defined as a mode of violating the rules of the code),[6] Cooke takes no notice of any of it – not even in opera, a world which is all conventions, codes and ambiguity. It is true that everything about opera conspires to give us the idea that the characters singing their hearts out on the stage are first and foremost doing exactly that: voicing their emotions. Some of the time they are, but this is only part of the story. Take the Act I Trio in Mozart's *Così fan tutte*, where Don Alfonso joins the two sisters in singing farewell to their lovers as they supposedly leave for the wars. The sisters are unaware, of course, that Don Alfonso has arranged the whole thing; while their feelings upon their lovers' departure, therefore, are perfectly genuine, Don Alfonso is obviously feigning. Can you tell this from the music? Not a bit of it. On the contrary, as he says in his recitative immediately after their departure, 'I have a flair for comedy. My acting, to judge from my performance, is convincing.' Opera loves these kinds of situation, the scenes of men's concupiscence, because this is exactly where men (and, consequently, women) are both most likely to dissimulate. Consider the case of the Duke in Verdi's *Rigoletto*. The man, we know, is a lecher: we discover him at the start of the opera boasting to his courtiers of bringing his latest amorous adventure to a successful conclusion – we soon guess that he is referring to Gilda, daughter of the eponymous hunchback jester – and in '*Questa o quella*', 'This one or that', he sings that he gives his heart no more to one beauty than to another. What, then, when we come to '*E il sol dell'anima*', when the Duke, posing as a poor student, protests to his chosen victim that fame and glory, power and throne, are but human frailties? Are we to suppose that here, when he declares his love to Gilda, these are his genuine inner feelings, or is this perhaps supposed to be ironic? It certainly doesn't sound it. We know that the Duke is posing, but there is no hint of it in the music. On the contrary: the aria is a consummate piece of macho self-projection. There is no entry in Cooke's lexicon for machismo, or for deception – nor could there be. His procedure does not allow for a world where feelings are not always true, where people dissemble, or by the same token where they explore different identities. In short, we need think only of the ambiguities of Mozart's operas, or of Schubert's songs, or of the shifting terrain of Chopin's nocturnes, to understand why the theory is lacking. Perhaps the process Cooke describes indeed takes place, but if so, it constitutes only one type of musical speech, limited, clipped, and with a particular ideological tendency: what Adorno calls affirmative music, music devoid of any sense of contradiction or struggle for truth.

The problem is not, as Cooke believes, that 'music is a language which has no dictionary', as if all we needed was to provide one.[7] First of all, this is to misconstrue the relation of the word to those peculiar hidden objects of signification called emotions, to which music, by so many accounts, has some kind of direct access. In the view of Henri Bergson, a philosopher particularly sensitive to the question, 'the word with well defined outlines, the rough and ready word, which stores up the stable, common and consequently impersonal element in the impressions of mankind, overwhelms or at least covers over the delicate and fugitive impressions of our individual consciousness'.[8] Music, however, is peculiarly suited to the expression of these fugitive impressions because its medium, like that of consciousness itself, is time: not objective, measured, chronometrical time, but what Bergson calls 'pure duration' [durée pure] – the subjective succession of our conscious states as they continually merge into one another, each itself yet not distinct. Music's embodiment of the continual flux of feeling remains inaccessible to verbalization, because, as Bergson has it, language cannot get hold of it without arresting its mobility. It was, of course, exactly this powerful but indistinct emotional flow which the Romantics celebrated.

This is not all. According to Bakhtin, the dictionary definitions of words are not meanings but only potential meanings, which come alive only in the course of dialogical utterance. Here the emotive expression of the music can hardly be said to exist outside the moment of performance; it depends on the situation which brings it alive, and the mental set of the subjectivities that perceive it. This is very different from Cooke's construal of music as a fixed language of emotions, which is like a garden of feelings laid out by the composer for the listener's delectation, rather than the culture of the emotions, the compost heap in which they grow. And there is more. Considered in historical perspective, the circumstances we have traced in the music of the nineteenth century constitute a process which admitted new dialogical currents into the musical sphere, bringing with them new terms of reference, connotations, meanings, and even – it seems – new emotions. As new musical publics took shape and old ones were transformed, and as they entered into rivalry and dialogue, what we seem to discover is a musical language becoming denser and richer. This is not intended as a value judgement, but as a commentary on the growing concentration of the musical language, which gives added resonance to the music. There is a qualitative change in the passage from the eighteenth century to the nineteenth. Technically speaking, there is an internal reconfiguration of musical syntax, which begins with a reduction of repetition and the heightening of harmonic tensions, and continues with the discovery of harmonic ambiguity and the introduction of processes of self-interruption and contradiction to create the fully fledged Romantic style of composition. The result is that Romantic music is in a very real sense more exciting than Baroque, more intensely pitched, so to speak (except, of course, for the work of a Bach or a Monteverdi). It seems to be denser, more pregnant, more full of meaning. But if this is best understood as the result of a multiplication of signifying elements, we are bound to ask where they come from.

Intertextuality and transgression

The character of artistic utterance, as Bakhtin sees it, is first and foremost that of an act of communication; and since communication implies communion and communion entails communication, all utterance is a kind of relation. Moreover, this relation becomes a constitutive element of semantic structure, not imposed from outside but its dialogical partner. This point was vividly demonstrated in a musical context by the Welsh baritone Geraint Evans in a master class on television some years ago, where the subject of study was Zerlina's aria 'Batti, batti' from Don Giovanni, where she tries to calm Masetto down after he has discovered her with the Don. Evans, a most gifted actor, insisted on rehearsing it with the students as a two-hander, explaining that it was not a solo aria at all, but a duet, a quarrel in which one of the pair remains silent. One saw the student Zerlinas, who all started by singing prettily but undramatically, learning how to act – to direct their vocal gestures not towards an invisible audience but at their dramatic partner.

In other words, the utterance is shaped as much by what is not said as what is, not because what is not said has been left out but because it cannot be put into words – it is the necessary envelope of non-verbal communication in which all speech is, so to speak, wrapped up, or situated. This is why Bakhtin often sits unhappily with the formal concept of the sign employed by semiologists, because the process he imagines is essentially open and – in his own word – unfinalized. This quality is even more prominent in music, where the attentive listener is always attuned to the expressive alterations which performers can produce at any moment in their conversation with the unheard co-locutor – who is none other than the listener, collectively and individually. But if the unfinalized quality of music is to be taken seriously, then this also means that musical communication may be constituted as much by transgressive and non-musical elements as by musical logic. Only a powerful ideological pull in the opposite direction, intent on protecting music as a domain of mystery and refuge from the everyday world, suppresses this realization.

Dialogue, for Bakhtin, is the natural condition of speech. The living utterance is shaped by the intention of eliciting a response in one form or another in the listener's subsequent speech or behaviour. Utterances are therefore not indifferent to one another, and are not self-sufficient; they are aware of and mutually reflect one another. The artistic utterance shares the same character: it is a link in a continuous chain of utterances. It takes shape and embodies meaning at a particular historical moment in a socially specific environment, and precisely for that reason cannot fail to brush up against thousands of living dialogical threads which weave themselves around it; it cannot fail to become an active participant in social dialogue. It is thus the very condition of artistic creation that each work is the product of a tacit conversation which lies embedded in the complex circumstances in which it occurs.

The musical utterance is the score interpreted by the performer in a social act addressed to a certain audience in a particular cultural and historical setting. It has a context, a subtext, and is related to other texts – both musical and non-musical. Precisely because of its dialogical nature it incorporates reference and allusion to numerous utterances of different types which it absorbs and transforms. The animation and stimulation of one text by another is a quality which the semiologist Julia Kristeva, evoking Bakhtin, has called intertextuality. The insight Bakhtin introduced into literary theory, she says, was to see the text as a mosaic of quotations and allusions, in which history, society and culture are themselves to be seen as texts 'into which [the writer] inserts himself by rewriting them'. In Kristeva's interpretation, the text is a three-dimensional space conjoining the subject who writes it, the reader who engages with it, and the other texts which it inevitably evokes. Since the relationship between reader and writer is asymmetrically mediated by this third dimension, 'the notion of *intertextuality* replaces that of intersubjectivity, and poetic language is read as at least *double*'.[9] To the extent that the musical text is essentially similar, it is therefore not shaped only by the logic of notation and the internal demands of compositional procedures.

These intertextual relationships are sometimes explicit and intended by the composer – when someone remarked to Brahms on the similarity between the main theme of the last movement of his First Symphony and that of Beethoven's Ninth, he is said to have replied: 'Any fool can see that!' They may also be intended but coded and oblique – as in various works by Schumann or Berg which use people's names to generate sequences of notes which are used as motifs. They may well be unconscious – as in certain instances in Mahler which I recount in a later chapter. A particular type of musicology makes its business out of tracing the biographical connections which occasion composers to invest specific musical elements with private associations. A recent radio talk by Callum MacDonald suggested, by tracing certain intricate connections, that Brahms intended his Fourth Symphony as a kind of private requiem for a friend of his. The symphony was written just after the death of Gustav Nottebohm, the first editor of Beethoven's composition notebooks, who had given Brahms the original manuscript of the Bach cantata (No. 150) from which Brahms derived the passacaglia in the last movement of his symphony. The words of the cantata (*Nach dir, Herr, verlanget mich*) give it the requiem-like connotation. This reading seems perfectly possible, and does not violate the solemnity of the music. But I have also heard a radio talk in which the driving rhythm of the scherzo of Bruckner's sublime Seventh Symphony was made out to be a portrait of one of the first steam engines to pull its way through the Austrian mountains, just because Bruckner was a railway enthusiast. Unfortunately, this is now an intertextual association every time I hear it.

The fact is that the intertextual dimension comprises the inevitable echoes which arise in the listener's mind in the course of their own particular dialogue with the work, which of course the composer cannot control. Because of this, intertextual relations are by no means limited to those texts which the composer could have known, and they may operate both forwards and backwards; as Borges once remarked of Kafka, some writers have the power to create their own precursors. Thus, if Brahms's First Symphony evokes Beethoven's Ninth, then the former becomes an intertext of the latter even if this is an anachronism. Similarly, Leonard Bernstein's *West Side Story* becomes an intertext of Beethoven's *Emperor* Concerto, since Bernstein – consciously or unconsciously – borrowed a telling phrase from the slow movement for one of the songs. There is no such thing as a text which resists this condition, and no way to avoid the listener bringing other texts to bear upon it, for the dialogical quality of a work is not limited to the situation of the composer, but is also present in its reception.

The paradoxical quality of intertextual relationships noted by Borges is beautifully illustrated by Anton Ehrenzweig's report of 'an unsettling joke' which the composer Alexander Goehr once played on him:

> Goehr claimed that he could demonstrate to me that Boulez, in spite of his deliberate destruction of traditional forms, really worked within an established French tradition. He played first the full recording of Boulez's *Le Marteau sans Maître* which was still unfamiliar to me at the time. This naturally conditioned my attention to the diffuse disconnected type of listening that this very new music required. Afterwards without much warning he continued with Debussy's *La Mer*. I did not recognise this well-worn piece of Impressionistic writing! Normally Debussy's tone-poem produces realistic associations, like the roar of the waves and the wind. Now I heard for the first time a constant variation and mixture of tone-colours so subtle and fleeting that they forced me to live eternally in the present as Boulez's music had done.

Not only, concludes Ehrenzweig, was he suddenly confronted with a hidden affinity between a familiar piece of musical Impressionism and a modern exponent of twelve-tone music, but he was also able to appreciate the huge antagonism originally aroused by Debussy's disruption of harmonic cliché.[10]

If every text is necessarily open to the absorption of intertextual relationships, and inevitably transformed by them, it thereby constitutes a virtual space where different voices overlap and compete, the condition Bakhtin calls heteroglossia. In this respect music is like any other language: 'At any given moment of its historical existence, language ... is the embodied coexistence of socio-ideological contradictions between the present and the past, between different epochs of the past, between different socio-ideological groups in the present, between tendencies, schools, circles and so on.'[11]

A striking demonstration of these various intertextual proclivities is provided by Edward Said's account, in the course of discussing the topic of music and recollection in Proust, of his response to a performance by Alfred Brendel of Brahms's Piano Variations Opus 18.[12] First, he recalls, came his pleasure in recognizing the piece as a piano transcription of a movement from the First String Sextet. Then, as he listened, he was 'reminded spontaneously' first of a work of very similar mood which he had heard a few days earlier – the 'Nimrod' variation from Elgar's *Enigma* Variations; then of an incomparable old recording of the Sextet from the Prades Festival featuring Pablo Casals, where you can hear the great cellist humming along with the music; then of Louis Malle's film *Les Amants*, where the sextet version of the variations provides the soundtrack music for a kind of French *Brief Encounter*. Said, a gifted amateur pianist, tells us how he played the work over several times for himself; now, in his written recollection, his musing leads him to the memory of his old piano teacher, a protégé of the great teacher Leschetizky, called Ignace Tiegerman, 'a Polish Jew who had come to Egypt (which is where I met him in the 1950s)'. (Here Said's own subtext breaks through to the surface, as the reader remembers that Said is a Palestinian intellectual, politically engaged in support for the struggle against the Jewish State for Palestinian independence.) It was from Tiegerman, and against the anomalous background of Cairo and the Arab nationalism of Gamal Abdel Nasser, that he learned about the force of tradition in this music: how 'to listen to or play a piece by Brahms is also to summon one's prior acquaintance with, say, Beethoven and Schumann to the task, along with experience of ballades, variations, rondos and rhapsodies generally ...'. In short, the experience of music – which his reading of Proust helped him to comprehend – is an unceasing shuttle back and forth between private moments and public settings, private and public associations and connotations, the disparate references and allusions which always enter into the musical experience unbidden, and in which the musical and the non-musical cannot always be easily separated. The truth is that everyone listens to music in this way; it is one of the ways we use music – but the canons of formal appreciation work to suppress such extra-musical associations.

Intertextuality implies that the work becomes its own *doppelgänger*; it leads a double, or even multiple life which merges and separates from it and gives it a discontinuous history that is partly hidden. It is constantly tempted to enter into new relationships as it meets with other texts, to reveal hidden faces (what Wittgenstein calls the dawning of new aspects) as it is placed in these new positions. From this point of view, although it originates in the composer, the privileged status conventionally accorded to the composer's intentions comes into question, together with the trust of the naive listener. The kind of semiotics we need must be able to take account of this situation – in other words, to elucidate not only the conditions of the production of musical meaning, but in Said's terms, also its transgression. And this, we shall find, will also enable us to grasp how the changing historical circumstances of music create new meanings to mingle with old ones, transform them, reveal them in a new light.

Music following Roman Jakobson

In the Introduction ('Overture') to *The Raw and the Cooked*, Claude Lévi-Strauss suggests that Roman Jakobson's account of language as a contextual system can be fruitfully applied to music, a suggestion followed up by the semiologist Gino Stefani.[13] Jakobson's schema derives from his insistence that the context of the utterance be admitted to the semiotic analysis, not just the text; we find the same emphasis in Bakhtin. According to Jakobson, natural language not only possesses grammatical and cognitive functions but also speaks through expressive, emotive and other non-verbal elements which all carry their own sense of significance. Indeed, Jakobson criticized the simple linear picture Saussure used to describe the chain of communication between speaker and hearer, and proposed instead a set of functions which arise from the internal structure of the act of communication, in which a speaker sends a message to a listener through a channel in which the content is shaped according to a code.[14] This is much more like the condition of music. The principal difference is that language is primarily referential and cognitive. As Bakhtin puts it, in a rare remark on music: 'Music is denied referential specificity and cognitive differentiation, but is profound in content: its form leads us beyond the boundaries of acoustical sound production, but does not lead us into an axiological void – content here is, at base, ethical.'

In Jakobson's terminology, communication consists in a *message* referring to a *context*, formulated in terms of a *code*, directed by an *addresser* to an *addressee*, through a channel of *contact* between them:

CONTEXT

ADDRESSER. . . . . . . MESSAGE . . . . ADDRESSEE
CONTACT

CODE

According to Jakobson, there is a different function corresponding to each of these six factors; the dominant character of an utterance will depend on which factor is emphasized at the expense of others, since they can never be found in perfect balance. This also means that the 'content' or 'meaning' of an utterance is not a simple given entity which passes untrammelled from sender to receiver; and this, as we are finding, is certainly true of music. This is the corresponding schema of functions:

REFERENTIAL

EMOTIVE   POETIC   CONATIVE
                          PHATIC

METALINGUAL

In this schema, if the communication is orientated towards the context, then the function which dominates is that of reference, or denotation. Here meaning is cognitive, as in a proposition like 'The distance from London to Tipperary is 400 miles'. Music is incapable of such statements, because music has no means of denotation. Musical reference can function only by means of connotation and association, a process which is not cognitive but, as we shall see, iconic. On the other hand, an emphasis on the speaker yields an inflected, expressive or emotive type of utterance, which is also typical of song – 'It's a long way to Tipperary' – and, indeed, quite central to music. An emphasis upon the listener Jakobson calls conative – that is, intended to persuade, or to induce an activity; in language this goes with vocatives and imperatives. These are not parts of speech in musical syntax, but in every other respect it is self-evident that music is highly conative. To distinguish an emphasis on the channel of communication or contact, Jakobson borrows from the anthropologist Malinowski the term phatic: here the primary purpose is to establish or sustain the act of communication itself (it is thus the first verbal function acquired by babies as they reach across the transitional space of infancy towards human intercourse); here too there are many musical parallels. Indeed, since music is pre-eminently a social activity, the phatic is also much to the fore: from the simple pleasure which people find in making music together to what Adorno would call the anthropological property of bringing communities together. An emphasis upon the message for its own sake provides the poetic function, to which corresponds the study of poetics, in which Jakobson himself is most interested. This function corresponds, as we shall see, to what Stravinsky used to call 'the play of notes', the inner working and reworking of the musical material which is the subject of 'pure' or 'absolute' music. A stress upon the code Jakobson calls metalingual, which at first seems difficult to recognize in music, perhaps because in the absence of cognitive reference it is not immediately obvious where a metalanguage could enter either. But a second and more critical look will reveal a much more subtle situation, in which we shall also discover that despite the absence of cognitive reference, music in fact possesses quite considerable metalingual functions.

Contact and persuasion

If, as Mahler said, the music is not in the notes, that does not mean it can be separated from them. Nor is it always possible to separate out neatly the functions described by Jakobson. There are certain difficult-ies, says Lévi-Strauss, in distinguishing the emotive from the conative, the conative from the phatic.

For ethnomusicologists, because musical forms are always simul-taneously ritual forms of social contact, the phatic is often the primary function of music; again Adorno's anthropological property of bringing communities together. It can even become the function of particular musical forms: from church carillons to national anthems, work songs to the sounding of the Last Post, the phatic uses of music to establish social identity stretch right across society, and the phatic takes on multiple aspects corresponding to the different estates of state, Church, military, community, and even labour. But at the same time it always has a conative aspect, that of persuasion, contained in the way the listener is carried along by the flow of notes in the call to participate. The conative function comes into its own in examples like hymns, military marches, solidarity songs and dance music, the main object of which is to inculcate a certain attitude or pattern of behaviour in the listener. This is purposeful public music-making.

Many forms of folk music, choral singing and chamber music are designed to give pleasure in the first place to the players themselves through the act of making music together. If this is not quite the same as Malinowski's concept of the phatic, says Lévi-Strauss, it can be called a 'subjectivized phatic function': 'Amateur musicians who get together to play quartets are not much concerned whether they have an audi-ence; and it is probably the case that they prefer not to have one.' Without an audience, the conative is directed exclusively to other players, and the playing of the group creates 'a harmony of gesture and expression which is one of its aims'.[15] This is intersubjectivity in its purest sense.

Phatic music-making has a long history in which its aesthetic charac-ter is bound up with its social functions and the site where it makes its appearance. Consider just one segment of this history, the tradition of unaccompanied part singing among the educated classes in eighteenth-century England which produced the catch and glee clubs. The prehistory of this tradition is inscribed in the very name of these gatherings. 'Catch' comes from the Italian *caccia*, a Renaissance hunting song in canonic style; the first recorded mention of the word 'glee', which comes from the Anglo-Saxon word for music, *gligge*, occurs in Playford's third collection of *Ayres and Dialogues*, published in 1659. These clubs are sometimes cited as predecessors of music hall, along with Victorian song-and-supper rooms and the penny gaffs described by Henry Mayhew, but their social milieu was more exclusive. The membership of the Noblemen's and Gentlemen's Catch Club, for example, founded in 1761, included seven earls, five dukes and numerous viscounts, generals and lords, as well as George IV as Prince of Wales and William IV as Duke of Gloucester. The Glee Club was founded in 1783 for the private post-prandial entertainment of gentlemen. Although its first public meeting was held in a coffee house and it afterwards moved to a tavern, its character can be judged from the names of its guests over the years (it was dissolved in 1857) – they included Samuel Wesley, Moscheles and Mendelssohn. The clubs should therefore rather be thought of as forerunners of Victorian drawing-room music – although as male gatherings they doubtless featured much bawdy.

Historical circumstances may turn the phatic into the political, a process which occurred in the French *sociétés chantantes*, which began in Paris and later spread throughout the country, where, before the Revolution, the repertoire was no more political than it was in England. But it also happened in the 1790s in England, where the habit of 'calling the tunes' in the theatre during the interval – a phatic expression of collective identity – became a confrontation in which rival political factions of Loyalists and Radicals provoked each other. In our own time, the political identification of the folklore revival movement in Chile in the 1960s with the left-wing politics of Popular Unity is only one example among many. But the politics need not be focused and explicit, and this is also the rubric under which we may see the analysis by sociologists in the 1960s and 1970s of postwar popular culture, and the use of the various kinds of rock music by sundry fractions of youth subculture as vehicles of social intervention with political overtones, in which expressive qualities are far outstripped by phatic functions.

When musical gatherings that were originally phatic in character become commercialized, however, then the phatic function is gradually overwhelmed by mercenary requirements, which not only favour spectacle rather than communion but promote the spectacular in the form of individual display. Hence the rise of the rock star. In the classical tradition this produces a double shift in musical values. On the one hand, the rise of the individualist virtuoso; on the other, that of the conductor. Both result in the dilution of the phatic purpose of the consort which originated in the domestic musical practice of the educated classes.

The discerning connoisseur turned instead to what was later simply called chamber music. Chamber music, remarks Adorno, practises courtesy: the first step in playing chamber music well is to learn not to thrust oneself forward but to step back. What makes the group function as a whole is not forwardness – that would produce only barbarian chaos – but reflective self-containment:

> Chamber music was the refuge of a balance ... which society denied elsewhere ... What makes such a homogeneous model space possible is the state of relative security enjoyed by individual, economically independent citizens, by entrepreneurs and, in particular, by well-to-do members of the so-called free professions. Obviously there is a relation between the flowering of chamber music and the peak period of liberalism. Chamber music is specific to an epoch in which the private sphere, as one of leisure, has vigorously parted from the public-professional sphere. Yet neither are the two embarked on irreconcilably divergent courses nor is leisure comman- deered, as in the modern concept of 'rest and recreation,' to become a parody of freedom. Great chamber music could come into being, could be played and understood, as long as the private sphere had a measure of substantiality, albeit one already fragile.[16]

It almost seems like a miracle, says Adorno, that it lasted so long.

Poetics and the emotive

The idea of a musical poetics, despite the long association between music and poetry, belongs in many ways precisely to the emergence in the early nineteenth century of new forms of instrumental music which purported to be self-sufficient and autonomous, dependent for their significance on no text or word associations but on the formal interplay of their own material, their themes, motifs, and harmonic and rhythmic structures – what Stravinsky was to call 'the game of notes'. Composers always played these games, of course, but until the nineteenth century they regarded them simply as their stock in trade. For certain nine- teenth-century critics, like Eduard Hanslick in Vienna, however, such self-dependent music was music at its purest: 'it is its own purpose and

not at all merely further means and material for representing emotions
and thoughts. . . .' It is not that Hanslick wanted to deny the emotional
content of music but, rather, to free it once and for all from association
and subordination to verbal descriptors and literary hegemony. 'What
part of the feelings . . . can music represent?' he asks. 'Only their
dynamic properties . . . the motion accompanying psychic action . . . its
momentum: speed, slowness, strength, weakness, increasing and
decreasing intensity.'[17] The logic of this position – even if Hanslick
would reject the idea for fear of letting slip in at the back door what he
had ejected from the front – is that music expresses its own poetry.
Stefani, for whom music is above all a poetic form which exists for its
own sake, takes this position, when he says that in this way music
manifests the characteristics of the poetic act to the highest degree,
and indeed the more complex it is, the less can music be reduced to
any of Jakobson's other functions; though here I cannot entirely agree.

Poetics considered as the study of rhythmic, metrical and phonetic
devices suggests obvious and extensive parallels with music, for which
Leonard Bernstein in his Harvard lectures serves as an excellent guide.
For Bernstein never generalizes but, rather, discovers in music what he
offers as equivalents to the gamut of poetic devices in language. For
example, rhyme – melodies with phrases which end with the same
configuration of notes; and alliteration – where successive melemes
begin with the same note. He even finds parallels with functions like
simile and metaphor, which would not at first sight seem to have musical
equivalents because of the lack of referential denotation. Bernstein does
not agree. As a simple example of metaphor he offers the opening
measures of Brahms's Fourth Symphony, where the second two bars [B]
are instantly perceived as a transformation of the first two:[A]

They are in fact the same, but with the treble transposed down a tone
and appropriate harmonic adjustments in the bass. Bernstein empha-
sizes that this is perceived immediately, whether you understand them
as transformations or not. Simple attention is all that is needed to
comprehend them: 'the only time required is the time it takes to play
the music'.[18] The trained musician is able to identify these things
formally, but hears nothing different from the ordinary listener, who

experiences its effect inarticulately but just as surely. Wittgenstein would say that they hear different aspects of the same thing. The same goes for ambiguity, and this is critical, since harmonic ambiguity is the very fountainhead of music in the nineteenth century. Bernstein offers the particularly beautiful example of the opening of the Adagietto of Mahler's Fifth Symphony, over which 'the whole world has been swooning . . . ever since *Death in Venice* invaded the silver screen'.[19]*

It is true that a large part of formal musical appreciation concerns the recognition of these poetic characteristics, and these are the very features privileged by theorists intent on emphasizing the qualities of what they call purely musical meaning. To this extent, Stefani is undoubtedly correct to foreground the poetic. He is mistaken, however, to suppose that it displaces other functions; this is to make the same mistake as the more conventional music theorists who, in privileging the formal properties of musical art, discount as unmusical accretions the transgressive and non-musical associations and connotations

* Here the preliminary vamping on the harp is syntactically ambiguous: we have no idea what the beat is nor what metre we're in. Secondly, the key is ambiguous, because the tonic, F, is missing, and the notes we hear could well turn out to belong not to F major but to A minor. All this lends great poignancy to the tune that emerges teasingly on top. When the basses move down to F on the first beat of the third bar, 'it feels good: we're home in F major'; but an unresolved appogiatura hanging above the melody tugs at the heart, and when this resolves 'we melt away with the pleasure of fulfilment'.

of intertextual interplay, which also have emotional effects which they regard as somehow illegitimate.

It is, of course, the emotive which the majority of listeners regard as the primary function of music. The first difficulty with this indubitable quality is to identify its source. The problem is an ambiguity over the identity of the utterer which follows from the separation of composition from performance. Expression is not only the prerogative of the composer. It is also embodied at the moment of live performance in or by the performer, who is never just the composer's representative but addresses the audience directly on his or her own behalf. Perhaps it should be said that the performer is the addressee of the score, the listener the addressee of the music, but the performer is more than the composer's surrogate, even though many conceive of themselves in this way. In fact the message the listener receives is authored twice over. Performance of a score gives it a kind of double voicing, in which the performer inserts their own measure of expression into what the composer inscribes in the matrix of the score. The listener receives a communication where the codes are recombined in a manner that is almost impossible to differentiate. The puzzle is present in the very image of performance. Where do the musicians' emotional gestures come from, and to what purpose? When pianists grimace and rock their bodies, is this because they are sensing the feeling in the music, or trying to put it there? Is it purely involuntary, or is it put on for the benefit of the audience? Or think of the conductor, whom Adorno calls 'the imago of power', whose gestures should certainly be conative, for is it not the conductor's primary function to communicate to the orchestra how the music should go? These are not either/or questions; performance is all these things at once in different measure. The truth, in short, is that the space of music is also the space of the body.

Musical icons

Whether or not it is possible to conceive of music without conative and emotive dimensions, with the category which in the case of language is primary, that of reference or denotation, we appear at first to be confronted with almost the opposite problem: that of identifying what would count as the referential function in music in the first place. In fact, as we shall see, it turns out that music has very considerable referential powers, but they function entirely on the plane of connotation, and this makes them slippery and elusive.

The simplest type of referentiality in music is a special case – let us call it ostensive reference – where the signified exists in the same medium – sound – as the musical signifier, but is not itself musical. A special case, but examples abound. The imitation of birds and animals and other natural noises like the wind is found in the earliest music. In European art music, there is birdsong in Jannequin's *Le Chant des Oiseaux*, Beethoven's *Pastoral* Symphony and numerous works from Vivaldi to Mahler, Delius and Messiaen; there is the braying of the ass in Mendelssohn's *Overture to A Midsummer Night's Dream*, but also the hammering of the Nibelungen in Wagner's *Das Rheingold*; trains in Honneger's *Pacific 231*, or *The Little Train of Caipeira* from the *Bachianas Brasileiras* of Villa-Lobos; even traffic noises in Gershwin's *An American in Paris*.

These are all instances of the *petits détails vrais*, the small touches of verisimilitude postulated in the eighteenth century by Diderot in the interests of cultural innovation, and in opposition to the alliance between Rococo art and the decadent aristocracy. The Germans called this imitation of acoustic phenomena *Tonmalerei*, tone-painting, and regarded it as aesthetically suspect if not repugnant; this is why Beethoven defended the *Pastoral* Symphony as 'more the expression of feeling than painting'. There was, however, ever since opera provided the rationale for such devices, a good deal of *Tonmalerei* around, especially in the form of storm pieces and the depiction of battles – there is even a *Battle Symphony* by Beethoven, a concoction written for a mechanical music-engine designed by Maelzel the metronome man. Yet it generally remains the case that for a musical sound to designate a non-musical sound at least the context must be articulate, therefore this is not proper denotation; some kind of semantic domination, however slight, is necessary to tell you what kind of thing you are supposed to be hearing. In short, ostensive reference in music is not strictly cognitive. If a comparison can be drawn with natural language at all, it is with the special type of word called onomatopoeic.

On the other hand, these examples of acoustic imitation represent a particular kind of musical icon. In the definition of the American philosopher C.S. Peirce, an icon is a sign that represents its object by means of a similarity between certain features, or 'fitness' of resemblance, like a drawing or a map. Umberto Eco adds that the similarities are culturally coded: he mentions a thirteenth-century artist who 'claimed to be copying a real lion, and yet reproduced it according to the most obvious heraldic conventions of the time'.[20] This is like the representation in Western music of birdsong: since birds do not actually sing in the diatonic scales in which our music reproduces them, so the musical imitation of birdsong has always followed pre-established musical conventions (at least until Messiaen).

The same reasoning that applies to the heraldic lion and to birdsong may be applied to the representation of emotion. The indicated emotion is reproduced according to certain governing conventions which stem from the musical idiom through which the subjective experience of emotion is channelled; for example, the falling pairs or cascades of intervals, representing sighs of sorrow or longing, which form the typical vocal gesture in madrigals by Gesualdo, where the imitation of feeling is mediated by the chromatic character of the musical discourse. If this means that music does not stimulate the nervous system directly, because the simulation is a coded one, it is none the less a form of coding of which we are not normally aware; it is like second nature. This kind of musical icon is kinaesthetic, for its imitation of bodily sensations: culturally coded imitations of kinaesthetic signals, like Dowland's weeping or Osmin's rage, which we encountered above.

To these auditory and kinaesthetic icons, however, we must add those which derive from the dialogical spaces of cultural discourse. This is a domain of symbolic connotation which began to draw the attention of music theorists in the eighteenth century. One of them was Mattheson, with his doctrine of affections; his *Der vollkommene Capellmeister* ('The Complete Music Master') was published in Hamburg in 1739 and subtitled 'Basic proof of everything one needs to know, to be aware of, and to understand thoroughly in order to direct a chapel creditably and profitably'. Mattheson depicts music as a form of 'sound speech', comprising a body of figures of two kinds: the descriptive (or affective) and the formal. The former clearly belong to the category of the kinaesthetic icon, impressions of the effect of music on the autonomic system. The latter comprise abstract musical procedures like imitation, inversion, repetition, and other common means of melodic organization. Themes and subjects are the musical equivalent of the orator's thesis or 'text', and the composer must have a store of formulae, a stock of the common musical figures, 'little turns, clever passages, and pleasant runs and jumps', to be combined in various ways into a continuous argument. These resources 'should be considered in the same way as the vocabulary and expressions used in speaking'.[21]

Now comes the interesting part. The paradigms of these figures were derived largely from the operatic aria, which in the classic form of the Baroque was usually designed to sustain a single dominant emotion. These operatic figures, laden with extra-musical connotations, were taken over by instrumental music, where they joined a range of conventionalized dance forms (minuet, German ländler, waltz, etc.) to create the interplay of contrasting sections and movements within the suite, the symphony, the concerto, and the sonata. They were not, after all, abstract musical subjects, monads of pure music. The material employed by the composer in this purely instrumental music comprised a family of configurations with a quasi-representational character, which constituted them as icons of various narrative, dramatic and emotional contexts and situations. The result is that the new music emulates the old, but in the process creates the conditions for a new level of signification to emerge, a field of connotation that gives the elements of music an entirely different dimension. Eco speaks of 'musical "signs" (or syntagms) with an explicit denotative value (trumpet signals in the army) and . . . syntagms or entire "texts" possessing pre-culturalized connotative value ("pastoral" or "thrilling" music, etc.)'.[22] David Osmond-Smith calls this 'the exploitation of the socio-historical connotations associated with a certain style or piece'.[23] Carillons and trumpet calls, chorales, marches, fugues, lullabies, waltzes and dances of different kinds all become, in opera and ballet, dramatic and symphonic music, the carriers of connotations derived from the implicit situation of the utterance. This kind of iconicity was already brought into play by a composer like Bach. The Passions, for example, are constructed around the contrast between the aria and the chorale, where arias, in the style of Italian madrigal or opera, are used for the dramatic expression of the individual protagonists, while German chorales are used for the devotional commentary of the chorus taken as representative of the congregation. In this way the music implies a powerful social statement.

Surprisingly, one musicologist who is aware of this process is Deryck Cooke, who speaks of it not in *The Language of Music* but in a short essay on Mahler's Eighth Symphony:

> The brass-band march was, of course, the central symbol of the humanistic attitude . . . The first great humanistic march was naturally the *Marseillaise* . . . March-music entered the classical symphony – bringing with it an unavoidable touch of vulgarity – when Beethoven used the march style for his three great humanistic statements: the ultimate march-like transformation of the graceful theme of the *Eroica* finale, the battering main theme of the finale of the Fifth Symphony, and, most significant of all, the unequivocal brass-band march, complete with drum and cymbals . . . in the choral finale of the Ninth. The funeral march also played its part, honouring the burial of humanistic heroes, in the Marcia Funebre of the *Eroica* Symphony, and in Wagner's mighty Funeral March for the death of his humanistic hero Siegfried . . . It was Mahler who brought this tradition to its head, by including in . . . all his symphonies either triumphal marches to celebrate humanistic aspirations, or funeral marches to lament the burial of humanistic hopes, or both.[24]

In the Eighth Symphony itself, however, musical and verbal symbolism do not simply go in harness, as they do in Beethoven's *Choral*, where the lines about the brotherhood of man are set to a rousing march, while the words 'Seek your Creator above the starry firmament' are given a hymn-like setting. 'In Mahler's Eighth, the verbal and musical symbols are crossed with one another, to amazing effect.' It is the setting of the medieval Latin hymn *Veni, Creator Spiritus*, 'Come, Creator Spirit, Dwell in our minds . . . Illuminate our senses' that is the great striding triumphal march in the humanistic tradition, and the final scene of Goethe's *Faust* which is based on a religious chorale. This, says Cooke, can mean only the humanizing of religion and the spiritualizing of humanism. In short, the symphony celebrates not divine but human creativity; thus 'the salvation of Faust's soul symbolises the indemnification of his humanistic quest, in spite of its failure; and this is granted because, as the angels sing, "He who is ever striving drives himself onwards, that man we can redeem"'.[25]

It is clear from this account that the musical icon is quintessentially historical – which also means dialogical – in character. Once we have realized that music's other functions – phatic, conative, and so on – are themselves subject to historical change, this should hardly surprise us. The fact that our examples are historically recent, however, could well be misleading, and a rider is necessary, a warning not to suppose that the iconic dimension is something new in music. Indeed, it is very likely that the earliest music was extremely iconic, including a high proportion of effects in imitation of both human cries and animal noises; music of this kind can be heard in ethnographic field recordings made in places like the Andes, where it has been preserved in ancient musical traditions which have survived into the acousmatic age. There is also a considerable degree of poetic iconicity in the largely vocal music of Europe between the late Middle Ages and the time of the Enlightenment, derived from widespread practices of imitation and direct borrowing of musical phrases and gestures, and even entire songs. None the less, our hypothesis is that the iconic field becomes greatly expanded through the process that begins with music's entry into the bourgeois public sphere – first because of the increasing articulation of the signifying elements; secondly because the increasing public circulation of music produces, so to speak, more and more intertextuality.

In the course of this process, the social reception of music and the uses to which it is put may also bring to it iconic and ideological meanings which are strange, sometimes alien, even contradictory. There are instances of naive projection, like the 'Hallelujah Chorus' from Handel's *Messiah*, a piece which the English have invested with special fervour, because, it is said, George III was so taken when he first heard it that he stood up in astonishment, so everyone else stood up too. The practice survives because when the performance is good, the effect can be thrilling: a phatic affirmation of a transient moment of collective identity. This is pretty benign. More worrying is the patriotic fervour injected every year on the Last Night of the Proms into the collective singing of Hubert Parry's exquisite setting of Blake's 'Jerusalem', which contrives to turn a powerful proto-socialist denunciation of the evils of the early Industrial Revolution into a jingiostic anthem.

Consider also the complex and contradictory example of intertextuality in the fourth movement of Bartók's Concerto for Orchestra, entitled 'Interrupted Serenade', which quotes a motif from Shostakovich's programmatic Seventh Symphony, the *Leningrad*. The Bartók was written in the United States in 1944; the Shostakovich three years earlier in Leningrad, while the city was under bombardment by the invading German forces: the resistance to the siege is the very subject of its programme. The circumstances of the war made the symphony immediately successful not only in the Soviet Union but also, when the score was smuggled out on microfilm, in the West, where the first performance was given in New York under Toscanini. Shostakovich became so celebrated in the United States as a result that *Time* put him on the front cover, wearing his fire warden's helmet. Bartók, we are told, had heard a broadcast of the symphony, and the suggestion has been made that when he borrowed one of its most prominent motifs, and used it as a rude and raucous interruption to a tender Hungarian melody, he was intent on satirizing the Soviet composer, to whom he felt some kind of antipathy. I have never been convinced by this interpretation: why should Bartók, a resolute anti-fascist, wish to satirize another equally anti-fascist composer, even if he thought him overrated? The truth is that the motif in question is already satirical in the Shostakovich symphony. It caricatures a fragment from *The Merry Widow* by Franz Lehár, a composer known to be one of Hitler's favourites, and Shostakovich's use of it could hardly have been an innocent accident. That this was the association Bartók intended becomes more obvious when you consider the tender melody which it interrupts: according to Bartók's compatriot, the conductor Solti, this is a variant of a well-known Hungarian patriotic song.[26] Rather than satirizing Shostakovich, this seems to me more like a demonstration of solidarity. If this interpretation is correct, however, the question arises whether the music is damaged by the wrong association, when in musical terms it is not impaired but functions with great effect. We should therefore introduce another rider. These dialogical connotations have a certain similarity to the dream symbols of psychoanalysis: they are susceptible to misinterpretation, and they exist in a kind of collective unconscious.

From icon to leitmotiv

If this argument is broadly correct, then the process not only nourishes the emotive function and the growth of the composer's subjectivity; it also forms an element as essential in the emergence of the Romantic symphony as internal musical processes like thematicism. The symphony as inherited by Beethoven was already the product of a complex process of evolution, which can be traced in the succession of one hundred and four of them that Haydn wrote, or the forty-odd by Mozart. In the earlier works of these two composers, symphony meant little more than an organized sequence of movements of different but balanced proportions, combining the French and Italian styles: the former decorative and based principally on dance forms, the latter both more dramatic and, in its use of new concerted textures, also more progressive. The range of movements included old forms like fugue and theme-with-variations, as well as the overture, the aria and the rondo. In the shape in which the symphony was passed on to Beethoven, these movements have become unified according to the new principles of tonal relations and thematic development, but not yet much else.

Among the symphonies of Haydn are a good number with names, only sometimes the composer's. Some are merely the places with which particular works are associated – *Paris, London, Oxford* (*Linz* and *Prague* in the case of Mozart) – which record their popularity. Some are anecdotal: *The Farewell*. Others identify a salient feature of the work in question: *The Drumroll, The Clock, The Surprise*. None of these seems to indicate anything essential about the affective nature of the music. *La Passione* and *Die Trauer*, on the other hand, are names which derive from the doctrine of affections: they belong to a group of minor-key symphonies which Charles Rosen aptly describes as dramatic, personal and mannered (these also include *The Farewell*).[27] Still other names are mere Baroque fancies: the early trio *Matin, Midi* and *Soir, The Hen* and *The Bear, The Philosopher* and *The Schoolmaster*. All these different kinds of names have only one thing in common: they never actually indicate a programme. The music of Haydn, as E.T.A. Hoffmann once said, appears to have been composed before original sin.

It was the marriage between thematicism and the iconic dimension, however, and especially the dialectical interplay between iconic themes and tonal structures, which created the possibility of the symphonic programme in the style of Beethoven's Sixth Symphony, which the composer himself called the *Pastoral*. Here the five movements have titles which are by no means arbitrary: 'Awakening of Cheerful Feelings on Arriving in the Country', 'Scene by the Brook', 'Happy Gathering of Peasant Folk', 'Storm', and finally 'A Shepherd's Song of Joy and Thanksgiving After the Storm'. Significant moments along the way are traditionally interpreted in terms of ostensive or onomatopoeic references: shepherds' pipes and village bands, lightning, thunder and bird calls – according to the score, Nightingale, Quail and Cuckoo; but as the commentators generally agree, the choice of key and the tonal schema are also important in welding the whole together.

The *Pastoral*, however, is almost a classical work in comparison to the Third, Fifth, Seventh and Ninth, where verisimilitude is entirely transcended. The programmes of these symphonies are not anecdotal, but spiritual. Take the case of the Third, which Beethoven himself called 'The Heroic' (*Eroica*). The story is one of the famous Beethoven anecdotes. According to his first biographer, Schindler, it was Napoleon's Ambassador in Vienna, Jean-Baptiste Bernadotte, who first gave Beethoven the idea of writing a heroic symphony. What happened subsequently is recounted by his pupil, Ferdinand Ries, who remembered how, in 1802, he had seen the score of a symphony on Beethoven's table, entitled simply 'Bonaparte'. 'I was the first', says Ries:

> to announce to [Beethoven] the news that Napoleon had declared himself emperor, whereupon he flew into a rage and cried: 'Then he, too, is nothing but an ordinary mortal! Now he also will tread all human rights underfoot, will gratify only his own ambition, will raise himself up above all others and become a tyrant!' Beethoven went to the table, took hold of the top of the title-page, tore it off and flung it to the ground.

Then he renamed it *Eroica*.[28]

This story has entered deeply into our understanding of the music. It is a cornerstone of the institutional meaning of 'Beethoven'. 'We know' – that is, his biographers all concur – that Beethoven was possessed of a keen sense of ethics, which often got him into trouble in his personal life, and which he translated in his creative life into grand artistic statements. This one word, *Eroica*, is thus enough to unlock the full humanistic drama of the symphony's programme: the action and heroism of battle in the first movement, the funeral of the fallen hero in the second, the exhilaration of victory in the Scherzo, the affirmation of the Finale. There is more: the Finale is a set of variations built on a theme of special iconic significance: a theme which

Beethoven first used for the ballet *The Creatures of Prometheus*, which clearly symbolized for him (as did the *Veni Creator Spiritus* for Mahler) the autonomous spirit of human creativity.

This symbolic content was selectively elaborated by Beethoven's hero-worshipping biographers, like his friend Schindler, the American scholar Thayer, the French literary Nobel laureate Romain Rolland, or the English science writer J.W.N. Sullivan; then projected by them on to other works – symphonies, sonatas and string quartets – like the Fifth Symphony or the *Grosse Fugue*. The result is to ideologize Beethoven by reifying his political spirit. This is what Adorno calls music as 'false consciousness'. It is no accident that Schindler, who edited the deaf composer's conversation books for publication, suppressed certain pages. What these pages contained, according to the best biographical evidence, was politically contentious. For Nietzsche, people like this 'show a dogged *innocence* in their moralistic hypocrisy. . . . These "good" people are so totally demoralized' that 'not one of them could face a *true* biography . . . Beethoven's biographer, the solid American Thayer, abruptly stopped in the middle of his work; having arrived at a certain point in this noble and naive life, he couldn't take it any longer.'[29] The ideological effect here is not so much a distortion or manipulation of meaning as the result of disconnection and repression. But somehow Beethoven still manages to break through.

The symphony becomes a discourse of icons which comprises a kind of musical realism that grows in dominance during the nineteenth century. Schubert, Berlioz, Mendelssohn, Schumann, Brahms, Bruckner, Dvořák, Mahler – the main line of nineteenth-century symphonic composers was dominated by the Beethovenian concept of the symphony as an organic unity, in which the form is first and foremost the implicit result of its content, its spiritual or narrative programme, and of the implacable logic with which the thematic elements impose their consequences upon the entire structure: from the drama of the first movement, through the contemplation and contrasts of the inner movements, to the fulfilment of this logic in the affirmative finale. This conception induces the composer to treat the genre with elasticity, to add movements or subtract them, and to hint at other kinds of content by means of a title (*Fantastique, Italian, Reformation, Rhenish, Spring,* etc.). These titles are often a sign of broad iconic references: the use of a national dance form, a chorale, a folk tune (real or imitated), a setting or a scene. In this way the symphony, which is built on the internal logic of the musical syntax, develops into a peculiarly nineteenth-century musical chronotope, literary in inspiration and adaptable as readily to a single-movement symphonic poem as to a full-scale work of several. In Liszt's symphonic poems and the concert overtures of Berlioz, it is as if music, having sought to break free from semantic domination and the literary public sphere, now seeks to make peace with literature, but on new terms – not by serving as a foil for poetry but by incorporating it directly into its own imagery, and even usurping it.

Programme music is thus not quite what it sounds like, for it is not as if the music is simply a form of coding, and the programme is the key to the cipher; or at least, this is only part of the story. The relationship is far more peculiar: the programme is in the music, but the music is more than the programme. Semantic domination gives way to a dialectical relationship between words and music. As Dahlhaus puts it, it is 'the music of an era when experience was shaped by reading and when literature on a subject was scarcely less important than the subject itself'; thus 'consciousness of music is determined, to no small extent, by literature about music'.[30] In other words, the idiom presupposes a sophisticated listener who has been tutored in the expressive powers of music, and who corresponds to the ideal type of educated bourgeois, equally at home in literary and philosophical culture as in music – and, indeed, politics, for as Dahlhaus comments, the adherents of programme music were enthusiasts of progress, 'and the zeal of nineteenth century efforts to justify programme music or even to declare it the goal of music history would be incomprehensible were it not for the interaction of esthetic and social motives'; especially in the example of Liszt, in whose aesthetic theories such motives play 'more than a minor role'.[31]

The paradigm of the programmatic symphony remains Berlioz's *Symphonie Fantastique*, written only three years after Beethoven's death. Here Berlioz turns the symphony, by means of the *idée fixe*, into something close to one of E.T.A. Hoffmann's fantastic and macabre musical tales. He tells the woeful story of a poet's unrequited love in the shape of series of visions which come to him after he takes opium. The *idée fixe* is initially heard as the first-movement main theme, unusually extended and very masculine, a sensuous undulating melody representing the Beloved; it then reappears in each successive movement in changing costume according to the setting. The second movement, 'A Ball', fetchingly employs a waltz; the third, 'Scene in the Countryside', begins with shepherds' pipes and distant thunder; the fourth, an ironic 'March to the Scaffold', is cut short by the guillotine, represented by a drum roll; in the fifth, the traditional tune of the 'Dies Irae' is parodied to evoke the Witches' Sabbath. Thus, in the first movement, the poet falls in love. In the second, the Ball, the *idée fixe* brilliantly captures the fleeting impression of the Beloved dancing. In the third, where the poet finds solace in nature, it appears in a slow and more winding tempo; he is tortured by the fear of deception, and ends up killing her. Justice takes its course in the fourth movement, and in the fifth, he is racked with guilt. What Berlioz achieved by this practice was definitive, but in the end it became what Adorno calls 'the ingenious illustrative technique of Richard Strauss' in works like the musical comic-strip *Till Eulenspiegel's Merry Pranks*, or, worst of all, the *Sinfonia Domestica*, where Strauss's command of his medium leaves you in no doubt how henpecked the German bourgeois felt by his wife.[32]

The *Symphonie Fantastique* points to the iconic effect to be found in the projection on to music of gender stereotypes, especially prevalent in the nineteenth century. Consider, for example, the definition of sonata form in a leading German music dictionary: 'Two basic human principles are expressed in each of its two main themes: the thrusting, active masculine principle (first theme) and the passive, feminine principle (second theme).' Are these mere extramusical stereotypes which become attached to elements of musical structure by a process of semantic domination? Or, as feminist musicologists like Susan McClary argue, something more profound and ingrained in our modern Western conception of musical art?

If gender coding has a definite iconic quality in nineteenth-century music, another powerful example is the *Faust* symphony by Liszt, a celebration of Goethe's play in terms of a masculine system of musical representation of sexual difference, where women are subjects only in so far as they are the object of male attention. The symphony apportions a movement each to Faust, Gretchen and Mephistopheles, with a last movement consisting in a vocal setting of the Chorus Mysticus (the same text which concludes Mahler's Eighth Symphony) from the end of Goethe's play. Consciously or not, Liszt follows the terminological convention that defines beginnings or endings of melodies as masculine if accented, feminine if unaccented.[33] Faust's theme is passionate and ascending, with leaping intervals with a strong rhythm, while Gretchen's descends in small intervals with the marking *dolce semplice*. This music, says Lawrence Kramer, 'projects Gretchen as unselfconscious and psychologically whole, Faust as reflective, self-divided, and conflict-laden'.[34] The relationship between them is portrayed in the development section of Gretchen's movement, when her theme intertwines with Faust's in a symbol of the lovers' union – a conceptual icon, this. Mephistopheles, however, has no theme of his own: to express the spirit of negation, he uses Faust's music in the form of parody, tearing the theme apart and tossing the fragments around from instrument to instrument. And when he gets hold of Gretchen's theme, 'she is roused from her rigid sweetness, released into self-transformation, imbued with a restless eroticism', only to be 'swept away in the rush of more Mephistophelian mockery'.

Liszt explained his general intentions in letters to Wagner. He had come to the conclusion that Faust was 'a decidedly bourgeois character . . . his personality scatters and dissipates, he loses his way'; and this is what he captures in the truly remarkable main Faust theme. Its thirteen notes include all twelve intervals of the chromatic scale; the melody is so arranged, in four successive ascending groups of notes, that the leaps which connect them produce a sense of tonal ambiguity: in this ambiguity we read the combined expression of Faust's questing spirit and a question mark about its implications. The stark contours of the principal Faust theme are designed to ensure that it remains instantly recognizable in all its transformations; it would be difficult to imagine a theme which retains its identity so uncompromisingly, even in the representation of sexual union. Yet it is Mephistopheles, not Faust, who endows Gretchen with erotic fullness – a touchy contradiction which Liszt attempted to erase with the closing chorus. In the end, this eternal feminine is nothing but the male expression of a feminine ideal.

A programme like that of the *Faust Symphony* is public knowledge; its musical icons are provided in the first instance by semantic domination – the title – and the rest is informed interpretation, though there is plenty of room to argue about the details. The procedure is related to that of the *idée fixe* in Berlioz, or the Wagnerian leitmotiv, which can be seen as an elaboration of Berlioz's *idée fixe*. From Berlioz to Wagner was only a small step. Wagner had an almost envious admiration for Berlioz's Dramatic Symphony *Romeo and Juliet*: Leonard Bernstein shows that there are thematic parallels between *Romeo* and *Tristan and Isolde* so close he believes them to be unconscious borrowings; they turn *Tristan*, he says, into a kind of huge metaphor for *Romeo* (which one can also sense without recognizing the thematic parallels). Indeed, the leitmotiv, a fully conscious device, also has its unconscious aspects: Wagnerians are wont to argue that some of the transformations his leitmotivs undergo are much too subtle and complex to have been consciously rendered; thus they also represent Wagner's ingestion of the principle of motivic working.

One thing is certain: the Wagnerian leitmotiv is a law unto itself, and a deeply ambivalent phenomenon, as Thomas Mann testified in his famous lecture of 1933, 'The Sorrows and Grandeur of Richard Wagner' (the immediate, though not the only, cause of his exile from Germany). On the one hand, said Mann:

> The device of the musical reminiscence, already used on occasion in the old operatic tradition, was gradually developed by [Wagner] into a subtle and masterly system that made music, to a degree never before realized, into an instrument of psychological allusion, elaboration and cross-reference ... [a complexity] that bears witness to the most extraordinary intuitive affinity between Wagner the psychologist and that other characteristic son of the nineteenth century, the psychoanalyst Sigmund Freud. The way that Siegfried's thoughts of his mother slide into eroticism in his reverie beneath the linden tree, or the way in which, in the scene where Mime tries to instruct his ward in the meaning of fear, the motif of Brünnhilde slumbering in the fire moves through the orchestra like a dark, distorted presence – this is pure Freud, pure psychoanalysis.

On the other hand, Mann reminds us what Nietzsche said after he made his break with the Master: that Wagner is 'the most impolite of geniuses – treating his listeners like fools and repeating a thing so many times until it drives you mad – and you believe it'. Wagner's art, he concludes, 'is a case of dilettantism that has been monumentalized by a supreme effort of the will and intelligence ... full of shrewdness and cunning ... music has here been pressed into service in imperiously dilettante fashion to portray a mythical concept'.[35] This, however, is exactly what so impresses Lévi-Strauss, who calls Wagner 'the undeniable originator of the structural analysis of myths ... when I suggested that the analysis of myths was comparable with that of a major musical score, I was only drawing the logical conclusion from Wagner's discovery that the structure of myths can be revealed through [music]'.[36]

It is not at all necessary that this should have been a wholly conscious process on Wagner's part, or anything like it; on the contrary, the genius of the method may well be precisely the way it mobilized the composer's unconscious – and continues to mobilize everybody else's. On the surface, however, the leitmotiv becomes a device for signposting the sprawling structure of the Wagnerian opera with melodic tags, easily remembered tunes and snatches which are distributed through the score at pertinent moments. This is what Adorno wittily calls their 'commodity-function, rather like that of an advertisement: anticipating the universal practice of mass culture later on, the music is designed to be remembered, it is intended for the forgetful'.[37] This is not unconnected with Wagner's frequent vulgarity. Wagnerites, however, resisting the implications of a lack of profundity in their hero, prefer to point to the structural function, in line with which they explain the tendency of the motifs to proliferate. One of the latest in this hermeneutic tradition, Robert Donnington, lists some ninety of them in the entire *Ring* cycle, and shows how they are related by means of inversion, variation, harmonic and rhythmic compression, and other techniques of motivic manipulation – techniques which belong generically to the symphony, and take their paradigmatic form in Beethoven.[38]

Unfortunately, in spite of his devotion to Beethoven, this is not what Wagner sounds like. On the contrary, his music presents the starkest contrast. 'That critics should regard this concatenation of symbolic motif-quotations,' says Mann, 'standing out like rocky outcrops in the torrent of primordial musical processes, as "music" in the sense of Bach, Mozart and Beethoven was too much to ask.'[39] Of crucial significance, the feeling of time is utterly different, and Wagnerian opera creates an entirely original chronotope. As Adorno puts it, Beethoven dominates time; Wagner revokes it. The Beethoven symphony follows a trajectory; the music of *Tristan and Isolde, Parsifal* and *The Ring* is static, a wave pattern which admits no sense of development, paradoxically unoperatic. Wagner knows, says Adorno, about motifs and large-scale forms – but not about themes, which are there to be developed. *The Ring*, however, proclaims that in the end nothing has happened: 'The Rhine maidens who are playing with the gold at the start of the opera and receive it back at the end are the final statement both of Wagner's wisdom and of his music. Nothing is changed . . .'[40] This makes Wagner both radically antihistorical and antisymphonic.

This is evident in the problematic nature of the leitmotiv as an icon, for it seeks to express quite definite notions and yet remains floating, unanchored. Its vocation is to be (in Adorno's words) 'a sign that transmits a particle of congealed meaning', like a theatrical gesture. Or like the elements which go to make up allegorical paintings, to which orthodox Wagnerian scholars, says Adorno, have inadvertently drawn attention by giving each one a name – Robert Donnington's list, following his Jungian line of interpretation, goes from 'The depths of the Rhine as undifferentiated nature' and 'Erda the Earth-Mother as ancestral wisdom' to 'Love as fulfilment' and 'Transformation' – like the labels attached to allegorical pictures by art critics to provide the keys to interpretation. The Wagnerphiles are not exactly wrong to catalogue the psychological and mythological meanings of the motifs in this way, but in so doing they both reveal and miss the contradictory nature of the leitmotiv as an iconic sign, the opposition between the musical function it resists and its theatrical purpose. For this purpose makes it totally at odds with the function of motifs in Beethoven, which is to generate themes, and thus the entire symphonic structure. The symphonic motif may be almost trivial (which is not the same as vulgar), like the door-knock opening of the Fifth; in itself, it is somewhat abstract, and not necessarily iconic at all: its function is to become a cell whose multiple transformations unify the totality. But the leitmotiv, in order to function as an icon, is exactly the opposite. It needs to retain its identity as a relatively complete and distinct unit, to detach itself from the musical continuum and stand out; it therefore resists symphonic transformation. Otherwise it will not wake the listener from the wonderful stupor which this formless wash of music induces.

Metamusic

We are left with the last of Jakobson's functions, the metalinguistic. In general, an utterance is metalinguistic when it refers, implicitly or explicitly, to its own code, and thus stands as commentary to the text within which it is embedded. Some semiologists, like Ruwet, find this hard to identify in music, on the grounds of logical difficulty: if music isn't referential, how can it refer to itself? Musical logic, however, is rather more subtle than this.

The epitome of the metalinguistic function is found, says Jakobson, in the way children learn language. Studies made in recent decades:

> have disclosed what an enormous place talk about language occupies in the verbal behaviour of preschool children, who are prone to compare new acquisitions with earlier ones and their own way of speaking with the diverse forms of speech used by the older and younger people surrounding them; the makeup and choice of words and sentences, their sound, shape and meaning, synonymy and homonymy are vividly discussed. A constant recourse to metalanguage is indispensable both for a creative assimilation of the mother tongue and for its final mastery.[41]

In a perfectly comparable way, learning music involves a continual dialogue with the teacher, whether the learning situation is a formal one or not: an interchange of demonstration and imitation takes place in the metamusical form 'like this, not like that', or 'this is the way to do it'. True, this dialogue is constantly interspersed with verbal speech and gesture, but these elements of non-musical communication continually refer back to the musical utterance itself in its sensual form, independent of its extramusical dimensions. Nor is this restricted to learning, for the process of rehearsal is essentially the same. Even if a certain amount of verbal instruction and suggestion is usually necessary, underneath it something much more delicate is going on, in both the rank-and-file of an orchestra and the democracy of a string quartet, let alone the jazz combo, which consists in a dialogue of nuance and musical gesture that leads to the fine-tuning of muscular and digital activity.

But there is another dimension to the question, which Lévi-Strauss discusses: the idea of a meta-music, or 'music about music'. Lévi-Strauss speaks of composers who use their music 'to expound and to comment on the rules of a particular musical discourse', citing J.S. Bach and Stravinsky as paradigms. This concern with the code he contrasts with Beethoven or Ravel as composers more concerned with a 'message', hence more referential; and with Wagner or Debussy as more concerned with myth, hence more poetic.[42] When Bach composes a set of preludes and fugues in every key in order to demonstrate the logic of tonality, it seems correct to call this metamusic. And Adorno agrees about Stravinsky, in whom 'the composition feeds upon the difference between its models and the use which it makes of them'; Stravinsky's music 'continually directs its gaze towards other materials, which it then "consumes" . . .'.[43] Adorno points the finger at *The Soldier's Tale*, a piece of chamber music theatre about a soldier, his fiddle and the devil, which Stravinsky wrote in Switzerland during the First World War, of which Bernstein gives a vivid description: Stravinsky's unique objectivity, he says,

> showed itself in dry, witty take-offs: a cartoon of military pomp; a wry tango; a squeaky ragtime . . . the transformation of these frivolous, lightweight materials, through Stravinsky's diamond-sharp intellect and sophisticated techniques, produced a music of unpredictable freshness, wit and humour . . . which . . . results from mismatched semantic components.[44]

This is exactly what incenses Adorno: 'Out of the externalized language of music, which has been reduced to rubble, *L'Histoire* constructs a second language of dream-like regression; this it does by means of constant manipulation . . . This second language of music is synthetic and primitive.'[45]

Nevertheless, it is a second language, another type of second-voicing, which is far from unique to Stravinsky. On the contrary, we shall find that it is one of the hallmarks of the musical language of the twentieth century, when the nineteenth-century musical public sphere has been transformed by a process of expansion, fragmentation, contention and recombination, which – since music is both a symptom and an agent in the process – the musical language both expresses and sharpens.

6

Nationalism and the Market

Nationalism

The iconic dimension of symphonic music – the chief form, alongside opera, of public musical discourse in the late nineteenth century – held particular resonance for the musical nationalism which is one of the strongest, but also most contradictory, ideological currents of the age. Music served as not only an expression but also a direct agent of this new secular religion, to which frustrated bourgeois aspirations for political emancipation and economic advancement found recourse. Naturally, the phenomenon carried different and even contradictory political connotations in different countries; this reflects, among other things, the different ways in which the tensions of the epoch were felt in the centre and on the periphery. Nationalism could thus become either monarchist or republican, as well as imperialistic, chauvinistic, elitist and racist or, contrariwise, anti-imperialist, democratic, populist and even socialist. In musical terms it was Wagner, said Adorno, who represented its most fatal form, and who would care to disagree?

German Romanticism, says Adorno, 'inclined to an aesthetic surrogation of the national because in German history the nation's birth was a miscarriage, as was bourgeois emancipation'.[1] In Britain, by contrast, where the nation-state had reached an advanced form, nationalistic traits in music were late to appear, and observed an entirely innocuous decorum when they did so. Yet if the English musical genius that flourished from Tallis to Purcell dried up in the eighteenth century (and reappeared only in the twentieth), nevertheless, for Adorno, the blanket exclusion of the English from music by the Germans 'is a pure resentment theory of German nationalism, an attempt to deny the inner kingdom to the older, more successful empire'.[2] It was entirely in keeping with the self-confidence of successful imperialism that

English musical culture became cosmopolitan early on, and readily adopted foreigners: Handel and Mendelssohn are only the most famous. France, as the model of the continental nation-state, also took foreigners in its stride, accepting the Italian Lully, the German Gluck, and the Jewish composers Meyerbeer, Halévy and Offenbach (only Halévy was born in France) as leading composers of French opera and operetta. Here, too, nationalism held no great sway in music; there is even a contradictory phenomenon, as composers like Bizet, Delibes, Debussy and Ravel turned for inspiration to Spain. On the other hand, there is no question but that France and Britain developed their own national musical styles, which were every bit as distinctive as those of Eastern Europe.

The context invites the inclusion of Meyerbeer, Halévy and Offenbach as Jewish composers, rather than German or French, because the early to mid-nineteenth century marks the stage where the liberalism of the bourgeois polity is matched by the Jewish emancipation movement and the entry of secularized Jews into the public sphere. Here, of course, we must add the name of Mendelssohn, grandson of the philosopher of Jewish emancipation Moses Mendelssohn, and a host of other performers and conductors. From this point on, the history of Jewish emancipation and its twin, the modern forms of anti-Semitism, become part of the history of the public sphere itself; in music, the latter begins infamously with Wagner. It also serves as a shadow over the history of nationalism, precisely because the Jews are not a nation – but eventually express the desire to become one. This occurs in the same Vienna, at the turn of the century, that produces artistic rebellion, psychoanalysis, and musical modernism, in all of which emancipated Jews play leading roles; if Zionism, however, which they must have known about because it was born in their midst, held no attraction for them, it should also be observed that nor did nationalism. Indeed, the role of the Jewish composer in the nineteenth century was to confirm not nationality but the universalism of bourgeois culture, but on one condition: that the emancipated Jew renounce every trace of his origins, and become completely secular. But again, it is Vienna at the end of the century – we shall see that this is no accident – where this equation breaks down, and Mahler, a convert and far from Zionism, confronts the bourgeoisie with the return of the repressed.

The contradictory and paradoxical nature of musical nationalism was inevitable. Adorno observed that music contains national elements to the same extent as bourgeois society as a whole. The history of music, and that of its forms of organization, occurred essentially within national boundaries and with national variants, which began to effect an influence when the Renaissance dissolved medieval universalism. This process allowed a sense of national character to develop in certain countries long before nationalism became an aesthetic programme, and even nurtured a succession of national schools (French, Spanish, Italian, English, Flemish and German) – naturally enough, says Adorno, since music is a universal language without being Esperanto; it does not crush qualitative peculiarities.

For the same reason, however, the national variants of European music remained from the very beginning highly permeable to foreign influence, especially since there was never a period when musicians were not migrants and successful composers did not travel. As a result, new regional styles were readily absorbed abroad; early French *chanson* was taken up in Italy; North Italian *frottola* incorporated the style of singing *alla napoletana*; the Italian madrigal was adopted in England, and so it went on. In this way, local peculiarities remained subordinate; regional and national tendencies were constantly transcended, flowing back into the universal (i.e. pan-European) course of musical development. These same dynamics, however, also mean that when the moment was ripe, and the conjuncture of the universal and the particular especially favourable, an essentially regional development could exert an inordinate influence. This, for Adorno, is exemplified by Viennese classicism, and especially by Mozart, who bequeathed to it the productive interaction not only of the German and the Italian, but also the French, which for some reason Adorno forgets to mention.

Here and there – for example, in France – chauvinistic tendencies appeared – a resistance to Italian influence before the Revolution, to German influence after it – but the new critical sensibilities of Romanticism retained a universal emphasis, fully in accordance with the idea of a universal bourgeois culture, and for the time being the inevitable contradictions remained subdued. In Schubert, says Adorno, the national element still had the innocence of a dialect. Conversely, Beethoven could still flatter a Russian patron by incorporating Russian themes in the string quartets he commissioned, while for the composer they remained mere thematic material, with no political overtones. These connotations came into force only later, after the middle of the century, when allusions to folklore became one of the principal iconic markers of musical nationalism. (Actually, German Romantic literature already included a significant folklore movement, exemplified by Arnim and Brentano's publication in 1805 of a German folk-poem collection, *Das Knaben Wunderhorn*, in which the cosmopolitan character of Herder's collection of folk songs became national. Curiously, no composer set these verses to music until Mahler, who found in them something quite different.)

Italy had a different kind of national identity, derived largely from the singularity of the Renaissance and the way it had promoted Italian culture to the fountainhead of humanism throughout Europe. Economically weakened, however, Italy had remained politically fragmented, torn between papal rule and foreign domination. When the time came for this condition to become a recipe for the development of nationalist sentiments, there was Verdi to provide the musical focus. This is nationalism in terms of musical populism, however, which explains the opposition in which he stands to Wagner, and the antagonism, both ideological and musical, between historical grand opera and mythological music drama. There is clearly more at issue here than a question of national temperament, even if this was Verdi's own opinion.

Verdi, like Mozart, was aesthetically cosmopolitan, taking his subjects and themes not only from national sources but from the entire European humanist tradition, including French, German and English sources. Wagner's acolytes denigrated Italy's leading composer as a musical reactionary, and waxed indignant over his plundering of German dramatic literature. For his part, Verdi held Wagner in great esteem for his stature as a composer, but found him aesthetically antipathic. Wagner, moreover, in spite of his nationalist pronouncements, held the German people in contempt and despised his public, while Verdi was not just an ardent but a true patriot: he took the popular verdict as a kind of divine judgement, and bore failure with equanimity. Wagner, who fumed over failure, inspired bitter feuding on his own behalf; Verdi participated zealously in the Unification movement, thus winning for himself the gratitude of his nation. The letters of his name became a call for union under the House of Savoy: 'Evivva VERDI' meant 'Evivva Vittorio Emmanuele Re D'Italia'.

To avoid censorship, Verdi learned to make political allusions in symbolic form, but with symbols which – unlike Wagner's mythical mysticism – were pregnant with realistic social and historical meaning. In his first great success, *Nabucco*, the Israelites' cries of revolt against the oppression of Nebuchadnezzar had obvious allegorical significance to Italian audiences. Verdi set the chorus of the Israelites yearning for their homeland to a broad, swinging melody in popular style, which immediately became the rage throughout Italy. There were similar parallels in his dramas of the struggle of the Lombard League in the twelfth century against the invading German emperor, as well as in the outcries against tyranny of the outlaw-heroes of *Il Trovatore* and *Ernani*; and it is no accident that the forms of popular Italian melody are present in almost every one of his works. That Germany, in contrast, no longer had a living tradition of folk music made it possible for its musical image to be completely remodelled – for this *The Mastersingers*, as Adorno mentioned, is already a manifesto, and already pregnant with the chauvinism and racism that prepared the way for Nazism. There is no way, however, that one can think of Verdi as a precursor of Mussolini, especially not after the profoundly humanist sympathies of his last two Shakespearean operas, *Otello* and *Falstaff*. However, it is not because the Moor is black that Verdi empathizes with him. His populist sympathies did not break the bounds of European – that is to say, Eurocentric – humanism. Witness *Aïda*: if Berlioz's magnificent *Trojans* is in part a paean to French imperialism, what are we to say of this opera commissioned to celebrate the opening of the Suez Canal, with its daft plot and mere pastiche of Oriental melody, which does nothing but confirm the peculiar silliness of opera?

There is the clearest of links between musical nationalism and the Balkanization of Europe, the struggle for the creation of nation-states out of the incipient dismemberment of imperial rule, a process which dominated European politics from 1848 until the First World War (and has now re-appeared in the wake of the colllapse of communism). The unification of Germany and Italy had a profound effect on the balance of power throughout Europe, and the growth of national states inevitably raised the problem of national minorities. No country was more affected than Austria, which now had to try to come to terms with the heterogeneous nations which made up the empire.

The challenge was twofold. The new champions of nationhood held that the state must be not only national but also progressive, the very model of modern liberal democracy. National movements accordingly became politicized, and, as Bartók was to write:

the discovery of cultural values implicit in popular music and poetry made a notable contribution to the development of national pride, even when . . . each people claimed that such treasures were its exclusive and peculiar privilege. Small nations, and especially those that were politically oppressed, believed that here they found a consolation for their condition and even the proof of national maturity, and they saw in the study and divulgation of these cultural values at least a means sufficient to reanimate national sentiment among the educated classes . . .[3]

Music thus became associated with patriotic literary movements, and the reform of educational and cultural institutions. These developments became linked in turn with political agitation for the advancement of the peasantry; thus the cultivation of folklore became a symbol of politically, though not necessarily aesthetically, progressive music, especially in peripheral countries like Hungary, Bohemia, Russia, Norway and Spain.

As Bartók demonstrated, however, the gypsy *csardas* which Liszt took to be the national music of Hungary was actually the creation of the middle classes. As for Smetana and Dvořák, or the Russians, like Borodin and Rimsky-Korsakov, even if they took their inspiration from more 'authentic' sources, their musical representation of these sources is none the less highly stylized: their melodies are essentially still diatonic, with only suggestions of the modes and inflections of a different *musica practica*. All of them – except perhaps Moussorgsky – 'civilized' the folk-like material, leaving iconic traces of national identity which are used to colour and inflect the substrate of a musical language which, in terms of the nineteenth-century public sphere, was indeed pan-European and universal. (The eventual appearance of a folklore movement in Britain is another story. Here the Industrial Revolution had long since invaded agriculture and altered the countryside, and the ancient folk tradition was already emaciated when it was still a living force in Eastern Europe and the Mediterranean. The English folklorists came late and, despite vaguely socialistic leanings, were never radicalized by a peasantry which still exerted strength within the social formation.)

The character of these movements is closely tied to a certain historical morphology. In large areas of southern and eastern Europe, the emergence of nationality – that is, a nationalist discourse – was simultaneously the emergence of a local public sphere, with its own associations and institutional life. The spirit that inspired the first Czech nationalist composers, for example, Smetana and Dvořák – despite their striking differences, both musical and political – was that of the well-organized urban middle classes of Prague which founded the Czech National University in 1882. But opposition to the old imperial centre was tempered by its very hegemony. When the National Academy of Music was established in Budapest in 1875, and Liszt was named as its first president, Hungary was taking as its national composer a reformed travelling virtuoso born in Hungary of German descent who spoke no Hungarian, made his name in Paris, settled in Germany, and retired to Rome. The ideological ambiguities of this situation corresponded to political confusions in the public, confusions which translated into musical susceptibilities. Politically, national supremacy under existing class relations was tantamount to the power of the gentry over the peasantry, which was not a good recipe for modernization; modernization, however, could not be achieved without national supremacy; therefore a strategic alliance was necessary. It is precisely this alliance which music is able to express and which allows it to become the very symbol of national unity, even while it simultaneously fills itself with differences. As a recent writer on Dvořák puts it: 'The metaphysics of the idea of nation, in all its monumental vagueness, could attach itself to the noncognitive aspect[s of music] and create massive tension.'[4]

This tension does not necessarily reside within the music – certainly not in the case of Dvořák – but forms a transgressive intertext. On this kind of reading, the music goes so far as to encode not only national but also sociopolitical differences. Consider the contrast between Smetana and Dvořák traced by contributors to a recent volume about the latter.[5] Smetana, under the spell of Liszt and Wagner, used the progressive musical language of the epic tone-poem to construct the dramatic patriotic narratives of Czech nationhood which make up the cycle *Ma Vlast*. Dvořák employed the musical icons of national identity within a classical symphonic discourse, following the model of Haydn, Beethoven and Schubert, which was now perceived as distinctly conservative, not to mention Germanic; when he later turned to symphonic poems himself, he adopted a different focus from Smetana, basing his subjects in folk tales without overt political symbolism. The oddity here is that while Smetana and Dvořák belong to different generations, the older is the more advanced in terms of education, economic standing, and cosmopolitan culture – and the more radical. Smetana, son of an estates manager, was twenty-four in 1848, when he openly sided with the Revolution, spending several years in self-imposed exile in Sweden to escape the prejudice and suspicion which enveloped Bohemian patriots in the following decade. Dvořák was born in 1841 of peasant origins; moreover, he did not encounter the music of the generation of 1809 – Schumann, Mendelssohn and Liszt – until his late adolescence. Smetana returned to become the modern who sought to critique the present through progressive and revolutionary positions; Dvořák was a conservative who was both a passionate Czech and a patriotic supporter of the Habsburg Empire, and out of sympathy with the renewal of radical nationalism. The Czech national cause signified personal advancement in social class and economic status, but left him feeling an outsider from the power structure of politics, culture and society in Prague. Indeed, he owed his success to imperial patronage, since it was as a beneficiary of an Austrian stipend for poor but talented artists that he came to the notice of two of the judges, the Viennese critic Hanslick and the adoptive Viennese composer Brahms, who brought him to the notice of the Viennese publisher Simrock, who published his work.

It cannot be said, however, that Viennese success influenced his musical orientation. It was precisely because of its traditional qualities that his music appealed to them in the first place. Dvořák himself said that he modelled his *Slavonic Dances* on the *Hungarian Dances* of Brahms (who was not a Hungarian); and Smetana, says the music scholar Beckerman, 'thought they were so un-Czech that he wrote his own Czech Dances as a moderately angry response'.[6] Dvořák later told a music critic in New York: 'You have all written so much about Smetana and myself and have tried to figure out what the difference is between us [but] it's really simple: Smetana's music is Czech and mine is Slavic.'[7] But though we might think of Dvořák's rendering of the Slavic spirit more authentic than Brahms's Magyarism, says another writer, he was not much more familiar with the source of his materials than was Brahms. That his music, says a third, was less radical, polemical or progressive than Smetana's only underscores the fact that he felt unable to utilize the weapons of a class to which he did not belong. In contrast to the 'overt, aesthetic polemical and literary habits' characteristic of middle-class composers like Schumann, Berlioz, Wagner and Smetana, Dvořák's mode of cultural advocacy was a more covert populist strategy which was equally original, says Leon Botstein, but more accommodating, and whose impact in terms of popular success was all the more impressive for its benign form. For the Germans and the English, Dvořák was 'a benign example of deviance': an exotic and primitive Czech peasant, whose rhythms and harmonies and folkish melodic patterns were tied to what was seen as a peripheral and backward culture, but who demonstrated how this backwardness could become civilized.[8]

The truest representative of radical nationalism in nineteenth-century music is arguably the Russian Moussorgsky; certainly he is the most consistent in carrying through the implied aesthetic commitment and, as a result, aesthetically one of the most revolutionary composers of the times. The group to which he belonged – which the critic Stasov, their apologist, dubbed the 'mighty handful' – is like a cross-section of the young progressive intellectual middle class in St Petersburg. They comprised a salon composer, Balakirev; a professor of chemistry, Borodin; a military engineer, Cui; a naval officer, Rimsky-Korsakov; and an army officer, Moussorgsky himself, a landowner's son who welcomed the emancipation of the serfs in 1861 even though it nearly ruined him financially. Nurtured on the debates between Westernizing and Slavic tendencies among the literati, the group defined itself by joint opposition to the Germanic leanings of the leading establishment composer, Anton Rubinstein, Tchaikovsky's mentor. But Moussorgsky went much further than any of the others, to achieve a formal freedom in his music greater than any other Russian composer before Stravinsky, together with an intensity of expression greater than any, other than Tchaikovsky, before Shostakovich.

In his own words, describing the orchestral tone-poem *A Night on a Bare Mountain* in a letter, Moussorgsky intended his music to be 'an independent Russian product, free from German profundity and routine . . . grown in our country's soil and nurtured on Russian bread' – in short, the 'historic truth' of the Russian folk tradition.[9] What he wrote was a Romantic *Walpurgisnacht* in which the setting is transposed from mid-Germany to the Russian steppes. Yet in so doing he incorporated idiosyncratic harmonic effects which were too much even for his friends. Rimsky-Korsakov spoke of people being baffled by the many peculiarities of Moussorgsky's harmonies, and Balakirev was so shocked by the tone-poem that he declined to perform it. Moussorgsky's friends persisted in advising him to study harmony, and he must have felt half-hounded to his alcoholic death. When Rimsky-Korsakov edited his works afterwards, he smoothed out the harmonies as he did so.

What Moussorgsky set out to do was unprecedented. Intellectually attracted by the new ideas of empirical psychologists, he conceived a new kind of musical realism sustained by an extraordinary sensitivity to the intonations and inflections of speech, the impulses, the lacunae, almost the intervals of spoken dialogue, as the basis for both song and opera. This empiricist realism, which is also found subsequently in Janáček, is at odds with all established conventions. Moussorgsky was equally critical of what he saw as the artificial style of Italian opera, its predictable melodic forms and restricted verse metres, and the German symphonic style, whose thematic working he regarded, like Debussy after him, as mechanical and pedantic. In short, he turned his back on what orthodoxy considered 'musical logic' and, instead of eight-bar melodies and modulation, invented a radical form of musical prose where, among other things, contrasting keys were to clash without transitions.

Boris Godunov also caused problems for other reasons. When it was first submitted to the selection committee of the Imperial Theatre, and they turned it down, they were put out by an opera consisting almost entirely of dialogue and choruses, with none of the traditional features of the historical genre piece: no parts for a prima donna and first tenor, no arias or vocal ensembles, no love interest, no dances. Even after extensive revision which included the addition of new material to appease the critics, and when the opera proved a triumphant success, the press notices were still unfavourable and the old guard continued to disapprove. This is not surprising: it was not only an extraordinarily bold work musically, it was radical in other ways too. First of all, *Boris* is opera as Shakespearean history, history as the tragedy of absolute power. The isolation and despair of the ruler are presented to us with an immediacy and vividness hardly equalled even by Verdi's portrayal of King Philip in *Don Carlos*. But secondly, the true hero of *Boris*, to a more pronounced degree in the opera than in the play by Pushkin on which it is based, is the Russian people themselves. The tension between the two explains Moussorgsky's indecision about the ending: to leave the audience with the tyrant or with the people? It was not just an aesthetic dilemma.

Dvořák and America

If the touchstone of musical nationalism lies in the use of folk materials, then the question is raised in particularly acute form by Dvořák's sojourn in America in the 1890s, when he incorporated ethnic melodies into his music and drew attention to 'Negro folk music', in which practically no one had yet shown any interest – except the minor but highly delightful pianist-composer Louis Gottschalk. Gottschalk was a child prodigy born in New Orleans who was sent to Paris at the age of twelve and then returned, garlanded with European fame, to make a career in America. The creole melodies with which he made his mark as a composer bear the stamp of the musical impressions of his childhood, and an ear which remains attuned to them, especially their rhythmic quality. Also, it seems, a heart, for during the Civil War the Southerner toured the North playing patriotic tunes in support of the cause of emancipation. Later he toured Latin America, again incorporating creole music into his own.

Looking back at Dvořák's visit a hundred years later, a group of American musicologists see the episode as a defining moment.[10] Dvořák went to the United States to become Director of the National Conservatory of Music in New York, the brainchild of a visionary named Jeanette Thurber, acting with the financial support of her wealthy food merchant husband. Thurber, like Gottschalk, had attended the Paris Conservatoire; later she came to believe, writes Joseph Horowitz, that

American musical life needed American musicians trained in America. Her radical agenda – which built on Gottschalk's example – was not just to develop local musical life but to encourage an American concert idiom based on native sources, something that could be called national American music. Her invitation to Dvořák – who was seen by the American musical establishment as the model of the modern composer, in whom the naive folk element had become civilized – was part of her political programme; Dvořák obliged by producing his most popular symphony, *From the New World*, and a number of other 'American' pieces.

Thurber's radicalism took practical forms. The Conservatory offered scholarships for women, minorities and the handicapped, and African-Americans were prominent students at every level. One of them, by the name of Harry Burleigh, sang Dvořák spirituals and Stephen Foster songs which he eagerly absorbed, adapting 'Swing Low, Sweet Chariot' for the symphony, or so it seems; while another of its themes, as Joseph Horowitz puts it, is 'a tune so resembling a spiritual that it later, as "Goin' Home", became one'.[11] Later, in a Czech community in Iowa, Dvořák encountered the singing and dancing of Native Americans (possibly Kickapoo or Iroquois, says Horowitz), and their traces can be found in other works. The first performance of the symphony was by all accounts, Dvořák's included, an extraordinary success; Horowitz calls it a moment when composer and audience were as one. No trace here, in other words, of the *fin-de-siècle* antagonism which was apparent in Europe by this time. But not quite everyone concurred about its significance. James Huneker protested, 'Dvořák's is an American symphony: is it? Themes from negro melodies; composed by a Bohemian; conducted by a Hungarian and played by Germans in a hall built by a Scotchman.'[12]

What is most interesting in the present context is the extent to which the polemic was the product of what the American scholars call, quite simply, public relations – in which, moreover, the normally reticent Dvořák happily implicated himself. 'I always envied Wagner that he could write,' he once lamented. 'Where would I be if I could write!'[13] In America he did not need to. In line with the latest journalistic trends, musical opinion was organized not only with the aid of well-briefed and partisan music critics, but through interviews and ghost-written articles, in which the composer could address the public directly in more or less his own words (and Dvořák spoke English rather well). Articles about him started appearing the month he arrived. The reception of the *New World* Symphony was well prepared. You had only to read the newspapers in the week of its premiere, observes Beckerman, to know that it was supposed to be an 'American' symphony, that Dvořák was fascinated with the various characteristic rhythmic and melodic features of African-American and Native American music, and that he believed they could be put to use as the basis of an American style. Dvořák seems eagerly to have embraced the modern methods of the American press. He was not, Botstein thinks, naive about it. He saw parallels between the issues of nationality and ethnicity in the Habsburg context and in the America of the 1890s, where it must have seemed to him that the breakdown of the remaining vestiges of caste structure and feudal privilege back home gave place to a democratic mingling of nationalities and cultures, an idealistic attitude which 'cannot be written off as merely sentimental'.[14] Moreover, his politics were conservative, but he was not antimodern; on the contrary, attached to modernity through the Czech national cultural revival, he saw America in similar vein as a new nation seeking its own cultural values. 'Dvořák's message to America', as Botstein calls it, was that it possessed a cultural potential equivalent in modernity to its industry; his advice was not to neglect its own native traditions.[15] Meanwhile, the same public relations machine projected him, in Botstein's account, as 'the family man, the antithesis of the image of the artist as an antibourgeois, deviant madman or Wagnerian-style decadent narcissist'.[16] And although this is true, still, on the ideological level, there seems to be a necessary connection: the acceptance of the musical programme is conditional upon the 'purity' of its motives. Otherwise, its rendering of the suppressed could become dangerous.

If Dvořák's American sojourn was indeed, for the Americans, a defining moment, this is not because it changed the course of history. It is significant here for two reasons. First, because it indicates a further stage in the composer's transformation as a public figure, when the methods of public relations first catch up with literary pretensions as a mode of addressing the public, educating the audience in the orientation of the music, and what the composer means by it. What we witness with Dvořák is a moment before the practice becomes corrupt, though it already displays a tendency to ideologize the composer's public utterances, both musical and verbal, according to its own agenda. Secondly, because the episode is prophetic of ideological contradictions which will present themselves anew, some decades later, when the same call for a music rooted in African-American culture is issued again – only this time by African-Americans themselves – in the course of the movement known as the Harlem Renaissance, and the question once more will be played out over the terrain of musical authenticity – but this time with different results.

*

Dvořák's visit to America was not an isolated foray by a European composer. Tchaikovsky had already been there in 1891, dispatched by the Berlin music agent Hermann Wolff to open the new Carnegie Hall. Indeed, as steamships had made the journey easier, agents and managers on both sides of the Atlantic had developed a profitable trade in fame and renown. As Horowitz writes elsewhere, what the New World lacked in indigenous resources it was prepared to entice with dollars and applause. By mid-century, New York had a Philharmonic increasingly staffed by expatriate Germans. As for soloists, from Jenny Lind to Paderewski the fortunes made in the United States by a succession of famous artists and their less well-known agents were out of all proportion to the composers', and economically more important than the publishers' share. Back in Vienna, Hanslick quipped that America was 'truly the promised land, if not of music, at least of the musician'.[17]

While the model for the traditional impresario was provided by the Italian opera industry, it is no accident that the paradigm of a new kind was found in the United States, where a huge untapped market was forming and old conventions had little meaning. Here in 1851, the circus showman P.T. Barnum demonstrated a new kind of business to be made by promoting the reputation of the musical artist as a type of freak. Failing to entice Liszt to undertake the trip, he nevertheless lured the soprano Jenny Lind across the Atlantic, just as she announced her retirement from the opera stage, for a gruelling nine-month concert tour, in which she earned more than $200,000 for herself, and more than half a million for him. Inventing for her the sobriquet of 'the Swedish Nightingale', and trading on her reputation for Christian charity, Barnum proceeded to raise the audience with a barrage of publicity handouts, high-falutin claims, and leaks to the press, topped by organized street processions to fête the celebrity when she arrived – the methods of ballyhoo, nowadays known as hype, which were part of the same huckster's trade that fed the new advertising agencies which first appeared in America in the same period. The purpose of advertising is intervention in the marketplace in order to capture and, if possible, create demand; Barnum was one of the first to show how to do it with music. Here we see again how music harbours the process which Habermas considers one of the principal forces in the transformation of the public sphere.

There were two aspects to Barnum's efforts. First – as Sol Hurok, a prominent post-Barnum impresario, once put it – an impresario doesn't make an artist, he makes an audience. Second, in the words of a popular history of the music business, Barnum was the first promoter to sell a singer as something more than a singer, but a star. [18] Where previously it was the person of the artist, preferably charismatic, who made the audience, now a gullible press is co-opted into a monster publicity campaign, using procedures already familiar to the playwright Sheridan: 'the puff preliminary, the puff direct, the puff collateral, the puff collusive, and the puff oblique, or puff by implication'. But in a constituency of millions who have had no means to formulate their own opinions, the product is a new relationship between the performer and the audience, in which the performer attracts a special fetish value.

Perhaps Marx had heard about the Swedish Nightingale. At any rate, he wrote:

> A singer who sings like a bird [in other words, freely] is an unproductive worker. When she sells her song, she is a wage earner or merchant. But the same singer, employed by someone else to give concerts and bring in money, is a productive worker because she directly produces capital.[19]

The results of Barnum's success had effects far beyond the shores of the USA. American musical promotion entered a symbiosis with a parallel process in Europe, where power became concentrated in the hands of a small number of agents who monopolized their own territories but competed for transatlantic contracts. The transatlantic trade was opened up by the first generation of New York agents, Europeans who arrived in the wake of the 1848 Revolutions and shared the same Central European Jewish background. When the piano manufacturer Steinway wanted the Russian pianist-composer Anton Rubinstein for an American tour in 1872, he had to deal with Jacob Grau, former aide to one of the pioneer New York music managers; his nephew Maurice Strakosch brought Offenbach. Another former Strakosch man, Bernard Ullman, now back in Europe, supplied the rival Boston firm of Chickering with Hans von Bülow in 1875. Their ranks were joined by a broadly similar breed of men who took root in the major European capitals, including Albert Guttman in Vienna and Hermann Wolff in Berlin. Both of them achieved their monopolies by capturing the business of the cities' principal orchestras. Wolff, who began his career in a music shop, learned his business travelling Europe as manager for Rubinstein, taking advantage of opportunities he discovered on his travels to obtain contracts for other musicians. By the time he returned to Berlin to set up an agency there in 1880, he had a list that included Rubinstein, Bülow, the violinist Joseph Joachim, French composers and Belgian tenors; he also scouted for the New York Metropolitan Opera, and served as a booking agent for orchestras in London, Paris and Copenhagen.

Orchestras were key players in more senses than one. Increasingly caught between conductors and agents, they developed a tendency to rebel – there were orchestral rebellions in Berlin in 1882, Prague in 1896 and 1901, even New York in 1903.[20] In Berlin, the court orchestra under Benjamin Bilse resigned *en masse*, complaining of low wages and other indignities, regrouped as the Berlin Philharmonic and went to Wolff for advice. Wolff ended up taking on their concert management at his own risk, appointing Bülow as chief conductor, replacing him with Arthur Nikisch when he resigned. Richard Strauss complained that the orchestra was 'in the gift of the agent Hermann Wolff',[21] but Nikisch raised their standards further, introduced Tchaikovsky and Bruckner, and led the orchestra on tours of France, Russia, Austria, Italy, Spain and Portugal – organized, naturally, by Wolff. If the Berlin Philharmonic was the first orchestra to travel widely, his artists went even further afield. He sent Fritz Kreisler round Scandinavia, the Mediterranean and America, and it was he who sent Tchaikovsky to New York in 1891. In the retrospective estimation of the violinist Carl Flesch, the development of German concert life under his influence, which lasted until the rise of Nazism, was not due to artistic or social need but was, rather,

> the outcome of Wolff's idea of the politico-economic correspondence between artistic performances and agricultural or industrial products. Why shouldn't a virtuoso be 'ordered' or 'despatched' in the same way as wheat or steel? It was simply a question of organisation; the concert-giving societies had to become accustomed to 'ordering' their artists through a central agency. Supply and demand were to fix the artist's fee just as stocks and shares were priced on the exchange . . .[22]

Again we find that one contemporary observer who perceived the relationship between musical life and the organization of capitalist production was the exiled German revolutionary quietly working things out in the British Museum. Marx saw the orchestra conductor as a representative of capitalist interests. The capitalist mode of production, he wrote:

> has brought matters to a point where the work of supervision, entirely divorced from the ownership of capital, is always readily available . . . An orchestra conductor need not own the instruments of his orchestra, nor is it within the scope of his duties as conductor to have anything to do with the 'wages' of the other musicians.[23]

Unless, one should add, he also owned the orchestra, like Leopold Damrosch and his son Walter in New York, whose musicians rebelled in 1903. They would doubtless have preferred to have had Mahler, on economic as well as musical grounds. Mahler was the exception to Marx's observation. Employed as chief conductor of the Hamburg Opera in the 1890s, when the impresario in charge, the piratical Bernhard Pollini, paid big money for his stars and kept the rest of the cast (not to mention the orchestra) on subsistence wages, Mahler formally objected when Pollini stopped paying the musicians in the summer months of 1894, when the theatre was closed, accusing him of 'shabby tricks' and writing in protest to the Burgomaster. Three years later, as the newly appointed director of the Vienna Opera, he was appalled when he discovered how little some of the players earned, and immediately took steps to raise their salaries, compensating for the expense by economies in other areas.

Mahler's situation reveals the effects of this politico-economic corre-spondence on the figure of the composer, precisely because we can see in his combination of the roles of conductor and composer the split which developed between them. As a conductor he achieved pre-eminence among his peers, as a composer he suffered rejection for being not modern but modernist. All the time, his podium career interfered with his composing. With the great success in the 1890s of mainstream composers like Dvořák and Tchaikovsky, who immediately entered the repertoire and never left it, the period has left the appearance of the symphonic tradition at its apogee, an ideal moment in the musical public sphere, representing the symbiotic unity of composer and public, before the composer adopted what the audience experienced as a negative stance, and they parted company. This image oversimplifies a much more complicated reality, for the truth is that the public has by now already begun to hand over responsibility for the formation of taste to surrogates: a handful of baton-wielders, the wily agents who manage them, the supposedly autonomous critics who lead the different musical camps. This is the last period in which the star conductors regularly and as a matter of course perform the latest music. Even the mainstream composer began to need a conductor to champion him, preferably one in charge of a major orchestra and supported by a powerful agent. If the figure of the composer-conductor will recur – the outstanding example in present times being Pierre Boulez – these functions were split by a political economy which prefers the proven, the track record of success on the podium, to the risk of the new; and in Mahler, paradoxically, the living composer's marginal-ization from the centre of musical life has already begun.

Composer's rights

The material source of this marginalization is the composer's peculiar economic position within musical life, which is quite different from that of both the rank-and-file musician, who is a simple wage-earner, and the star singer, the virtuoso, and the conductor, who draw the crowd and are paid a fee, the value of which is geared to the market in much the same way as a footballer's transfer fee. According to the economist Jacques Attali, the fact that the composer produces an object in the form of a written score does not make him a productive worker. The composer is positioned not inside the system of exchange value within organized musical life, but at its point of origin. The composer is 'reproduced' and economically sustained in the printed copy and its audition, in performance and mechanical reproduction, by virtue of copyright and royalties. Copyright, legally speaking, is a form of property; the compensation provided by royalties is a kind of rent. Hence, while performers are wage- or fee-earners, impresarios and publishers are the entrepreneurs of music, and the composer is a rentier.[24]

Musical copyright before the middle of the nineteenth century was either nonexistent or a fragile and precarious affair, and composers were legally worse off than writers. The literary author is at the very epicentre of the emergence of the literary public sphere, and its changing conceptions of authorship, which advance the status of the writer both intellectually and juridically, as the very model of the private individual in the public sphere. The first public edict designed to protect authors was proclaimed in Venice in 1545, but it was in England a hundred years later that the issues were first seriously enjoined, in an Edict of 1642, in response to the flood of anonymous publications which followed the abolition of the Star Chamber. The primary intention was thus to hold authors and printers responsible for books which Parliament deemed libellous, seditious or blasphemous. Milton's *Areopagitica* two years later is the poet's angry response to Parliament's reimposition of censorship, the proud defence of the autonomous author whose authority is based not on public office or sanction but on personal experience, study and deliberation. Milton, says the scholar Mark Rose, 'presents himself as a private man and author protesting an act of state that is insulting to the dignity of authors'.[25] Milton is followed by Locke, who frames the argument against pre-publication censorship, writing in a memorandum to a Member of Parliament to provide him with arguments against licensing: 'I know not why a man should not have liberty to print whatever he would speak.'[26] These arguments coincided with rising commercial interests which perceived the monopolistic system of privileges derived from royal prerogative as an archaic obstacle to expansion; thus England makes the evolution of copyright law part of a process of legal reform aimed at rendering the law responsive to the needs of a commercial nation. As the seventeenth century draws to a close, Parliament fails to renew the Licensing Act, and censorship lapses, again leading to a flood of print in the radical spirit of the coffee house – a situation which could hardly endure. In the 1700s, Daniel Defoe, newly released from pillorying and imprisonment for his satiric *Shortest Way with the Dissenters*, publishes pamphlets and articles in his journal, the *Review*, opposing the reintroduction of both licensing and pre-publication censorship on grounds of liberty and democracy, because it subjected the press to the interests of the party in power, arguing: 'A Book is the Author's Property, 'tis the child of his Inventions, the Brat of his Brain';[27] Addison takes up the issue in *The Tatler* and its successor, *The Spectator*. In 1709, Parliament reimposes licensing but recognizes the rights of authors.

The Statute of Anne made authors into the prior owners of literary property, but limited the term for which their rights should last in the same way as patent rights. It was the first modern copyright law. In theory, at least, ownership of the text now belonged to the private individual who wrote it, not the person who printed it, and the author joined the ranks of the propertied classes by virtue of the product of his brains. Not so in the case of music. There was no similar legal protection for musical works anywhere until late in the eighteenth century. The product of the composer's pen was not protected by author's rights simply by virtue of the intellectual labour of getting it down. In the conditions under which most music was traditionally composed and performed, the composer was not on a legal par with the literary author: either the composer was a salaried employee, or perhaps in receipt of opera house commissions, or maybe a self-managing virtuoso, but in any case a performing musician first, a composer second. And when music was printed, copyright was vested in the publisher, who drove a very hard bargain.

This is not all. The form of copyright law introduced by the Statute of Anne is based on a curious contradiction, which emerges over the ensuing decades as publishers try to ignore the new legislation and authors challenge them in the courts. In 1759, while one judge speaks of 'the idea of the composition, as it lies in the author's mind, before it is substantiated by reducing it into writing', another acknowledges the author's right to his composition before it was published but maintains that the act of publication necessarily made the work common: 'I allow, that the author has a property in his sentiments till he publishes them . . . But from the moment of publication, they are thrown into a state of universal communion.'[28] This, of course, is the natural condition of music, where the very sign of a song's popularity was that everyone sang it and played it and even made arrangements of it for free. The main protection for the composer of written musical scores was the fact that they physically owned their own manuscript, a commodity for which theatres and publishers comprised the primary market; but the composer's claim ceased when they bought the manuscript.

In the eighteenth century, the composer was lucky to find a publisher prepared to pay in advance. A common practice was publication by subscription, by which the expenses could be cushioned; otherwise composers either relied on the generosity of patrons or had to share or even shoulder the costs themselves (as we saw, there is an excellent account of these conditions in the letters of Mozart). In the case of opera, composers often kept their own full scores and sold copies of the parts to the theatres (or the impresario) for a fee or commission. If the result was a more-than-average success, the system worked against the composer and in favour of the impresario, who took all the profits; but the composer could increase his rates as his track record improved. The composer could also lose out, when the opera was a hit, to unscrupulous publishers, who were quick off the mark in bringing out unauthorized arrangements. Mozart was caught out like this by the huge popularity of *Figaro*.

Relations between publisher and composer began to alter with the expansion of the trade in printed music in the latter part of the eighteenth century. This development, by capitalizing the publisher, allowed him to take the risks involved in exploiting the market and bid for the composer's services. As publishers began to provide a growing proportion of a successful composer's income, the growth of their business enabled them to begin to capitalize the composer, replacing the patronage of the aristocracy as the bedrock of his livelihood. What the publisher paid the composer, however, was not an advance but a flat fee which, according to the music publisher Ernst Roth, was essentially an informed guess

> based on the chances of the work's success as the publisher saw them. If he sold more copies than expected he had a good bargain and the composer lost; but the reverse was more frequently the case, because failures are always more numerous than successes, although history does not register them. There was no need to sign formal documents; an exchange of

correspondence was sufficient. If, like Beethoven, the composer had the public behind him the publisher could not bargain. He probably did not even try because he had to outbid five or six other competitors. If the composer was less well established the publisher secured for himself a premium for the risk that he took.[29]

Publishers called this system, with a hint of sarcasm, *à fonds perdus*. Its workings were logical enough. In a world where the markets for printed music were principally amateur, domestic and religious, once the music was sold it left the market just like any ordinary commodity, and no one made anything from it when it was played; performance was free. With the demise of patronage there was no other way to make money from composing – apart from a commission or playing it yourself to a paying audience – than to get it printed. But the publisher's advantage was unassailable, and his profits, when a piece sold well, were enormous.

The growth of concert life changed these arrangements only slowly. Orchestral music, and the various forms of opera and ballet music, lay outside the publisher's main circuit, except as transcriptions and arrangements, which indeed comprised a significant part of the trade. But large-scale scores often circulated, when they did so, in manuscript. Opera houses would guard their commissioned scores to prevent piracy; in any case, it was not the composer who would benefit if they sold the work to another house. Thus if such a state of affairs became increasingly anomalous with the growth of commercial musical activity, the effects first became obvious in the theatre, where considerable sums of money could be earned very fast by successful productions. In France, Beaumarchais (author of a play which Mozart and da Ponte 'borrowed' for the opera stage without payment of rights) spearheaded a rebellion by a group of dramatists and opera composers, who formed a *Société des auteurs et compositeurs dramatiques* to demand the payment of royalties for performance of their works. (This was not the first time Beaumarchais had concerned himself with intellectual property rights; the son of a watchmaker, he made his literary reputation through a series of polemics he wrote in the course of litigation over patents when he invented an escapement mechanism himself.) A few years later the French Revolution, with its ideology of natural justice, would decree a performance right, which would be followed by a revision of copyright that favoured the authorial rights of composers.

Similar rights were gradually granted by various other countries during the course of the nineteenth century; in Britain a theatrical performance right was enacted in 1833 (the 'Bulwer-Lytton Act'). The grant of a right, however, is not the same thing as exercising it. A performance right has to be *collected*; agencies to collect it were needed, and legal judgments to make people pay up. Again the first performing rights collection agencies were French: the *Société des auteurs dramatiques*, founded in 1791 by the musician Framery, well known in his day as a writer on music, and the *Société des Auteurs, Compositeurs et Editeurs de Musique*, or SACEM, dating from 1851. The former had little clout. Significantly, the latter owed its birth to the initiative of an author of *chansons*, Ernest Bourget, who in 1847 started taking his claims for authors' rights against *café-concerts* and similar establishments to the courts, and winning. SACEM was set up four years later by 'a group of creators and publishers' mainly involved, according to the sociologist Pierre-Michel Menger, 'in the genres of light music'. In short, the growth of popular urban entertainment brings a new interest group into the business, and while 'serious composers' soon affiliated, the administration of the society was controlled mainly 'by the creators and publishers of the undemanding music which was the most consumed'.[30] Gradually similar author-and-publisher agencies appeared elsewhere, depending on the state of the business and the law in different countries. Italy's SIAE dates from 1882, the German GEMA from 1903; Britain's Performing Rights Society was not founded until 1914.

According to a study of the composer in the marketplace by two neoliberal economists, Alan Peacock and Ronald Weir, the British delay is revealing. In Britain both publishers and composers thought of performance rights as inimical to the main business of selling copies – especially after John Boosey pioneered a new relationship with the composer, when, in the interest of spreading the risk, he introduced percentage royalties on sales. The more a piece of music was played in public, it was thought, the more people would buy it; and the payment of publisher's royalties was a more important part of a composer's income than it was in countries where performance rights were already established.[31] But if the sheet music market was growing, it was also fragmenting, and this process is reflected in the specializations developed by different publishers. Boosey's, for example, traded mainly in songs, ballads and duets for popular consumption. Of their two main competitors, Chappell's had a high proportion of dance music, while Novello's specialized in sacred music, instructional music, and textbooks. The same rules did not apply in all markets – notably, they did not apply in the same way to the music which, in the hierarchy of genres, had the most prestige but often the smallest of buying publics. For the market, in becoming fragmented, also became divided against itself. New forms of stratification translated the social and class divisions into aesthetic susceptibilities in a manner that left the composer exposed. The results upset the established hierarchy of genres. At first, the proliferation of the salons and a growing middle-class pianistic public together encouraged, through the medium of the publisher, the development of the less elevated genres of the piano repertoire. From the publisher's point of view, the business involved risk, judgement and a certain amount of luck. As Roth explains: 'Imagine seeing for the first time the first of Chopin's Preludes, Op. 28, in manuscript, a graphic image such as had never been put on paper before, and having to decide whether publication would be a sound investment.'[32] But Chopin had a monied following. The young Wagner, on the other hand, was unable to find a publisher for his grandiose operas – first Schott refused him, then Breitkopf and Härtel – and was left no choice but to finance publication himself; it took him thirty years to overcome the resulting debts, in spite of a growing income from the performance of his works. Mahler, too, with his enormous symphonies, had to pay the costs of publishing them himself; for him the price was the constant battle of sustaining a career as a supremo conductor, in order to finance his work as a composer, but leaving him only his summers to compose in.

Another factor to shape the musical economy as the century draws to a close is the growing internationalization of musical life. The juridical framework for the moral and intellectual rights of the author begins as a national and domestic matter. The economic pressures in the industry in which the author is the primary producer, however, grew more and more international. In the countries which led the production of the written word, publishers became increasingly concerned with the problem of foreign protection – for both their own authors abroad and the foreign works which they published at home. Here, music publishers and composers were worse off than authors and publishers of the word: music does not need translation; artists, too, since lithography and other advances in graphic reproduction, were also in trouble. Lack of international co-ordination meant that piracy was endemic. In the case of commercial successes, the sums involved could be very considerable, especially across the Atlantic. The first American copyright laws were statutes passed by the newly independent colonies in the 1780s, most of which viewed copyright as an author's right. When the first Federal copyright law was passed by Congress in 1790, it left out any protection for foreign works. (Indeed, the USA was totally recalcitrant about protecting anyone except its own, and only in the 1990s did it join the Berne Convention.) As a result, a European success could be introduced without paying a penny for book or music. It happened to Gilbert and Sullivan, and the huge popularity of transatlantic pirate productions induced their manager, Richard D'Oyly Carte, to take on the expense of mounting simultaneous premieres of new operettas on both sides of the ocean himself, in order to beat the pirates.

France was again the country which took the lead on the international stage: first by seeking bilateral copyright treaties, and then in 1852 by declaring piracy of foreign works in France illegal. The measure was not exactly altruistic: the problem of piracy is most acutely felt where a language is shared by neighbouring countries, as French is in Belgium, where Belgian printers sold their pirated editions (so did the Dutch, whose typographers have always worked in different languages). Six years later, the first international congress of authors and artists met in Brussels, and called for uniform worldwide copyright legislation. It was a non-government organization, the International Literary and Artistic Association, founded in 1878, which prepared the draft text for the meetings at government level which Switzerland agreed to convene in Berne. When the Berne Convention was established in 1886, the signatories agreed to extend the same protection to works by authors belonging to the member countries as to works by its own nationals (though the dues would still have to be collected). The irony, with the benefit of hindsight, is that the invention, less than ten years earlier, of the phonograph was regarded in the same light as musical boxes and Barbary organs, and since the manufacture of these instruments was mainly a Swiss industry, the Convention agreed that the mechanical reproduction of music should not count as infringement of copyright.

By the end of the nineteenth century, then, the political economy of music has been redrawn in a manner which seriously disadvantages the composer in the high tradition, in several ways. The situation was transformed by performing rights, but not entirely in the composer's favour. As we have already noted, a musical economy that is based on performance fees depends on an effective system of collection. Because of the growing multiplicity of performance sites, the individual composer is in a weak position to collect the dues, and the publisher steps in to do it for him. The principal beneficiary is the publisher who, in order to improve returns from performance rights, turns the thrust of their operations towards promotion, teaming up with impresarios and agents to obtain performances. For works of prestige, printing becomes almost secondary to performance. Since publication royalties were not yet common, the composer benefited from further and – ideally –

higher advances, while the publisher ensured his position as a keystone of the music business as it then operated, tying the composer into a form of musical economy which was weighted against him but which he could not do without: without getting his music published, he was simply not a composer.

This situation produces a growing mismatch between the mercenary values which increasingly governed sociomusical relations, and those of music's autonomy. Bourgeois culture – to follow Habermas – was not mere ideology: it expressed an authentic aspiration to a spiritual life which transcended the utilitarianism of the economic realm. The elements of ideology which accompanied these aspirations lay largely in the orientation of cultural consumption towards the cultivation of a particular kind of individual subjectivity, even though, especially in such domains as music, it none the less served vital collective needs. Commercialization functioned initially as a means of distribution – the working of the market lay in the distribution of cultural goods beyond the exclusive audience of wealthy patrons and high-born connoisseurs – and the public which thus gained access to culture related to it 'as objects of judgement and taste, of free choice and preference'.[33] At this stage, commodity value did not yet influence the quality of the cultural object in itself, which retained a certain indifference to the market; this would later turn into either resistance or acquiescence. Although something of the incompatibility between cultural value and the commodity form continues down to our own day, the terms of this relation would be altered decisively by the transformation of the market for cultural goods into the organized leisure market catering to the growing urban masses which first developed during the second half of the nineteenth century. For here the laws of the market begin to penetrate into the substance of the work itself, which is increasingly shaped from within, as Habermas puts it, by the need to facilitate access *psychologically* as well as economically. Habermas takes the model for this process to be the transformation of the literary public sphere, through the introduction of the new technologies of mass printing, into the popular press – which then becomes an agent in the promotion of new forms of urban mass entertainment. But it also has profound effects in the domain of high culture, through the growing incommensurability between individual subjectivity and commodified psychology.

In the course of the growth of the literary public sphere, the bourgeois public was able to cultivate a new form of subjectivity in which the expression of intimacy was orientated towards a public. In this form the individual interpreted their new form of existence which was based, as Habermas puts it, on the liberal relationship between public and private spheres. This experience of audience-orientated privacy encouraged a search for novelty, and hence artistic experimentation, which would come into conflict with the process which animated it. The original relationship between the domain of interiority and the public sphere is upset. The commodification of the art work in a world of cultural consumption increasingly mediated by the principle of psychological facilitation had determinate effects on the figure of the artist who produced these works. An inner life orientated towards a public audience tends to give way to reifications of the inner life. 'The public sphere becomes the sphere for the publicizing of private biographies', which produces a growing 'sentimentality' towards an idealized type of artist far removed from the growing alienation of the life of creative endeavour.[34] A case in point is that of Tchaikovsky. 'Alas!' he wrote to his patron, Madame von Meck:

> when I begin to reflect that with an increasing audience will also come an increase of interest in my personality, in the more intimate sense; that there will be inquisitive people . . . who will tear aside the curtain behind which I have striven to conceal my private life, then . . . I half wish to keep silence for ever, in order to be left in peace. I am not afraid of the world, for I can say that my conscience is clear, and I have nothing to be ashamed of.[35]

If this is a reference to his unstated homosexuality, there is of course no doubt that the difficulty of coming to terms in nineteenth-century Russian society with what his brother called his 'abnormally neurotic tendency' has a great deal to do with his periods of depression and misanthropy. But these comments are also interesting for another reason: they indicate the extent to which the journalistic invasion of privacy had already become the inevitable concomitant of artistic success.

Recognition in print and success with the public were not the same thing, however, and any artist or composer bent on challenging the process of psychological facilitation in the name of higher or deeper imperatives ended up more infamous than famous. There now arises a stratum of artists, says Habermas, who explain their progressive isolation from the educated bourgeois public to themselves 'as an – illusory – emancipation from social locations altogether', and who, accordingly, see themselves as 'free-floating intellectuals'.[36] Arnold Hauser, in his *Social History of Art*, traces the origins of this stratum back to the middle of the nineteenth century and the gestation of the *bohème*. The first generation of bohemians (that of Théophile Gautier and Gérard de Nerval) were children of bourgeois society: 'in whom the opposition to the prevailing society was usually a product of mere youthful exuberance and contrariness,' and functioned like a rite of passage. Balzac, in *Un Prince de la Bohème*, saw it as a transitional stage, consisting 'of young people, who are still unknown, but who will be well known and famous one day'.[37] They undertook their excursions into the world of outlaws and outcasts in the same way as their cousins went on journeys to exotic lands; they returned to the comforts of bourgeois society when they wished. They knew nothing of the misery of the fully fledged *bohème* of the following generation (that of Rimbaud and Verlaine, Gauguin and Van Gogh), which became 'an artistic proletariat, made up of people whose existence was absolutely insecure . . . who stood outside the frontiers of bourgeois society, and whose struggle against the bourgeoisie was no high-spirited game but a bitter necessity'.[38]

The composer is drawn into this struggle no less surely than the poet or the painter. Liszt is the representative musical figure of the first-generation *bohème*, Satie of the *bohème* as artistic proletariat. The transformation of the social functions of music, which accelerated in the second half of the century, placed contradictory demands on them. To pursue the call of musical autonomy, subjective exploration, and novelty – this path entailed increasing difficulty, in terms of both obtaining performances and the demands the music made on the audience's concentration and goodwill. It also confirmed the so-called serious composer in a certain identity, a figure in the sphere of high culture, to be increasingly distinguished from those whom the publishers courted plainly and simply for their popularity. At the same time, a separation of musical languages begins to develop in accord with the social stratification of consumption. Popular composers attune themselves to the idioms and skills of the popular singers and musicians who become professionalized by the growth of popular urban entertainment. Up to the time of Brahms and Dvořák, classical composers might subsidize themselves, so to speak, by coming up with, say, sets of national dances for domestic consumption; the popular parlour trade, however, was quite another matter. By the next generation, the distance between the most advanced composers and the popular idiom was too great to be bridged in the same way, and according to Roth, among the avant-garde at the turn of the century 'only Debussy seems to have had no difficulty in finding a proper publisher'.[39]

Debussy and the origins of the avant-garde

In late-nineteenth-century public musical life, you could be a nationalist and a cosmopolitan at the same time. But in a world which was becoming together – propelled by capitalist expansion, innovations in transportation and communication, and the drive of the European powers for imperial conquest – cosmopolitanism would soon take a new turn. This is not just a matter of the ease with which European musicians now traversed the Continent and crossed the Atlantic; musicians have always travelled. There is a shift in focus, observable in the rise of a science of anthropology as a concomitant of European imperialism and, in matters aesthetic, of exoticism. Music is deeply implicated in this process. If the explosion of radical new musical idioms in the new century is the outcome of the growing frustrations of previous decades, of a growing feeling that the inherited musical language was incapable of expressing the anxieties and desires of modernity, then exotic musics reaching Europe played a critical part in liberating its composers from too much interiorization.

Thus, while the New York musical public in the 1890s debated the source of a possible new American music in its own 'native' ethnic heritage, in Paris the musical twentieth century begins in 1889 at the World Exhibition, when a number of young composers, including the twenty-seven-year-old Claude Debussy, first encountered the music of Africa and Asia. Debussy's response was a striking contrast to that of Berlioz to the Far Eastern music he had heard at the Great Exhibition in London less than forty years earlier. Where Berlioz had been dismissive, demonstrating the limits of even progressive ears in the mid-century, Debussy was fascinated and seduced by the exotic orchestras, singers and dancers to be heard beneath the new tower built for the occasion by the military engineer Gustave Eiffel. Three years later, he produced one of the most singular short pieces in the history of modern music, the *Prélude à l'Après-midi d'un Faune*, based on a poem by the symbolist Mallarmé, in which he abandons the structural function of triadic harmony which had ruled Western music since long before Handel. Since triadic harmony is the mark of the established chronotope of the civilized music of opera house, concert-hall and salon, the *Prélude* prophesies the birth of a new musical chronotope. In spite of being shorter than many a movement in Beethoven, a snippet beside the gigantism of Wagner, Bruckner or Mahler, Debussy's orchestral prelude seems to float, purified, in a kind of timeless acoustic space. This is the moment when the surface of European music begins to dissolve, the established forms start to break up.

The significance of this signal shift in perception is symbolized in the paradox of the setting which inspired it. Walter Benjamin signals the Great Exhibitions as festivals of capitalist production and the universal reach of nineteenth-century imperialism, 'places of pilgrimage to the fetish Commodity', with all the glitter to distract the masses.[40] The Paris Exhibition of 1889 dramatized the official optimism with which the French government, celebrating the centenary of the Revolution, boasted of the country's status as one of the great colonial powers. Yet as Max Raphael observed – concerning Picasso's discovery of African sculpture fifteen years later – in the wake of the very imperialism symbolized by the World Exhibitions comes 'a certain decomposition' in the unity of European consciousness, and the hallowed Greek and Christian canons of its art.[41]

The Great Exhibitions were invariably accompanied by music festivals, and included competitions for musical instruments. At one of the Paris exhibitions in 1867, the American piano firms of Chickering and Steinway each spent some $80,000 on brochures and advertising, entertainment, the engagement of pianists, and 'the judicious insinuation of favourable anecdotes and references into newspapers' – in short, public relations.[42] This was an enormous sum for the time. Both manufacturers were rewarded with medals. News of these American successes were among the first messages to be transmitted over the new transatlantic telegraph cable. This, too, indicates the incursion of forces which would seriously impinge on the public role of the composer, becoming a source of deep anxiety. For the final decades of the century saw what Georg Simmel, writing towards its end, called the accelerated development of 'external civilisation', and 'the preponderance that the technical side of life has obtained over its inner side', which produces diverse and contradictory effects.[43] With inventions like the telephone, electric light, mass reproduction of print and image, cinematography and, of course, the phonograph, the world becomes, in its very modernity, increasingly fragmented and illusory, a world whose perception of itself is hindered by the very means which render it accessible. Moreover, as David Harvey reminds us: 'Modernization entails ... the perpetual disruption of temporal and spatial rhythms', and if the rapidly evolving technologies of transport and communication brought about the reduction of geographical space and the contraction of time – and a veritable transformation of the social chronotope – then modernism, which is born in this moment, 'takes as one of its missions the production of new meanings for space and time in a world of [increasing] ephemerality and fragmentation'.[44] Debussy's music, seen in this perspective, was deeply symptomatic of the generation which was the first to feel the impact of these transformations, in the city which Walter Benjamin called the capital of the nineteenth century, where modernism finds its first stirring.

The Polish musicologist Stefan Jarocinski spotted in a letter written by Debussy in 1886 the echo of an idea which Baudelaire expressed in the dedication of Le spleen de Paris to Arsènne Houssaye almost twenty-five years beforehand, where he proclaims that modern life requires a new artistic language: 'As to the kind of music I want to make,' the young composer wrote, 'I would like it to be flexible enough and sufficiently accented to correspond to the lyrical impulses of the spirit and to the capriciousness of dreams.'[45] 'Who among us', Baudelaire had asked, 'has not dreamt, in moments of ambition, of the miracle of a poetic prose, musical without rhythm and without rhyme, supple and staccato enough to adapt to the lyrical stirrings of the soul, the undulations of dreams, and the sudden leaps of consciousness?'[46] Walter Benjamin regarded this dedication as especially significant. It tells us, he wrote, about the close connection in Baudelaire between the sense of impact of modernity and contact with the metropolitan masses, an index of the growing alienation of artistic sensibility in the midst of the prosaic and banal reality of the modern metropolis. The continual and repeated shock of this encounter intensifies the artist's sense of isolation, reflected in Baudelaire's identification of the poet with the postures of the bohemian and the dandy, in whom the terror of assimilation, and of the loss of creative freedom, leads to an exaggerated and exasperated individualism. Dandy and bohemian, says Renato Poggioli in his study of the avant-garde, are equal and opposite manifestations of an identical state of mind and social situation: that of alienation, whose expression in such garb cannot but provoke antagonism in the public.[47] Debussy – who, in his photographs, tends to appear as the dandy – is a child of the same Paris as Baudelaire; here he grew up, practised his art and died, his life and the life of the city forever intersecting. In the quest to comprehend the dialogical situation of musical creation, these intersections are more than characteristic.

Debussy's destiny was first joined with that of the city when he was scarcely nine years old, in the momentous events of the Paris Commune; since he never spoke of his childhood even to intimates, these events came to light only much later. Immediately after the Siege of Paris, his father, the son of a cabinet-maker, joined the National Guard, and was rapidly promoted to the rank of Captain. On 8 May 1871, in one of the decisive battles of the Commune, when the Versailles forces took the fort of Issy, Captain Debussy found himself leading the Communard battalion after his superior had been wounded, but his men deserted him and he gave himself up. After the collapse of the Commune two weeks later, he ended up in the infamous military prison at Satory, and a court martial sentenced him to four years' incarceration (though a plea for clemency from his wife obtained his release). In the jail at Satory, he struck up a friendship with a musician, Charles de Sivry. Sivry's mother, Antoinette-Flore Mauté, a piano teacher of exceptional pedagogic gifts and mother-in-law of the poet Verlaine (who was accused of Communard sympathies), was the first to discern the child's musical talents, and undertook to teach him gratis. A year later, at the remarkably early age of eleven, Claude Achille entered the Paris Conservatoire.

The Commune became a formidable symbol not for what it achieved but for what it prophesied: in two words, the dictatorship of the proletariat. It is true, says Arnold Hauser, that the Commune ends with complete defeat, but it is the first revolution to be sustained by an international labour movement, and to leave the bourgeoisie with a feeling of acute anxiety.[48] Paris soon recovered its reputation as the city of fashion, glamour and luxury, which other capitals sought to emulate, yet it was not quite the same city as before, in the heyday of the Offenbachiade. Reconstructed during the Second Empire – in advance of Vienna's Ringstrasse – according to a new urban ideal, given the revolutionary history of Paris, the real aim of Haussmann's boulevards, says Benjamin, which contemporaries christened 'strategic beautification', was to secure the city against civil war, to render the erection of barricades impossible because of the width of the streets, and 'to provide the shortest route between the barracks and the working class districts'.[49] Yet the barricades returned during the Commune, stronger than ever, and shielding trenches behind them. Afterwards the masses went back to their passive role as consumers of entertainment and commodities, but certain illusions had been shattered. This mood is reflected in new artistic and intellectual trends, both idealistic and mystical, which are progressively reinforced and inflected by the furious speed of industrial and technological development which now, at the height of European imperialism, overtakes society. In the aftermath of the Commune, while the Parisian intelligentsia continued its outward life as before, the artist gained a new sense of the uncertainty and disharmony of bourgeois existence, and of the contradictions of seeking to satisfy a confused and fearful bourgeois audience. As Mallarmé put it: 'In a society which lacks stability and unity it is impossible to create an art which is stable and well-defined.'[50]

The artists in their cafés, cabarets and salons formed coteries and cliques, and increasingly became, as Benjamin says of Baudelaire, secret agents – agents of the secret discontent of their class with its own rule. It is precisely this moment and this milieu to which Poggioli has traced the emergence of the term avant-garde (in which Baudelaire saw the predilection of the French for military metaphors) to describe a new sociocultural phenomenon, 'the modern concept of culture as spiritual civil war'.[51] It is surely no coincidence that young French artists who had flirted with anarchism and socialism in the Commune were the first to call themselves, defiantly, 'decadents'. As Poggioli mentions, Théophile Gautier shows in his essay on Baudelaire 'that the decadent spirit is in harmony with the crisis of civilization';[52] in which case it is inevitable that antagonism to the public will become antagonism towards tradition. As for Debussy, who was not very militaristic, he expressed his opposition to received ideas in his own characteristic image: 'Let us cultivate only the garden of our instincts, and trample disrespectfully upon the flower-beds in which ideas are all lined up symmetrically in full evening dress.'[53]

A bifurcation develops between the drive for aesthetic experiment and the normalizing aims of the public sphere. Where once the public sphere functioned to discover problems, it now suppresses them, and the artist is driven deeper into antagonism. Again this was expressed by Mallarmé, who declared in a press interview that this was an epoch in which the artist finds himself 'on strike against society'. Poggioli comments that in order to be on strike, one has to be employed; and this is the problem with bohemianism. What started as a rite of passage for mostly well-to-do young artists and students turned into a chronic condition at the margins of bourgeois society – what Hauser called 'a real *bohème*, that is, an artistic proletariat' – made up of those whose existence was insecure because they stood at the edge of respectability, cast out by mutual antagonism. On the whole, says Hauser, the bourgeois regards the *bohème* as an underworld which both attracts and repels, and is romanticized and idealized at the very moment when it ceases to be Romantic.

Debussy entered the bohemian world through the famous cabaret of the Chat Noir (where his friend Erik Satie later played the piano), which opened its doors in 1881; from here it was only a few steps to reach the famous Tuesday gatherings of Mallarmé in the rue de Rome. The Chat Noir served as headquarters for the Friday meetings of a literary circle founded by Goudeau, under the patronage of Charles Cros, the poet and amateur scientist who – in the same year as Edison, but unknown to him – had conceived of a talking machine on the model of Léon Scott's phonautograph. As for the rue de Rome, here Mallarmé had created a true refuge. As André Gide recollected: 'Ah! how far away one felt in that little room ... from the empty rumours of the busy town, political gossip, scandals and intrigues. One entered with Mallarmé a supra-sensitive region where money, honours and public acclamation no longer counted. . . .'[54] As if, on entering, one left the public sphere behind. In this reduced space, a widening gap opens up between the conventional cultured taste outside and the dissident anti-bourgeois rebels whose experimentation the public sphere finds increasingly threatening, inaccessible, and scandalous (for they sometimes breach the boundaries of public sexual order). The artist is confronted with what Eric Hobsbawm calls 'the problem of combining reality with subjectivity', which ends up in a pure subjectivism which verges on solipsism.[55] This solipsism is reflected in the audience for this art, which is divided between two small publics, one of them the immediate coterie, the other, dispersed, atomized and anonymous. As Paul Valéry wrote:

> I sometimes said to Mallarmé: 'There are some who blame you, and some who despise you. It has become an easy thing for the reporters to amuse the people at your expense, while your friends shake their heads . . . But do you not know, do you not feel, that there is, in every city of France, a youth who would let himself be cut into pieces for your verses and for you? You are his pride, his craft, his vice. He cuts himself off from everyone by his love of, faith in, your work, hard to find, to understand and to defend.'[56]

One should not overlook those reporters, however, for they are precisely the ones who decide whether the public shall hear of you or not.

Around 1890 there is a shift in sensibilities from 'decadence' to 'symbolism', from sensualism to the realm of the idea, where experience is accessed artistically through the symbol. In Mallarmé's words: 'It is not *description* which can unveil the efficacy and beauty of [archaeological] monuments, seas, or the human face in all their maturity and native state, but rather *evocation, allusion, suggestion*.'[57] Artistic language must undergo a transformation which renounces the reproduction of what is given in order to regain a sense of reality from a deeper and fuller perspective – in order, in Simmel's words, 'to experience in the individual phenomenon . . . the fullness of its reality'.[58] As a programme, this implies a rejection of the methods of naturalism and a move away from realism. Impressionism had already extended the Symbolist programme to painting where a new agenda developed, found in the writings of Van Gogh, of Cézanne, of Gauguin: the need to recover a primitive sense of vision, to discover pure colour, pure form, to sweep away the falsity of the pictorial vision of civilized art, the falsity of civilization. It was also from this imperative that European artistic sensibility derived its empathy for Oriental art. The painters' renovation of their language became exemplary for music, too, and implied the relevance not only of Oriental forms but also of other forgotten kinds of musical experience. Debussy not only discovered renewal in the Oriental music performed at the World Exhibition, but also made a special journey to Cambrai, a hundred miles north of Paris, to hear the revival of Gregorian Chant by the Benedictine monks of Solesmes, the godfathers of the contemporary ancient music movement.

The term Impressionist was first used in relation to Debussy's music as early as 1887 – with derogatory intent. Debussy had won the Prix de Rome, and one of the compositions he sent to the Académie des Beaux-Arts was an orchestral suite with female chorus, *Printemps* (of which the original score is now lost). The report of the Secretary declared: 'He clearly has a strong feeling for colour in music which, when exaggerated, causes him to forget the importance of clarity in design and form. It is very much to be hoped that he will be on his guard against the vague "Impressionism" which is one of the most dangerous enemies of truth in any work of art.'[59] The wording is significant. According to Schoenberg some decades later:

It was the harmonies of Richard Wagner which had disrupted the logic and constructive powers of harmony. One of the consequences of this state of affairs was the use of what were called 'impressionist' harmonies such as we find especially in Debussy. Devoid of any constructive significance, these harmonies are often used to produce effects of 'colour'; their object is to express atmosphere and pictorial images. In this way, however, atmosphere and images, though of extra-musical origin, do become constructive elements, and in the end take their place among other musical functions . . .[60]

This constructive quality was less in evidence to begin with, however, than its destructive aspect – at least from the point of view of the academicians; Jarocinski is therefore broadly correct when he says that nothing very precise was intended by the comparison with painting, and the use of the word was primarily ideological. Yet ideologically the term is quite appropriate, for it was Impressionism which began the process by which the inherited order of pictorial space was progressively decomposed, and perspective and the stable outline were dethroned. In due course the German critic Richard Hamann declared that the disappearance of tonality reminded him of the lack of perspective in Impressionist paintings.[61]

For their part, the painters readily drew comparisons between colour and music. Gauguin, for example, spoke of colour in a painting 'vibrating just like music', and advised painters to 'aim at suggestion rather than description, just as music does'.[62] Even Eugène Chevreul, the French chemist whose research into the polarization of light and the composition of the spectrum the Impressionists incorporated, spoke about colour harmonies. These parallels invite the suggestion that Debussy's radical conception of timbre entered into musical perception in the same way as the Impressionists' discoveries about the constitution of colour intruded into visual artistic awareness: in both cases they disrupted the constancy of the traditional perceptual categories. The revolution in the rendition of colour dislodges the Florentine system of linear perspective, and leads to the break-up of the picture surface in Monet and Cézanne. It is a momentous development. In the same way, the incursion of aharmonic sonorities – including the 'exotic' harmonic colour which Debussy took from the gamelan orchestra – contributed decisively to the demise of the musical equivalent, the system of diatonic harmony; and thus Debussy's discoveries anticipated those of Schoenberg, and influenced both Bartók and Stravinsky who, between them, would completely overturn the sound of the music of the bourgeois public sphere in the nineteenth century.

7

Modernism, or *Nervenkunst*

Mahler

Like nationalism, the idea of the modern was a confusing and contradictory one. In 1894, the Viennese writer Hermann Bahr, one of the
group known as *Jung Wien* (Young Vienna), identified four distinct
and by no means compatible meanings of the term.[1] To be modern
was to pursue the urbane and artificial; or, to yearn feverishly for the
mysterious and mystical; or in Wagnerian fashion, to run to
unbounded emotion; or, finally, to practise *Nervenkunst* -- the art of
the nerves. While Bahr himself did most of these at one time or
another – Karl Kraus poked fun at him for changing his aesthetic and
political positions in the way most men change their shirts – what is
interesting about his formulation is how characteristic it is of Vienna,
the birthplace of psychoanalysis and the breeding-ground of modernism – the city, moreover, where music was the most universal art form
and the very model of subjectivity at the moment when it became the
representative locus of the altering subjectivity of modern European
culture. Carl Schorske, in his absorbing study of politics and culture
in *fin-de-siècle* Vienna, distinguishes two phases in the development of
modernism: the first characterized by growing Oedipal revolt against
the authority of the paternal culture; the second, after the turn of the
century, by breakthrough and rupture with the past, bringing the
explosive and revolutionary overthrow of the inherited artistic
language – the moment, in music, of the birth of atonality.[2] In the
passage from one to the other, traditional categories lost their clarity
and function; boundaries became indeterminate and artistic consciousness in the throes of crisis embraced the dissolution of the ego.
Plural modes of vision which blimpish bourgeois aesthetics had
blocked off were opened up. Time and space took on a new plasticity,

leading to the transformation of artistic chronotopes. In music, the exemplary figures in this process are Mahler and his spiritual son Schoenberg, possibly the two most nerve-racked composers in the history of music.

The Austrian metropolis, where these issues came to a head, was not only the musical capital of the German-speaking world; it also became the forcing-ground for diverse – often contradictory – intellectual and aesthetic preoccupations of decisive importance for twentieth-century culture. It was not only the city of Freud, Mahler, Klimt and the young Wittgenstein, but also that of the architects Otto Wagner and Adolf Loos, whose thinking prefigured the Bauhaus and modernist architecture; of the physicist and philosopher of science Ernst Mach, of special importance for his influence on Einstein; and the economist Karl Menger, whose theory of marginal utility – according to the intellectual historians Allan Janik and Stephen Toulmin – is 'so characteristically Viennese in its emphasis upon the psychological and subjective factors which underlie value'.[3] It was also a city with a large immigrant Jewish population, the city of Herzl and the birth of Zionism. In short, Vienna, like Paris, exemplified the multiple features of *fin-de-siécle* metropolitan life to an unusual degree. It was a city of many faces, a medley of ideologies, movements, parties and programmes, and several fictions about what it meant to be Viennese. It was a city of industrial and financial wealth rebuilt according to modern precepts of urban planning, which continued to outgrow itself and secrete proletarian slums; a city which, politically repressed, gave itself up to operettas and congenial *Gemütlichkeit*; a city of cafés where tightly knit groups of artists, musicians and writers were accustomed to meet and argue the issues of the day.

At the same time, Vienna's peculiarities, in the last decades of its rule over the hopelessly backward and unstable Habsburg Empire, gave a radically different slant to the experience of metropolitan modernity from that of Paris. For one thing, although there had been fighting on the city streets in 1848, when Metternich was put to flight, Vienna symbolized in the political realm the very opposite of Parisian revolutionism. Its very identity as a cosmopolitan metropolis was due to a policy of political compromise by which the imperial dynasty managed to shore up its rule. According to Janik and Toulmin, what we see in the political and social character of 'gay Vienna' in the last decades of the Habsburg monarchy is 'a superpower plagued by problems of rapid economic change and turbulent racial minorities, a power whose established constitutional structure was ... incapable of adapting itself to the novel demands of its changing historical situation'. As the stability implied by the outward show of the imperial regime became progressively more illusory, it became 'a petrified formality . . . barely capable of disguising the cultural chaos that lay beneath it'.[4] State and society were in contradiction. As Robert Musil put it in *The Man without Qualities*: 'By its constitution it was liberal, but its system of government was clerical. The system of government was clerical, but the general attitude to life was liberal.'[5] The rule of Franz-Josef was antidemocratic and deeply patriarchal, and the system was so repressive that in the view of Stefan Zweig, any thought or activity not in explicit conformity with traditional authority was liable to become a source of guilt.[6] Here was one of the sources of the intense anxieties which fed both psycho-analysis and artistic experiment.

This condition became so acute, say Janik and Toulmin, that on every side conventional public discourse was robbed of its capacity to perform its proper functions. From the language of politics to the principles of architectural design, the established forms and means of expression were divorced from their intended 'messages', and rhetoric, intellectualism, or aestheticism took their place. The disintegration of Austrian liberal values, squeezed out between the entrenched imperial court and the rise of the mass political parties, thus left its children with a narcissistic preoccupation with their psychic life; for the same reasons, their psychic life was prone to feelings of frustration and impotence. So the acceleration and fragmentation of modern metro-politan experience combined with economic crisis and the failure of liberal ideology to induce a crisis of culture; and in the city of Freud, as Schorske puts it, this crisis was characterized by collective Oedipal revolt and alienated narcissism.

Perhaps, says the historian Eric Hobsbawm, nothing better illustrates the identity crisis of bourgeois society in the years leading up the First World War than the history of the arts:

> Contemporaries, ever since Nietzsche, had no doubts that the crisis of the arts reflected the crisis of a society – the liberal bourgeois society of the nineteenth century – which in one way or another was in the process of destroying the bases of its existence, the systems of value, convention and intellectual understanding which structured and ordered it.[7]

A tension develops, first among the bohemian and then in the avant-garde; an estrangement between artistic innovation and the public sphere, and a growing contradiction between the critical and the normalizing functions of the cultural domain. Psychic perplexities which the political domain repressed found expression in artistic experiment, where they aroused the hostility of a congealed public sphere whose norms and susceptibilities were thereby attacked. The antagonism was mutual. It was also projected upon ideological shifts in the political domain, for the public sphere was strained when it came to sharing rights and privileges with the subaltern classes; and these, in lacking the education and cultural capital which the cultural sphere assumed in the public, helped to drive the avant-garde into isolation at the very moment of its bid to break with the past.

In musical Vienna, as in Paris, the salon still had its place. One of the great salons of *fin-de-siècle* Vienna was that of Karl Wittgenstein, leading industrialist and father of the future philosopher, whose childhood experience was thus peopled by musicians of the calibre of Joachim, Brahms, Mahler, Bruno Walter and Pablo Casals – no wonder music surfaces in Ludwig's philosophy as a paradigm of meaning and its puzzles. The public sphere, however, was dominated by its teaching institutions and the press, and by the Imperial Opera and the Philharmonic Orchestra where, from 1897, the commanding figure was Mahler. Born in 1860 in a village in Southern Bohemia, Mahler was brought up in the small town of Iglau (now Jihlava), about a hundred miles from Prague, a region within the Austro-Hungarian Empire associated with the struggle for Czech independence. His native tongue, however, was German, and he ranked as an Austrian subject of Jewish descent – in other words, he belonged to an Austrian minority among Bohemians and to a Jewish minority within the Austrian one. Years later, after serving his apprenticeship as a conductor in a series of positions the length and breadth of the German-speaking world, he expressed a deep sense of permanent dislocation in the most often-quoted of Mahler's aphorisms: 'I am thrice homeless, as a native of Bohemia in Austria, as an Austrian amongst Germans, and as a Jew throughout the world. Always an intruder, never welcomed.'

Iglau provided a favourable environment for a child as musically gifted as Mahler. It had a strong musical tradition dating back to the Mastersingers of the sixteenth century, and a school (which he attended) where the pupils had included Stamitz, Dussek and Smetana (the latter being not only the founder of Czech musical nationalism but also one of Mahler's favourite composers). There was a theatre where he could hear operas and operettas by composers from Mozart to Offenbach, and the Jewish child also belonged to a church choir which performed the masterworks of the classical composers like Mozart and Beethoven, whose rehearsals he sometimes accompanied on the piano and whose director gave him lessons in harmony. He thus arrived in Vienna at the age of fifteen to study at the Conservatoire with a wealth of musical experience already behind him.

In the music which he now began to compose, childhood and death quickly became major themes. In his late teens, he spent two years writing a large-scale cantata based on a popular folk tale that he may well have heard in childhood. *Das Klagende Lied* ('The Song of Lament') is the story of the singing bone which tells a tale of murder, familiar from fairy tales by Ludwig Bechstein and the Brothers Grimm, reminiscent of Heine's *Belsazar* and the medieval morality play *Jedermann*. Mahler wrote his own libretto, after an intense study of the literary sources. The work is steeped in the musical medievalism of Carl Maria von Weber, a predilection he shared with his friend the painter Gustav Klimt, leader of the dissident Secession and foremost Viennese exponent of *art nouveau*. The Secession, as its name implies, was an organized break with the authoritarian institutions of academic art. Mahler nevertheless invited one of its members, Alfred Roller, to join him as stage designer at the Opera when he himself was appointed director in 1897. The productions they mounted together – Mahler serving as his own producer – became a byword of modern staging.

The gallery built by the Secessionists the same year (and financed by Karl Wittgenstein) bore above its entrance the inscription TO THE AGE ITS ART, TO ART ITS FREEDOM. It was designed internally as an open space, externally as a strange new kind of ancient temple. Here, in 1902, the artists of the Secession held a group exhibition around a much-fêted contemporary statue of Beethoven by the Leipzig artist Max Klinger, an exalted image of the composer as a Promethean. For the opening, Mahler conducted a performance of the Choral Symphony in a specially condensed arrangement. In retrospect, the whole affair is like the last public act of affirmation of the past before the moment when artistic revolution breaks out.

Mahler as a public figure expressed pan-German – indeed, pan-European – sentiments, but his music constantly harks back to his Bohemian Jewish origins. It is marked throughout by the poignant alternation of major and minor which is characteristic of Bohemian folk music. According to one testimony, there is a striking similarity between the jaunty march tune of the First Symphony which interrupts the parody funeral march, and the Hatschô, a characteristic dance of the Iglau district. But it is more than a question of musical archaeology. It is not as if the music contains only a few such traces; it is so full of them that it would seem beside the point to uncover their origins individually. The entire fabric of Mahler's music is a weird tapestry woven of the most disparate threads, made up of popular and cultured musics of every genre, apparently combined in such an indiscriminate and illogical manner that many of his first listeners could find nothing coherent in it at all. As Adorno puts it in his peerless study of the composer, from this potpourri of shop-soiled music, from this mixture of melodic scraps from the classics and the most hackneyed popular tunes, lumped together with unsettling fanfares and bandstand music, Mahler constructs what amounts to a new musical language, in which the fragments acquire a new life. The unity of this second language is created by the very laceration of the borrowed material, through the impression of familiarity it brings with it. In this way, says Adorno, Mahler pitilessly denounces the illusion that the reconciliation of contraries is possible in a non-reconciled world.[8]

For this stylistic amalgam, Mahler offers a striking image of his own, which again takes us back to his childhood. Natalie Bauer-Lechner recalls a visit they made together to a fair, with swings, shooting-galleries and puppet shows, where barrel-organs blared out from merry-go-rounds while a military band and a men's chorus were performing separately, creating an incredible musical pandemonium. Mahler exclaimed:

> You hear? That's polyphony, and that's where I get it from! Even when I was quite a small child, in the woods at Iglau, this sort of thing used to move me strangely, and impressed itself upon me. For it's all the same whether heard in a din like this or in the singing of thousands of birds; in the howling of the storm, the lapping of the waves, or the crackling of the fire. Just in this way – *from quite different directions* – must the themes appear; and they may be just as different from each other in rhythm and melodic character . . . The only difference is that the artist orders and unites them all into one coherent and harmonious whole.[9]

This is a very modern way of hearing. Charles Ives heard the world in the same way, and John Cage after him, with the difference that the Americans, in the end, abandoned the artistic aim of welding these disparate elements into a cohesive totality.

Mahler's music never repeats itself. In Adorno's words, 'he never says the same thing in the same way'. Or as Deryck Cooke puts it, a Mahler theme is 'one continuous, seamless melody, which never retraces its tracks'.[10] It is the clash of leaping counterpoints, the vivid orchestration, the irregular length of the phrases and the resulting rhythmic contractions, which together account for 'the pungent Mahlerian personality', half-affectionate, half-satirical, full of key switches which 'disrupt the tonality of the melody so severely that it seems as if it will never find its way back to the main key'.[11] For Adorno, Mahler's 'tenaciouos idiosyncrasy' of playing with the alternation between major and minor not only gives the music its sense of heartbreak but imbues it with a modal feel.[12] Leonard Bernstein once demonstrated this in a television essay on Mahler. He showed how Mahler often had resort to the 'heart-rending' semitones of the Phrygian mode that belong equally to Arabic music; to flamenco, with its Moorish influence; and to klezmer, the music of itinerant Jewish musicians in Eastern Europe, which combines the ancient modal traces that are found in peasant music from Croatia to Georgia. He pinpointed a paradigmatic instance of these Phrygian melodic twists in the song *Das irdische Leben* ('Earthly Life'), which protests the death of a child from poverty and starvation in its constant chromatic wheeling; it sounds, says Bernstein, like a child of the ghetto.

The personality which could bind all these widely disparate elements together provoked in certain of Mahler's detractors a racist response. According to a certain Rudolf Louis in an item published in Munich in 1909:

> If Mahler's music spoke Yiddish, it would be perhaps unintelligible to me. But it is repulsive to me because it *acts* Jewish. This is to say that it speaks musical German, but with an accent, with an inflection, and above all, with the gestures of an eastern, all too eastern Jew. So, even to those whom it does not offend directly, it cannot possibly communicate anything. One does not have to be repelled by Mahler's artistic personality in order to realize the complete emptiness and vacuity of an art in which the spasm of an impotent mock-Titanism reduces itself to a frank gratification of common seamstress-like sentimentality.[13]

Mahler's biographers correctly emphasize the growth of anti-Semitism which dogged the rising tide of Jewish social participation in Vienna. They are generally vague, however, about the extent of Mahler's Yiddishkeit, his Jewish culture, accepting the cynical judgement of Alma Mahler in her memoirs. 'The Jewish question', she says, 'touched Mahler very closely. He had often suffered bitterly from it.' He never denied his Jewish origin, but showed a certain leaning, she says, towards Catholic mysticism, 'whereas the Jewish ritual had never meant anything to him'.[14] But this can be misleading, and it would be simpler if he had never written the Second Symphony, with its setting of Klopstock's *Resurrection* Ode. Theodor Reik has shown that Mahler did not take over the poem Klop, stock and barrel, but adapted it, omitting stanzas and altering it so as to remove its 'theological message, its eschatology'.[15] Add to this the fact that the Nietzschean pantheism of the Third Symphony which followed is the very converse of Catholic orthodoxy, and the circumstances suggest that when Mahler became a convert to Catholicism early in 1897, it was not from conviction but in order to secure the post of the Director of the Vienna Opera. (In the same circumstances and the same Vienna, Freud, who was neither more nor less Jewish than Mahler, resolutely refused the well-meaning advice of Christian friends to convert, knowing that this would imperil the appointment he desperately wanted; and somewhere it is said that he was privately critical of Mahler.)

Biographers find the mix of religious elements in Mahler's childhood confusing, but here the facts are straightfoward. If the child was allowed to sing in a church choir, his parents' attachment to their religion clearly did not extend as far as the rabbinic prohibition against Christian music; and the synagogue they attended, if they did so, would have belonged to the German reformist movement, not to the more orthodox tradition. Adorno allows that Hebraic melodies, both sacred and profane, turn up in Mahler's music, but its Jewish feel, he says, is much more than this: a spiritual quality, intangible in its detail but pervasive at the highest level.[16] Jews retain a certain sensitivity to these questions. Leonard Bernstein is guilty of projective identification – of reading his own susceptibilities into his hero – when he finds that because Mahler lied about his conversion, backdating it several years, he was not so much ashamed of being a Jew as ashamed of being ashamed. Perhaps. But he was evidently right when he demonstrated at the piano the proximity of various passages in Mahler to certain traits of popular Yiddish culture.

What both these versions leave out, however, is Mahler's affinity with what the historian Isaac Deutscher called the marginal identity of the non-Jewish Jew, the type of Jewish heretic whose prototype was the Enlightenment philosopher Spinoza.[17] Baruch (Benedict) Spinoza, the scion of a Netherlands family of Marranos (Spanish and Portuguese Jews expelled by the Inquisition), educated in a *yeshiva* (a religious seminary), was excommunicated in 1656 by the Amsterdam Beth-Din, the Jewish religious court, for his secular and pantheistic thinking, which married Kabbalistic ideas with Cartesian philosophy. For such a mind, to leave the ancient faith behind to enter the world of embattled Christendom only affirms a vocation for philosophical and cultural critique. It is not, in other words, some special 'Jewish genius' that is responsible for the decisive contributions to modern culture of thinkers and artists of this mould – Marx, Freud, Wittgenstein, Mahler, Schoenberg, Kafka, Chagall, Modigliani, and the rest – but the fact of living on the borderlines between cultures, nations and religions, exposed to all their contradictions. Placed at the concatenation of different cultures and ideologies, struggling with internal conflicts which they are forced to negotiate daily, Jewish intellectuals conceive reality as a dynamic process, and see society in a state of contradiction and flux. This condition was especially acute in *fin-de-siècle* Vienna.

It is Mahler's lieder which contain the most explicit expression of his sense of social critique, especially those, like *Das irdische Leben*, which come from the folk collection *Das Knaben Wunderhorn* ('The Youth's Magic Horn'). Despite the Romantic medievalism of this anthology, published many decades earlier, Mahler discovers in his settings of these texts what the historian E.P. Thompson, in another context, calls a Brechtian sense of solidarity with the oppressed, of the tenacity of self-preservation, and of irony in the face of homilies from on high.[18] Moreover, the world of these songs is in no way separate from that of the symphonies, for the musical motifs are the same, and Mahler frequently borrowed from the former to provide material for the latter (indeed, vocal settings of *Knaben Wunderhorn* texts occur in both the Third and Fourth Symphonies).

The affinity between Mahler and his chosen verses is an expression of the presentiment he finds in them – doubtless inspired by the misery he saw around him as a child – of the underlying barbarity of imperial rule, in which soldiers are simultaneously representatives of an occupying force, and as much its victims as the civilian population. As Adorno puts it, Mahler 'pleads musically on behalf of peasant cunning against their masters; of those who go AWOL at the prospect of marriage; of those who live on the margins, of jailbirds, the children of poverty, the persecuted, losers'.[19] Moreover, in taking the music of the people to provide his own work with its musical iconology, he refuses to romanticize the image of those for whom he sings. In Adorno's opinion, the vulgarity into which a composer like Tchaikovsky falls involuntarily becomes in Mahler 'a provocative alliance with vulgar music', in which 'the low-brow elements erupt upon the elevated style with Jacobin violence'.[20] Through this direct affront, Mahler speaks to the bourgeoisie of its coming doom; in Tchaikovsky it is only the composer himself who is doomed.

Mahler's disapproval of Tchaikovsky's subjectivity, as of programme music in general, expresses the same philosophical suspicion as Nietzsche's towards the composer who 'recites to us the entire chromatic scale of his passions and appetites', or to music that tries to 'beguile the listener with external analogies'.[21] Any such tone-painting, says Nietzsche, is at the opposite pole from the deep 'mythopoeic power' in music. It is here that Mahler makes his stand, equally distant from the antiprogrammatic nature of Brahms or Bruckner or the aesthetics of Hanslick. For Mahler conceives the symphony – and its chronotope – in a completely different way from anyone before him. He gives it a narrative quality uniquely akin to the novel. This is the real significance of his well-known remark to Sibelius that the symphony 'must be like the world, it must embrace everything'.[22] There is also the matter of his special sympathy for Dostoevsky and the Russian novelist's treatment of the tragic meaning of life. This is not simply a question of Mahler's pessimistic outlook and Dostoevsky-like pity for human suffering, but of the musical language itself. In the same way as in an epic novel, says Adorno, 'the musical material is prosaic, the discourse sublime'.[23] Furthermore, Mahler's sense of form (or lack of it, in the eyes of his critics) is also, like that of the novel, a question of scale and duration. It is not just that Mahler treats symphonic form with a freedom more typical of prose narration, but the characteristic way in which the music drives towards catastrophe – unless this is averted by some chance intervention; or how, whenever suffering seems to recede behind a moment of good humour, this is soon interrupted by the menace of some fresh anxiety.

Mahler was not unique in combining the influence of Nietzsche with socialistic leanings. During his student years in Vienna he was drawn into a group of young intellectual tyros known as the Pernerstorfer Circle (after the editor of the group's newspaper), which revolved around the teachings of Schopenhauer, Wagner and Nietzsche and which, under the influence of a curious article by the ageing Wagner, became, for a period, vegetarian. This group formed an inner circle within the Vienna German Students' Reading Club *Leseverein der deutschen Studenten Wiens* to which Freud also belonged. In 1877 the *Leseverein* wrote a collective letter to Nietzsche to tell him of their devotion to his philosophy, especially his *Schopenhauer as Educator*.

Prominent in the *Leseverein* and later as a leader of the Austrian Social Democrats, the popular party of the Left, was Viktor Adler, who became a lifelong friend of Mahler. In 1882, Adler was one of the young intellectuals on the radical wing of the liberals who broke away and drafted the so-called Linz Programme. Adler had been a medical student with Freud, and his experience as a young doctor treating the poor in Vienna radicalized him and turned him towards Marxism; he became the organizing spirit behind the formation of the Austrian Social Democrat Party in 1888, and a delegate to several International

Socialist Workers' congresses. A correspondent at that time of Friedrich Engels, he later gravitated towards the opportunistic wing of the Second International. Ironically, this is the same Adler who cropped up in what Freud called his 'Revolutionary Dream', the night after seeing Count Thun in the railway terminal, when he found himself whistling Mozart.[24] Schorske mentions that Freud, in analysing this dream, 'recalled having defied Adler, toward whom he had had strong feelings of envy and rivalry, in a German nationalist student organisation to which they both belonged in the 1870s'.[25] There is no hint that Freud and Mahler met as students, but the dream-link is intriguing. Revealing Mahler, Viktor Adler and Freud as contemporaneous members of the same radical pan-German student society, it not only shows how closely knit was the young Viennese intelligentsia of the 1870s. If Freud was the relative outsider (because he wasn't musical and couldn't take Wagner), nevertheless it makes it 'inconceivable', as one biographer puts it, 'that Freud ... was as totally uninfluenced by Schopenhauer and Nietzsche as he liked to think'.[26] Conversely, it presents us with Mahler as a figure who is like Freud with music added. But in that case, what we shall find of special interest in Mahler is not the individual psychobiography, but rather, given the iconic nature of his musical language, music as a form of social psychoanalysis.

Mahler also retained a political sympathy for the Left which was lacking in Freud. Alma recounts a touching indication of it which occurred in 1905. The composer Pfitzner rudely left a rehearsal of Mahler's and returned to the Mahlers' apartment. He arrived in a terrible temper:

> It was the first of May and he had met a procession of working-men ... Furious at the sight of proletarian faces, he darted down a side street and scarcely felt safe from pursuit in my room. Mahler soon followed ... He was too happy to care [about Pfitzner]: he too had met the procession ... and had even accompanied it for some distance. They had all looked at him in so brotherly a way – they *were* his brothers – and they were the future! That was enough to start the battle. It raged for hours, with ill-nature on both sides and me in the middle.[27]

(Mahler did not live to see Pfitzner become a Nazi.)

Mahler came to Nietzsche and *Das Knaben Wunderhorn* at about the same time; the one meshed with the other, for this is the anthology which Nietzsche praises in *The Birth of Tragedy* as a prime example of the Dionysian element in folk song, whose multicoloured images, with their rapid pace and abrupt transitions, are in 'the most marked contrast to the equable movement, the calm illusion, of epic verse'.[28]

In the two vocal movements of the Third Symphony, Nietzsche and *Das Knaben Wunderhorn* stand side by side. First a solo contralto intones the Midnight Song from *Also Sprach Zarathustra* ('O man, take heed/What does the deep midnight tell . . . The world is deep/And deeper than the day would think . . .'), then, in complete contrast, she is joined by a chorus of women's and children's voices, singing a ditty about a trio of angels who set the heavens ringing with joy and delight at their song. The depth of human despair is matched by a parodistic heaven (an image repeated in the last movement of the Fourth Symphony). Mahler originally thought of calling the Third Symphony *Meine fröliche Wissenschaft*, after the title of another work by Nietzsche, 'The Gay Science'. He wrote to a correspondent about the conception behind it: 'for me Nature includes all that is terrifying, great and also lovely . . : I always feel it strange that when most people speak of "Nature" what they mean is flowers, little birds, the scent of the pinewoods, etc. No one knows the god Dionysus, or great Pan.'[29]

This appropriation of the Dionysian bespeaks a much more profound grasp of Nietzsche than Richard Strauss's symphonic poem on Zarathustra which, in spite of its advanced musical idiom, is puny by comparison. Some of Mahler's biographers, however, are perplexed about the Nietzschean influence in his work because a few years after this symphony, when he was courting Alma, he got so angry (she tells us) at finding a complete edition of Nietzsche in her library that he 'demanded abruptly that it should be cast then and there into the fire'. (She sensibly refused, and told him that 'if his abhorrence had any justification it would be easy to convince me'.)[30] Opinions differ concerning the reasons for this rejection; Mahler would certainly have found Nietzsche's condemnation of Wagner displeasing, but this was already old news at the time of the Third Symphony. What really turned him off Nietzsche – and shows the integrity of his socialistic leanings – was the concept of the *Übermensch*; as he put it to Alma in a letter afterwards: 'the whole deceitful and viciously shameless immorality of Nietzsche's [idea of the] superiority of an elite'.[31]

In the summer of 1910 (the year before he died) Mahler, distressed about the state of his relationship with Alma, was urged by a relative of hers, a psychoanalyst, to consult Sigmund Freud; Freud was an acquaintance of her family and already knew Alma personally. Both Alma and Ernest Jones give accounts of what happened, and Theodor Reik devotes a chapter to it. Freud was on holiday in Holland, where Mahler contacted him by telegram. Three times Freud gave Mahler appointments and Mahler called them off. Finally Freud, who naturally recognized this behaviour as symptomatic, summoned him with the message that this was his last chance for the present, as he was about to go off on a trip. 'So they met in a hotel in Leyden,' says Jones, 'and then spent four hours strolling through the town and conducting a sort of psychoanalysis. Although Mahler had had no previous contact with psychoanalysis, Freud said he had never met anyone who seemed to understand it so swiftly.'

In the course of the conversation Mahler suddenly realized why he constantly interrupted the flow of his music with:

> the intrusion of some common-place melody. His father, apparently a brutal person, treated his wife very badly, and when Mahler was a young boy there was a specially painful scene between them. It became quite unbearable to the boy, who rushed away from the house. At that moment, however, a hurdy-gurdy in the street was grinding out the popular Viennese air 'Ach, du lieber Augustin'. In Mahler's opinion the conjunction of high tragedy and light amusement was from then on inextricably fixed in his mind, and the one mood inevitably brought the other with it.[32]

Ironically, Mahler never used this tune, but Schoenberg did, in his Second String Quartet.

It is hardly surprising if the various factors to emerge in Mahler's meeting with Freud have tempted so many writers to psychoanalyse his music. The most curious attempt is undoubtedly that of Reik, a Viennese-trained psychoanalyst who found himself haunted by snatches from Mahler's Second Symphony, which led to an obsession with Mahler; the book is the result. The different interpretations are mostly Freudian, emphasizing one or other aspect of Oedipal revolt, but one or two incline to the psychodynamic theories of Melanie Klein and D.W. Winnicott, which emphasize maternal links.[33] Adorno warns of the dangers: that musical signifiers and those of the world they may seem to be modelled upon are not to be confused with each other; in musical space they have another dimension. But if, he continues, the interior space of music does not so much express – that is, *externalize* – an internal content but, on the contrary, assimilates external reality, then this also means that 'psychoanalytic theory is right to interpret music as a means of defence against paranoia: it protects the subject from submersion in reality by means of subjective projection'.[34] But this subjective projection is not a private matter for the composer, because music serves the same functions for the listener. According to Winnicott, the aspects of the infant's confrontation with reality which are internalized in the course of psychodynamic conflict reappear in cultural products in the symbolization of schizoid experiences, so that on this reading Mahler's 'almost schizoid' inner tensions and strivings deal with the same problems as the wider social disintegration of the time – what Schorske calls the crisis of the liberal ego: 'the groping for orientation in a world without secure coordinates' by a generation in the throes of Oedipal revolt.[35]

Mahler saw exactly how the musical establishment – and there was none more socially powerful than the Viennese – ideologized music, and he resisted with a streak of black humour which was responsible for moments of satire and parody more biting and grotesque than in any music before him. With determination and even savagery, he attacked the hierarchy of forms which had once been fluid but were now congealed into rigid conventions. His music was duly decried, the critics declaring that any composer who used such material as he did was evidently lacking in inspiration. This did not worry him unduly. On the contrary, he scoffed back at them with parodies of academic musical procedures like counterpoint and fugue – the very devices Brahms had treated so respectfully – burlesquing the musical and social establishment in one fell swoop. He played havoc with everything which that establishment regarded as sacrosanct – even when he himself was deadly serious – and did so in the name of an art which would joyfully, positively, defiantly embrace everyone and the force of life itself: a full-blown Dionysian vision.

Mahler does not express only an acute sense of *fin-de-siècle* alienation. Where Brahms escaped into the past, and Tchaikovsky remained enclosed within his own surcharged emotionalism, Mahler has a unique and original sense of objectivity, which doubtless comes from his combined awareness of the outer and inner worlds. Adorno considered it not the least of Mahler's merits that he turned the wound within himself into the aesthetic means of expression of objective contradictions. Subjectivity in Mahler is not the seismograph of the soul that it becomes in Expressionism – especially in certain works by Schoenberg, Berg and Bartók – but the arena of objective events whose origins, lost in the unconscious, keep breaking through to the surface. That is why Mahler understood psychoanalysis so readily; he had already psychoanalysed himself in his own music. His symphonies are like a musical talking cure.

If Mahler's music presupposes a soul that inspires it in the same way as Tchaikovsky's, then it does not remain imprisoned in the private individual who makes the music merely an instrument of personal expression. Even when Mahler seems to be speaking in the first person, says Adorno, the I that speaks, like the latent I of the literary narrative, 'is separate from the person who writes the work across the chasm of the aesthetic'. He cites Schoenberg on the Ninth Symphony in evidence: 'most strange . . . the author hardly speaks as an individual any longer. It almost seems as though this work must have a concealed author who used Mahler merely as his spokesman, as his mouthpiece.'[36]

'My time will come in fifty years,' Mahler once said of himself, more ironically than prophetically. In the 1970s, Pierre Boulez asked: 'Are we drawn to Mahler's music only because he knew how to convey accurately certain sentimental, bizarre reflections on a damned world? Would that be enough to retain and enthrall us?'[37] Mahler, he says, is much more than the last representative of a certain tradition, even though he still belongs to a world by then incapable of renewing itself, obsessed with forms of expression that reflected a disappearing social order. This music that was once rejected as too ambiguous is now esteemed precisely for its ambiguity. It has become for us a document – a source – in which we perceive the birth of a process of transformation and transmutation which yields up our own point of departure.

Schoenberg

Freud voiced the sentiments of a whole generation when he placed a rebellious motto, taken from Virgil's *Aeneid*, on the title page of *The Interpretation of Dreams*: 'Flectere si nequeo superos, Acheronta movebo.' Roughly translated (Acheron being one of the rivers of Hades): 'If I cannot bend the higher powers, I shall stir up hell.' We can think of the publication of this book in 1899 (but bearing the more symbolic date 1900) as a signal confirmation of the dominant subjective feelings to permeate the society which produced it, indeed, the pivot of the altering subjectivity of modern European society. As well as establishing a new theoretical paradigm in psychiatry, *The Interpretation of Dreams* points to the constant anxiety of a world where social being provides only a false identity; where individual experience – hidden from view by the forms of social existence – becomes neurotic; and sexuality suffers not only frustration and the defeat of desire, but loss of contact with both inner and outer reality. Exposing such home truths, Freud's ideas could hardly fail to arouse fear and repulsion, as his own reasoning predicated. However, by probing the depths of the psyche with therapeutic intent, and revealing the signs in conscious psychic life of primal experience and behaviour, psychoanalysis not only allowed access to the irrational mentality hidden behind the mask of rational civilization, but contributed decisively to the revaluation of instinct – a quest scientifically sanctioned by Darwin in which poets, artists and composers were also implicated. As Freud himself once said: 'Not I, but the poets, discovered the unconscious'. It is no accident, then, if, in the cauldron of late Habsburg Vienna, psychoanalysis articulated the same sense of frustrated impulse and instinctual insight that nurtured artistic movements like Symbolism and Expressionism; or that – despite Freud's unmusicality – it should also show an affinity to the emergence of atonal music. Nor did the fascination of psycho-analysis depend on a theoretical grasp of its principles. For Schoen-berg's generation its preoccupations were part of the intellectual discourse of the day. To this ambience of instinctive and unconscious desire and frustration also belong the psychosexual themes of operas like *Salome* and *Elektra*, by Richard Strauss, the latter to a libretto by Hugo von Hofmannsthal; *Wozzeck* and *Lulu* by Alban Berg, based on plays by Franz Wedekind; and only a little further afield, in Budapest, Bartók's *Duke Bluebeard's Castle* to a libretto by Béla Balázs. Indeed, music after Wagner was especially apt, says Adorno, for the expression of these intimations. In this sense Schoenberg could hardly help but be a Freudian.

It was not until the 1920s that psychoanalysis achieved world renown, but in Vienna, Freud, like Schoenberg, was already infamous long before the First World War. His influence in his home city was greater than many of his biographers have allowed for; it was disseminated not only by the reports of his associates but also through his patients. Its sphere included musical circles. In one famous case history, published in 1909, the patient, 'Little Hans', was the child of the music critic of the *Neues Wiener Journal*, Max Graf, who was a member of the 'Wednes-day Psychological Society', the discussion group which began to meet in Freud's consulting rooms in 1902. To provide the libretto for *Erwartung*, Schoenberg turned to a young woman, Marie Pappenheim, whose combination of talents was fully characteristic of her place and time. About twenty-six years old when she entered the Schoenberg circle, in around 1908, Pappenheim was a medical student who had had some poems published by Kraus in *Die Fackel*. Schoenberg asked her if she would write him a libretto; she responded, drawing on her knowledge of psychoanalysis, with the monodrama of a woman search-ing for her lover in a wood at night, who eventually discovers his bloody corpse – whether real or fantasized is uncertain; perhaps the whole thing is a dream or, rather, a nightmare.

The concentrated language of the libretto is an extraordinary interior narrative of high avant-garde intent, an early example of the stream-of-consciousness technique. It has practically no grammatically complete sentences – the fragmented phrases are linked only by free-association, like the flow from a patient on the psychoanalyst's couch. Only free association music could hope to deal with such a text, and Schoenberg composed it in seventeen frenetic days of white-hot inspiration – a fact mentioned by several critics, as if it explained why the work resists musicological analysis. It only seems this way, however, because in this case the musicologist is looking for the wrong thing: Schoenberg derives his musical structure directly and only from the text. While the woman wanders distractedly through the forest, the music runs the gamut of her emotions – often within the space of a few bars – from subdued calm and self-reassurance to nervous tantrums and shrieking hysteria. Adorno believed that here the passions are no longer simulated but are registered without disguise through the medium of music. Like all the early atonal works, he says, *Erwartung* is like the dream case study of psychoanalysis.[38]

Schoenberg a Freudian? Yes and no. There is a puzzle here. Schoenberg's biographer Stuckenschmidt mentions in passing that from 1913 onwards Schoenberg kept a catalogue of his books. Among the literary authors he listed were numerous volumes of Balzac (12), Dehmel (10), Rilke (9), Kraus (12), Ibsen (5), George (11), Hauptmann (6), Maeterlinck (18), Strindberg (28); in philosophy, Kant (11), Schopenhauer (6), Bergson, Nietzsche and Plato (4 each). But as Stuckenschmidt laconically observes, Schoenberg never possessed any book of psychoanalysis,[39] despite his psychological acuity in the matter of musical theory, and *Erwartung*'s clear and strong affinity to psychoanalytic methodology. Indeed, in the whole of Schoenberg's voluminous writings, he refers to Freud only when he mentions his name as one of the Jewish intellectuals vilified, like himself, by the Nazis – while Kraus, who was another, is mentioned several times. In short, while Schoenberg could compose *Erwartung*, he was never a Freudian.

The puzzle is all the greater when one remembers that his devoted pupils Berg and Webern, like their shared musical mentor Mahler, both had crucial encounters with psychoanalysis. Berg was highly impressed by Freud when he was treated by him in 1908 – they were both holidaying in the same place – for an asthma attack, and according to his pupil Willi Reich, he came to believe that music was the 'representation and illumination of the unconscious'.[40] That this was not just a vague feeling is demonstrated by the psychological acuity of his two operas *Wozzeck* and *Lulu*. As for Webern, he was psychoanalysed in 1913 for a period of three months by Alfred Adler, and wrote several letters to Schoenberg about the experience; however, since he was somewhat suspicious and resistant, Adler was able to give him only limited assistance in dealing with the acute hypochondria which kept on making him genuinely ill, so that he often had to withdraw from conducting engagements.

It is Schoenberg's allegiance to Kraus that explains his resistance to psychoanalysis. Kraus was more than a satirist; he was a philosopher in satirical garb, with a philosophy of language which – if Janik and Toulmin are right – strongly influenced Wittgenstein. In Kraus's philosophy, language, being the vehicle of thought, belonged first and foremost to the moral world. The fallacies of someone's logic, the very defects of their character, were reflected in the way they expressed themselves – indeed, in the very structure of their sentences; to expose these defects was to expose the corruption of the spirit by which Vienna was plagued. Obviously, only absolute moral integrity could produce authentic art, free from the hypocrisy that was inseparable from the contemporary malaise. (To Kraus, Offenbach was genuine but Lehár was a fraud.) The implication of this stance is to link the critique of language with ethics and artistic utterance with personal integrity, and for Kraus the aesthetic form and the moral content of the work of art were totally identified with each other. He therefore shared with Schoenberg, Loos and Kandinsky the disavowal of aestheticism and, like them, indicted the loss of integrity produced by aesthetic decoration and ornament. And at first he thought that Freud's concerns were in line with his own.

There was a crucial difference, however. Kraus was antiscientistic, and spiritually conservative to boot (Freud was never that, but a pessimist). Philosophically an idealist, Kraus had no wish to deny the recognition of the unconscious as the source of creativity – quite the contrary – but Freud's conception of it was the exact antithesis of his own, even if both found their ideas prefigured by Nietzsche. Freud's id was a seething mass of irrational, egocentric, antisocial impulses which could at best be held at bay by reason; aesthetic and moral values were the result of frustration, the very product, through sublimation, of the socialization of these impulses. To Kraus, this amounted to an inadmissible break with creative fantasy as the source of both individual and social health. (As for his famous aphorism which holds that 'psychoanalysis is the disease of which it purports to be the cure', Freud himself was quite as capable of the same sense of irony; in 1909, on a visit to the United States, he remarked sardonically to his fellow-travellers Jung and Ferenczi: 'We are bringing them the plague.')[41]

Schoenberg – whose holistic sense of the psychological domain came far closer to Kraus than to Freud, and who wanted so desperately to believe in the ethical character of his own undertaking – was caught, in

Freudian terms, between the Scylla and Charybdis of his id and his superego: the compulsion to be true to the inner life in the face of the rule of musical law. Intellectual integrity demanded the affirmation of the role of unconscious compulsion: 'The artist's creative activity is instinctive,' he wrote.

> Consciousness has little influence on it. He feels as if what he does were dictated to him. As if he did it only according to the will of some power or other within him, whose laws he does not know. He is merely the instrument of a will hidden from him, of instinct ... this intuition, moreover, is dependent upon preconditions, upon the influence of my inborn and acquired culture.[42]

He therefore pinned his colours to the ethical wager that somewhere within these depths law and instinct meet, and the musical explanation must also be psychological. For Schoenberg, therefore, the composer need only seek to be musically truthful, and should not consciously aim at beauty and aesthetic effect. The artist attains to beauty without willing it, he says, *because* he is striving after truthfulness. Beauty with a capital B 'exists only from that moment in which the unproductive begin to miss it. Before that it does not exist, for the artist does not need it. To him integrity is enough. To him it is enough to have expressed himself ... according to the laws of *his* nature.'[43]

The results sometimes provoked tumult in the audience, like the orchestral concert Schoenberg conducted in Vienna on 31 March 1913 which ended in a commotion comparable only with the first perform-ance in Paris, just two months later, of Stravinsky's *Rite of Spring*. The Vienna programme consisted of new works by Webern, Zemlinsky, Schoenberg and Berg, with some Mahler to finish off, but the Mahler was never reached – the performance had to be called off. Each successive work only produced more laughter and increasing uproar as detractors and supporters battled with each other, exchanging insults and fisticuffs, until finally the audience stormed the platform. A lawsuit followed in which a doctor who was called as a witness gave it as his opinion that the effect of such music on a large part of the public was 'enervating and injurious to the nervous system ... and that many of the audience showed exterior signs of deep mental depression'.[44]

Despite such scenes, Schoenberg always saw himself as a reluctant revolutionary, who knew that the course he pursued was not merely private and personal. But it was only because he had the highest conception of his calling that this ideologically conservative composer arrived at the overthrow of tonality. What we see in Schoenberg is the relentless pursuit of the critique of musical language carried through to its logical conclusion as if this were the only ethical way to proceed – like a musical Wittgenstein, with his vision of the logic of logic.

The same sensitivity towards colour that we find in Debussy plays a large part in the powerful attraction that the music of Schoenberg held for the group of Expressionist painters in Munich before the First World War who called themselves *Die Blaue Reiter* ('The Blue Rider') – an attraction which led to the composer's participation in their activities. There is a deep affinity between Schoenberg's theory of the emancipation of dissonance and Kandinsky's concerning the emancipation of colour, and it is no accident that the two of them formed a close personal relationship precisely at the moment when the composer was evolving atonality and the painter abstraction. Their association before the Great War is a pivotal example of cross-currents between the different arts, like Debussy's with Mallarmé.

It was Vassily Kandinsky, the Russian expatriate leader of the Munich Expressionists, who discovered the affinity when he read an extract from *Harmonielehre* while he himself was writing the essay *Concerning the Spiritual in Art*. Here Kandinsky not only advances ideas in a Symbolist vein about the fundamental spiritual unity of the arts; more importantly, he presents the first sustained argument for abstraction in painting. Reading Schoenberg led him to believe that he had found a kindred spirit, and hearing Schoenberg's music at a chamber concert in Munich at the beginning of 1911 convinced him of it. He wrote to the composer, saying: '[the] independent life of the individual voices in your compositions is exactly what I'm trying to find in my painting'.[45] Another member of the group, Franz Marc, who was also hearing Schoenberg's music for the first time, wrote to a third, August Macke:

> The audience behaved like rabble, like silly children; they snuffled and coughed, giggled and squirmed so that it was difficult to follow the music. Can you imagine music in which tonality (that is, the maintenance of a key) is completely abandoned? I kept thinking of Kandinsky's great composition, which hasn't any tonality either . . .

Each tone in the music, he said, speaks for itself – like Kandinsky's 'springing spots' which stand out from the white canvas: 'Schoenberg works on the principle that consonance and dissonance don't exist at all. So-called dissonance is only a consonance which has been stretched.' And like themselves, Marc concluded, he seemed convinced of the dissolution of the laws of European art and harmony.[46]

When Kandinsky discovered that Schoenberg also painted, some of his work was included in the first *Blaue Reiter* exhibition. The following year, 1912, the group published an Almanac which included reproductions of two of Schoenberg's paintings and, along with songs by Berg and Webern, the score of *Herzgewächse* ('Foliage of the Heart'). This short piece of vocal chamber music is an exquisite atonal setting for high soprano, celesta, harmonium and harp of mystical verses by Maurice Maeterlinck (the author of *Pelléas et Mélisande*, the Symbolist play which inspired several composers of the period: Fauré and Sibelius wrote incidental music for it, Debussy turned it into an opera and Schoenberg wrote a symphonic poem). The instrumentation of *Herzgewächse* reflects Schoenberg's experiments in tone-colour-painting; the text expresses a powerful leaning towards spiritual symbolism which also strongly appealed to Kandinsky. For both of them, colour was at one and the same time the plastic material of composition and a symbolic domain, and their interest in each other's medium was a function of this mutual perception.

While Schoenberg, as an amateur painter, had a certain talent for the bizarre,[47] Kandinsky was a gifted amateur musician influenced by the mystic (and socialistic) Russian composer Scriabin. He shared with Scriabin the gift of synaesthesia, the mental association of colour and musical sound which was explored during the same period by a number of psychologists (indeed, it appears that this whole generation was especially sensitive to these qualities). Scriabin went so far as to devise a table in which colours were listed against chords and, in his *Prometheus* Symphony, to employ the projection of coloured light in the performance. Schoenberg and Kandinsky pursued the same path, quite independently of each other, in their two experimental theatre pieces, Schoenberg's *Die glückliche Hand* ('The Hand of Fate') and Kandinsky's *Der gelbe Klang* ('The Yellow Sound', for which Thomas von Hartmann wrote the music); both are highly symbolic pieces of Expressionist music theatre, a mixture of psychological depth and literary pretension almost impossible to bring off successfully, in which, among other things, colour projection is written into the stage directions. Schoenberg, says Stuckenschmidt, wanted this piece to have 'the greatest unreality', to be a 'play with apparitions of colours and forms', and suggested as the designer Kokoschka, Kandinsky or Roller (Mahler's designer at the Opera).[48]

Central to Kandinsky's aesthetic was the essentially abstract nature of musical expression. Kandinsky argued that just as notes are the autonomous material of music, colour and form should be considered as the material of painting independent of representation (and hence of tradition). For Schoenberg, tone-colour is one of the three necessary properties of every musical sound, along with pitch and intensity, and therefore deserved in turn to be treated as an independent quality. While Kandinsky spoke of certain visual effects in painting as *Farben-klänge*, 'colour-sounds', Schoenberg spoke of the converse, *Klangfarben*, 'sound-colours', and thus arrived at the radical musical concept of *Klangfarbenmelodie*, or tone-colour-melody, which plays a significant role in the evolution of atonality by supporting, like Debussy's sense of timbre, the withdrawal from functional harmony. Alma Mahler records in her *Memoirs* that he once discussed with Mahler 'the possibility of creating a melody from one note played successively on different instruments'.[49] Mahler, she said, strenuously denied that it could be done, though he always supported Schoenberg in public, aligning himself with the struggling young composer against the incomprehension of the Philistine mob. In fact he twice took a prominent part in quelling disturbances at concerts. He also helped Schoenberg financially by anonymously purchasing one of his paintings when they were exhibited in a Viennese bookshop.

The idea of *Klangfarbenmelodie* is posited in *Harmonielehre* and realized in the third of the *Five Pieces for Orchestra* (Opus 16, 1909), entitled 'Summer morning by a lake (Colours)': the piece consists in little but a softly shimmering atonal chord which undergoes various transformations, both of timbre and of its constituent notes, as the instruments playing it alter. Schoenberg instructs the conductor that 'the chords must change so gently that no emphasis can be perceived at the instrumental entries, and so that the change is made apparent only through the new colour'. This music was so advanced that Mahler admitted, when Schoenberg showed him the score, that he could not read it (meaning that he could not hear it in his head). Richard Strauss turned down Schoenberg's invitation to conduct it, leaving it to the adventurous Henry Wood at a Promenade Concert in London in 1912; not surprisingly (as Ernest Newman reported), the work was rejected as incomprehensible dissonance. Today it can be heard as perhaps the closest music in Schoenberg to Debussy, and at the same time, the first instrumental approximation of a process of sonic transformation that has since been perfected by electroacoustics.

But there was something paradoxical about Schoenberg's musical colour sense. In another letter from Marc to Macke, a few weeks after the one quoted above, he reports a conversation about Schoenberg with Kandinsky, telling him of the conclusion of his wife Maria, 'which for me was rather surprising'. She claimed that Schoenberg worked with completely unresolvable mixed tones, without any tonal colour, only *expression*. (The concert of his music that they heard had included

string quartets and piano pieces, whose monochromatic sound colouring would have encouraged this perception.) 'Kandinsky enthusiasti-
cally agreed! He said that that was his own goal; "beautiful colour", the
merging of his colours into a single grand harmony, was a *faute de mieux*
in his work which he still had to overcome.'⁵⁰ Schoenberg's paintings
throw this paradox into relief by revealing his preoccupations through
a different medium, in which, because of his very lack of technique, his
intentions appear in a peculiarly stark form.

Macke, who was critical of Schoenberg's technical ineptitude as a
painter, described the imaginary faces which Schoenberg called
'Visions' and 'Gazes' as 'those green-eyed dumplings with an astral
stare'.⁵¹ Kandinsky, however, who considered conventional technique
and traditional forms a barrier to the direct expression of feeling, took
these paintings more seriously. He was interested precisely in what
Schoenberg's lack of conventional painterly technique allowed him to
do, and wrote that Schoenberg as a painter sought to eliminate
superfluous decoration just as much as he did as a composer. He
eschewed beautification of style and aesthetic effect, going straight for
what was essential and necessary to communicate his idea. A self-
portrait 'is painted with the so-called dirt from the palette, but what
other kind of paint could he have used in order to achieve this strong,
sober, precise and laconic impression?'⁵² Schoenberg's music, as he
descended into atonality, began to leave a similar impression: as if the
ugliness which so disturbed people was that of the dirt from the palette
of sound normally discarded as noise.

Schoenberg's sense of the lonely and isolated position to which his
pursuit was leading him comes out vividly in his Second String Quartet,
composed in 1907–08, just before he turned to painting and at the
same time as he embarked on the first atonal music. The Quartet
begins in a highly strung vein, post-Brahmsian in its thematically
organized counterpoint, post-Wagnerian in its acutely chromatic tonality. The second movement, a feverish scherzo, includes a snatch of the
popular Viennese song *Ach, du lieber Augustin*. This has sometimes been
described, with an eye to what follows, as an ironic farewell to tonality;
but in that case it suggests a strange continuity between Viennese
tradition and the language of psychological extremity, towards which
this music pushes so relentlessly. Then, in the last two movements,
Schoenberg introduces a solo soprano singing two poems by Stefan
George which distil the experience of anxiety, leading to a paradoxical
resolution in the abjuration of tonality. In moving beyond the hyper-
chromatic but still basically tonal-harmonic world he had inhabited
until then, Schoenberg now, for the first time, dispenses with key

signatures: though each movement still ends with a tonal cadence, the music has no tonal centre. Instead there are melodic progressions with accompanying voices whose purpose, according to the composer himself, 'is not harmonic at all'. Not only do they defy harmonization by triads, they do not even aim for chord production: but perhaps, says Schoenberg, their function and derivation may be discovered in the near future, for their author 'found them psychologically comforting when he wrote them'.[53]

The first of these two movements, *Litany*, is a wistful metaphorical reflection on the artist's unrelenting search for fulfilment: 'Long was the journey, weak is my body,/ bare are the coffers, full but my pain.'[54] The second announces in appropriately floating tones the inevitable consequences of Schoenberg's explorations for musical language:

> I feel the air of another planet
> the friendly faces I knew so recently
> now fade into darkness.
> The trees and pathways I used to love
> grow pale . . . I am dissolved in swirling sound . . .
> soaring, floating, swimming
> into a sea of crystalline radiance,
> I am but a spark of the holy fire,
> a murmuring of the holy voice.

There is no trace here of alienated narcissim, but of the avant-garde composer's utter isolation, at the edge of both society and music, lost in religious nostalgia with Kabbalistic associations ('a spark of the holy fire, a murmuring of the holy voice'). Not a comfortable position to be in, according to Schoenberg himself, who henceforth adopted towards the public sphere the persona of a reluctant and ironic prophet.

When *Harmonielehre* was published, Schoenberg sent a copy to Karl Kraus, publisher, editor and chief author of the satirical fortnightly *Die Fackel* ('The Torch'), with the inscription: 'I have learnt more from you, perhaps, than a man should learn, if he wants to remain independent.'[55] Kraus was an intellectual maverick who became the chief spokesman for certain deep and intractable feelings of suspicion cultivated by a whole generation towards the society they lived in. In the words of Walter Benjamin, *Die Fackel* served as the thermometer 'of the chronic sickness of which all attitudes and standpoints merely mark the temperature curve: inauthenticity'.[56] According to the testimony of the Viennese-born composer Ernst Krenek, who belonged to the circle of Kraus's intimates, there is a close analogy between Kraus's thoughts on language and Schoenberg's on music, especially in terms of the moral value each attached to the integrity of expression.[57]

In 1910, a meeting of the Vienna Psychoanalytic Society heard a paper by Fritz Wittels psychoanalysing Kraus's character. Wittels explained that the *Neue Freie Presse*, the leading Viennese newspaper which was Kraus's favourite target for satire, was 'the father's organ, which corrupts the whole world; *Die Fackel*, on the other hand, is but a small organ, which is, however, capable of destroying the big organ . . .'.[58] This proposition had at least as much wit and justification as some of the barbs Kraus directed against his own targets, but still, he responded with the very kind of righteous indignation he condemned in others. His attacks on his attackers were fierce and sneering. According to a typically paradoxical comment he made in 1913:

> Adolf Loos and I – he literally and I grammatically – have done nothing more than show that there is a distinction between an urn and a chamber pot and that it is this distinction above all that provides culture with elbow room. The others, those who fail to make this distinction, are divided into those who use the urn as a chamber pot and those who use the chamber pot as an urn.[59]

The violent hostility towards psychoanalysis which this dictum betrays was probably inevitable. In spite of the defence which the anti-Freudian psychiatrist Thomas Szasz has recently made on his behalf, Walter Benjamin gets closer to the truth when he remarks that Kraus's very capacities 'are maladies, and . . . his vanity makes him a hypochondriac'.[60]

Schoenberg's most notorious atonal composition, *Pierrot Lunaire*, inhabits the same world of hypochondria. A setting of German translations by Otto Erich Hartleben of verses by the Belgian Symbolist poet Albert Giraud, *Pierrot* was composed in 1912 at the behest of Albertine Zehme, a Berlin actress and *diseuse* who liked performing 'melodramas' – a strange musical form in which a speaker is accompanied by a musical background. Schoenberg had earned his living for a period as a young man in the Berlin literary cabaret, conducting, arranging and composing songs; the Überbrettl, where he led a small instrumental ensemble, was the Berlin equivalent of the Chat Noir in Paris. When he received Zehme's commission, the memory gave him what Boulez describes as 'the idea of a superior, "intellectualized" cabaret',[61] in which, instead of singing, the vocalist uses a special form of delivery halfway between singing and declamation which Schoenberg called *Sprechstimme* ('speech-voice'). He had already tried out the technique in *Gurrelieder*, a massive cantata which had not yet been performed. It is indicated in the score by a cross instead of a notehead; the contours of the voice are supposed to follow definite pitches, but not to sustain them. The exact sense of nuance needed, which is somewhere between exaggerated speech and *parlando* singing, stands out strongly from the intricate instrumental accompaniment, which is given to five musicians playing seven instruments in different combinations.

Pierrot is in fact a piece of *cabaret noir*, which Zehme performed in the costume of Columbine to the accompaniment of an ensemble hidden behind a screen. Giraud's poems, says Boulez, are 'closely allied to the period of French symbolism when the Moon and Pierrot were remorselessly exploited . . . giving rise to Mallarmé's irritated "La lune, ce fromage!" '[62] They exude a sense of the bizarre, and a mood of malaise and sadomasochistic perversity, in which the poet is a moon-struck harlequin who drills a hole in the bald head of his enemy Casander in order to smoke tobacco out of his skull, and blood flows from the thin breasts of the Madonna while poets are crucified by their verses. In *Mondfleck*, near the end of the cycle, Pierrot walks out one evening, and finds a white spot on the back of his dark coat; he rubs it furiously but cannot get rid of it: it is the moon. One of Schoenberg's paintings from a few years earlier evokes exactly the same sense of paradox – the 'Self-Portrait from Behind'.

Schoenberg made a canny agreement with Zehme that instead of her paying him a fee for the commission, they would mount a tour and share the performance rights. Rehearsals – twenty-five of them – began in August 1912. In October, Webern wrote to Berg that the first performance in Berlin was 'an unqualified success'.[63] The tour began with small audiences and a few adverse critics, but word got around, and it quickly took off. Otto Klemperer heard the performance in Hamburg, and later said it made 'an overwhelming impression. The sound effects . . . were indescribable . . . sometimes it sounded like an orchestra of a hundred'.[64] One testimony is of special interest. Back in Berlin at the end of the tour, the final performances coincided with a visit by Diaghilev's *Ballets Russes*. Some fifty years later, Igor Stravinsky recollected that this was the first time he had heard Schoenberg's music. Schoenberg joined Stravinsky to watch a performance of *Petrushka*, and Stravinsky went to hear *Pierrot*:

> Albertine Zehme . . . accompanied her epiglottal sounds with a small amount of pantomime. I remember that and the fact that the musicians were seated behind a curtain, but I was too occupied with the copy of the score Schoenberg had given me to notice anything else. I also remember that the

audience was quiet and attentive and that I wanted Frau Zehme to be quiet too, so that I could hear the *music* . . . The real wealth of *Pierrot* – sound and substance, for *Pierrot* is the solar plexus as well as the mind of early-twentieth-century music – was beyond me as it was beyond all of us at that time, and when Boulez wrote that I had understood it *d'une façon impressioniste*, he was not kind but correct. I *was* aware, nevertheless, that this was the most prescient meeting in my life . . . but we never met again.[65]

Stravinsky

When Debussy was approached by Diaghilev to write the music for a ballet conceived by Nijinsky to be called *Jeux* ('Games'), he at first refused, on the grounds that the idea – the portrayal of flirtatious tennis players – was idiotic and unmusical. He obliged only when Diaghilev doubled the fee, yet the result was one of his most remarkable scores. If the ballet was not a success – partly because it was eclipsed by the scandalous premiere two weeks later of Stravinsky's *Rite of Spring*, for which Nijinsky was also the choreographer – it was none the less remarkable as one of the first ballets to be conceived with a modern scenario. Moreover, it appeared to some critics as a work conceived in the vein not of Impressionism but of Cubism. Nijinsky had intended to create 'an apologia in plastic terms for the man of 1913'[66] – in terms not only of the subject matter but also the choreography, which he termed 'stylized gesture', and which struck Debussy as 'a peculiar kind of mathematics'[67] – he did not like it at all, any more than he approved of Nijinsky's scandalous version of *L'Après-midi d'un Faune* a year earlier, with its scarcely disguised sexual innuendo at the end. Nevertheless, Diaghilev's Russian Ballet constituted a unique convergence of modernist currents in which Debussy himself was deeply implicated; the moment when ballet became an avant-garde art form and prompted, above all in Stravinsky, further decisive musical developments of the day.

Diaghilev made his first foray to Paris in 1906, with an exhibition of new painters from St Petersburg, and met the French impresario Gabriel Astruc, who became his backer. A major concert season in 1907 enlivened the Parisian musical scene with the sounds of a new anti-Wagnerian national school of composers whose music was tinged with an Oriental strangeness which made it devastatingly attractive to a public seeking both novelty and relief. After a concert series in 1907, and Russian opera and ballet in the theatre, Diaghilev came up with an even grander scheme for the *Ballets Russes*, which made its hugely successful debut in 1909, combining new music, choreography and stage design from Russia and France alike. Astruc's brilliantly managed press campaigns added to the success, which induced him to build a new theatre, the famous Théâtre des Champs-Élysées – though Diaghilev's uncontrolled expenditure drove him into bankruptcy on the eve of the 1914 War.

The whole venture was paradoxical. Created in Paris by expatriates, the most traditional and decorous of bourgeois art forms fell into the hands of a group of avant-gardists with strong homoerotic sympathies suddenly granted the resources to mount their most ambitious projects, who proceeded to map exotic dreams upon the stage of the metropolis. This venture became another wrench in the reconfiguration of subjectivity in the cauldron of modernism; it would hardly have been possible in Russia itself, yet it was possible only because of the achievements of the Russian Imperial Ballet, its technical perfection, its introduction of scenic design by easel painters, the commission of original scores for which the elegant and sumptuous ballets of Tchaikovsky stand as the paradigms. The unique status of ballet in St Petersburg is reflected in Stravinsky's recollection that when he was taken as a child of seven or eight to see *The Sleeping Beauty*, he not only knew the plot and the music in advance, but was already 'able to identify the dance positions and steps'.[68] At the same time, these conditions themselves produced dancers who became dissatisfied with the traditional artificialities of classical ballet, and began dreaming of new forms. Foremost among them was the man whom Diaghilev had the good sense to call upon as his first choreographer, Michel Fokine. Fokine brought with him the most outstanding young dancers from the Imperial Ballet, including Nijinsky, in whom the male dancer found not only a new exemplar, almost scandalous in the magnetism of his physical attraction, but one who combined his extraordinary agility with a great gift for dramatic pantomime perfectly suited to Fokine's aesthetic. For Fokine, influenced by the free form and spontaneity of Isadora Duncan, who visited Russia in 1904, had begun to create a new kind of choreography which abandoned classical ballet's conventional sign language, and even began to eschew orthodox ballet steps.

Nijinsky, when he turned to choreography, went further. If Fokine was influenced by Isadora Duncan, Nijinsky found inspiration in the eurhythmics of the Swiss composer and educationalist Émile Jacques-Dalcroze. Intended by its inventor as a pedagogical method of instilling the physical feeling of rhythm in children, and later widely taken up for just this purpose, eurhythmics was also adopted by Rudolf Steiner, secretary of the German branch of the theosophical movement, a modern transcendental philosophy with minor cult status which found its inspiration in a marriage of third-century Roman pagan mysticism with Eastern philosophies of reincarnation and belief in the paranormal. Nijinsky may well have felt drawn by it, too, and would not have been alone among modernists if he did – Schoenberg knew all about theosophy. In any event, Nijinsky was able, by using eurhythmic ideas, to establish a much freer relationship between dance and music than had ever existed before.

It is another paradox of the *Ballets Russes* that, as Nijinsky's biographer Richard Buckle puts it, it appeared not so much as a modernist venture so much as the last flowering of Romanticism. It was only later that it acquired the reputation of a reaction to Wagner; this was not the impression it produced before the First World War (or at least, before the notorious season of 1913), when it seemed to represent another attempt at the synthesis of the arts, combining Wagnerian ideals with the poetic aims of the Symbolist movement and the vigour of the Impressionist painters, captured in the decor and costumes of Benois and Bakst before their counterparts at the Opéra and the Opéra-Comique. This is why André Boucourechliev, in his study of Stravinsky, is able to say of *The Firebird*, the first ballet Diaghilev commissioned from Stravinsky, that although it was his first completely personal work, nevertheless it is 'paradoxically an end rather than a beginning'.[69] It is composed to a scenario by Fokine based on an idea by Diaghilev, and there is nothing revolutionary about its sumptuous and bewitching but harmonically unenterprising musical language. While this is doubtless part of the reason for its immediate success, it also represents a further ingredient in the overall success of the Russian Ballet, the element of exoticism derived from the Oriental tinge of Russian folkore which Diaghilev also exploited in such ballets as the *Polovstian Dances* and *Scheherezade*. And it is precisely around this ingredient that the paradox revolves, for what started as Diaghilev's 'export drive' of Russian colour and folklore (as Buckle puts it) became in *Petrushka*, and above all in *The Rite of Spring*, a Dionysian eruption of unparalleled force.

Although Stravinsky conceived *The Rite* before *Petrushka*, it was the latter which reached the stage first. Here, everyone in Diaghilev's team excelled themselves, for they were creating on the Parisian stage a collective memory of the popular culture of their childhoods, which in certain senses had already ceased to exist. As Benois reflected: 'The fact that the *balagani* [fairground booths] had for some ten years ceased to exist made the idea of building a kind of memorial to them still more tempting . . .'[70] Benois endowed Petrushka with a soul: he was no longer merely an insensitive bully but became the pathetic Pierrot, capable of imagination, love and sorrow – a Hamlet among puppets, as Buckle puts it.[71] Nijinsky discovered his greatest dramatic powers in the part, in which the biggest difficulty, according to Benois, is for Petrushka 'to express his pitiful oppression and his hopeless efforts to achieve personal dignity *without ceasing to be a puppet*'.[72]

According to Benois: 'If Petrushka were to be taken as the personification of the spiritual and suffering side of humanity – or shall we call it the poetic principle? – his lady Columbine would be the incarnation of the eternal feminine; then the gorgeous Blackamoor would serve as the embodiment of everything senselessly attractive, powerfully masculine and undeservedly triumphant.'[73] This schema, it is true, seems like a glaring example of a typology which has since been exposed for its racialist and sexist stereotypes. Yet because these are puppets being played by ballet dancers, the work still retains its pathos. For Stravinsky responded by finding in Benois's scenario a release from conventional narrative psychology. The double stylization of human emotion allowed him to purge the music of all subjectivity and, in the process, to discover in himself new and original musical resources. *Petrushka* is rhythmically unorthodox: it employs perpetually varying time signatures and even polyrhythms – that is, different rhythms simultaneously in different parts. It is also harmonically experimental, entering a new musical realm that was simultaneously explored by composers such as Bartók and Prokofiev, and goes by the name of polytonality – music employing more than one key at the same time or, in other words, tonal simultaneity; here there is indeed a very real affinity to Cubism. *Petrushka*, as a series of visual tableaux, is the realization of the Freudian dream-world inherent in the pantomimic form of balletic narrative. Ironically, this means that Adorno, in spite of his aversion for Stravinsky, is correct when he says that the impending disintegration of the subject itself is evident in the situation represented on the stage, in which the puppet characters are turned into psychic archetypes, possessed of an inner life which escapes the control of the master of ceremonies to run amok amid the hurly-burly of the life of the fairground.

If Stravinsky's compositional techniques are comparable to procedures to be found in the visual art of the same period, then *Petrushka* is especially reminiscent of Chagall, the precursor of Surrealism, who arrived in Paris the year after Diaghilev's first ballet season and filled his nostalgic canvases with dissociated symbols of his Russian-Jewish childhood: his forms are often truncated; there are huge disparities in the size and position of the images, which sometimes float in space or are even upside down. At the same time, if the simultaneity of Stravinsky's polyrhythms and bitonality evokes the splitting of images in the Cubist inventions of Picasso and Braque, these techniques are greatly expanded in the third of his Diaghilev ballets, *The Rite of Spring*. The Dionysian frenzy of *The Rite* stems from a vision he had, while he was working on *The Firebird*, of 'a solemn pagan rite – sage elders, seated in a circle, watched a young girl dance herself to death. They were sacrificing her to propitiate the god of spring.'[74] This visionary quality extended itself to the difficult process of composition: 'I was guided by no system whatever in *Le Sacre du printemps*,' Stravinsky has said, comparing this lack with the theoretical basis of music by Schoenberg, Berg and Webern: 'these composers were supported by a great tradition, whereas very little immediate tradition lies behind *Le Sacre du printemps*. I had only my ear to help me. I heard and I wrote what I heard. I am the vessel through which *Le Sacre* passed.'[75] One suspects that in large part it was precisely this raw immediacy which communicated itself to the audience at the premiere and provoked their infamous reaction. Boucourechliev is doubtless correct when he says that the social background of the audience played an important part, for 'the dress rehearsal, where the audience consisted of professionals, had been perfectly calm', but it hardly makes sense when he adds that their reaction was therefore of no special historical significance, especially when, a few pages later, he comes up with the insight that it was the whole bewitching harmonic poetics of Romanticism which is consumed in the sacrificial fire of *The Rite*.[76]

Several people who were present have left descriptions. According to the artist Valentine Gross: 'The theatre seemed to be shaken by an earthquake. People shouted insults, howled and whistled, drowning out the music. There was slapping and even punching . . . I cannot think how it was possible for this ballet . . . to be danced through to the end . . .'[77] Stravinsky himself wondered the same thing as he watched Pierre Monteux, the conductor: 'It is still almost incredible to me that he actually brought the orchestra through to the end.'[78] He left his seat and went backstage, where he found Nijinsky standing on a chair in the wings, shouting numbers to the dancers. Jean Cocteau considered this reaction inevitable: 'All the elements of a scandal were present. The smart audience in tails and tulle, diamonds and ospreys was interspersed with the suits and *bandeaux* of the aesthetic crowd. The latter would applaud novelty simply to show their contempt for the people in the boxes . . .' Every shade of snobbery, super-snobbery and inverted snobbery was manifest: 'the audience played the role that was written for it . . .'[79] Perhaps the most amusing reminiscence is that of the music critic Carl van Vechten: 'The young man seated behind me in the box stood up during the course of the ballet to enable him to see more clearly. The intense excitement under which he was labouring betrayed itself presently when he began to beat rhythmically on the top of my head with his fists. My emotion was so great that I did not feel the blows for some time.'[80]

The rhythmic brutality of *The Rite* belonged to a crude idea of pagan savagery – or, rather, its stereotype – long repressed in Western music, which the breakdown of the musical tradition suddenly made available. It is precisely this stereotype which explains what happened that night in the Théâtre des Champs-Élysées. To begin with, *The Rite* evokes the image of an antihumanistic primeval world to be played off against civilization, akin to the embrace of African sculpture by avant-gardists like Picasso, which seems to promise the liberation of plastic art from the worn-out formulae of external imitation – in other words, the logical – that is, internally necessary – extension of Post-Impressionism into inner psychic reality. In this way, 'the wild portrayal of the primitive . . . gratifies the longing for the end of social illusion . . .'[81] Thus, the idea of human sacrifice, which proclaims the domination of the primitive collective, evokes the insufficiency of the individualistic condition of civilized society. The progressive aspect of the endeavour is simply stated: it is not merely that the work seems to resound with the noise of impending war, but that 'In the Third Reich – with its astronomical sacrifice of human beings – *Le Sacre du printemps* could never have been performed'[82] – because it was much too close to the bone. At the same time, however, in the evocation of 'archaic impulses which threaten the very life of the bourgeois principle of individuation', *The Rite* is like a piece of magic, an attempt to gain control over regression merely by offering an image of the forbidden. This image is not just highly charged – it makes such an assault upon the nerves that there is no longer any room here for catharsis, which requires a certain Apollonian distance in which to resolve the Dionysian impulse. Instead, it becomes totemistic, while the pleasure which the music harnesses, says Adorno, is virtually sadomasochistic. As a result, *The Rite* becomes 'the virtuoso composition of regression'.[83]

Bartók

Perhaps, from Adorno's Central European perspective, in which Paris and Vienna were the twin stars of European musical culture at the beginning of the twentieth century, the polarity between Schoenberg and Stravinsky may have appeared logical. The problem is the way this reduces other currents in twentieth-century music to the status of footnotes. There is indeed a particularly revealing footnote in the *Philosophy of Modern Music* which comes close to giving the game away. Here Adorno mentions Janáček and Bartók, and calls their music 'extra-territorial'. He means no ill towards them; on the contrary, he considers the music of Janáček 'magnificent', and that of Bartók among the most progressive in European musical art, 'in spite of his folkloristic inclinations'. Such music, he says, was like a bulwark on the eastern periphery against the blood-and-soil ideology of Nazism; it has 'a power of alienation which places it in the company of the avant-garde and not that of nationalistic reaction'.[84]

Now it is perfectly true that Fascism could make no use of this music, but that leaves the question of why it should be called peripheral. Peripheral to what? From the geographical position occupied by a composer like Bartók, the perspective is altered, and the whole business looks different; the Schoenberg/Stravinsky polarity, while it is deeply symptomatic of contradictions at the centre, is by no means the prime concern that it is for the likes of Adorno. Both the geography and the very genealogy of new music take another form, in which Bartók himself is a much more pivotal figure.

First there had been Wagner, the composer of German imperialism, music's Bismarck (while Verdi was Italy's musical Cavour). The anti-Wagnerite cause was not to be found in Brahms, who represented alienated cultural conservatism in the heartland, but out on the periphery, in Moussorgsky, the progressive voice of the Russian intelligentsia. The next generation produced a similarly progressive voice in Mahler, composer of the marginal classes of the metropolitan hinterland, a Jew from Bohemia who took up residence in Vienna. Politics: socialistic, democratic.

Debussy, in this schema, is the composer of the metropolitan *petite bourgeoisie*, who encountered the music of the remote periphery of empire at the World Exhibition of 1889, and discovered in it liberation from the oppressive weight of both Wagner and the French academicians. He is apolitical, though patriotic in time of war against the metropolitan neighbour. Schoenberg, in turn, is the composer of the migrant ethnic minority in the heart of the metropolis, the Jew born in Vienna; the breeding-ground of alienation. Politics: humanist, but frankly elitist. Later he becomes a neglected prophet in a foreign land. Stravinsky, coming from St Petersburg to be adopted in Paris, is a composer from a capital of the near-periphery who finds fame and fortune in the metropolitan heartland. Ten years later, as a result of

The essay is a salutary one: a modest tribute by someone for whom music was 'difficult', but with more to say than volumes of musical analysis. For Lukács, Bartók's artistic development was exemplary. He entered the arena in 1903 as a champion of Hungarian nationalism, his manifesto pinned to a symphonic poem on Lajos Kossuth, the revolutionary hero of 1848. (We can add that the piece was composed under the influence of Bartók's first encounter with the music of Richard Strauss; and a famous incident occurred at its first performance, when an Austrian trumpet-player in the orchestra refused to play a parodistic version of the Austrian national anthem.) Although Hungarian folk music then became the foundation of Bartók's art, 'he did not stop at this first and powerful impulse: he went further, towards a comprehensive and artistic utilization of all folk music'. The early *Kossuth* Symphony, even if it sprang from revolutionary sentiments, could still be welcomed by conservative Hungarian critics. But then, through his discoveries in the field and their repercussions on his own style of composition, he exposed the pretensions of so-called gypsy music cultivated by the urban middle classes, like the *csárdás* which had passed as *all'ongarese* in the music of Liszt and Brahms: 'Here the right wing ceased their praise; it is well known that he was even accused of high treason because he praised Rumanian folk music. Nor did he stop there; he included Czech, Slovak, Arab, Portuguese, indeed all folk music among the ever-broadening and deepening basic elements of the new music.'

Bartók, says Lukács, considered the peasant class 'a natural force' in the artistic struggle to transcend the alienation of modern society. He makes Lukács think of what Lenin said to Gorky about Tolstoy: 'before this Count there was no real peasant in our literature'. But Bartók had more 'historical universality' than Tolstoy, because of the way his music was able to objectivize the deepest subjective attitudes. This makes it an exemplary instance, he tells us, of his own concept of 'undetermined objectivity', which is the key to the artist's power to lay bare the symptomatic features of the epoch.

Bartók's first field trip dates from 1906. Together with Kodály he made the discovery that the folk music of Eastern Europe was essentially non-diatonic. In other words, the notes did not correspond to those of the chromatic scale in the system of equal temperament which European music had adopted by the middle of the eighteenth century.[90] The scales were either modal or, in more remote parts, even pentatonic; intonation, both vocal and instrumental, was sensitive to microtonal inflection, rhythm was often asymmetrical. These discoveries had a profound effect on Bartók's musical thinking: melodic, harmonic, rhythmic and colouristic. Within two years he had abandoned the lush orchestral language of Strauss, full of modern effects but essentially diatonic and in the end conservative, and had begun to discover a new idiom. In one of the *Bagatelles* for piano (1908) the separate voices represented by the two hands are written with different key signatures. The resulting clash of keys is precisely calculated: this is how Bartók creates the feel of folk music, its 'false' intonation, its non-diatonic idiom – a similar trick was later evolved by jazz pianists in order to render the blues.

At times, this new musical idiom comes close to the highly chromatic Expressionist gesture exemplified by Schoenberg, which in turn is only the sharp end of a process of harmonic experiment to be found among composers in several different countries. In *Harmonielehre* Schoenberg cites one of Bartók's *Bagatelles* as an example of a crucial tendency to be found 'in the works of some of us'[91] – himself, Berg, Webern and Schreker in Vienna; Debussy and Dukas in France; and perhaps Puccini in Italy (whose idiom was close to that of Mahler, Schoenberg's mentor). He could also have mentioned other exemplars, like Scriabin in Russia. All were moving towards chords of seven notes and more which annulled the traditional pull of dissonance towards resolution.

In Bartók's case these chords were often constructed from a synthesis of the intervals in the melodic motifs he derived from folk music, and he himself found the same thing at work in Stravinsky. These motifs, considered separately, may be pentatonic, modal or unambiguously diatonic. When they are superimposed, or otherwise combined, the overall effect is not so much *a*tonal, without key, as *poly*tonal – that is, in two or more keys simultaneously. The difference is crucial. In the dodecaphonic method of Schoenberg and subsequent serial music, the triad is wholly abolished. There is none the less a large part of contemporary music, neither serial nor dodecaphonic but running in parallel, in which the triad no longer reigns supreme in the old way but still operates, in dissonant recombinations: not only in Bartók and Stravinsky, but also in Prokofiev, Milhaud, Hindemith, Ives, the Brazilian Villa-Lobos, the Mexican Revueltas, and a good many more. In short, this polytonal sound was far more prevalent in new music before the Second World War than dodecaphony, and Bartók was one of its most representative figures.

*

By the First World War Bartók had carried out fieldwork in the Middle East, North Africa and the Western Mediterranean. From such music, he wrote, 'we may learn unique terseness of expression and inexorable rejection of all inessentials – and that is exactly what we have been longing for after the prolixity of Romanticism'.[92] He immersed himself, on these trips, in the rich anthropological experience they proffered; in between, in his travels as a virtuoso to Berlin, London, Paris or Madrid, he critically assimilated the experience of the metropolis. His own music was never merely folksy, but equally impregnated by these two forces, metropolis and periphery, and he joined the tribe of avant-gardists whose music is greeted by both cheers and catcalls.

Branded in the press a 'young barbarian', Bartók replied in 1911 with the *Allegro Barbaro*, a short piano piece of relentlessly pounding rhythms and hammering dissonant chords of greater ferocity than any piano work hitherto. Naturally he was vilified, his music dismissed as 'ugly' and 'incoherent'. A critic in London in 1923 compared his keyboard touch to a village blacksmith hammering a horseshoe; in the words of a Boston critic in 1928, 'He has gone after beauty with hammers and sticks'.[93] These are curiously apposite comments. The originality of Bartók's piano music – the exact opposite of Debussy's – lies precisely in its percussiveness. But the savagery upon which the reviews harp is only the half of it. The other half is the recovery of the percussive domain as a field of musical expression, not just of added colour: percussion as an integral element of the texture; and the percussive use of string instruments, as the very titles of two works from the 1930s indicate – the *Sonata for Two Pianos and Percussion* and the *Music for Strings, Percussion and Celesta*. The discovery of percussive sonorities in melody instruments – and, to produce these sounds, the introduction of new playing techniques – derives directly from the example of folk musicians. Bartók had found that their peculiar timbre and intonation were not, as conventional wisdom supposed, a matter of careless and untutored execution, but of a spontaneous expressive nuance far more subtle than orthodox notation was able to transcribe. In the musical system articulated through orthodox notation, all such effects had become transitive inflections between the fixed notes of the chromatic scale, those stepping stones twelve in number, as John Cage calls them; with the result that they disappeared from conscious attention into the interstices of the musical fabric. Bartók never asks his performers to try to imitate the folk musician; he reinvents their technique.

For Bartók, says Lukács, 'the irreconcilable contradiction between the natural life lived by the peasant and the distorted and alienated life of modern man provided [him with] the point of departure'. In three stage works written between 1911 and 1919, a one-act opera and two one-act ballets, he explores the forces of alienation and the psychological distortions which result. The first is *Duke Bluebeard's Castle*, with Balázs the librettist of an Expressionist, psychoanalytic reading of the popular folk tale as a study in sexual politics and the concupiscence of alienated masculinity. It was rejected when it was first submitted for production in Budapest, and its reputation as a masterpiece of Expressionist opera is retrospective; none the less it is like Bartók's *Erwartung* or, as Kodaly called it, Hungary's *Pelléas et Mélisande*. Like the composers of both those works, Bartók eschews traditional operatic formats such as arias and duets, and *Bluebeard* consists in practically continuous recitative, of deep lyricism and perfectly adapted to the inflections of the Hungarian language. The declamation is moulded by folkloric nuances, and floats above a shimmering orchestral texture with a certain similarity to Debussy or Dukas, but more dissonant. The action is symbolic. Bluebeard brings his new spouse Judith home to his castle, where she persuades him to give her the keys to seven doors; they are the doors to Bluebeard's soul. Behind the first is a torture chamber whose walls bleed; behind the second an armoury full of weapons; behind the third a treasury full of coins and jewellery; behind the fourth a secret garden. The fifth opens on to his kingdom; the sixth reveals a pool of tears. Behind the last is a chamber where his three previous wives are locked up, and Judith must now join them.

Balázs was again the librettist for *The Wooden Prince*, a ballet based on a fairy tale about a curious game of love between a prince and a princess. To win the love of the princess, the prince makes a wooden doll dressed like himself to catch her attention; the doll comes alive with the aid of a supernatural helper – a figure not unlike Lorca's *duende*, a kind of creative prankster-demon. The prince promptly falls into his own trap as the princess falls in love with the doll instead of him; it is left to the *duende* to put things right again at the end. This tale becomes, in the telling, a poignant metaphor for the alienation of the artist through the very act of creation. Despite its happy ending, this is Bartók's *Petrushka*, with a musical idiom to match, full of iridescent instrumentation and impetuous rhythms, and the xylophone playing an almost solo role. Mounted in Budapest in 1917 only with the greatest difficulty, it was an immediate triumph.

The last of this trio of theatrical works, a wonderfully grotesque pantomime called *The Miraculous Mandarin*, though closer to the world of *Bluebeard*, has a scenario by a different writer, Melchior Lengyel (who ended up writing scripts in Hollywood, including Garbo's *Ninotchka*). The setting is the garret of a backstreet prostitute where, every time the girl brings in a trick, he is set upon by three pimps. The first victim is an elderly drunk, the second a timid youth; then comes the third, a mysterious mandarin from the East whom the three pimps find much more difficult to vanquish. Three times they try to kill him, but he refuses to stay dead until the girl has submitted to him. This work was prohibited by the Hungarian authorities, and when it was premiered in Cologne in 1926, the scandal and outrage in the press and the Church were so violent that the mayor, one Dr Konrad Adenauer, banned it after one performance. It is Bartók's most uncomprising statement on alienation, more immediate, disturbing and profound than either *Die glückliche Hand* or *The Rite of Spring*. The mandarin is an alien force, a figment of our divided consciousness, a cipher for the dangerous power of sexuality and instinct: in our average civilized world, says Lukács, in which alienation has become second nature to us, 'natural forces' can break in only from the outside.

However, the mandarin is not a personification of peasant revolution against the 'conquests' of capitalist civilization, as Lukács suggests. Here his lack of ear and his Romantic literary bias tell on him (not to mention his masculine susceptibilities). The music of the city is chromatic and dissonant; the mandarin is characterized by Oriental pentatonicism; and the music to which the girl dances is modal. The mandarin is thus an Oriental stranger in the Western metropolis who falls prey to its wiles; but the girl is as much a stranger to the metropolis as the mandarin, a migrant from a peasant village forced by misfortune into prostitution in the city.

Lukács also mentions the *Cantata Profana*, dating from 1930 and the work which Bartók himself called his most personal profession of faith. Based on a Romanian folk ballad, it recounts the legend of nine brothers, sons of a hunter, who are bewitched and turned into stags. When their father, in his ignorance, is about to shoot at them, the eldest cries out to stop him, but they reject his entreaties to return home: ('We shall not go with you, for our antlers cannot go through doors, only through forest groves. And our mouths no longer drink from crystal glasses, only from mountain springs.') Lukács calls this work an open protest again alienation, in which the youths who have turned into stags are right to prefer the world of nature to the human world. Musically, this is expressed in a kind of nostalgia for the pentatonicism of the 'natural' way of life, though since Bartók regarded himself – being a product of urban culture – as a man of dissonance, the accompaniment to this pentatonicism is generally dissonant.

The mix of musical modalities in these works – the pentatonic, the modal and the chromatic – signals the breadth of Bartók's mature idiom, which follows a very different curve from that of either Schoenberg or Stravinsky. The works of his maturity range all the way from a tender pentatonicism more lucid than Stravinsky's neoclassicism, to the most dissonant chromaticism, virtually indistinguishable from dodecaphony – the string quartets in which such passages occur have been compared, for the concentrated intensity of their construction, to the late quartets of Beethoven. But Bartók feels the need neither to systematize his compositional techniques, nor (despite his interest in early keyboard music) to revive archaic forms. Nor does he proceed from one style to another, or follow a linear trajectory. His folk-song arrangements, which range from the very simple to the rather complex, are never exercises in nostalgia, like those of the English folklorists. In his original works he always chooses the style for each in accordance with its function and genre, and with a discriminating ear for the susceptibilities of both performer and audience.

This is what enables him to respond with equal success whether he is writing piano pieces for children or folk settings for amateur choruses; or fulfilling commissions from virtuoso soloists (Benny Goodman, Yehudi Menuhin) or from conductors for their orchestras (Paul Sacher and the Basle Chamber Orchestra, Serge Koussevitsky and the Boston Symphony). In the last of these, the Concerto for Orchestra (1944), Bartók attains a modern diatonic language so simple, so direct and so rich, that like certain works by Shostakovich – to whom it ironically alludes – or Prokofiev, it immediately became part of the repertoire of orchestras normally resistant to anything beyond Debussy. Yet he had only just written the Sonata for Solo Violin, a work of intense, dissonant, contrapuntal lyricism that makes few concessions to the uninitiated ear, which Yehudi Menuhin, who commissioned it, has called the most remarkable work for unaccompanied violin since Bach. It is Bartók himself who invites the comparison, by incorporating elements of chaconne in the first movement and fugue in the second; and where the fugues in Bach's unaccompanied violin sonatas are all in three parts, Bartók composes one in four. As for the last movement, in its original version, says Menuhin, Bartók wrote the rondo theme in quarter-tones; unfortunately, Menuhin found the demand of accurate quarter-tones in fast tempo 'too intimidating', and opted for the semitone alternative which Bartók thoughtfully provided.[94] (This is a pity, but his recording of the work none the less confirms his high claims for it.)

8

The Jazz Age

Milhaud and the lure of the exotic

If the early years of the twentieth century are marked by the scandals of modernism, the rift between the artist and the public is also aggravated, according to the historian Eric Hobsbawm, by other major intellectual and cultural developments of the decades leading up to the First World War.[1] There is a massive advance in popular education, the creation of a popular reading public, and a huge expansion in popular urban entertainment, especially the rapid rise of a radical new form of diversion in the shape of the cinema, and the introduction of mass production in the record industry.[2] This process of cultural massification, which created enormous tensions 'between the hope of general renewal and the pessimism of educated middle classes faced with "mass society"',[3] has profound effects on the musical lifeworld, which now splits three ways: an ageing conservative elite which controls the institutional forms of patronage; a radical and youthful avant-garde which enjoys the support of the fashionable intelligentsia and each other; and, rapidly outstripping both, the populism and psychological facility of the entertainment industry, which is about to spring surprises on both the other two.

From the traditionalist perspective, the musical language came under attack from all sides – from within, from below, and from beyond. Indeed, no sooner had internal pressures brought the age-old harmonic idiom to the point of collapse than a whole range of peripheral influences began to enter the equations of European musical consciousness. In technical terms, because diatonic harmony entailed the subservient interdependence of both melody and rhythm, the rupture of harmonic equilibrium affected both rhythmic and melodic sensibilities. It is as if natural forces, like Bartók's Miraculous Mandarin, began to break in upon European musical sensibilities from outside. The breakdown opened the door not only to atonality but also to non-functional harmony, the recovery of modal melody, microtonal inflection, and polytonality; and in the domain of rhythm, to experiments in polymeter and polyrhythms, and the subversion of European rhythmic susceptibilities by schemata found in other musics, like the syncopations of jazz.

The process is crystallized in the middle of the First World War in the figure of the young composer Darius Milhaud, a French Jew from Provence, when he finds himself in Rio de Janeiro as secretary to the French Ambassador, the poet-playwright Paul Claudel; Milhaud is befriended by a Brazilian counterpart, Heitor Villa-Lobos, who takes the Frenchman under his wing and introduces him to *choros* and carnival music, and explains *macumba* fetishist rites. This music, with its subtle syncopations – which, Milhaud says in his autobiography, he at first found hard to grasp – is a manifestation of Afro-Brazilian culture. Similar characteristics explain the impact of another African-American music, from the North, on a whole host of European composers – Stravinsky, Ravel, Weill, Martinů, Hindemith, Walton, and the rest; in both cases, the double-barrelled appellation indicates a transformation and fusion of musical features in the process of transplantation from one continent to another.

Milhaud was musically the most radical of a group of composers who shared concerts together in Paris after the First World War, and was dubbed by a critic *Les Six* (the others were Auric, Durey, Honegger, Poulenc and Tailleferre). Stimulated by his exotic sojourn, he produced a series of ballets which incorporated and developed his experience in Brazil. Claudel provided the scenario for the first of them, *L'Homme et son Désir*, set in a rainforest where the figure of Man is liberated by a phantom Woman; in this polytonal and polymetric evocation of the tropical jungle with a completely original concept of instrumental colour, the band consists in a quartet of wordless voices, a string quartet, two quartets of mixed wind instruments and two batteries of percussion. 'I wanted to preserve absolute independence, melodic, tonal, and rhythmic, for each of these groups,' Milhaud wrote.[4] To this end, the different melodic parts were written in different time signatures, while the percussion, coming from two sides, was used unaccompanied to evoke the nocturnal sounds of the rainforest. The result surpasses mere colonialist expropriation, transcending the conventional language of exoticism through a sound in many ways as startlingly new and fresh as Stravinsky in and after *Le Sacre*.

As for *Les Six*, the only thing they had in common, Milhaud told his hosts on a visit to the Soviet Union in 1927, was that they were all children of the bourgeoisie.[5] The group never shared any consistent or coherent aesthetic programme, only general tendencies. They were *à la mode*, they spurned the music of the older generation (Fauré, D'Indy, even Debussy); their collaborators were Cocteau, Picasso and Braque. Above all, their mascot, as Milhaud called him, was the highly eccentric Erik Satie, who went from playing the piano at the Chat Noir to writing Dadaist ballets – not such an odd career for the friend of Debussy who responded to the latter's criticism of a lack of form in his music by writing *Trois morceaux en forme de poire* ('Three pieces in the form of a pear'). *Parade*, the most notorious of his ballets, was presented by Diaghilev in Paris in 1917. With its music-hall scenario by Cocteau and designs by Picasso, Apollinaire described it as surrealist. With its megaphones used for shouting advertising slogans and nonsense syllables, and its orchestra including sirens, a typewriter and a revolver, it invokes the Futurist claim to make music out of noises but without the earnestness of the Futurists – more as a kind of deliberate bad joke. *Les Six* cultivated the same attitude of irreverence as Satie, and drew on the same bohemian milieu of music hall, café and cabaret. Indeed, they met for a time at a nightclub named after Milhaud's second Brazilian ballet, *Le Bœuf sur le toit* (1919; produced in London the following year as 'The Nothing Doing Bar'). The scenario, again by Cocteau, consisted in a pantomime set in a bar in America under Prohibition, but the music was a racy polytonal collage of popular dance tunes, mostly South American in origin, including examples of tango, maxixe and samba, thrown against each other in such a way that two, three and even four different tonalities were juxtaposed at the same time. Since the individual tunes are full of simple diatonic cadences, the result is a highly dissonant but quirkish charm, which Milhaud himself thought might make an appropriate accompaniment to a Charlie Chaplin film.

It is instructive to contrast the effect of Rio de Janeiro on Milhaud with that of Paris on Villa-Lobos. In the wake of the exotic elements in Debussy and Ravel, of Stravinsky's Russian primitivism, and now the example of Milhaud, Villa-Lobos was taken up in Paris in a big way, but his experience there makes a cautionary tale. Stravinsky, coming from St Petersburg, had felt very much at home in Paris. Villa-Lobos was convinced that his appeal in the French capital remained merely an exotic one. 'I am not a folklorist,' he told Alejo Carpentier in the 1920s. 'Folklore doesn't interest me. My music is the way it is because I feel it that way. They find my music very Brazilian! It is, because it reflects an absolutely Brazilian sensibility.' He did not borrow folkloric melodies, he said, he composed his own, and if someone thought they heard a popular song from São Paulo in his music, it was because those were the songs which rocked him to sleep as a child. 'I feel them the same way the Russian feels the coachmen's chorus in *Petrushka*.'[6] What these suspicions of the Brazilian in Paris reveal is how the relationship of periphery to metropolis remained problematic even when there was a certain receptivity. Carpentier reflected ironically that the question of exoticism often worried the Latin American artist too much – like Heine's pine tree dreaming of the distant palms, only the other way round: 'we are the palm, sometimes growing in virgin forest, and we try and disguise ourselves in hoarfrost . . . For the European the exotic is a landscape by Gauguin . . . For our temperament, it ought to be Montparnasse . . .'[7]

The third of Milhaud's postwar ballets, *La Création du Monde*, followed a visit to North America in 1922, when he told reporters that the kind of American music that interested Europeans was not Edward Macdowell or John Alden Carpenter but jazz, earning himself headlines like 'Milhaud Admires Jazz' and 'Jazz Dictates the Future of European Music'.[8] It is clear from his description in his autobiography of his first live encounter with jazz in 1919 – the Billy Arnold band from New York at the Hammersmith Palais in London – that the diverse features of jazz presented themselves to his ears as an organic unity, even when the ensemble was a white, well-rehearsed and less than fully spontaneous dance-hall band:

> In the course of frequent visits to Hammersmith, where I sat close to the musicians, I tried to analyse and assimilate what I heard . . . The new music was extremely subtle in its use of timbre: the saxophone breaking in, squeezing out the juice of dreams, or the trumpet, dramatic or languorous by turns, the clarinet, frequently played in its upper register, the lyrical use of the trombone, glancing with its slide over quarter-tones in crescendos of volume and pitch, thus intensifying the feeling; and the whole, so various yet not disparate, held together by the piano and subtly punctuated by the complex rhythms of the percussion, a kind of inner beat, the vital pulse of the rhythmic life of the music. The constant use of syncopation in the melody was of such contrapuntal freedom that it gave the impression of unregulated improvisation, whereas in actual fact it was elaborately rehearsed . . .[9]

In America, he heard the real McCoy:

> Harlem had not yet been discovered by the snobs and aesthetes: we were the only white folk there. The music I heard was absolutely different from anything I had ever heard before, and was a revelation to me. Against the beat of the drums the melodic lines criss-crossed in a breathless pattern of

broken and twisted rhythms. A negress, whose grating voice seemed to come from the depths of the centuries, sang in front of the various tables. With despairing pathos and dramatic feeling, she sang over and over again, to the point of exhaustion, the same refrain, to which the constantly changing melodic pattern of the orchestra wove a kaleidoscopic background ... I resolved to use jazz for a chamber music work.[10]

This he did in the shape of *La Création du Monde*, with its extraordinary combination of syncopation and fugue, in which the Judaeo-Christian creation myth becomes an icon of the encounter with a musical culture that was completely Other.

La Création du Monde, as the musicologist Glenn Watkins points out, shares many of the same melodic blue-note figurations that appear in 'St. Louis Blues' and Gershwin's *Rhapsody in Blue* of the following year.[11] But if it represents the beginnings of a new idiom of 'symphonic jazz', it is also the product of a trend which goes back to the 1890s, when black American dance music first reached Europe. Gabriel Astruc – Diaghilev's French producer – first came across the cakewalk at the World's Fair in Chicago in 1893, and danced it in Paris a little later; in 1900 John Philip Sousa was playing ragtime selections on his European tours, and Satie was incorporating ragtime into his music; four years later Cocteau reported Negro dancers at the Nouveau Cirque in Paris; by this time the cakewalk had reached Russia: according to one account, the steps were demonstrated at a gathering of Rimsky-Korsakov's pupils by – among others – the twenty-one-year-old Stravinsky, leaving the master's wife somewhat scandalized.[12] Shortly afterwards Debussy produced his *Golliwog's Cakewalk*, one of a suite of piano pieces called *Children's Corner*. The piece is a trifle, but its title and locus remind us that the category of what the French called *art nègre* was profoundly contradictory, feeding off racial stereotypes while evoking the allure of the exotic.

Exoticism is not just a matter of the strangeness of the foreign; product of the metropolis that defines the exotic as the Other which peoples its colonized domains, it is a relation to strangeness as both alien and seductive. To classify and control the Other, the West develops the cognitive practice of anthropology, but the exotic is essentially an aesthetic category which goes through several phases from the moment it first appears as a theme in European consciousness as far back as the seventeenth century. In the eighteenth-century construct of the noble savage, it becomes the imagined locus of lost instincts. At the beginning of the twentieth century comes the discovery of its capacity to upset the order and reasoning of the metropolitan culture. Here music plays a special function within the cultural sphere at large, as the privileged site of subjectivity and the emotions, and the back door to irrationality. This is the guise in which a new black music from America first arrives in Europe early in the new century, in the form of scores, then records, and then, at the end of the First World War, the bands themselves. In Paris, where Picasso and others had already discovered in African art a resource for reshaping their own sensibilities, a veritable cult of *la musique nègre* would grow up; Berlin and London would follow suit. The Orientalism of Debussy, or Mahler in *Das Lied von der Erde*, recedes, and African-American music becomes the European composer's Other.

The musical appeal of jazz is complex; so too are the contradictions which this appeal set in motion, as jazz is released into a musical domain vastly extended by radio and records, invading the traditional spaces of popular music (where the bourgeois composer went slumming) with its special qualities of rhythm, tonality and improvisation. Jazz is *par excellence* a form of disciplined improvisation inflected by a non-European syncopated rhythm and tonality – in other words, the rhythm called swing, and the melody called the blues. The blues is not a transplant of traditional West African music, which is basically pentatonic, but the result of the clash between different senses of musical temperament (tuning, tonality) in the context of a particular social history. The African scale has a natural temperament, and its intervals are therefore pitched differently. The Western intervals of a third and a seventh become ambiguous because the system of equal temperament installed in the mid-eighteenth century has given them a peculiar inflection; and the encounter with pentatonic sensibility flattens or sharpens them. The consequence, around the interval of a third, is that the blue note hovers between major and minor, and at the seventh, becomes distinctly modal. The effect is all the greater for syncopation, which strengthens the natural tendency to sharpen accented beats and flatten unaccented ones, so that the syncopated shift from strong beats to weak ones also tends to flatten the note. Bartók found analogous inflections in the folk music of Eastern Europe and the Mediterranean, with the result that on hearing live jazz at a speakeasy in Chicago during his first US tour in 1927 ('they played from a score but many times they improvised and this was fascinating'), he had no need, he said, to fling himself into its arms; essentially, there was nothing there he hadn't already learnt about from his detailed studies of Eastern European and Mediterranean folk music.[13]

Improvisation, according to some accounts, was originally limited to brief 'rags' by individual members of the band which occurred at clearly defined points, but it soon developed into a leading structural feature of the jazz idiom. What improvisation means is that nothing is fixed: each time the piece is played it is likely to vary and evolve, but improvisation was never 'free', never lacking in preparation, design and method. It was cleverly based on the harmonic structure of the tune and, as the idiom evolved, better and better rehearsed. Command of these skills is what enables jazz musicians to sit in with new bands and jam with them, and this process became the driving force behind the evolution of jazz as a musical language.

Last, the exotic tonality of jazz came across not only in its blue notes but also in subtle alterations of instrumental articulation, and the discovery of new sonorities in what were, after all, conventional European instruments. The jazz musician achieves this result through techniques such as vocalization – playing the instrument in such a way as to give it a vocal quality. The inflections of the human voice which the jazz instrumentalist imitates are those of the raw, untrained singer, full of vibrato, portamento, and the effects known in jazz terminology as smears, falls, bends, growls, and all the rest. In short, the articulation of jazz lies at the opposite pole to European art music; it is a carnival-esque and Dionysian force whose influence accordingly became not just a stimulant, but by turns also naughty and subversive. For Hindemith, incorporating foxtrot, shimmy and the like into his chamber music as early as 1922, it was a stimulant which intensified his fluency, rhythmic drive and instrumental skill. It was naughty when William Walton, at the age of twenty-one, composed a sophisticated salon entertainment called *Façade*. It became subversive – and was openly indicted as such – a few years later in Berlin, in the work of Kurt Weill, and when Krenek wrote his opera *Johnny spielt auf* ('Johnny Strikes Up') about the amorous adventures of a black jazz musician on tour in Europe.

Kurt Weill: Weimar to Broadway

Live jazz first came to Europe in 1918 in the shape of the Original Dixieland Jazz Band, soon followed by other mostly white musicians, but it was through its rapid diffusion by means of records and radio that it became – mostly in the derivative form of big band dance music – the sign in postwar European culture of everything American. Not the least important ingredient was its sense of energy, which Lion Feuchtwanger captured in a parodic poem called 'Music' from a book of poetry called *Pep.J.L. Wetcheeks americanisches Liederbuch*:

> In executing modern music the turnover of energy
>   is immense.
> Whereas for a song by *Brahms* the energy expended
>   has been reckoned
> At 32 to 35 kilogram-metres per minute, that
>   required for a *jazz hit* has been found to be
>   much more intense,
> Amounting *in the case of the drummer alone* to
>   between 48 and 49 kilogram-metres *per second.*[14]

It was in Germany that, for a period in the 1920s, this kind of Americanism was most potently invested with special mythical value. Witness in particular the theatre of Bertolt Brecht, and his invention of a city somewhere 'twixt Florida and Alaska called Mahagonny, set to music by Kurt Weill first as a short piece of theatre and then as a full-scale opera, a strange new kind of opera with angular rhythms, catchy tunes, and choruses in broken American English. It is true that Mahagonny was meant as a thinly veiled portrait of Berlin, but America was the land where the modern city found its quintessential form; Weill's music was American and jazzy, while remaining at the same time completely impregnated with the spirit of Berlin.

Americanism served in Germany as a peculiar counterpoint to the proximity in time and place of the Bolshevik Revolution. It was this proximity which spurred the revolutionary movement in Germany at the end of the 1914–1918 War, and politicized the emergent generation of German composers. (Weill would later write his *Berliner Requiem* for the Communist revolutionaries Karl Liebknecht and Rosa Luxemburg, who were killed in the aftermath of the Spartacist insurrection of 1919.) Some of them, for instance, joined the Berlin-based *Novembergruppe*, which took its name from the uprising of November 1918, and consisted mainly of painters, sculptors and architects belonging to the more socially conscious wing of the Expressionist movement. Aiming to establish closer links between artists and working-class audiences, the November Group promoted exhibitions, lectures, film screenings and concerts of new music. Musicians who joined the group included Kurt Weill, Hanns Eisler, Stefan Wolpe, Jascha Horenstein and H.H. Stuckenschmidt; their concerts also included music by non-members, such as Berg, Webern, Schoenberg, Hindemith, Bartók, Stravinsky, Krenek, Ravel, Kodály and Satie.

In Vienna, by contrast, Schoenberg, who remained apolitical, created a Society for Private Musical Performances. Its aim was to escape the hostility to new music on the part of overweening critics and lazy audiences by promoting private concerts for the confraternity and its sympathizers, where composers could feel free to experiment. In the three years before raging inflation put an end to it, hundreds of works were performed for the first time. Members undertook neither to applaud nor to show displeasure, and to publish nothing about the music they heard – naturally the press was also excluded, except for a small number of open concerts each year intended to drum up publicity. Here, in a step that is both logical but also extreme, the composer turns his back on the public sphere, finding it hostile to musical values, demonstrating in the process the extent to which the musical lifeworld was now deeply split by internal schisms.

In Berlin, however, these same schisms – and the perception of a lack, a void in the relationship between the composer and the wider community – exercised the entire generation emerging into the Weimar Republic, and initiated an intense debate on exactly the central topic of the present study: the figure of the composer in the public sphere – the function, the role, the responsibility attached to the métier. The composers involved in this debate argued over terminology and music's relation to politics, but all of them attacked the traditional apparatus of professional musical culture, which reduced the audience to passivity, separated musicians into a confraternity of their own, and marginalized the living composer. They also distinguished themselves from commercial music production precisely by insisting on the social responsibility of music and the composer. This principle was enunciated in Hindemith's concept of *Gebrauchsmusik*, or socially 'useful' music, a utopian concept born of intense consciousness of the radically altered nature of the musical public sphere in the postwar world, and hence the responsibility of the composer in answering to its needs. The term is intended to draw a double contrast, with art music on the one hand and, on the other, *Verbrauchsmusik*, 'consumption music' – that is to say, commercial music, or what French publishers dismissively call *musique-papier*, 'paper music'. *Gebrauchsmusik* proposed to resolve the frustration of divided camps by breaking out of the orthodox categories of musical life, rejecting the bourgeois concept of music's autonomy, and pulling down the barriers between the professional art musician and the audience. It would seek to find a way around the division between commercial music and art music by taking seriously precisely that music which was employed not for its own sake but for its utility, such as music for the theatre and the cinema. As Weill put it in 1929 – a year or two after the huge success of *The Threepenny Opera* – the composer of *Gebrauchsmusik* aimed to satisfy the musical needs of a wide public without giving up artistic substance, without renouncing 'the intellectual bearing of the serious musician' in order to compete with the hit: to write music – including music for radio, cinema and theatre – with a sense of social purpose, promoting the participation of amateurs in choirs, festivals and schools, and any other musical activities that would help break down the barriers with the wider public. This, he said, required the use of 'an entirely perceptible, understandable language', one designed to be not catchy but, rather, 'bitter, accusing, and ... ironic'[15] – the very qualities, of course, that he succeeded at the time in exemplifying in his own music.

In terms of cultural politics, *Gebrauchsmusik* was not so much an artistic movement as a political idea in search of a party. There was little stylistic unity among the composers and commentators who became involved, and the polemics went back and forth. The composer, said Hindemith, 'should only write today if he knows for what purpose he is writing. The days of composing for the sake of composing are perhaps gone forever. On the other hand, the demand for music is so great that the composer and the consumer ought most emphatically to come at least to an understanding.'[16] For Hindemith, this meant a return to the practical values of pre-Romantic music, when professionals and amateurs performed together. Others disparaged this kind of *Gemeinschaftsmusik*, or community music – works for amateurs, choruses for youth festivals – which Krenek sneered at as *Blockflötenkultur* – 'recorder culture'. But the Communist militant Hanns Eisler, who had studied with Schoenberg, also disliked the stylistic implications of this position and, detecting a certain vagueness in Hindemith's utterances, counterattacked: 'When I hear talk of "building community spirit" through "joy in playing" then I become suspicious and immediately wonder what sort of community is going to be built and why these pieces of music, mostly pseudo-baroque, should arouse that joy ...'[17] He would have had a difficult time, however, in the Soviet Union, and did so, like Brecht, in East Germany after the war. Both regimes would have been happier with the more conformist music of Carl Orff, if he had not lent his musical talents to the Nazis.

Another who criticized Hindemith's ideas, as a means of saving the established structures of music from deeper social change, was Brecht, though as late as 1929 they worked together on a *Lehrstück*, a piece of didactic music theatre with a political theme for the Baden-Baden Festival. What they shared was the mental set of *Neue Sachlichkeit*, the anti-Expressionist tendency of postwar German art usually translated as the 'New Objectivity' or, in John Willett's more subtle rendering, the New Sobriety:[18] an ethos first identified with painting, said to reflect 'a radical commitment to the modern environment and everyday life',[19] which quickly revealed aesthetic correlations throughout the cultural sphere. The corresponding edge in Hindemith's approach to music of utility, topicality and social commitment served Brecht's theatrical purposes rather well. Kurt Weill, however, served him even better, for Weill had thought long and hard about the nature of the musico-dramatic gesture, the *gestus* which also figures centrally in Brecht's theory of epic theatre, and perceived its relation to melody, with marked effect on his own style of composition.

Before he began his collaboration with Brecht, Weill had already written two one-act operas and was at work on a third. His librettist for two of these one-acters was the Expressionist playwright Georg Kaiser. In the first, *Der Protagonist*, the title role is the leader of a company of strolling players in Shakespeare's England, in the process of rehearsing for a command performance before a Duke and his guests; since the players are foreign and have no knowledge of the language, the play will be in mime. In the Pantomime music which Weill provides for the rehearsal scene, the players sing wordlessly to the accompaniment of an onstage wind band. The style of the music is deliberately distinct from what surrounds it, predominantly grotesque and distorted, like an Expressionist parody (says the Weill scholar David Drew) of the *buffo* music of the rest of the opera.[20] Significantly, the score carries the instruction to be played '*ganz tänzerisch, unrealistisch, mit übertriebenen Gesten*' – 'dance-like, unrealistic, with exaggerated gestures'. A few years later, Weill reflected on the problem of the gesture in an essay written while he was composing the full version of *Mahagonny*. The form of opera is an absurdity, he says, if it does not succeed in granting music the predominant position in both the overall structure and the details. Therefore, the music of an opera must not abandon the task of drama to the text and the staging, it must take an active role in the presentation of the proceedings. The one capability of music which is of decisive significance in this endeavour is its capacity to embody the *gestus*, which elucidates the events onstage. 'It can even create a type of fundamental *gestus* which prescribes a definite attitude for the actor and eliminates any doubt or misunderstanding about the respective incident.'[21]

According to Weill, the basic musical means of gestic music lies in the rhythmic fixing of the text, in mapping the accents of the language, the distribution of syllables, 'and above all, pauses', around which the composer spins the musical web. Good examples, he says, can be found in the recitatives of Bach's *Passions*, in Mozart's operas, in *Fidelio*, in Offenbach and Bizet. In *The Magic Flute*, in the aria *Dies' Bildnis ist bezaubernd schön*, when Tamino sees a picture of Pamina for the first time, 'the attitude of a man who is gazing upon a picture is fixed by the music alone. He can hold the picture in either his right or left hand; he can raise or lower it; he can be illuminated by a spotlight or he can stand in the dark – his basic *gestus* is correct because it is correctly dictated by the music.' If the music thus accomplishes the fusion of words and gesture, this is also close to the way Mozart himself thought about it, to judge from the letter to his father where he describes his music for Osmin's rage and Belmonte's throbbing heart in *Die Entführung* which we encountered above.[22] As we saw then, this is something quite distinct from orthodox notions of characterization through the psychological effect of the music, which Weill, along with Brecht, dismisses.

In fact Brecht and Weill were both aiming at much the same thing, but from different directions; arguments about which of them dominated the partnership are therefore fruitless: they complemented each other. For Brecht, the *gestus* is more than a gesture; it is that part of the actor's stance (deportment, intonation, facial expression) which can be 'quoted' by another, because it corresponds to the social and external rather than the individual and interior element in the action. By emphasizing the *gestus*, Brecht wished to shift the emphasis from the inner life of the characters to their public existence and interaction, the way they behave towards each other – an essential step towards a more political theatre. The two men met on the opera stage because opera, in Germany, was the most public form of the aesthetic communicative act, addressed to an audience not of private individuals but of social subjects.

Brecht's predilection for songs is closely related to this intention. As Martin Esslin writes, he 'used to point to the way street singers render the more vulgar kind of popular song with large and simple gestures. His own ... were designed to achieve a similar effect on actor and audience alike by crystallising an essential, fundamental attitude and exhibiting it with the utmost clarity: despair or recognition, defiance or submission.'[23] Weill's genius lay in translating this material (which could be musical as well as verbal, for Brecht sometimes provided tunes to go with the words) into a novel form of music theatre which returned to the primacy of song; or in operatic terms, to the aria or ensemble which had been banished by Wagner and Debussy, and even by Verdi in *Falstaff*, though it is still sometimes present in Puccini. Thus, as Weill explained in a letter to the avant-garde music journal *Anbruch* ('Daybreak', edited by Adorno), *The Threepenny Opera* represented a 'return to a primal operatic form' which

> brought with it a far-reaching simplification of the musical language. It was necessary to write a kind of music that could be sung by actors – that is, by

musical laymen. But what seemed at first to be a limitation proved in the course of the work to be an enormous enrichment. It was above all the shaping of a comprehensible, easily perceived melodic line that made possible what was achieved in *The Threepenny Opera*, the creation of a new genre of musical theatre.[24]

Weill's Brechtian music theatre naturally made ample use of the forms of commercial popular music – street ballad and blues, foxtrot, shimmy and tango, combined with the parody of the musical-box waltz, hymns, chorales, and *opéra comique*. The elements in *The Threepenny Opera* go all the way from the parodistic fugal overture with which it opens, to the thanksgiving chorale which Weill uses for the fairy-tale happy ending. Along the way are hurdy-gurdy music in the famous *Moritat*, blues in the *Anstatt-dass* duet, foxtrot in the *Kannonensong*; Mackie and Polly's anti-romantic love duet is at one point marked 'Boston-Tempo'. The 'Barbara Song' is in cabaret style, and the 'First Threepenny Finale' is a combination of opera and vaudeville. There are even moments reminiscent of Gilbert and Sullivan patter ensembles, but the beat is harsher and more satanic, in the Berlin manner of the 1920s. There is one other number in Act I: the text of 'Pirate Jenny' is a burlesque of Senta's ballad in *The Flying Dutchman*, with its vision of a redeeming lover who will mysteriously come from over the sea; but here the music completely eschews any temptation to parody. Instead it is utterly anti-Wagnerian, scored for piano and banjo, wind and percussion, with dark sustained chords and piano arpeggios.

In the second act, after a musical-box waltz melody recalling the love duet, we get the 'Ballad of Sexual Need', a piece of Berlin satirical cabaret, followed by the 'Tango-Ballad', one of the best of all Weill's many tangos. The 'Ballad of the Good Life' is marked 'Shimmy Tempo' and comes off the vaudeville stage, while the 'Jealousy Duet' is operatic parody again. The 'Second Threepenny Finale' – 'What keeps a man alive' – is a nightmarish version of a Salvation Army hymn, with a strange echo in this stark music – punctuated by booming trombones and trumpets answering each other in strophe and antistrophe – of Mozart's *Don Giovanni*. The 'Solomon Song' in Act III is a waltz disguised as a street ballad, and 'Lucy's Aria' another operatic parody. Macheath goes to the gallows to a solemn oratorio-like processional, and then comes the third 'Finale': like the Beggar's final announcement in the original, Peachum steps foward and declares: 'since this is opera, there will be a happy ending', for which Weill turns out a pastiche of Handelian opera, revivals of which were then all the rage in Weimar Germany.

Musically, there is a certain affinity between *The Threepenny Opera* and Stravinsky's *Soldier's Tale*, with its pastiche of jazz, café and salon music, full of waltzes, polkas, rags, foxtrots and tangos. However, what Adorno regards in Stravinsky as a 'regressive tendency' embraces in Weill the politically radical dramatic concept provided by Brecht, and a strange thing happens: time and again, in works like *The Threepenny Opera* and *Happy End*, the music passes completely beyond pastiche and parody, and transcends itself to become the very model of the genre it imitates and, more, the paradigm of a new style of intelligent popular music (indeed, Weill's songs would be taken up within jazz, alongside numbers by popular composers on Broadway – a destiny which was never shared by Stravinsky). *Anbruch*, which was published by Weill's publishers, inquired of the composer's response to his enormous success:

> Dear Mr. Weill,
>   The sensational success of *The Threepenny Opera*, which allows a work of totally novel style that points to the future suddenly to become a box-office hit, confirms most gratifyingly prophecies repeatedly expressed in these pages. In this beautiful and exemplary model, the new popular opera-cum-operetta, which draws the proper inference from present-day artistic and social assumptions, has succeeded. May we ask you, since you have the advantage of . . . practical results . . . to comment theoretically . . .

To which (in the same letter quoted above) the composer replied, concerning the sociological significance of this success:

> here a breakthrough into the consumer industry, which until now had been reserved for a completely different type of composer or writer, has been accomplished for the first time . . . we addressed a public that did not know us at all . . . which far exceeded the boundaries of the musical and operatic audience . . . Theatre has decisively turned in a direction that one can characterize accurately as socially creative [*Gesellschaftsbildend*]. If the frame of opera does not allow an approach to this kind of contemporary theatre, quite certainly that framework must be exploded.[25]

Weill wrote in a letter to his publisher around the same time that he did not know 'how many more pieces I'll be able to write as effective as the "Alabama Song," the "Kanonensong," the "Tango Ballade," the "Ballade vom angenehmen Leben," and the "Moritat." '[26] (Fortunately for us, quite a few.) This correspondence is very revealing. A recent scholar calls it a 'dramatic narrative' of a career animated by questions and difficulties which confronted a whole generation of composers; he adds – usefully – that other sets of correspondence in the Universal

Edition (UE) archives are the same. It is clear, says Christopher Hailey, that this publisher was not at all passive towards the composer 'but exercised considerable influence on the genesis, planning, and shaping of individual works, as well as on the overall trajectory of entire careers'.[27]

Universal Edition played a key role in the reconstruction of musical life after the First World War, linking with other initiatives, like music festivals, to promote the new composers whom established publishers were abandoning. Under the guidance of a Budapest-born textile magnate by the name of Emil Hertzka, who had bought the Viennese publishing house a few years after it was founded in 1901, UE became the midwife of musical modernism. According to Ernst Roth, who worked for him, Hertzka, who was no doctrinaire, followed a policy guided by public opinion – he was no doctrinaire: everything it was offended by, he published: 'All new music of no fixed abode' found a home under his roof – Schoenberg, Berg and Webern, Bartók, Kodály, Krenek, Weill, Milhaud, the Italians Casella and Malipiero, and many more. 'Anyone who had a grudge against "old" music – or against its representatives – was welcome at Universal Edition', and successes like Krenek's *Johnny spielt auf* and Weill's *Dreigroschenoper* were as welcome to Hertzka 'as the riots and fisticuffs which surrounded *Pierrot Lunaire* and [Berg's] *Wozzeck*'. If UE seemed to specialize in works rejected by other publishers, nevertheless there was a logic behind this apparently loss-making formula, which reveals a canny reading of the nature of the modern musical lifeworld. Hertzka did what no comparable publisher for the classical market was doing any longer. Instead of relying on the newly consolidated systems of international copyright and performance rights to rake in profits from back catalogues of now dead composers, while shying away from living ones, Hertzka considered the long-term prospects for new investment. He may have had the feeling, as Roth puts it: 'that a new art was about to arise, and that he could seize an opportunity which older and wealthier publishers were sure to misjudge and therefore miss'; but he operated not on the basis of personal taste but on the principle of literary publishers that a few big successes would pay for what was less successful, knowing that some of the latter would in due course produce long-term bestsellers; as a safeguard, he also subsidized his investment through subsidiaries which published dance music and pocket scores of standard classics. He did not just leave it up to the public opinion he defied, however. UE was highly proactive, spending considerable sums not only on engraving, printing and publicity, but also 'on supporting financially the struggling prophets of the new art'.[28]

As part of this policy, Universal published the journal *Anbruch* and supported the International Society for Contemporary Music (ISCM), whose summer festivals became a showcase for UE composers. Here the publisher becomes allied to a new kind of international network corresponding to a new balance of power within the cultural domain. The ISCM grew out of a festival organized by young Viennese composers in Salzburg in 1922, one of a number of initiatives in the German-speaking world to promote new music – like the Donaueschingen Festival, which ran from 1921 to 1926, and Baden-Baden, which replaced it, both dedicated to chamber music by contemporary composers. The genius of the ISCM was to internationalize itself: founded at an international congress in London in 1923, it operated through national branches under an English president, the musicologist Edward J. Dent, with an annual festival held in a different country each year, featuring works submitted through the society's national branches. By the time of the London festival, 1938, there were twenty-five national sections, including eight outside Europe (in Argentina, Australia, Columbia, Cuba, Japan, Palestine, Peru and the USA). A composer who entered this circuit encountered a very different world from the orbit of the previous generation.

Weill's relationship to Universal Edition changed with the success of *The Threepenny Opera* and *Mahagonny*, since at that moment he stopped needing the subsidy with which the publisher nurtured such promising young composers, and instead began to earn both himself and them considerable sums. An amusing account is given by Hans Heinsheimer, a colleague of Roth: 'A lot of people who had avoided us through all of our professional lives like a boring plague, tried to find out how we spelled our names and were surprised to discover we had a telephone.' Hertzka was approached by 'a man who looked like the personification of His Master's Voice and turned out to be just that', who offered him money to record a show album of *Dreigroschenoper*. 'He did not *ask* for money to record one of our publications – he *offered* it. It was a shattering experience . . . a delicious disgrace.'[29] UE lost no time exploiting their successes, as arrangements were prepared for dance bands, jazz ensembles and movie-house orchestras, recording contracts were signed, and the numbers were issued individually as hits. Weill urged that these arrangements should be kept as simple as possible, for the market was no longer a sophisticated audience of new music enthusiasts, but the broader and less musically tutored music-lovers of the mass public. Universal Edition were nevertheless sceptical of the long-term viability of the direction his music was taking, advising him that his popular song style could not be copied indefinitely. Weill, for his part, was intensely conscious of the problem of style as commodity – 'of the market value of novelty', as Hailey puts it, and 'the twin perils of repetition and competition in the fast turnover' of commercial music economics.[30] Indeed, all these are issues he discusses in the column he wrote from 1925 to 1929 in the weekly radio magazine *Der Deutsche Rundfunk.*

The fact that Weill should write for a publication that pioneered a new domain within the public sphere – the magazine combined programme listings with articles on technical, social and aesthetic issues, plus music and theatre criticism – is itself a characteristic marker of his social conception of the composer. Staking his claim to the tradition of composer polemics which goes back to Schumann, he directly confronts what has become of this tradition, when there are composers 'who, filled with disdain for the audience, continue to work towards the solution of aesthetic problems as if behind closed doors'. Instead – in an article for a Berlin newspaper in 1927 under the title 'Shifts in Musical Composition' – he calls for a 'departure from individualistic artistic principles', and a turn from the role of a socially exclusive art towards a broader audience – the only one through which music can maintain its social viability.[31] The first question for the composer, he writes two years later, is this: 'Is what we do useful to a general public? It is only a secondary question if what we create is art, for that is determined only by the quality of our work.'[32]

What we find in these writings is a highly condensed but extremely cogent outline of what amounts to an interrogation of the musical public sphere from the composer's point of view. Art music – *Kunst-musik* – is composed for an audience of 'music societies and organizations devoted to the cultivation of new music whose sphere of listeners is made up primarily of musicians'. *Verbrauchsmusik* – commercial music – is a simplified music for immediate consumption. The desire to mediate between them generates *Gebrauchsmusik* – music for social use – which embraces social aims, and the new domains of radio and film music. *Gebrauchsmusik* has certain stylistic implications. It does not seek to compete with *Schlagerkomponisten* – hit composers – and does not sacrifice the intellectual bearing of the serious musician in order to compete in the market with V*erbrauchsmusik.* It represents a deliberate 'lowering of aesthetic sights', but only in the search for a musical language that is comprehensible to a broad audience. The issue is not 'tonal' or 'atonal', and originality is no longer a primary concern; the idiom Weill seeks is enticing only in order to be provocative; it is conceived against a background of ethical and social concern, and is therefore 'thoroughly serious, bitter, accusing, and even in the most pleasant context, ironic'.

If Weill describes his own musical aims here with great accuracy, Adorno perceives his solution as a kind of negative time bomb, which will implode to destroy its own transgressive potential. In a polemical and partial reading of the musical situation on the eve of Hitler's ascent to power, Adorno differentiated four tendencies in contemporary music. The first was the preserve of Schoenberg and his school; for Adorno (who himself was a composition pupil of Schoenberg's pupil Berg), this was the only trend which merited being called 'modern music'. The second, 'objectivism', was represented by Stravinsky, but also corresponded to the anti-Expressionist tendency of postwar German art known as *Neue Sachlichkeit*. Later, Adorno would make the antithesis of Schoenberg and Stravinsky into the central axis of his *Philosophy of New Music*. A third type he calls 'community music', a cousin of *Neue Sachlichkeit* and objectivism but directed at fulfilling particular social functions, whose chief exponents are Hindemith, Weill, and Eisler with his 'proletarian choral works', which, despite Adorno's political sympathies, he considered musically empty. Indeed, for Adorno, any type of *Gebrauchsmusik* was symptomatic of 'false rationalization'; yet when it came to Weill and *The Threepenny Opera*, he was forced into uncharacteristic ambivalence.

In Weill, he identifies a fourth type of contemporary music which he calls – somewhat oddly – surrealism. It is difficult to square this use of the term with the character of Weill's musical world, which is as far as could be from the psychological, the unconscious and the Freudian. Stephen Hinton associates Adorno's reading with Krenek's interpretation a few years later of the polemical essence of surrealism as 'the intention of unmasking the illusion': a process of 'refunctioning', 'whose essential means is a montage technique [which] consists of splitting up the usual unity of text and music and imposing on each half a new meaning opposed to the earlier one'; a procedure Krenek mistrusts because, he says, it is too easily reversible – 'one has only to rectify a couple of wrong bass notes and . . . it becomes rather cozy'.[33] The truth is that Adorno was nonplussed by Weill. His bewilderment is evident in his review of *Die Dreigroschenoper*, where he finds that Weill has written '*Gebrauchsmusik* that can really be used', because of its critical distortions of the atrophied material of dance music and jazz; so that in the face of Weill's 'force and originality', any objection pales.[34] In short, he cannot fail to perceive the delicious incongruity between the rough and common characters on the stage and the sublime melodies which issue from their mouths, but he finds the experience discombobulating. Nevertheless, there is a crucial truth in his later critique, when he writes:

The misunderstanding on the part of the public, whereby the songs of *Die Dreigroschenoper*, which after all are their own and their public's enemy, are peacefully consumed as hit tunes – this misunderstanding may be legitimate as a means of dialectical communication. The further course of things, however, reveals ambiguity to be a danger: the unmasked appearance turns into false positiveness, destruction into the community art of the status quo.[35]

It would seem consistent with Adorno's critique that Weill's music would lose its edge when he took exile in New York and tried to translate his philosophy on to Broadway; and that former collaborators, colleagues and admirers, like Brecht, Eisler, the conductor Otto Klemperer and the philosopher Ernst Bloch, should join Adorno in disdain for the 'new' Weill. David Drew suggests that Weill in America did away 'with his old creative self in order to make way for a new one'.[36] He suppressed his identity as a German composer – he even refused to speak German – and asserted that his only roots were those he had now established in the USA; that his responsibilities were to the American musical stage in its popular form, where the composer he now saw as his chief rival was not Hindemith but Richard Rodgers. He himself, says the Weill scholar Kim Kowalke, believed that he had no options. His métier was theatre music. He could not join Schoenberg, Hindemith, Krenek and Milhaud in their academic shelters, nor accept the film industry's treatment of its bevy of skilled émigré composers, so California held no appeal, and instead he made for the heartland of the theatre.[37] He therefore remade himself as an American composer, aided by a gift he shared with that other émigré composer of opera who arrived in England via Italy in the early eighteenth century: an acute ear for the phrase structure and accent of the language. Krenek would sum up retrospectively:

If Kurt Weill in America seemed to exchange the aggressive, bald, and sarcastic style of his Brecht period for the sumptuousness, the mundane sentimentality, and the, if at all, circumspect irony of the Broadway manner, he was probably hardly aware of the fact that in doing so he descended in our eyes below the level of his tradition and his earlier works. Rather he did, as he himself told me, what seemed necessary to comply with that natural, invincible urge of his to communicate via the musical theatre: he adapted this communication to the only vehicle at his disposal, namely the Broadway stage.[38]

In the end, the issue is not the musical quality of Weill's Broadway musicals; as Weill himself put it, these are only secondary questions. The interest of these works is their paradigmatic role in expanding the parameters of the Broadway musical, the most prestigious 'native'

American musical genre, and the apex of a career as a popular composer from George Gershwin to Leonard Bernstein and beyond; the cornerstone of the claim of such composers to greater impact as public figures, at least in their own country, than any number of so-called serious composers who lacked such a knack for the popular idiom.

Gershwin, Ellington and the Harlem Renaissance

Established notions of the composer come into question in America from the opposite direction. If Weill pursues a trajectory which starts with the adoption of a populist aesthetic, *pour épater le bourgeois*, and ends with a lowering of aesthetic sights (and a loss of political acuity), then in figures like George Gershwin and Duke Ellington a composer emerges from popular origins to claim the respectability and cultural status of high art, a challenge with its own political overtones.

The case of Gershwin is a counterpart to that of Weill, a sequel to Offenbach and a precursor to Bernstein. Is it merely coincidence, in the century after Meyerbeer and Mendelssohn, that all four emanate from Central European musical Jewish families? Or is it, rather, that the history of the Jewish composer constantly repeats the problematic of the cultural passage from outside in, from the cultural margins to the centre of the musical lifeworld? Perhaps of equal importance, their common background was one in which musicality took the form of singing: Offenbach's and Weill's fathers, and Gershwin's grandfather, were all synagogue cantors. But where Offenbach and Weill both received a classical training, Gershwin had little formal musical education, and began his professional career in Tin Pan Alley. In subsequently seeking to embrace, on his own terms, the concert platform and the opera house, he became, like Weill, a transgressive composer: Weill is accused of betraying his heritage; Gershwin of attempting something for which he is ill-equipped. The debate which began with the success of *Rhapsody in Blue* in 1924, when Gershwin was still only twenty-six, addressed directly the changes which mass culture brought about in the scope for the composer's cultural interventions – indeed, the very possibility of the 'popular art composer', and the issues of national and ethnic identity which this raised in 1920s America. All these matters excited contemporary comment.

Some saw Gershwin in a line including Offenbach, Sullivan and Johann Strauss, composers who were said to evoke an immediate response 'in the hearts of their contemporaries', who became 'the articulate expression' and even 'symbol' of their age.[39] According to

Olin Downes, music critic of the *New York Times*, Gershwin's rise from Tin Pan Alley to Carnegie Hall, 'his emergence from the stage of a highly promising purveyor of popular entertainment to the higher realms of art', might be seen as 'a manifestation of a certain phase of democracy and American opportunity'.[40] For another critic, Paul Rosenfeld, however, the Americanism of *An American in Paris* (1928) was a highly dubious quality:

> Momentarily we feel the forces of ambition and desire; imperious, unmitigated appetites, yearnings for tenderness, intoxications flowing from the stimulation of novel, luxurious surroundings ... from the joy of feeling oneself an American – Americanism apparently conceived as a naive, smart, inept, good-natured form of being, happily and humorously shared by other good fellows like oneself ...

The 'atrocious dreams' which this music articulates could be compared, he believed, with advertising: 'most American art is advertising, glorifying the material objects and fanning up the appetite directed upon them; and this category of aesthetic products is dangerously close to that of George Gershwin ...'[41] This could almost have been written by Adorno.

Some of the criticisms were musically sensitive to the dilution of black musical traits by white musicians of the kind to be found precisely in dance bands like Paul Whiteman's, which premiered some of Gershwin's concert music. They hardly distinguish between Gershwin's musical aims and the racial stereotypes of the black minstrel tradition continued by entertainers like Al Jolson, or shows like *Amos 'n Andy*. The ethnographer Zora Neale Hurston, for example, decrying the white musician's failure to assimilate the true Negro accent in song and dance, judged Gershwin as a *faux* Negro rhapsodist, 'just about as Negro as caviar'.[42] In these circumstances, when Gershwin passed over a commission from the Metropolitan Opera to write an opera based on a Yiddish play, Ansky's *The Dybbuk*, in favour of one about black Americans taken from a novel by DuBose Heyward, then – as musicologist Glenn Watkins writes – 'the spectre of a New York Jewish composer treating a story of Southern blacks written by a white novelist that associated African Americans with crime, violence, and shiftlessness ... could only have been seen as a perpetuation of racial stereotypes'.[43] Black intellectuals, like Hall Johnson writing in the 'New Negro' magazine *Opportunity*, treated *Porgy and Bess* with circumspection, suggesting that such a venture was probably beyond the reach of any white composer; while Alain Locke, noting Gershwin's mix of Afro-American music with the methods of grand opera, suggested: 'it is not certain how well such musical oil and water can be made to mix'.[44] Similar reservations were expressed by whites. The critic and composer Virgil Thomson summed up: 'With a libretto that should never have been accepted on a subject that should never have been chosen, a man who should never have attempted it has written a work of some power and importance.'[45] Perhaps it is not surprising that the original production in 1935 was not a success; even when it was revived eighteen years later, many still found it unacceptable. According to jazz critic and record producer Rudi Blesh:

> Gershwin's *Porgy and Bess* is not Negro opera despite a Negro cast, a liberal use of artificial coloration, and the inclusion of some street cries. It is *Negroesque*, and earlier travesty of minstrelsy is continued in a form more subtle and therefore more invidious . . . By enlisting actual Negroes for the public performance of these Tin Pan Alley potpourris, a new stereotype . . . is being fitted to the Negro in which he is set forth as an able entertainer singing a music that the white public finds to be just like *its own*. In these works, as in virtually all of the movie output which pretends to present Negro music, the public never hears fine, real Negro music . . .[46]

Back in 1935, even Duke Ellington, who was normally reticent about such things in public, was drawn into the controversy when the subject was broached in an interview by a reporter named Edward Morrow from the left-wing magazine *New Theatre*. 'Grand music and a swell play,' said Ellington, 'but the two don't go together.' Pressed by Morrow, he added: 'it does not use the Negro musical idiom'; it was not the music of Catfish Row 'or any other kind of Negroes'; Gershwin's style was derivative, 'taken from some of the best and a few of the worst'; he did not discriminate, 'he borrowed from everyone from Liszt to Dickie Wells' kazoo band'. The account finally prompts Ellington to the conclusion that 'no Negro could possibly be fooled by *Porgy and Bess*' and its superficial tricks, 'cooked-up, flavoured and seasoned to be palmed off as authentic'.[47] Ellington was apparently so upset by the way the interview was written up that he had his agents issue a rebuff, where he expressed the hope that 'Gershwin didn't take any stock in those things I was supposed to have said'. The article is none the less highly indicative of contradictions not only in the reception of the opera itself, but running right through the debate about authenticity in which Ellington himself was embroiled. In the course of the interview, Ellington turned to the piano and demonstrated how, in *Rhapsody in Blue*, Gershwin borrowed from a Negro song called 'Where Has My Easy Rider Gone?'. He then played what he called a 'gut-bucket waltz' in a Negro idiom, to demonstrate how you can apply what he called 'the method' of a musical style without stealing or borrowing.

Morrow represents these illustrations as a straightforward confirmation of his own arguments, but in fact they are highly problematic – or, to put it another way, they indicate the high degree of intertextuality in popular musical idioms. As Watkins mentions, various musical authorities have shown that Ellington's 'Creole Rhapsody' contains subtle borrowings from Gershwin's *Rhapsody in Blue*; while 'Cotton Tail' takes off from 'I Got Rhythm'.[48] It would be amazing, says Watkins, if Ellington failed to realize that both Gershwin and he himself actually did the same thing, picking up musical ideas wherever they found them and turning them to personal account – or what Watkins calls 'transformative emulation' rather than 'surface imitation'. Nor is this kind of emulation at all unusual; on the contrary, it was nurtured by the very dynamics of popular music and its disrespect for the idea of private sources of inspiration. Moreover, this free exchange of musical elements and ideas – which always goes on despite the regulation of copyright and intellectual property – is in stark contrast with the purism implied by criticisms like Locke's; this points to a critical blind spot in the aesthetics espoused by the generation of African-American intellectuals who inspired the ideals of the New Negro, an issue to which we shall have to return.

Porgy first reached the New York stage as a play in 1927. A year later, Heyward completed a novel, *Mamba's Daughters*, which – Watkins says – is reminiscent of Israel Zangwill's play *The Melting-Pot* (1908), which relates the tale of a Russian-Jewish composer living in New York whose ambition was to write a symphony 'expressing the vast, harmonious interweaving of races in America'.[49] Ironically, there is another link here which Watkins misses: a connection with the film celebrated as the first talkie, *The Jazz Singer* (also 1927), where Al Jolson plays the son of synagogue cantor who leaves home to become a blackface singer; the film is a latter-day version of Zangwill's portrait of immigrant aspirations seen through the eyes of the Hollywood production machine which was itself another outgrowth of the same process. It is to Gershwin's credit that he rejected Al Jolson's proposal for a blacked-up Porgy, and for his own version he insisted on an all-black cast (at one time he hoped for Paul Robeson as the lead). Indeed, he intended *Porgy and Bess* as a critical comment on a tradition of racial stereotyping, a bold attempt to give voice and dignity to characters taken from the very bottom of the social pile, dating from a time when both Jews and Blacks were subject to comparable misrepresentations in the mainstream media, but also when both used music and entertainment to cross certain social barriers. One of Ellington's biographers, John Edward Hasse, comments on the common attraction of Tin Pan Alley for Jewish singers, songwriters, publishers and musical theatre producers, with the result that 'the two groups, blacks and Jews, formed a symbiotic relationship'; of which one example was Ellington's albeit troubled relationship with his publisher, Irving Mills.[50] This observation serves as a reminder that what is represented in both Gershwin and Ellington are benign versions of a complex about racial and ethnic identity which, then and now, is central to the character of American culture. It also points towards a critical aspect of popular music as a cultural public sphere, the element of truth in the melting-pot theory of American culture, which is formed by the fusion and integration of multiple foreign cultures interacting in a new ferment, for which music provides a privileged and paradigmatic site.

When Stravinsky first laid hands on black American music during the First World War, while he was composing *The Soldier's Tale* in Switzerland, what he encountered was ragtime, in the form of sheet music and records which his friend, the conductor Ernest Ansermet, brought back with him from touring America. The ragtime in *The Soldier's Tale*, the *Piano Rag Music*, and the piece called *Ragtime* (where Stravinsky uses the cymbalom, an Eastern European folk instrument, to imitate the sonority of a brothel piano) – these Stravinsky calls 'concert portraits'; they are like a 'snapshot of the genre – in the sense that Chopin's *Valses* are not dance waltzes but portraits of waltzes'. A year or so later Stravinsky heard his first live jazz, and discovered that 'jazz performance is more interesting than jazz composition' because of its improvisation.[51]

Ragtime proper was not an improvised form; it originated among a group of young black pianists working in the clubs, bars and brothels of the Mississippi Delta towards the end of the nineteenth century, who took to writing down their music in the same way as composers south of the Rio Grande, like Joaquim Antônio da Silva Callado in Brazil and the maxixe, or Manuel Saumell in Cuba and the *danzón*. This was a new type of musically literate popular composer who sought to emulate the respectability which was the norm of bourgeois music, but using popular dance forms; the most successful of the North American composers, Scott Joplin, who modelled certain features of his rags on Sousa marches, even wrote an opera.

The broader idiom which came to be known as jazz, and included ragtime among its forebears, is commonly traced back to the small street bands, made up mainly of wind instruments, found around the turn of the century in New Orleans, a city with a past both Spanish and French which afforded particular cultural advantages to black musicians. Even before it was promoted to prominence by King Cotton, New Orleans was a major port for international traffic passing through the Caribbean and Central America, and accordingly developed an exceptionally rich musical culture with diverse inputs. It became a point of intersection where three different European traditions – French, Spanish and Anglo-Saxon – came in contact with a creole music in which black African influences were especially strong: the French influence had meant, among other things, that plantation slaves in the New Orleans hinterland were often allowed a degree of cultural expression denied by Anglo-Saxon slave-owners. With the rise of cotton, after the USA had bought Louisiana from the French in 1803, New Orleans rapidly became the only sophisticated metropolitan centre in the American South: an entrepôt, a marketplace, a city of leisure, creole cuisine, theatre, music and vice, which encouraged a large body of both professional and semi-professional musicians; and as in the other great Caribbean entrepôt, Havana, free black musicians comprised a major element in the city's musical rank-and-file. A black symphony orchestra had been formed in New Orleans as early as 1830, and the city supported as many as three opera companies, as well as the marching bands among which jazz originated.

That a new form of *musica practica* took root here and began to flourish as an autonomous musical domain was due to a series of favourable circumstances. First, the early jazz musicians enjoyed a direct and close relationship with their audience: they were essentially semi-professional local musicians employed to play at picnics, funerals, weddings and holiday parties, who then became professionalized as the new music caught on. While this was happening, the geographical isolation of New Orleans from the centres of musical entertainment in the north-east of the USA protected its first manifestations from both extraneous influences and the interest of big musical capital. As Mike Hobart, a writer on the 'political economy of bop', explains, once the early jazz musicians became dependent on music for their livelihood they came into relations, equally direct but relatively benign, with the owners of the clubs, dance-halls and shows which made up the black entertainment circuit; thus the geographical spread of jazz beyond New Orleans was rapid.[52] Publishing, however, at the time the dominant form of musical capital, by its very nature had little interest in an improvised music, and in any case did not regard black America as an exploitable market beyond filching some of its songs and arranging them for white audiences. Ironically, therefore, because the social and economic segregation of black Americans extended into the cultural sphere, they were able to develop a new and distinctive music unhindered. Indeed, it is not until the intangible performance is transmuted by recording into a material commodity that jazz enters the world of full-scale capitalist relations and begins to escape into the wider community. It was at the culmination of the First World War that the record industry started producing 'race labels' aimed specifically at a black audience; the initial effect was to boost the popularity of the classic blues.

The early development of jazz thus remained independent of Tin Pan Alley, which was dominated by the publishers. Instead of the stock arrangement, jazz was free to develop a series of different musical models and incorporate improvisation. Elements of march, hymn, rag and blues became fused into a musical discourse of unified diversity, consisting of dense contrapuntal ensemble playing with breaks for individual improvisation. In European music, extemporization was a lost art, practised by the beginning of the twentieth century by precious few (mostly organists, though Elgar recorded some piano improvisations in his later years, on twelve-inch 78s, one per side). This is one of the reasons why European composers were both stimulated and nonplussed by jazz: they were intrigued by its improvisatory elements, which they recognized at the same time as beyond their reach. In many respects, improvisation became the main trait of jazz which enabled it to resist the full encroachment of capitalist production techniques. Even when big bands emerged in the 1920s, stimulating the art of arrangement, the publisher's control over the music remained limited; notation could transcribe only the skeleton of performance, leaving its realization to the musicians themselves much more radically than did the standardized scores of white music. For example, Duke Ellington's first New York band, The Washingtonians, avoided 'stock' arrangements and worked out their own instead. The mobilization of this collective oral–aural composition became the essential element in Ellington's skill as a bandleader, earning him within a few years the status of the foremost jazz composer.

The status of jazz composer is paradoxical. At first sight – and precisely to the extent that the music is improvised – there is something incommensurable between the idea of jazz and the notion of the composer as the singular author of the music being played. This paradox, however, is in large measure the result of the process described in earlier pages: the institutionalization of the function of the composer within a musical domain configured by a division of function of labour induced by progressive commercialization. Musically speaking, this is a distortion, depending on what the composer-conductor Lukas Foss once called the very unmusical idea of dividing what is essentially indivisible – music – into two separate processes: composition, or the making of music, and performance, which is also the making of music. What Ellington represents is their reunification, in a situation which allowed for something like the resuscitation of the functions of the Baroque *Kapellmeister* transposed to the secular domain of commercial entertainment.

On the other hand, even as the process of commercialization drove the composer to the economic margins, the figure is invested with a form of cultural prestige and social status to which jazz, as a subaltern music, was foreign. The disparagement of jazz was found not only in the white world but also in the black – at least among the intelligentsia whose flowering, known as the Harlem Renaissance, coincides with Ellington's rise to fame as a composer, and with whom he had an ambivalent relationship. As pianist Willie 'the Lion' Smith recalled, Renaissance figures rejected the 'Negro image created in the South' which was 'constantly given a showcase by both white and colored show business'.[53] To the intellectuals, says Samuel Floyd, editor of a volume on music in the Harlem Renaissance, the 'antics' of some jazzmen who perpetuated the posturings of the minstrel tradition were embarrassing, while for jazz musicians, the intellectuals were a source of amusement: known as the 'dicty' set, says Floyd, they served as inspiration for Henderson's 'Dicty's Blues' (1923) and Ellington's 'Dicty Glide' (1929).[54]

In the white world, it was not the composer's credit on the phonograph record or the song which aroused controversy, but the celebration of his music by a small number of critics and foreign composers – notably Percy Grainger and Constant Lambert, who were well known for their cultivation of exotic musical connections, and who intended to scandalize when they mentioned Ellington alongside Delius, Debussy, Ravel, and even Bach. In the black world, the question went far deeper. The ascent of jazz was part and parcel of an upsurge of black American creative activity at the end of the First World War, which was centred in the industrial cities of the North as they grew to take in waves of Southern migrants and returning soldiers, and constituted the emergence of a vibrant new black public sphere, with distinctive features of its own. Within just a few years, clubs and meeting-halls, theatres, movie houses and dance-halls sprang up in the black sections of Chicago, Detroit, Cleveland, Philadelphia and especially New York, while there was growing interest and debate among educated African-Americans over questions of black history, literature and art. According to Ron Eyerman and Andrew Jamison, a cultural milieu was created which mixed the high and the low, the serious and the popular, and connected them through magazines, journals and newspapers which served to link a widespread and socially diverse racial community.[55] The distinctive character of this movement was its re-creation of the conviviality and literary bias of the early forms of the bourgeois public sphere, but mapped against a dominant and highly commercialized public sphere which was fast developing the new cultural formations of the mass media. This reconfiguration would produce particular tensions around music, as the leading form of black American artistic prowess both within the black community and beyond.

When W.E.B. DuBois, a few years into the New Negro movement, wrote: 'until the art of the black folk compels recognition they will not be rated as human', he was not thinking of the blues of Bessie Smith and the jazz of 'King' Oliver; his musical model was that of spirituals, as sung by trained choirs or singers of lieder. The tradition goes back to the 1870s, when the Fisk University Jubilee Singers of Nashville, Tennessee, first brought the black 'sorrow song' or spiritual to the concert platform and to international audiences, when they went on tour to raise funds for their new institution. This is the moment which Paul Gilroy, in *The Black Atlantic*, identifies as the entry of black music 'into the public domain of late nineteenth century mass entertainment'.[56] Their success spawned a host of similar companies who took to the road in Europe, South Africa and elsewhere, projecting an image of choral dignity in explicit opposition, says Gilroy, to the stereotypes of the flippant minstrel show. In America their example would inspire the liberal intellectuals who invited Dvořák to New York, and the black intellectuals of the new century, including DuBois, who was a student at Fisk and devoted a chapter to the Jubilee Singers in *The Souls of Black Folk*.

Yet the concert spiritual is not as pure as it sounds, and its musical idiom is contradictory; it claims the authority of authenticity, but there is nothing musically primitive or illiterate about it. Indeed, for Hurston, the success of the Fisk choir represented the triumph of formal musicianship over the vital, untrained, angular spirit of the rural folk who 'care nothing about pitch' and 'are bound by no rules'. 'The spirituals that have been sung around the world', she wrote, 'are Negroid to be sure, but so full of musicians' tricks that Negro congregations are highly entertained when they hear their old songs so changed.'[57] It was the Fisk Singers themselves, she thought, who originated what she calls 'this Glee Club style'.

By the 1920s, the raw music of the South had invaded the North, and in New York it was rapidly incorporated into Harlem life. The black population of New York had outstripped that of Washington as the largest black urban community in the country, and Harlem became the cultural capital of black America. Just as in New Orleans and Washington, where Ellington grew up, music was everywhere: the music of the black theatre shows, the dance music of the cabarets, the blues and ragtime of the speakeasies and the rent parties, the spirituals and art songs of the recital and concert-halls – all created an ambience for the activities of the Harlem Renaissance. The Harlem Renaissance has been treated primarily as a literary movement, says Floyd, 'with occasional asides, contributed as musical spice, about the jazz age and the performances of concert artists', but the role of music was crucial.[58] David Levering Lewis, in his introduction to a collection of Renaissance writings, agrees: 'The very centrality of music in black life, as well as of black musical stereotypes in white minds, caused popular musical forms to impinge inescapably on Renaissance high culture.'[59] When the visiting Russian film director Sergei Eisenstein enthused about new black musicals, Charles S. Johnson and Alain Locke expressed mild consternation, but eventually 'the Renaissance deans' made a virtue out of necessity: 'they applauded the concert-hall ragtime of "Big Jim" Europe and the "educated" jazz of Atlanta University graduate and big-band leader Fletcher Henderson, and took to hiring Duke Ellington or Cab Calloway as drawing cards for fund-raising socials'.[60] The irony of the situation was that Ellington was the very model of Locke's concept of the 'New Negro', which he represented, according to one description, 'in his dignified manner and cultivated persona, his social consciousness, his use of vernacular sources . . . and his deep pride in the Afro-American heritage'.[61]

Mark Tucker argues that Ellington received what amounted to the basic framework of a Renaissance-type education growing up in Washington, where he was born in 1899 into a secure black middle-class home. Popular biographers make much of the encouragement he received from his mother; Tucker's point is that social culture as well as individual psychology is at issue here: the black Washington middle class cultivated 'a public persona that commanded respect by its inherent dignity and decorum' – which, moreover, was considered 'essential for blacks working in popular music who wanted to be taken seriously'.[62] The musical lifeworld of black Washington ran the gamut from pianists and small ensembles, choral societies and glee clubs, military bands, a symphony orchestra and one of America's earliest black opera companies; advanced formal musical education was provided by the Washington Conservatory. It seems that Ellington kept his distance from formal music, heading instead for the popular music of the less educated. Nevertheless, he found tutors and models in conservatory-trained black musicians, like Oliver 'Doc' Perry, who moved fluently between different types of performance venue – as Ellington himself was to do. In the 1920s, a brief but strong influence on Ellington would be Will Marion Cook, composer of one of the first all-black revues, *Clorindy, The Origin of the Cakewalk*, back in the late 1890s; Cook, who had studied in Berlin and been a pupil of Joachim and Dvořák, taught him about compositional values. Ansermet wrote about Cook's Southern Syncopated Orchestra, which he heard in London in 1919, in what was probably the first piece of writing about jazz – though he still calls it ragtime – by what he himself terms a learned musician. Cook himself, writes Watkins, took pains not to describe the music they played as jazz – the term was derogatory. The etymology of the word is unknown; some think it derives from the French *jaser*, to jabber. According to one source it was first used in print as early as 1909 in reference to dancing, but in the slang of the deep South it also had sexual connotations. One story has it that it became attached to the music in Chicago in 1916 when an inebriated retired vaudeville entertainer, excited by the music, leaped to his feet and yelled 'Jass it up, boys!': he was immediately paid a retainer to come back every night and repeat his performance, and the term caught on. The story may even be true, though it is hardly singular. The words 'jazz song' appeared on sheet music as a subtitle to Clarence Williams's 'Brown Skin, Who You For' a year or two earlier. In any event, the word had an aura of disrepute which it did not quite shed when it transferred itself to the music, and was only reinforced when Prohibition linked its natural home in the nightclub and cabaret with other forbidden fruits. The mature Ellington, who expressed dislike of hierarchies and pigeon-holing, objected to the word jazz when he thought it represented a limiting attitude towards the music; he once declared, in defiance of the widespread notion of folk music as the anonymous repertoire of a people (and echoing what Villa-Lobos told Carpentier): 'I don't write jazz, I write Negro folk music.'[63]

In New York Ellington began by writing songs and taking a composer's credit for arrangements worked out with his own band using his own tunes. His engagement at the Cotton Club in 1927 gave him the opportunity to develop his skills in the favourable conditions of secure employment, good pay, and public exposure, even though it was a practically whites-only audience; but Ellington was nothing if not pragmatic; the club's policy was not unusual at the time, it gave him a regular slot on the radio, and above all an eager audience, for the Cotton Club's social cachet made it a safe place for white socialites (and composers like George Gershwin) to encounter black culture face to face. Encouraged by the club's penchant for exotic floorshows – and its décor of African motifs – he developed an expertise in the style known as 'jungle music', where, under the veil of exotica, it was possible to do all sorts of raucous, bold, unconventional things. Exotic chord progressions, and so-called jungle effects involving the use of special mutes (the growl and the plunger) – the specialities of trumpeter James 'Bubber' Miley and trombonist Joe 'Tricky Sam' Nanton – were combined with disparate musical material. Watkins mentions the example of 'Black and Tan Fantasy', which introduces the cry, the field-holler, the Easter hymn 'Holy City' played in the minor, a profusion of blue notes, and a coda quoting Chopin's Funeral March, alongside African tom-tom effects, unusual harmonies and primitive-sounding scales (actually pentatonic and whole-tone).[64]

As Ellington's fame increased, the press revealed the limits and confusions of popular understanding. A writer in the *Christian Science Monitor* in 1930 expresses bewilderment on interviewing him: on the one hand he seems musically naive, on the other 'It is a little hard to get precisely at what he means when says he wants to "develop legitimate humor" because wailing and moaning and the hollow laughter of brass instruments is debatable humour.'[65] An English critic, writing in a popular music magazine after Ellington's first European tour in 1933, sets out to disabuse the naive who marvelled at the fact that the band mostly played without written music, and supposed the incredible flights of the soloists to be pure improvisation. If the key, he explained, was *rehearsal*, the term took on a wider meaning in a process which began with an idea from Ellington, where the players made their own suggestions and Ellington organized the composition, sketching a rough score as it evolved through argument and exchange of ideas.[66] Ellington contributed his own account in another British publication, a magazine aimed at dance-band musicians, in 1931: 'Long association between players should result in their being able almost to anticipate each other's thoughts, so that the first desideratum, *viz.*, that they should play as one man, is not hard to attain.' Published orchestrations were much too stereotyped; a top-flight band had to be original: 'What little fame I have achieved is the result of my special orchestrations, and especially the cooperation of the boys in the band.'[67] In fact, his genius as a composer was inseparable from his ability to discover and develop the individual gifts of the players who made up his orchestra; this is why both his autobiography and biographies devoted to him turn into a portrait gallery of the band's musicians.

It is R.D. Darrell, in a classical record magazine in 1932, who elaborates the rationale for considering Ellington something more than a bandleader and arranger, but in the terms ascribed to the composer in classical music. Where the normal situation of popular music was a production line, 'with one man writing a tune, another harmonising it, a third scoring it, and a fourth called in for the actual performance', Ellington's music 'bore the indelible stamp of one mind . . . primarily occupied . . . with . . . tapping the inner world of feeling and experience'.[68] Darrell's account of Ellington is a signal attempt to accommodate the phenomenon he represented to what is both a traditional cultural construct and the confirmation of the aspirations of the 'New Negro', though not without repeating certain myths. 'Where the music of his race', he writes, 'has heretofore been a communal, anonymous creation, he breaks the way to the individuals who are coming to sum it up in one voice . . .'. But his argument is a musical one. There is not only a unity of style, says Darrell, but also harmonic subtlety; and in the exploitation of new tonal colouring, Ellington goes 'further than any composer – popular or serious – of today'. Naming those he considers his peers, Darrell judges that 'The larger works of Gershwin, the experiments of Copland and other "serious" composers are attempts with new symphonic forms stemming from jazz, but not of it.'

As he warms to his theme, Darrell's claims get bolder and bolder. Ellington has the gift of melody, at a time when 'noble, spontaneous, unforced melodies' have become rare: 'whereas Ellington's finest tunes spring into rhapsodic being as simply, as naturally as those of Mozart or Schubert'. Here he compares an effect to Wagner, there to Stravinsky, adding that 'the most daring experiments of the modernists rarely approach the imaginative originality, mated to pure musicianship, of a dozen arresting moments in Ellington's works . . . To me the most brilliant flights of Rimsky's or Strauss's orchestral fancy are equalled if not surpassed' by many passages in Ellington. He even compares him to the composer of the last century he reveres, he says, above all others, Frederick Delius: 'Ellington's scope is vastly smaller, his atmosphere is sustained only over small canvases, but to me intensity and not size is the true measure of musical worth.' This is music criticism as aesthetic confessional, which invites us to be scandalized by the comparisons, but what it signals is a real shift in the musical lifeworld, the emergence of jazz as an image of musical restitution, and the restoration of alienated musical relations to something like their proper balance. When Darrell describes what he calls 'the fusion of content, form, and medium in Ellington's work' in terms of an ideal chamber ensemble composing its own music, one is inevitably reminded of Adorno's description of chamber music as 'the refuge of a balance which society denied elsewhere'. But where classical chamber music expressed the ideal of free individuals in the peak period of liberalism, a time before leisure was 'commandeered, as in the modern concept of "rest and recreation," to become a parody of freedom', jazz comes to represent a new utopian ideal arising, as a Hegelian might say, from the negation of the negation, by commandeering alienated entertainment in the name not only of racial pride but of liberation from the repression of vital instincts throughout society.

9

Towards Postmodernism

Composer and critic in the acousmatic world

In the 1930s, confronted by the Great Depression, capitalism behaved substantially as Marx believed it did, pursuing the revival of the economy by stimulating demand for consumer products, or what he called secondary production, in order in turn to stimulate the primary sector of heavy industry, and the production of the means of production. Along with new brands of canned foods, domestic cleaning materials, toiletries and drugs came developments in the mass media, whose new and evolving communications technologies not only reinforced the process but brought an expansion of advertising, which was designed as much to stimulate the desire for consumption as to promote individual products. Largely through the growing utilization of public relations, a practice intended to mould and bend public opinion by less than honest means – by influencing editorial content without appearing to do so – the shape of the public sphere, both political and cultural, was redrawn. And with cinema, radio and the record industry as major economic players, no insignificant part of this effort was directed towards consumption in the culture industry, and especially music, which was deeply implicated in the development of all three media.

Reconstruction following the Second World War rapidly picked up where the 1930s left off. Consumer expansion began with the relaunch of television and magnetic tape recording, which had both made their first appearance in the 1930s, and the introduction of the LP and EP record formats.[1] Like radio at the end of World War I, the rapid spread of television in the late 1940s and early 1950s was the result of the reconversion to consumer goods of the huge productive capacity in electronics which had been developed to fight the war. New record formats were the record industry's fight-back against television, just as the sound movie had been cinema's response to radio; the relaunch of the tape recorder was a by-product of military victory, when entrepreneurs in the United States pounced upon German patents which defeat made available as part of the spoils. Becoming both a low-cost means of production for new independent record companies and also a means of privately copying both records and radio broadcasts, the tape recorder extended the circulation of both beyond the marketplace. (When illicit copying was carried out for gain, it was called piracy, an activity which would grow steadily over the next fifty years in line with the development of the technology.) Then came transistors, which helped to facilitate the development of computer technology, another product of wartime military investments, since the computer chip represents the miniaturization of the transistorized circuit; the computer would begin to affect musical production in the 1950s and 1960s, when it first became one of the instruments of the electronic music studio; by the 1980s the relation was reversed, and the computer became the universal electronic musical instrument, subsuming all types of electronic and electro-acoustic music production.

By the end of the century, the result of the technical convergence between the media which has been brought about by computers and the digitalization of information was also to produce a rupture in the conventional workings of the cultural market, since it is now possible for any form of work to be copied and reproduced in any format with great ease and at low cost given possession of the necessary hardware, which is cheaper and more powerful than ever before. This technology is unequally distributed but still has several effects on music. It not only speeds up the circulation of music that has entered the public sphere as a merchantable commodity – nowadays thought of as software – it also allows it to escape control even before it has properly entered the market, through large-scale piracy: a situation which renders the laws of copyright and intellectual property unstable but, in an era of globalized media markets, is increasingly crucial to the forms of economic and financial domination of the world market. Meanwhile, the same need for globalized profits propels the producers of hardware to market not only the very equipment which makes the infringement of copyright so easy but also the means of production – the video cameras, the music synthesizers, and so forth; while the pairing of the computer and the telecommunications industry has spawned the Internet, with which these devices are now integrated. These conditions make it possible, at least in theory, for original producers of music – composers and musicians – to bypass the established structures of the music industry in the attempt to reach the ears of an audience, albeit by placing themselves in hock to another, more advanced sector of capital. If one is to believe the hype, however, then anyone can do it. The commercial focus of all this activity is the teenage pop market, but by the early 1990s it was possible for a student at a film school in London to conceive and carry out a plan to shoot an original opera on film, for which he himself wrote the music. He composed it himself, on a synthesizer, producing both a computer-generated score and a sound-track to use as a playback track for shooting the film, which was later replaced by a richer version, and finally, when the film was sold to television, rerecorded by a symphony orchestra.[2] (By the end of the decade, he could also be sending it out on the Internet if he wanted to.) There is a catch of course: to bypass the industry is not yet a way to make a living. But then this is nothing new for composers of any type of music.

In short, the media do much more than simply carry music to new and wider audiences. It is undoubtedly true, as the music critic Hans Keller used to observe, that more people nowadays hear a single broadcast of a new work by an avant-garde composer than would have heard all Beethoven's symphonies in his own lifetime. But the effects are not only quantitative; they also include radical alterations in the relationship between the audience and the object of aesthetic consumption, which seriously affect the situation of the composer, whose audience may now be wider and larger, but also becomes even more fragmented and anonymous.

At the same time, the consumption of music has become embedded within a huge interconnected cultural market which has radically altered its uses. The world fashioned by the mass media, says Habermas, is a public sphere in appearance only, for media like film, radio and television 'curtail the reactions of their recipients in a peculiar way. They draw the eyes and ears of the public under their spell but at the same time, by taking away its distance, place it under "tutelage".'[3] In part, this is because they provide no means for the recipient to interrupt the flow, say anything back, or register disagreement. Partici-pation in the conversations and debates of this pseudo-public sphere is accomplished through surrogates, thus granting cultural power and authority to presenters and pundits and stars, who are courted and manipulated by a huge public relations industry, while critical discus-sion of the old kind gives way to exchanges about tastes and prefer-ences, and more or less tasteful gossip about personalities, where even the talk about what is consumed becomes part of the process of consumption.

In all this, the public discourse of music remains trapped in old and outmoded pre-technological habits of listening, in which different musics were kept apart because they generally belonged to different kinds of space, both social and physical, and now remain so because they have become the product of an intense division of labour between musical specialisms. These specialisms become a mechanism for organizing the market – or, as the philosopher Michel Foucault put it, in a conversation with the composer Pierre Boulez in the early 1980s:

> What is put at the disposition of the public is what the public hears. And what the public finds itself actually listening to, because it's offered up, reinforces a certain taste, underlines the limits of a well-defined listening capacity, defines more and more exclusively a schema for listening. Music had better satisfy this expectation . . .[4]

Paradoxically, therefore, the same divisions are maintained and even refined by radio programming schedules and station specialization, even though this is no longer the way music is heard. For nowadays, we experience wherever we go an acoustic world saturated with recorded sound suffused with invisible music and disembodied song. Whether we like it or not, music now comes to us from any direction and in any environment in the form of discs, radio, tape, cinema, television, Muzak, and the tinny tunes of telephone prison. Yet at about the same time as Foucault's conversation with Boulez, a small group of music producers on the French cultural radio programme were fired because they began mixing up musics from different levels of the hierarchy of styles, like opera and jazz, sonatas and pop music, thus upsetting – as Foucault might call it – the official order of things.

The process began with the invention of recording. The record did not only become the focus of the music industry; it also had the most profound effects on the whole musical lifeworld by disturbing the age-old dialogue of musical communication: by separating performance from audition, removing the performer from the presence of the listener, robbing the listener of participation in the act of performance, depriving the performer of the listener's response; in a word, by bringing about – together with radio – the disembodiment of music. The effects of this disembodiment were indicated by Walter Benjamin in his crucial essay of the 1930s, 'The Work of Art in the Age of Mechanical Reproduction': by taking copies of the original into situations that are out of reach of the original itself – like a choral performance played in a drawing-room – it thus creates new ways of using music, both domestically and in public.[5] In short, reproduction detaches the music work from the domain of the tradition that gave birth to it, destroying what Benjamin calls the aura which signals its authenticity. Moreover, reproduction is not just an adjunct to the musical lifeworld. Our musical experience is now predominantly what the pioneer of *musique concrète* in the 1940s, Pierre Schaeffer, called 'acousmatic': sounds that are heard without seeing their source.

The constriction of the recording format proved a forcing ground, especially for the artistry of new types of musical object which do not belong to any particular domain but, rather, anywhere a loudspeaker (or earphones) may be found. In the domain of art music, Schaeffer's own recorded-sound compositions of the late 1940s, known as *musique concrète*, are among the first self-consciously novel types of musical object created for the loudspeaker, followed in the 1950s by the first computer-aided compositions and the creation of a new branch of compositional art in the form of electronic music, largely supported by cultural radio stations in Europe and universities in the USA. Pop music, in the same decade, became increasingly driven by techniques designed to ensure an effective recorded sound, and which are the product of recording technology itself and cannot be created in live performance. But the broader process of adaptation to the medium in fact began much earlier, with the compliance of popular musical forms to the three- or four-minute format of the 78 rpm record. The constriction of the record proved a forcing ground for the artistry of the blues singer and the jazz musician, who responded by evolving highly concentrated forms. At the same time, the good musician, listening to the result, is struck by the problems of acoustics, and turns their attention to the question of sound projection; that is to say, the relation of the instrument to the microphone (or, in the case of crooning, the voice). There is a telling footnote in Darrell's 1932 apologia for Ellington, where he speaks of the Duke's 'keen under-standing of microphone technique', and observes that some of his records reveal his work better than a performance in the flesh[6] – a comment which is of more than passing interest in the present context, and serves as an early pointer to the manner in which many popular musicians, unhindered by the weight of tradition but informed by great technical skill, responded readily to the special demands of the new medium – albeit in what was primarily, from the perspective of the composer's art, an intuitive and untheorized fashion.

For the composer of art music, creating music which is supposed to be autonomous, and for which the media are supposedly merely carriers, the acousmatic world is a threat mitigated only as long as there is still direct contact with the audience in the concert-hall. At the same time, however, the identity of the concert audience undergoes a subtle but drastic shift: it is no longer quite as representative of a traditional musical lifeworld as it used to be, it becomes a fragment carved out of a largely estranged public, which is more passive than active, more untaught than cultured, and riven by demarcations of taste which are ideologized by the media themselves, as audiences are turned into consumers of targeted products, and the public sphere becomes less a space for negotiating social difference and more an arena in which those differences are exacerbated.

The emergence of the acousmatic world first became the subject of reflection and commentary – alongside the question of the composer's public responsibility – in 1920s Germany, where the musical tradition was a matter of the highest cultural prestige, and the civic radio stations of the Weimar Republic commissioned special radio works from composers of every tendency. The leading figures in the debate were a new generation of composers: Kurt Weill, Paul Hindemith, Schoenberg's pupil Stuckenschmidt and, above all, Berg's pupil T.W. Adorno. Philosopher, sociologist and trained musician, Adorno contributed a subtle, intricate analysis of the musical condition of the time. Using the method he later called negative dialectics, which produced controversial results, he uncovered the process by which the commercialization of music through the medium of recording leads to fetishization, as business values overwhelm the process of production, and market values overwhelm creativity. Music coming from loudspeakers develops a liability to decompose. It becomes a stream of highlights: striking melodic intervals and turns of phrase, memorable modulations and conspicuous harmonic progressions, special instrumental effects, insistent rhythmic patterns, certain quirks of interpretation. In this way, individual and often incidental features of the music attract a fetish value, and composing is reduced to the manipulation of formulae designed to isolate and exaggerate these fetish objects. This in turn promotes an atomized kind of listening, distracted instead of attentive and centred, which Adorno considers the enemy of musical intelligence.

Some of Adorno's own music has recently become available on CD; it shows a modest but genuine musical gift, superior to both Rousseau and Nietzsche. It serves in the present context above all to situate Adorno the theorist, the pioneer in the analysis of the culture industry, not as a precursor of the late-twentieth-century cultural theorist, whose position within the culture is that of an ironic consumer, but as a creator *manqué*. This makes the charge against him of elitism too easy, an evasion which confuses questions of production and consumption. (Perhaps it is not the music which is elitist, but the audience.) What

Adorno perceived all too clearly was how the industrialization of culture, in extending the social reach of the high musical tradition, also transformed the conditions of both composing and listening. The negativity of his attitude towards popular music is not simply the manifestation of some kind of intellectual superiority complex, but a political critique of populism.

By the mid-1920s, according to Weill, many German musicians lived entirely off their radio work, and for others it had become a vital supplement to concert and theatre earnings.[7] Reflecting on the task of writing pieces for the Frankfurt radio station, he considered the first prerequisite to be a 'knowledge of the acoustic restrictions of the broadcasting studio, the orchestral and instrumental capabilities of microphones, the distribution of vocal registers and harmonic limitations [of] a radio composition'. (The radio stations set up laboratories and research units to investigate these things.) But it was also 'impossible to apply the assumptions of the concert hall to radio music' for another reason: because 'concert music was meant for a definite and limited circle of listeners of the cultured and affluent classes', whereas 'the radio audience is composed of all classes of people'. This imposes stylistic demands: 'the task of creating works which can be taken up by as large a circle of listeners as possible', and the requirement that the means of musical expression must not cause difficulty for the untrained listener.[8]

If Weill came to different conclusions from Adorno, Weill was a composer who wrote a newspaper column, not a critic who also composed. The general character of music criticism, as Weill saw it, fitted logically and consistently into the overall pattern of the press. Reportage and politics predominated over the function of appraisal, and was either corrupted by personal opinion or degenerated into what Brecht called copywriting for the entertainment industry.[9] The analysis remains thoroughly pertinent more than half a century later. The evolution of these functions was a direct consequence of the peculiar nature of specialized markets like high culture, where until recently it has been the conventional wisdom that hard-sell advertising techniques are ineffective (in Europe; the USA is a different matter). As a result, concert promoters, music publishers, artists' agents, record companies – all were forced to rely on the critic as a purveyor of information, a former of opinions, a trendsetter; in short, an adjunct whose autonomy and independence were generally tolerated, but not much savoured. Since the critics, down to the present day, have always depended on these very business interests for constant favours, the relationship is a delicate one, and professional rules and conventions

Britten was writing music for plays by Auden, Isherwood and MacNeice; worse still, a *Pacifist March* for the Peace Pledge Union in 1937 and a Popular Front choral marching song, a setting of Randall Swingler's *Advance Democracy*, in 1938. These activities did not escape the watchful eye of the man from *The Times*, who wrote of Britten's Piano Concerto (1938):

> It is the content that raises doubts. . . . There are . . . moments of seriousness and genuine romantic feeling. . . . But satire kept breaking in, and . . . satire is a dangerous element in music. For one thing it sets the hearer on his guard against taking anything at its face value . . . The second movement . . . is elegant, and would make an effective contrast to more serious matter elsewhere, but the Finale seems to have some 'ideological' motive behind it which merely betrays the composer into an angry blatancy. The anger may do credit to his feelings, but his expression does less to his taste.[17]

Britten's later career, of course, tells a different story: after the war he joined the establishment, and came to be celebrated as the 'country's leading composer'. This he achieved partly by swapping his social conscience for a religious one, which the establishment was able to accommodate – it was certainly not the critics who changed very much. It is hardly fair, of course, to denigrate his music for this reason. On the contrary, his popularity was due largely to the originality with which he handled the traditional idiom, unequalled by any similar composer in England except Michael Tippett. The two contrasting operas *A Midsummer Night's Dream* and *Curlew River*, for example, are highly original and sensitive experiments in the deployment of carefully chosen resources: the former one of the finest of Shakespearean operas, the latter a highly atmospheric re-creation of medieval church drama achieved by a novel imitation of the Japanese Noh play. Yet one aspect of Britten's creative personality remained completely beyond the pale, tolerated but never spoken of, for the approving chorus of critics wholly concealed their subject's homosexuality, and avoided in their commentaries the implications of the roles and words which he provided for his lifelong companion, the tenor Peter Pears; or – as Andrew Lumsden put it in a review of the obituaries for Pears in 1986 – 'the erotic wellsprings of the Pears–Britten achievement' and the theme of gay sensibility which runs throughout his work.[18] For Britten repeatedly turned for sources to homoerotic authors, choosing texts from Michelangelo, Melville, James, Rimbaud, Owen, Mann, Auden and others, to create such works as the *Michelangelo Sonnets, Billy Budd, The Turn of the Screw, Les Illuminations*, the *War Requiem*, and finally *Death in Venice*. But there is never a word about it, never more than praise for the fit of the notes to Peter Pears's vocal physiognomy, and Britten's extraordinary sensitivity to different languages. Not all these works are of equal musical quality by any means, but as for the rest, says Lumsden, don't consult the quality press for clarification.

Audiences and listeners

Even Adorno admitted that theoretically, the record represents a great benefit. In principle, he says, the medium makes all of the musical literature available, and even though records become fetish objects, nevertheless the 'potential abolition of educational privilege in music should socially outweigh the disadvantages which hoarding records as a hobby of an audience of consumers involves under present conditions'. The present conditions, however – he is writing in the middle of the postwar consumer boom – are such that the recorded repertoire 'mirrors the official life of music in its most conventional form'.[19] At the centre of this official musical lifeworld, mounted on a podium, stands the conductor, one of whose less visible functions is to determine this repertoire – no longer alone, but nowadays subject to the sanction of the committees which run the orchestras, and the commercial pressures which operate on the economics of the undertaking. For most conductors, capable of imposing themselves on a hundred people, bending the will of these committees to their own ends is not a great problem, though it frequently requires more tact than is needed on the podium. And as commanding personalities with the capacity to magnetize an audience while standing with their back to them, they are also well able to turn the commercial pressures to their own advantage. In the course of developing these capacities, the conductor eclipses the composer. The former's worldly success and popularity seem to be bought at the latter's expense, as the two roles, unified in the nineteenth century in figures like Mendelssohn, Berlioz and Wagner, part company in the twentieth, and new music is progressively excluded from the orchestral concert platform. Behind the comparative merits of a Toscanini, a Beecham or a Karajan as interpreters of the classics, therefore, stands another question: the elimination from their repertoire of the composers who were their own contemporaries. Even those, like Klemperer or Monteux, who were champions of new music in their early careers left it aside in their later years, when their authority was at its height. The same pattern was found among their accomplices, the soloists, who had their own careers to look after, and equally chose to bask in the reflected glory of the dead (white male) composer, rather than take the risk of alienating a public which wanted music above all to be comforting, not to make them think. These are generalizations – there are many artists who are exempt from these charges – yet the trend is clear. The living composer has become the performing artist's *Doppelgänger*.

Paradoxically, despite the rise to predominance of acousmatic music over the course of the twentieth century, the concert-hall has not been eclipsed. Nor is it exactly correct to say that it has been reduced to a nineteenth-century leftover. The conductor reigns supreme, together with a number of charismatic soloists, and the music they play is predominantly old and well known, yet it clearly satisfies a real social need. As Christopher Small observes, the last fifty years have seen 'a doubling of the number of professional symphony orchestras around the world, as the Western classical music tradition has moved into regions where it was previously unheard', and there has been an explosion of concert-hall building to house these orchestras. Moreover, says Small, many cities in Western countries 'have decided that their existing nineteenth- or early-twentieth-century hall is too small, or insufficiently specialised, or that it projects an image that is not up to date' and have therefore built a new one, so that today modern concert-halls greatly outnumber old ones.[20] What they all have in common, however, is first that they convey an impression of opulence, wealth and power, though always with a careful avoidance of any vulgarity: what is to happen here, says Small, 'is serious and important and will not appeal to the vulgar'. Secondly, they allow no communication with the outside world: 'performers and listeners alike are isolated from the world of their everyday lives'.[21]

Nevertheless, the concert-hall is more democratic than the opera house – at any rate, more bourgeois. The opera-house horseshoe had a triple function: to project the musical sound forwards; to allow the members of the audience themselves to be on visual display; and to minimize the diffusion of their chatter. The concert-hall works differently. The spatial–acoustic arrangement developed during the nineteenth century, and embodied in the halls of cities like Vienna and Amsterdam, is intended to create a balanced sound, while the seating arrangement, with the audience now mostly facing the orchestra directly, suppresses individual display in the auditorium and displaces it to corridors, bars and salons. The arrangement gains from refinements in the arraignment of the band which help to focus the sound acoustically, to create what one writer calls 'the unity of a single, corporate source'.[22] Architecturally, these halls are masterpieces of both acoustic and social engineering; seating an audience between two and two and a half thousand, of a size and shape which produces a pattern of sound reflection and resonance such that the sounds are fused without being muddied – above all, they are halls to embody the ideals of bourgeois democracy: it is true that the size of the audience is limited, but inside they share a uniformly warm and responsive acoustical state of being.

At the same time, the modern concert-hall is built on the assumption, says Small, that a musical performance is a system of one-way communication, from composer to listener through the medium of the performers: 'The very form of the auditorium tells us that the performance is aimed not at a community of interacting people but at a collection of individuals, strangers even, who happen to have come together to hear musical works. We leave our sociability behind at the auditorium doors.'[23] Indeed, Walter Benjamin called the concert-hall a school for asocial behaviour. The concert audience is thus a paradoxical form of collectivity: a social gathering which is devoted to the cultivation of interiority, with a certain resemblance to church-going, except that in church the public participates in the music-making. This paradox of public interiority, as it was manifest in the Edwardian concert audience on the eve of the First World War, is beautifully captured by E.M. Forster in his novel *Howards End* (1910), with its witty description of a party of friends attending a performance of Beethoven's Fifth Symphony at the old Queen's Hall in London:

> ... the Andante had begun – very beautiful but bearing a family likeness to all other beautiful Andantes Beethoven had written, and, to Helen's mind, rather disconnecting the heroes and goblins of the first movement from the heroes and goblins of the third. She heard the tune once through ... and then smiled at her cousin Frieda. But Frieda, listening to classical music, could not respond. Herr Liesecke, too, looked as if wild horses could not make him inattentive; there were lines across his forehead, his lips were parted, his pince-nez at right angles to his nose, and he had laid a thick white hand on either knee. And next to her was Aunt Juley, so British, and wanting to tap ... the Andante came to an end. Applause, and a round of 'wunderschöning' and 'pracht' volleying from the German contingent ... Helen said to her aunt: 'Now comes the wonderful movement: first of all the goblins, and then a trio of elephants dancing'; and Tibby implored the company generally to look out for the transitional passage on the drum.

This passage confirms what we all know: different types of people have different ways of hearing music. But this is a question which can be approached either as a matter of psychology or as Adorno sees it, from a more sociological angle. As the starting point of his *Introduction to the Sociology of Music*, based on lectures at Frankfurt University in the early

1960s,[24] Adorno's typology of listening addresses the contradictory and contrasting traits which are found mixed up together in contemporary listening habits, at a time when the audience is fragmented and estranged by a cultural public sphere that is fully redefined by the acousmatic media. But this is not an empirical analysis, and the different types which correspond to these habits 'do not occur with chemical purity'; the typology is posited on the subjective relationship between listener and music, especially in terms of the adequacy or inadequacy of the act of listening to that which is heard.

Adorno's first category is the 'expert', who listens structurally, 'tends to miss nothing and at the same time, at each moment, accounts to himself for what he has heard'. Expert listening is facilitated by the specialist training of musical faculties like perfect pitch, and such listeners are more or less limited, as Adorno admits, to professional musicians, though by no means all of them (there are plenty of good musicians who don't have perfect pitch, for example). It is also the kind of listening to which the modern professional critic aspires (but not all attain).

In any event, expert listeners are rather few in number compared to Adorno's second type, the 'good listener', who still follows many of the details, is able to make connections spontaneously, and therefore judges for good reasons. The good listener, albeit not always fully aware of technical and structural devices, has unconsciously mastered music's 'immanent logic'. This is the type of listener Adorno thinks we mean when we talk about a 'musical person' – both Frieda and Herr Liesecke in *Howards End*, for instance. Historically, says Adorno, such musicality requires a certain homogeneity of musical culture, of the kind that used to be found in the courts and the salons: 'Characters of this type are drawn by Proust in the Guermantes sphere – Baron Charlus, for example.' But he presumes that this type of listener is growing rarer and more isolated: 'in the past . . . there was a far better understanding between good listeners and experts than exists today between the so-called educated class and the products of the avant-garde'.

If Adorno is right in thinking that a distance has grown up between the good listener and the contemporary composer, there is also another kind of distance which separates all but the most expert of modern listeners from the composers of the past. Consider the example of Mozart's *Dissonance* Quartet, which acquired its name from the character of the opening chords. How many listeners nowadays, bicentenary or no bicentenary, being accustomed to much more dissonance than in former times – including music which is completely atonal, even if they hear it only in the form of background music at the movies

– how many listeners in these conditions are able hear the opening of this work as dissonant at all, at least without a certain effort? If this degree of dissonance is immediately obvious nowadays only to the expert or highly experienced listener, this suggests that ways of hearing, not just ways of listening, must have changed since the time when the quartet was first given its name – an awkward conclusion. The very idea that alterations in the musical idiom correspond to shifts in the listener's mode of hearing is anathema to a system of values which is predicated on absolutes. The mere possibility of such a transformation is completely alien to the normative character of the bourgeois public sphere.

Adorno's third type of listener is the 'culture consumer' which, he believes, makes up the bulk of concert and opera audiences. Many are voracious, well-informed, enthusiastic record collectors. But for listeners like these, who hoard up information and discuss the merits of interpreters for hours on end, 'the structure of hearing is atomistic: the type lies in wait for specific elements, for supposedly beautiful melodies, for grandiose moments'. Like Tibby in *Howards End*, this type's relation to music has a fetishistic touch, and for such a listener 'the standard he consumes by is the prominence of the consumed'. This group, says Adorno, furnishes not only subscribers to concert series and pilgrims to festivals like Salzburg and Bayreuth, but also the Philharmonic concert committee ladies in the United States who are responsible for selecting programmes.

Next in line comes the 'emotional listener', exemplified in *Howards End* by Helen, since for this kind of listener music triggers 'instinctual stirrings otherwise tamed or repressed by the norms of civilization'. The type extends to those in whom music stimulates visual notions and vague reveries, and akin to it is the typically culinary taste of the 'sensuous' listener (in the narrow sense of the word) for isolated sonic stimuli. However, readers who feel belittled by finding themselves in this category may take consolation from the company of the poet Heine, who wrote: 'Berlioz's music reminds me of extinct species of animals, of fabulous kingdoms and fabulous sins, of sky-storming impossibilities, of the hanging gardens of Semiramis, of Nineveh, of the wonderful constructions of Mizraim'.[25] But then, of course, music like that of Berlioz is deliberately intended to evoke this kind of association.

Fifth comes the simple 'entertainment listener', who is generally completely passive and can hardly be said to listen at all, but uses music merely as a background to cut off silence and kill time. A vast chunk of the output of the culture industry is intended for such use, says Adorno, prepackaged into standard genres in consideration of the minimal vestiges of differences of taste in the anonymous consuming public. This is perhaps Adorno's most problematic category, not because passive entertainment listeners do not exist – indeed, they probably comprise a majority – but because entertainment listening also comes in other, more active forms. As Foucault remarks about rock music, for example, it is not only an integral part of many people's lives, but 'a cultural initiator: to like rock, to like a certain kind of rock rather than another, is also a way of life, a manner of reacting; it is a whole set of tastes and attitudes'.[26] Here, the act of listening is mediated by all sorts of peer-group pressures and predilections which have now been studied by a large group of sociologists of popular culture;[27] but is this any less true of classical music? The main problem with analyses in the former group is that they often lack any concrete consideration of the musical notes and values of the music; the main problem with the latter is the reverse: they often fail to perceive any relation between the notes and their sociological projection.

Sixth, with his penchant for paradox, and since he believes that there is no type of listener who escapes the social construction of music, Adorno includes the unmusical, or 'tone-deaf'. The roots of musical indifference, he says, are not – as conventionally supposed – a matter of some naturally occurring deficiency, but can only be a question of negative processes experienced in childhood. Indeed, what other view is possible if the gift of music is as universal a human faculty as speech? It remains open, of course, what 'negative processes experienced in childhood' might consist in, but there is certainly evidence of the converse: that a person with deficient hearing may still be musical, even outstandingly so. It is a curious historical irony that the physicist who introduced the word acoustics in the early eighteenth century, Joseph Sauveur, had a serious hearing deficiency. But this was not a mystery to his contemporaries. At any rate, Rousseau pointed out in *Émile* that you can tell whether a cello is playing a high note or a low note by laying a hand on its body; and his contemporary, Pierre Desloges, author of one of the earliest memoirs by a deaf author, wrote: 'if I put my hand to a violin or flute being played, I can hear them'.[28] One is reminded of Helen Keller's description of how she learned to love music by standing at the side of a piano, her hand on its rim, feeling the vibrations. Today, the most famous example is the deaf percussionist Evelyn Glennie, who began to lose her hearing soon after she started playing in her early teens, and yet went on to become a virtuoso soloist; she has demonstrated in a television programme how a highly developed sense of touch enables her to feel pitch as well as rhythm: she is able to tune the timpani by placing the tips of her fingers on the drumskin and feeling the vibrations of the overtones going in and out of alignment as she presses the tuning pedal. These examples strongly suggest that Adorno is right in supposing that a lack of musicality is the result not of deficiency but of an induced aversion.

Adorno's most curious and paradoxical category is the 'resentment listener', a stark antitype to the emotional kind. These are listeners whose musical preferences are the expression of emotional manifestation rather than indulgence, and may be found among the followers of many different types of music; like the stern Bach purist or the ancient music lover, who scorn the established repertoire on which emotional listening nourishes itself. The category extends to militant devotees of the contemporary avant-garde who reject the classical tradition it stems from because they despise its easy emotionalism; contrariwise, it also includes populist opponents of the avant-garde who militate in favour of the established repertoire – what these people resent is intellectualism. At all events, Adorno is particularly fascinated by this category, which he discusses at greater length than the others, and more speculatively. However, when he comes to the typical jazz listener, whose resentment, he says, may be equally directed against the classic–romantic ideal on the one hand, and unadulterated commercialism on the other – here again he runs into trouble. One senses that he only reveals the limitations of his own ear when he wonders if there is any real distinction between 'pure jazz' and the commercially disfigured kind. It is doubtless true that 'the jazz realm is tied to commercial music by its predominant basic material, the hit songs, if by nothing else'. But he continues with the contestable comment: 'Part of its physiognomics is the amateurish incapacity to account for things musical in exact musical terms – an incapacity which it is futile to rationalize with the difficulty of nailing down the secret of the irregularities of jazz, long after the notators of serious music have learned to fix fluctuations of incomparably greater difficulty.'[29] A recent account suggests that this scorn is the unfortunate result of the kind of amateur jazz culture which Adorno encountered in Britain in the mid-1930s, when he was at Oxford writing a doctorate on Husserl. In that particular context, says Evelyn Wilcock, what he writes about jazz is directed against the evaluation of the music in terms of the predominant racist myths of the time.[30] On the one hand, he argued that jazz bore little relation to indigenous African music; on the other, he attacked the charge that jazz was primitive because Blacks were intellectually inferior by correctly insisting that, on the contrary, jazz demanded instrumental virtuosity and technical skill. At the same time, while himself condemning the work of Gershwin as synthetic, he accused the jazz world of playing up a stereotypical representation of the Jewish jazz musician. And so they did. 'Most jazz', wrote Constant Lambert tendentiously in 1933, from his upper-class perch in London, 'is written and performed by cosmopolitan Jews. The nostalgia of the negro who wants to go home has given place to the infinitely more weary nostalgia of the cosmopolitan Jew who has no home to go to.' Perhaps the conclusion to be drawn from this debate is that even the most expert listeners – Lambert or Adorno himself – may be consumed by resentment; and the history of musical resentment would explain a good deal about the dubious history of music criticism.

Probably the main force of Adorno's typology of listeners, however, is the realization that each of us harbours different types of listening within ourselves. As we move through the modern acousmatic musical lifeworld, we experience continual shifts in our listening identity; our listening becomes distracted and decentred (and often traced by resentment). And since the heterodox diet of musics to which we are constantly exposed belongs to every style, idiom, dialect, age and genre, uprooted and disconnected from their original lifeworld, deprived of their aura, our old responses have become confused and largely dysfunctional. When ubiquitous mechanical reproduction pushes music into the realms of noise pollution, it seems that musical values become relative – a condition which is nowadays often considered one of the defining characteristics of postmodernism, and which sows the seeds of great confusion. But perhaps the crucial problem is not relativism at all but, rather, rampant heterophony – not whether one thing can be judged against another but, rather, being able to hear them at all.

Adorno as the Devil

Adorno got under people's skin. In the late 1940s, when they were all German refugees in America, Schoenberg bitterly attacked Adorno in the press for helping the novelist Thomas Mann to insult him in his new novel *Dr Faustus*, a study in the pathology of German culture. The book's protagonist, Adrian Leverkühn, is a theological student turned composer who enters into a Faustian pact with the Devil: his soul for twenty-four years of musical genius. Taken together, the narrative of this highly polyphonic novel, and the character of Leverkühn and his music, form a composite derived from the biographies and works of a pair of literary figures – Nietzsche and Dostoevsky – and a bunch of composers – Schumann, Wolff, Tchaikovsky, Mahler and Schoenberg –

who all had something of the air of the tragic artist about them, and in certain instances madness (in Nietzsche's case, the possible result of syphilis). Mann tells us, in his memoir *The Genesis of a Novel*, how he thought of the theme – the artist's demonic intoxication, with its self-liberating but finally catastrophic effects – as a metaphor for Germany's moral self-destruction.[31] To ensure the authenticity of technical details – an account is given of each of Leverkühn's compositions – he sought assistance from a number of German musical figures who had also been exiled in the States. They included Schoenberg, the conductor Bruno Walter, and, most importantly, Adorno, whom Mann called his Privy Councillor in matters musical. Mann had already written several chapters when Adorno sent him a manuscript 'whose startling pertinency to the world of my novel instantly arrested me'. The manuscript in question was the first part of *The Philosophy of Modern Music*. What Adorno wrote hit home to Mann, who recorded in his diary: 'Finished reading Adorno's essay. Moments of illumination on Adrian's position. The difficulties must reach their highest peak before they can be overcome. The desperate situation of art: the most vital factor.'[32] He added: 'Ideas about death and form, the self and the objective world, may well be regarded by the author of a Venetian novel of some thirty-five years ago as recollections of himself.'[33]

Mann ascribes to his fictional composer the invention of a technique of composition in all essentials identical to the twelve-tone method which Schoenberg had introduced in the early 1920s. Schoenberg, in a letter to *The Saturday Review of Literature*, strongly objected. He was piqued that the conductors Bruno Walter and Otto Klemperer were mentioned in the book by name, but not himself, yet he was the intellectual author of Leverkühn's compositional technique. Moreover, Leverkühn 'is depicted from beginning to end, as a lunatic. I am now seventy-four and I am not yet insane, and I have never acquired the disease from which this insanity stems. I consider this an insult . . .'.[34] As for Adorno, whom Schoenberg calls the author's 'informer' and 'a former pupil of my late friend Alban Berg': 'Mr Adorno is very well acquainted with all the extrinsic details of this technique and thus was capable of giving Mr Mann quite an accurate account of what a layman – the author – needs to tell another layman – the reader – to make him believe that he understands what it is about.' But if Schoenberg is Leverkühn, then perhaps, as Lyotard has suggested, the character of the Devil in the novel – the travesty of an intellectual who delivers whole phrases from the *Philosophy of Modern Music* almost as they were written – is Adorno.[35] Indeed, the novel's justification for Leverkühn's music – 'that *it has taken upon itself all the darkness and guilt of the world,* that *it finds all its happiness, all its beauty in forbidding itself the appearance of the beautiful'* – is the same as Adorno's justification for Schoenberg's.[36]

So – Schoenberg should not have complained. In the great rift which divided the avant-garde before the war – the split between Schoenberg and Stravinsky, atonality and neoclassicism – Adorno was on Schoenberg's side. For Adorno, an aesthetic was defined not by what it aspired to but by what it denied, and Schoenberg's genius lay in his denying the appeal of beauty. He praises Schoenberg's stance because it acknowledges the force of history. Stravinsky, said Adorno, denies history, by consuming it through infantile regression. At the same time, the terror Schoenberg spread was not the result of his incomprehensibility but came from the fact that he was all too correctly understood: his music gave form to that anxiety and insight into the catastrophic situation of the time which others – Stravinsky was not the only offender – evaded by regressing. On the other hand, Schoenberg after Mann and Adorno was no longer himself, but became an aesthetic imaginary named 'Schoenberg'.

For the new generation of composers emerging just as the novel was published, Schoenberg and Adorno were alter egos, and the choice of idiom was hardly in question. Amid the great hunger on the European Continent for spiritual rebirth after the ravages of Fascism, musical art showed its extraordinary resilience in the renewal of pre-fascist modernism and the rapid burgeoning of a new avant-garde. This happened, the music publisher Ernst Roth recalled, virtually unassisted. The promotional support which publishers had been used to giving composers for a century had dried up in the economic and political troubles of the 1930s. When serial music rose from the ashes of the war, 'there was no publicity at all. Its . . . supporters were themselves surprised.'[37] The reason is assuredly pinpointed by Umberto Eco when he compares Schoenberg's concert piece *A Survivor from Warsaw* (1947) with the *Warsaw Concerto* written by Richard Addinsel for the film *Dangerous Moonlight* in 1940. Schoenberg, commemorating the Warsaw Ghetto, is able to express 'an entire culture's outrage at Nazi brutality' only because he is using a new musical language:

> Had Schoenberg used the tonal system he would have composed not the Warsaw Survivor but the Warsaw Concerto, which develops the . . . subject according to the most rigorous laws of tonality. Of course, Addinsel was not a Schoenberg, nor would all the twelve-tone series of this world suffice to turn him into one. On the other hand, we cannot attribute all the merit of a composition to the genius of its creator. The formal starting point of a work often determines what follows: a tonal discourse dealing with the bombing

of Warsaw could not but lapse into sugary pathos and evolve along the paths of bad faith.[38]

But if Schoenberg (or, rather, 'Schoenberg') provided their formal starting point, the postwar generation also perceived that to escape the Faustian trap they needed a music which released its subjects from the burden of their subjectivity; nor could there be any going back. How to compose such music that would escape the weight of a tradition annulled by the years of catastrophe; what forms and techniques would satisfy the objective measure of modern history – these became the primary concerns of the generation who lived their adolescence and their schooling against the background of Fascism and war. Even Schoenberg, laying claim to the mantle of the German tradition from Bach to Brahms, became a negative model, and it quickly appeared to the new generation of composers who rediscovered him after the Second World War that Schoenberg the prophet was imprisoned within formal schemata which his own methodology rendered invalid – or, at least, this was what the young French composer Pierre Boulez argued in his scandalous obituary article of 1952, 'Schoenberg is Dead'.

The spirit of Darmstadt

Schoenberg and Weill, at the end of the war, had stayed in America (where they died within a year of each other at the mid-century). Other such exiles, including Mann, Brecht, Eisler and Adorno, returned to Europe. Mann went to Switzerland; the others returned to Germany. But whereas Brecht and Eisler went to the East, Adorno stayed in the West, and became a crucial intellectual figure behind the emergence of the postwar avant-garde which grew up this side of the Iron Curtain. While the unity ascribed to any avant-garde is always something of a myth, for a period following the Second World War the Western European musical vanguard was closely identified with the New Music Summer School established in Darmstadt in West Germany in 1946: here Adorno was to hold seminars and exert a strong philosophical influence.

Darmstadt belonged to a new musical situation in postwar Europe, where a number of cultural radio stations keen to re-establish their credentials began to provide material support for experimental music; in due course the resurgent avant-garde managed to eke advantage from the market growth of capitalist reconstruction – despite strong hostility in traditional cultural quarters, and the aggressive nature of the challenge which their music threw down to the audience. According to Stuckenschmidt, the original intention of the Darmstadt summer school was to rectify the isolation imposed in Germany by the years of Nazi *Kulturpolitik*; it very quickly became an open forum which drew young composers from all over Western Europe, and later further afield, who soon established themselves as leaders of the avant-garde in their respective countries. Here in Darmstadt, in a local school where the guests were housed and fed, they met, learned from each other, and argued everything out, sometimes (according to the gossip) quite fiercely (a few reports even tell of fisticuffs). Luciano Berio, who became one of Darmstadt's most consistently accomplished alumni, recalled that by 1953 'Stockhausen was the theoretical pivot . . . Pousseur provided the speculative machinery, Boulez the analytical spirit'; while his compatriot Bruno Maderna, he said, was like a benign father figure. The place swarmed with 'musical adventurers . . . merchants of sonic carpets . . . graphic extravaganzas, political gestures and musical cure-alls', but quite apart from all that, 'those years were, to say the least, fundamental'.[39]

According to the Italian musicologist Andrea Lanza, the teaching of Adorno and the Frankfurt School provided the composers associated with Darmstadt with the principles they needed to assimilate certain historical models. Adorno 'saw in the avant-garde a last attempt to flee from capitalist commercialisation of the aesthetic product' at a time when the seduction of the market was daily growing stronger. It was a desperate flight, and deeply contradictory. The distance which the vanguard maintained from the market allowed a protected existence, but gave them an isolation not unlike that of the museum – an institution they often criticized – which carried with it the incipient danger of leaving them neutralized. In Adorno's scheme of things, however, this flight contained its own justification, for 'its aim consisted in negation, its power to communicate negation of the modern world'.[40] It was a risky argument but a powerful one, precisely because it invoked the historical crisis of the first avant-garde half a century earlier – a crisis of language, communication and the relation between art and public. But in taking the moment of modernism as the given condition of contemporary music, it identified the critical solution wholly with its highest peak, its most extreme manifestation in the school of Schoenberg. In this way, dodecaphony was converted from a crisis of language into the language of crisis; with the clear implication that any other musical language was anachronistic and historically irrelevant. As Boulez put it in 1952: 'every musician who has not felt –

we do not say understood but indeed felt – the necessity of serial language is USELESS'.[41]

Ten years later, Darmstadt was a movement in international ascendancy, which had already conquered a number of centres of cultural power in the domain of contemporary music, like the music station of the BBC (the Third Programme, later Radio 3), even though the conservatoires remained hostile and the mass media continued to treat such weird doings and alien sounds with the greatest suspicion; such antagonism, of course, only reinforced the conviction of the musical revolutionists. The cultural establishment had at first no alternative but to fall back upon composers who, one way or another, retained the prewar idioms of chromaticism or polytonality, which now began to sound familiar. Rather than *A Survivor from Warsaw*, concert planners preferred to programme Richard Strauss's *Metamorphosen*, the private lament of the ageing one-time Nazi sympathizer for the bombing of his home city of Munich and its opera house, which, from a moral-aesthetic point of view, is little better than Addinsel: a late example of chromatic expressionism incapable of registering the true scale of the Nazi horror.[42] Such patronage, apparently forgiving of past political indiscretions of both Left and Right – but not the indiscretions of the present – turned the best composers slowly but surely from *enfants terribles* into mainstays of tradition, thereby alienating them from the new generation, who now saw relatively little difference between Richard Strauss, Hindemith, Milhaud, Copland, Walton or even Benjamin Britten. It was partly in order to save himself from this fate that Stravinsky, who was politically no radical and creatively a long-time servant of Apollo, now abandoned tonality and took up twelve-tone technique – an aesthetic conversion which the music critic Hans Keller called the most profound surprise in the history of music. The effect of this infamous transmutation of style in legitimizing a musical idiom which had failed to catch the imagination of the broader public demonstrated the deference which the official cultural public sphere still granted to the individual authority of the great composer.

Darmstadt represented the most successful example of a new kind of cultural association adapted to the transformation of the public sphere in the postwar world. Conceived as a public project in cultural recuperation, the summer school earned its prestige by dint of special circumstances. It used a national base to secure the allocation of cultural resources but had an international function, purpose, life, and public relations profile. For the composers, it represented a model of a new

accurate to call "intensities" – are now free-floating and impersonal, and tend to be dominated by a peculiar kind of euphoria'.[45] The description is particularly apt for music, where what is left, when conventional emotions are stripped away, is pure sentience, feeling in the sense of the kinaesthetic sensations which music produces within us. The euphoria of which Jameson speaks is just such a kinaesthetic sensation, pretty much equivalent to what Boulez means when he talks of music as 'controlled delirium'. On the other hand, this phenomenon is not new to music. Music has always manifested this kind of geometrical impersonality; indeed, the controlled delirium created by composers like Nono, Boulez, Berio and Stockhausen often evokes the very intensity found in old-time composers like Perotin, Tallis, Palestrina, Monteverdi, Bach or even Beethoven, at least in the readings of certain symphonies by certain conductors. (Try listening to Beethoven's Fifth in the recording conducted by Boulez.)

Boulez, Cage and the politics of new music

Boulez demonstrated his own approach to integral serial technique in *Polyphonie X* (1951), a work which fared badly at its premiere at the Donnaueschingen Festival of that year, apparently because it was too difficult to be mastered by an orchestra who were not yet convinced by such music, and a conductor (Hans Rosbaud) who was fully sympathetic but not yet fully in command of the score. It is perhaps not irrelevant to know that Boulez had excelled as a schoolboy as much in mathematics as in music, and even entered university as an engineering student, before prevailing over his provincial bourgeois parents and dedicating himself to music; but where the popular biography makes a psychologistic meal out of this kind of anecdotal information, it is significant here primarily as the sign that he came to music in a constructivist spirit which already situated him firmly within a modernist aesthetic. Constructivist does not mean scientistic, however: he will later, in a lecture at Darmstadt in 1960, scorn what he calls 'the "parascientific" mania' that imagines music to be a wholly rational affair.[46] Also of significance is the biographical fact that this schoolboy grew up and went to university under the shadow of war and the Occupation, in which this dedication of spirit was itself an act of resistance; it is a link which Boulez himself would make a few years later, in a work he wrote for a radio performance in 1948, *Le Soleil des Eaux*, a setting of a text by the poet and fighter in the French Resistance, René Char.

'What I was after', Boulez later said, 'was the most impersonal material. Personality had to be involved, of course, in bringing the mechanism into action, but then it could disappear after that. To have the personality not at all involved was a necessity for a while.'[47] He called this the 'zero point' of composing, alluding to Roland Barthes's first book, *Writing Degree Zero* (1953), where Barthes says that literature is like phosphorus: 'it shines with its maximum brilliance at the moment when it attempts to die'.[48] It also turns out, however, to be a zero point of listening – the down side, as it were, of postmodernism's impersonal euphoria; somewhat like the full emptiness of an ocean in which the listener is riding on a raft: surrounded by constant movement, without seeming to go anywhere. Boulez was conscious of reaching this point in 1952 with a work for piano duet, *Structures I*, to which he appended the title of a painting by Klee, 'At the edge of fertile country', as if to say: in this direction there is no further to go, all is barren. Three years later came the breakthrough to a new, richer and above all more sensuous idiom, with the completion of his shimmering cantata *Le Marteau sans Maître*, which Stravinsky – no less – singled out as the best work yet by a postwar composer. The trick which Boulez had learned was a new *diabolus in musica*, an element of controlled chance, which he evoked with the Latin word *alea*, dice. A close observer, Umberto Eco, identified the same trend in other composers, including Stockhausen, Berio and Pousseur – all were composing music which, in appealing to the initiative of the performer, rejects 'the definitive, concluded message' and constitutes a new type of 'open work', where 'every performance makes the work an actuality, but is itself only complementary to all possible other performances of the work'. Here, 'the very fact of our uncertainty is itself a positive feature: it invites us to consider *why* the contemporary artist feels the need to work in this . . . direction'. The poetics of the open work, he believes, 'posits the work of art stripped of necessary and foreseeable conclusions' in which the performer's freedom functions as an element of discontinuity: a condition like that to be found in contemporary physics, where discontinuity is not perceived as disorientation, but belongs to the pattern of events in the subatomic world.[49]

For some of the survivors of prewar modernism, however, serialism had gone too far. Stuckenschmidt, for example, wrote that the impression it made 'even on a listener who has read the commentaries beforehand' was one of chaos, in which melody and harmony were suppressed in favour of shock effects of dynamics and timbre. 'The fact that these shock effects were organised according to pre-chosen series was only of theoretical interest.'[50] Besides, it was based on a fallacy, since the number 12 in any other parameter than pitch is arbitrary, perhaps even fetishistic. True, some critics felt forced to admit that serial technique nevertheless generated its own special beauty – especially in the hands of a composer like Boulez. On the other hand, there were also far more hostile attacks, seemingly motivated by Cold War ideology, which reveal the potency which high musical art still retained as an ideal model of the moral order. It is the fashion, wrote Herbert Eimert in 1957, 'for empty-headed critics to make out that the systematic "management" of musical material is identical with the terrorist rule of force in totalitarian political systems'. One such 'social critic' held that serial technique produced the programme music of the concentration camps, or that of a Kafkaesque world of inhuman bureaucracy. But to hear in this music, says Eimert, 'the counterpart to political totalitarianism, is just as witless as to appeal to "Nature" when what one really means is textbook harmony'.[51]

For Stockhausen, writing in 1958, the problem with total serialism came from its density, in which, because everything is in constant rapid flux, 'one finds oneself in a state of suspended animation'.[52] While this is by no means an unpleasant experience – after all, many listeners have always treated music in this way – it is liable to become quickly self-limiting. For a while, the constant play of changes on the same spot holds a certain fascination, like watching a fountain or a kinetic sculpture; but let your attention wander, and when you come back to it, you have the feeling of not having missed anything. In other words, all sense of direction and teleology has been suspended. Such a piece cannot even be criticized for being too long, since it becomes impossible to say what the right length would be. Critics found themselves at sea. The listener, wrote one is:

> faced with a strange anomaly, for *everything* in the music is significant to the composer, insofar as everything is subjected to some kind of serial necessity which he has established, yet *nothing* is significant to the listener, who is incapable of divining that necessity and hence of relating each entity to the morphology of the whole. Consequently the music has nothing to offer but its surface.[53]

This was still some time before surface reflection and the exploration of its properties was identified as one of the characteristic modes of postmodernism.

In sum, as the New York composer Christian Wolff put it:

> Complexity tends to reach a point of neutralization; continuous change results in a certain sameness. The music has a static character. It goes in no particular direction ... It is not a question of getting anywhere, of making

progress, or of having come from anywhere in particular, of tradition or futurism. There is neither nostalgia nor anticipation.[54]

From this we might conclude that what such music proposes is a chronotope so purified of dialogical content that it almost denies its own chronotopic character, and pretends to nothing more than an abstract slice of time. Or perhaps, as Eco put it: 'Here are no privileged points of view, and all available perspectives are equally valid and rich in potential. Now, this multiple polarity is extremely close to the spatiotemporal conception of the universe which we owe to Einstein.'[55] The point is not which of these descriptions is more cogent; they are all once again metaphors for the power of music as an ideal model of a higher order.

From America came John Cage, who brought the example of a different kind of experimentalism to Darmstadt in 1956, and in the process helped to change the direction of the European avant-garde, turning it towards a more ludic approach. Cage, who found his inspiration largely in the Orient, was a child of California, a deceptive place where the frontier ends and the west points to the east, and native intellectuals cultivate naivety and dream of ancient Oriental wisdom. As a student in Schoenberg's composition class at UCLA in the mid-1930s, he learned from the master that he had no talent for harmony.[56] According to one story, Schoenberg declared that he was no composer, but an inventor of genius. This prediction was borne out in the invention of the prepared piano, where assorted objects like pencil rubbers or screwdrivers are placed inside the instrument, wedged in between the strings, which modify the sound emitted when the key is struck; and in the composition between 1939 and 1952 of the series called *Imaginary Landscapes*, using novel combinations of percussion and electrics: turntables playing frequency test records, contact microphones made from electric guitar pickups, and so forth. The most notorious was No. 4 for twelve radios, dating from 1951, whose effect depended entirely on what the radios picked up at the moment of the performance. By this time Cage had enrolled in the Japanese philosopher Daisetz Suzuki's class in Zen Buddhism 'back east' at Columbia University, and begun to use chance techniques derived from the Chinese *I Ching* to determine the values of the notes and sounds of his music. His object was 'to free sound of all psychic intentionality . . . let sound be itself, rather than a vehicle of human theory and feeling'.[57] This evacuation of the subject position of the composer, which pre-echoes the French literary theorists' idea of the death of the author, is clearly cousin to the impersonality sought by Boulez, and probably explains the affinity which the two composers originally felt for each other. They first met when Cage went to Paris in 1949, and Boulez arranged a private performance of his *Sonatas and Interludes* for prepared piano. Here the role of chance took a very particular form: the notes to be played are fixed by the score, but preparing the piano makes the sounds that are made when these notes are played unpredictable.

Cage belonged to the tradition of the American eccentric, a fraternity which makes a special showing in music. His confrères include figures like Charles Ives and Carl Ruggles; Henry Cowell, with his tone clusters; Harry Partch, with his 43-note scales and home-made instruments; and Conlon Nancarrow, forced after fighting in the International Brigade in Spain, when the US government refused to renew his passport, to live in Mexico, where he composed the most beguiling and rhythmically intricate pieces for player-piano. Ruth Crawford Seeger shared much of this sensibility; Edgard Varèse, as an adoptive American, was an honorary member, and Satie was their mascot. The eccentric, however, is by no means the innocent he or she may try to seem. In Cage's case, to express the desire for spiritual liberation by rifling the conceptual apparatus of the great mystical philosophies of the East is a clear symptom of the loss of selfhood in the West. It is indeed a deeply ambivalent position, which combines (to follow Edward Said) certain habits of thought rooted in the mentality of the colonizer, typical of Orientalism, with the desperate need to escape from them. Cage, it must be said, mostly succeeds in escaping; perhaps because behind the manifest form of whatever compositional technique he employs, including the refusal to bother with any technique at all, the guiding spirit – Lorca's *duende* – is that of transgression, the wilful violation of sanctioned norms of which the prepared piano, with its bizarre collection of unmusical objects stuck in between its strings, is the very image.

When Boulez criticized Cage for the 'adoption of a philosophy tinged with orientalism serving to mask fundamental weaknesses of compositional technique', it was partly because the French composer had become worried that his own total serialism was only the obverse of throwing dice: both were forms of number fetishism, the one relying on arbitrary and mechanistic automatisms, the other on extreme nonchalance.[58] Boulez, in attempting to distinguish serial music from chance music and distance himself from American experimentalism, advanced the concept of aleatoric music to describe the use of controlled choice as an integral element of the musical structure – in contrast to the randomness cultivated by Cage. The term caught on for music which played with elements of chance and choice alike, ignoring the differences Boulez was trying to bring out. (The same thing, of course, had happened with the word 'atonal' which, in defiance of Schoenberg's disapproval, was widely used without differentiating between heavy chromaticism, polytonality and twelve-note music.) Composers of different tendencies – Cage and other American experimentalists, Europeans like Nono, Berio, Stockhausen, Ligeti, Penderecki, and Xenakis – were lumped together regardless of different compositional techniques and the different-sounding music that resulted (not to mention their varying ideologies). There were splits and divisions between camp followers, but not everyone denied the broad similarity between them. To Morton Feldman, 'The fact that men like Boulez and Cage represent opposite extremes of modern methodology is not what is interesting. What is interesting is their similarity. In the music of both . . . what is heard is indistinguishable from its process. In fact, process itself might be called the Zeitgeist of our age.'[59]

There is, however, a strong contrast between Cage and Boulez in their relation to the public sphere, and the public model they offered of the role and function of the avant-garde composer. Cage consistently maintained his position at the margins; Boulez steered for the commanding heights. Cage represented an iconoclastic American tradition of composers who remained outside both the highly conservative established circuits of classical music and the universities where a new avant-garde academicism took root: instead, they taught in liberal arts colleges, without becoming tenured academics, and made a living as performers by forging close links with visual artists, the dance world and independent film-making, thereby drawing on support and funding from the galleries, museums and arts centres which comprised the American modern art circuit. Politically, Cage represented a libertarian credo which is summed up in texts like the diary entries entitled 'How to improve the world (you will only make matters worse)', written in the mid-1960s:

> Hearing my thoughts, he asked: Are
> you a Marxist?   Answer: I'm an
> anarchist, same as you are when you're
> telephoning, turning on/off the lights,
> drinking water.   Private prospect of
> enlightenment's no longer sufficient.   Not
> just self- but social-realization.[60]

Boulez was similarly a man of the Left, but he was much more attracted to power. His writings and interviews suggest a theoretical position which is more *marxisant* than anarchist; in practice, he used his skills as polemicist, organizer, conductor, theorist and educator to create opportunities, establish positions, supervise forces and run campaigns on behalf of the musical cause he represented as a composer. As with Cage, the style of his polemics made him known among intellectuals outside the narrow arena of modern music, first in France and then beyond. In the process he moved from the shock tactics of his youth to a position that was still articulate and uncompromising in its cultural political critique, but more pragmatic in its recognition of the contradictions in the cultural public sphere, and the opportunities they provided. As he expressed it in a film which the present writer made with him in 1972, when he had conquered the heights and was simultaneously chief conductor of the BBC Symphony Orchestra and music director of the New York Philharmonic: 'You want to expand liberalism, but you have to force the situation to happen, so at the same time you have to be a kind of dictator to bring people to more freedom.'[61] To another interviewer he observed that in politics, this is called entryism. Remarks like this contributed to an image of manipulation which would be seen by many, especially by a later generation with different preoccupations, as a kind of aesthetic Stalinism. More recently Boulez has put it differently: 'When the dog is outside the house, he barks. When he's in the house, he no longer barks – he bites.'[62]

In the first phase of his career, that of his rise to fame, Boulez is remembered as a young tyro who engaged in 'terrorist' actions like demonstrating at concerts, and wrote polemical articles against the musical establishment. As one account has it, he propounded 'the avant-garde principle that innovation, by definition, involves a refusal of immediate gratification of the general audience'.[63] Writing as an anthropologist, Georgina Born argues that in chiding those who seek to satisfy the mass public – which, like Adorno, he considers to be the aesthetic of the supermarket – Boulez epitomizes the value of disinterestedness in the analysis of the French cultural theorist Pierre Bourdieu, where the merit of artistic culture, with its long-term investment of specialist knowledge, is separated from the immediately pleasurable experience proffered by the entertainment industry, and is therefore classified as elitist. Here one might add that the whole analysis of the musical public sphere could indeed be recast in accordance with Bourdieu's sociology of culture, in terms of the accumulation of cultural capital and the competition for cultural legitimacy; the danger of such an analysis, however, would be to underestimate those forms of value that escape the economic metaphor, precisely because they escape any reduction to exchange value – these include the values which Boulez deems to lie in the crucial irrationality of music, its capacity to ignite perception and comprehension through experiment with new materials and the exploration of new domains of sensibility.

In 1954, in pursuit of this vision, Boulez founded a concert series in Paris called the *Domaine Musical*, originally modelled on Schoenberg's Society for Private Musical Performances in Vienna at the end of the First World War. But where Schoenberg's Society lasted only two years, the *Domaine* was born under more propitious circumstances, and by the mid- to late 1960s it had become a central feature of high cultural life in the French capital, thereby adding further to Boulez's international renown. Originally funded by the Renaud–Barrault theatre company, of which Boulez was then musical director, the *Domaine* began as an esoteric meeting-place of the avant-garde, with the intention of mounting a fight against the irresponsible lack of interest in postwar France in contemporary music, both public and private. The aim was to get the music heard, and by this means return contemporary music to both the public cultural agenda and the consciousness of its audience. At first Boulez did everything himself: he decided the repertoire, selected the performers, issued invitations, collected the patrons' cheques and paid the musicians, wrote the programme notes, even put out the chairs and music stands; the only thing he did not at first do much of was conduct – a task which was mainly taken on by Hermann Scherchen. The repertoire established a new model for the lineage of the new avant-garde, a new order of legitimacy for the postwar composer just as the establishment had cast the composer adrift. New works by Messiaen, Stockhausen, Nono, Pousseur, Maderna, Cage, Wolff and others – over fifteen years, the series premiered more than two hundred pieces by around sixty composers – were presented alongside their precursors, particularly the still rarely performed works of Debussy, Stravinsky, Bartók, Varèse, Schoenberg, Berg and especially Webern, together with key compositions from previous centuries which played a crucial role in the historical evolution of music, like the motets of Machaut and Dufay, the madrigals of Gesualdo, and Bach's *Musical Offering*. This didactic form of programming by demonstration, which opened unexpected vistas and perspectives, would reach its most adventurous form during the 1960s in London, in the so-called Invitation Concerts at the BBC's Maida Vale Studios, where enlightened patronage allowed the combination of different musical forces without regard to economic logic or box-office appeal – nevertheless, the studio, which had a seating capacity for an audience of a few hundred, was invariably full, and the radio audience reached several hundred thousand. A tiny figure, to be sure, in terms of ratings, but enough to justify the public-service role of the institution. Now that the concept of public-service broadcasting has suffered a beating from the neoliberal deregulation of the airwaves, a distorted history remembers only that the music controller in charge of the programming, William Glock, was the perfect combination of a paternalist Reithian and a Boulez camp follower; as early as 1952 he had published Boulez's attack on Schoen-berg in the journal he then edited, *The Score*. This blinkered memory, however, represents another episode in the history of musical resentment.

The fact the *Domaine Musical* had thrived was due largely to the support of a wealthy Parisian patron, Suzanne Tézenas, whose recep-tions were later remembered as 'the last salons in Paris', with a mix of society people, writers, painters, art dealers and visiting foreigners – a combination which conferred a certain social legitimacy and provided a circle of patrons who supported the *Domaine* through subscriptions. Tézenas would hold receptions after the concerts, where the composers 'used to stay talking until two in the morning'.[64] The *Domaine*, says Born, thus became 'a point of contact, merging and conversion between cultural and economic power', and by the early 1960s it also attracted government funding. 'As well as a platform for Boulez's own career,' she continues, 'the *Domaine* became a gateway to success for other composers, an arena in which careers were made or broken, since a successful debut bestowed legitimation and recognition.'[65] As one of these other composers put it: 'At the time of the Domaine, the only sanction worth giving to a work was not the reaction of an anonymous public but the judgement of equals; the notion of success didn't exist, only recognition by one's peers.'[66] This observation gives the lie to the accusations of aesthetic Stalinism directed at Boulez and his camp followers. Such feelings, another aspect of the category of disinterestedness analysed by Bourdieu, can hardly be attributed to the influence of any one person. They are the structural result of a situation which Boulez himself has described as ghettoization, which acts like a double-bind. As he explained in the conversation with Foucault, the contemporary music circuit functions like other circuits comprised of chamber music, opera, Baroque music and so forth, each of them partitioned off and specialized to an extent that makes one ask if there is any longer such a thing as a general musical culture. Recording should in principle bring down the walls but, in fact, only reinforces specialization in both public and performers. Contemporary music does not escape this development.

Foucault suggests that different circuits of music represent different relations between contemporary culture and music; rock music, for example, offers the possibility of a relation which is intense, strong, alive, 'dramatic', 'with a music that is itself impoverished, but through which the listener affirms himself'. There is a plurality of musics, where each is worth as much as the group which practises or recognizes it. To this Boulez replies:

> Will talking about musics in the plural and flaunting an eclectic ecumenicism solve the problem? . . . This discourse, as liberating as it may wish to be, on the contrary reinforces the ghettos . . . The economy is there to remind us, in case we get lost in this bland utopia: there are musics which bring in money and exist for commercial profit; and there are musics that cost something, whose very concept has nothing to do with profit. No liberalism will erase this distinction.[67]

The *Domaine Musical* also served as a model for a crucial tendency in postwar avant-garde music: the effort to restore the composer to an integral relation with the performing group. If orchestras and their managements were resistant to the new music, composers had no option but to gather devoted musicians around them however they could – in some cases with the help of cultural radio stations, but often without any kind of institutional backing at all. The result was the formation of a new type of performing group, somewhere between a large chamber ensemble and a small orchestra, either conducted by a composer or closely linked to composers whose works they regularly premiered; they played in small halls for groups of devotees. Composer–performer groups sprang up everywhere, around composers as diverse as Pousseur, Lukas Foss, Peter Maxwell Davies and Harrison Birtwistle. At the same time, smaller and more experimental groups appeared, around figures like LaMonte Young, Cornelius Cardew and Karlheinz Stockhausen, which dispensed with the role of conductor and brought the composer into the group as a performer. Since these initiatives took place necessarily in the interstices of the musical life-world, and were not accompanied by any wider change in the musical sphere at large, they acquired political significance. And if they represented protected sites of experimentation where composers and performers working together could develop new models of musical interaction, free of hierarchy, authority and prohibition, this was a stance which joined the new music of the 1960s to the wider social movement of the decade, and gave it, for the establishment, an odour of scandal and disrepute.

*

In the late 1950s, at the height of his powers as a composer, Boulez began to conduct more widely, turning his attention from the chamber ensemble towards the very different locus of the symphony orchestra; a decade later, he was in demand on the podium throughout the world, and poised to take on the position of chief conductor of two of the world's leading orchestras, the BBC Symphony in London, and the New York Philharmonic. Even more remarkable than the rapidity of his rise was the fact that he achieved his reputation as the most authoritative conductor of contemporary music – almost the only one capable of filling a concert-hall with an entire programme of twentieth-century music – on the basis of a singularly delimited repertoire, restrained not by any lack of musical prowess but by reason of a certain cultural politics. The orchestra – which for the establishment represented the apex of musical life – was for Boulez and his generation a lethargic institution, a museum devoted to preservation instead of creation, where the living composer was a foreigner, an alien presence. Musical life had been decentred; the orchestra had become an institution fixated on a form of dissociated perfection which represented a kind of progressive death.[68] 'Perform new works,' he told an interviewer for the London magazine *Time Out* in 1972, 'then arguments can start, but if you don't perform them, there is nothing to talk about.'[69] The repertoire he developed as an orchestral conductor again provided an education for both audiences and orchestras: model performances of model works of the twentieth century, illuminated by selected classics going back to Mozart, Haydn or Handel. Even those critics who doubted his gifts as a composer admitted his superiority as a conductor, his command of sonority, lucidity, and rhythmic energy in old war-horses and new masterpieces alike. The only thing they criticized was a lack of something they called feeling.

Inevitably, the figure of Boulez invites comparison with other musical Bs of the same generation – Britten and Bernstein – who also tried to live out the problematic role of the composer-conductor. Boulez never sought stardom, but has never shied away from media attention – or rather, from using his exposure to the media to further his cause on his own intellectual terms. Britten was an altogether retiring personality who kept away from the gossip columns and television cameras. Confronted by the threat of marginalization, he created a musical community of his own, a summer music festival in the East Anglian fishing village of Aldeburgh, which acquired an international reputation for the refined quality of its small-scale music-making, promoted Britten's standing as a public figure at home, and eventually turned him into a national institution. His quiet genius on the podium was realized through an even narrower repertoire than that of Boulez; it was also entirely the opposite of that of Leonard Bernstein, whose repertoire was probably wider than that of any other conductor alive. Bernstein, born in America in 1918, the son of Eastern European Jewish immigrants, was everything that both Boulez and Britten avoided: vulgar and flamboyant, a magnet for the show-business crowd, 'the kind of man you read about in the glossy magazines and saw on the Johnny Carson show'.[70] Conductor-composer-pianist-lecturer-socialite, Bernstein was the very model of the modern media personality, the type that takes to television like a proverbial duck to water. As early as 1956 – and a year before the huge success of his best-known musical, *West Side Story* – he won an Emmy, American television's equivalent to Hollywood's Oscars, in the same year as Sid Caesar and Edward R. Murrow. When CBS started televising his Young People's Concerts at Carnegie Hall, the weekly audience reached ten million.

Yet Bernstein was no respecter of convention or conformism. During the 1940s, while he was establishing his reputation as an all-round musician of exceptional gifts, he linked his name with left-wing causes like the American Youth Congress, the Civil Rights Congress, the Spanish Anti-Fascist cause, and the American–Soviet Friendship organization, which was associated with the Communist *Daily Worker* newspaper. The same instincts found aesthetic expression in his adoption as a composer of a populist style, which brought him his first theatrical successes in the 1940s: a ballet, *Fancy Free*, at the Met, and the musical *On the Town* on Broadway. Without mentioning his politics, *Time* magazine waved a wagging finger: 'Bernstein has still not decided whether he wants to be a composer or a conductor, a jazzman or a classicist.'[71] A year later, Virgil Thomson – composer, conductor and music critic, and himself a man of leftist credentials – attacked him in the *New York Herald Tribune* with the charge that he would be a delightful conductor if he could stop behaving like a potential film star.[72]

This kind of suspicion would not only accompany Bernstein throughout his career but clearly reveals the same tensions and contradictions aroused before him by both Gershwin and Ellington, composers who similarly sought their identity through crossing boundaries. Like them, Bernstein was sustained by popular success. He went on to create a paradigm of the symphonic jazz film score in his music for Elia Kazan's *On the Waterfront* in 1954 and, two years later, his masterpiece, the musical *West Side Story*. The establishment succumbed to his talents, and by the end of the decade he was brought in to rescue the ailing New York Philharmonic. It seems – without wishing to psychologize – that this went to his head. At any rate, his aim as a composer now began to falter. He started to identify publicly with Mahler, whose music he conducted with a unique mixture of ferocity and tenderness, but who gave him an inferiority complex as a composer. His own music descended into symphonic bombast. He also paid the price of relentless exposure to the media limelight, and the resentment that goes with it. In 1970, when he hosted a fund-raising cocktail party for the Black Panthers, a *New York Times* columnist who infiltrated the event made his own name by coining the term 'radical chic' to describe the phenomenon of the rich and famous getting their kicks from mixing with the rough trade.[73]

That Boulez should have been invited to take on the New York Philharmonic when Bernstein retired as musical director after twelve years at the helm was an unexpected move for both parties, orchestra and conductor. By contrast with Bernstein, everything in Boulez's stance constituted a stark refusal of both the distorting mirror of the public sphere and the normative values of tradition. To a reporter from *Time* he explained: 'The dilemma of music is the dilemma of our civilisation. We have to fight the past to survive.' Or as he put it to a *Newsweek* correspondent – 'I must abandon the past. In the beginning in the womb you are tied to an umbilical cord. You're fed through it. Eventually you cut it. You can still love your mother but you have to feed yourself.' The time he gave himself to see if New York would respond ended in a standoff – he left, and nothing seemed to have changed; a living example of Bob Dylan's paradoxical line that there's no success like failure, and failure's no success at all. On this reading it was not Boulez's failure but that of the New York musical sphere to respond to his provocation. He would now return to France – to the Paris where he first made his mark, and where the government of Georges Pompidou now rewarded the prodigal son with the director-ship of a new institute, the Institut de Recherches et de Coordination Acoustique/Musique or IRCAM, where music, science and technology could enter into a new collaborative dialogue, protected from the reductionism of the market and the media, in the name of the progress of musical art according to its own internal agenda; its evaluation, however, would take us beyond the span of the present study, and must therefore be left for another occasion.

The strange case of Piotr Zak

The peculiar susceptibility of music critics to resentment listening explains the case of Hans Keller, who used to speak (especially in his two-minute talks on the radio) of the problem of the modern critic's self-confidence – or, rather, lack of it. Nobody, he claimed, was 'at home' in the new music, but they had to pretend that they were. He added somewhat cynically that compared with the kind of writing that was supposed to bridge the gap between contemporary music and its audience, the music itself was easy. And to demonstrate this thesis, he carried out a hoax.

In 1961, the BBC's quality music station transmitted a concert which included music by Petrassi, Webern, Nono, Mozart and Zak. Piotr Zak, said the announcer, is of Polish extraction but now lives in Germany. He was born in 1939; his earliest music was conservative, but he recently came under the influence of Stockhausen and John Cage. *Mobile* takes its name from the aerial sculptures of John Calder. It consists of an electronic tape, against which two percussion players play music written down but giving scope for improvisation. The tape exploits the full range of the aural spectrum, controlled by strictly measurable quantities – frequency ratios, velocity graphs and decibel indices.

A few weeks later, Keller explained in a discussion programme 'what actually happened': he and the pianist Susan Bradshaw

> recorded a performance, if you can call it a performance, which was completely spontaneous . . . without a composer . . . [we] went into a studio and . . . bashed about on percussion instruments for about twelve minutes. We also had a special mike in a corner screened off and put through an echo chamber, where we produced the electronic noises . . . and the purpose of it all, and here I'm getting serious, was not a hoax. It was really an experiment, or if you like, I wanted to pose a problem. How far would this kind of thing be taken seriously?[74]

The incident subsequently turned into a little legend, in which the critics supposedly proved their gullibility. In fact, their reaction to what they had no reason to doubt was a genuine piece of music was on the whole fairly hostile. The anonymous critic in *The Listener* described it as 'a *farce d'atelier* which . . . has no possible claims to be considered as music . . . a series of the more unpleasant kinds of kitchen noises, accompanied by bangs and thumps, hisses, shrieks and whistles'. Donald Mitchell in *The Daily Telegraph* found it an unrewarding and limited enterprise, though he failed to distinguish between Keller's joke piece and the Nono: 'There was nothing, one felt, to "understand" here. It was only the composer's ingenuousness that was mysterious. . . . How demanding Mozart seems after the innocence of Mr. Nono and Mr. Zak!' *The Times* was more discerning:

> It was certainly difficult to grasp more than the music's broad outlines, partly because of the high proportion of unpitched sounds and partly because of their extreme diversity . . . Without some idea of what could be irrelevant, it is not easy to say what is not. It was more disappointing that such recognisably musical events as did occur seemed trivial and that the texture made so little sonorous appeal. Beside it, Nono's early Polifonica-Monodia-Ritmica shone as the model of clarity and controlled fantasy.

According to the man from *The Times*, Jeremy Noble, in the subsequent discussion programme, Keller had vividly demonstrated that in consequence of the total compositional freedom accepted by most contemporary composers, there was no difference in kind, only in degree, between a bad piece and Piotr Zak. Keller was gleeful. This showed, he claimed, that contemporary music had become self-defeating. Stockhausen, he pontificated:

> hasn't really faced this problem of communication at all, and therefore produces sounds which have exactly the same effect as Zak, although there is more behind them. Now, if it were a matter of a time-lag, if these sounds would gradually become comprehensible, I wouldn't regard it as a very serious problem, but in my opinion, this kind of thing is destined to remain partly incomprehensible. That is the contemporary problem in its extreme form.

But if the critics were not entirely taken in, what about the listeners? Some of the comments reported by the audience research department were naturally adverse, but there were also listeners who had found it stimulating, refreshing and enjoyable. According to one: 'If you could freeze this music, it would be printed circuits or racing bicycles. Completely fascinating . . . I enjoyed every hiss, whistle and bang. The contrast in musical cadence was wonderful, from the musical notes with harmonics to the almost totally dead sounds made by the tape recorder.' Another said: 'The ideas startle, shock, and yet coruscate in the mind after the performance.' And a third: 'What made me think this was more than a random assortment of squeaks, bashes and tinkles was that one waited expectantly for the next noise.'

Are these comments to be dismissed as the untutored and therefore irrelevant responses of merely emotional, visual or sensuous listeners? Do they sound like the attitudes of resentment listeners? (A not dissimilar 'experiment' was carried out in a concert of new composers in Oxford in 1969, when a young composer called Nigel Osborne led an improvising quartet in a totally unrehearsed performance with a tape of a piece of *musique concrète* which had been created quite independently. As maker of the tape I remember our glee when the item was rewarded with the longest round of applause of the evening.) Or is this Keller's 'contemporary problem' the other way round: not the fact that phoneys are possible but that everything John Cage says is true, and non-musical sounds are capable of becoming music? In that case, the critics, detecting the absence of structure in Piotr Zak, demonstrated only the structure of their own minds. The listeners, on the other hand, demonstrated a different way of listening altogether, in which music is not merely speaking to itself but finds itself in dialogue with the wider world.

This is more exciting, but entails more risks. As the philosopher Stanley Cavell puts it – as if in answer to Keller's amateur philosophy of the phoney, and with well-judged irony:

> I do not see how anyone who has experienced modern art can have avoided such experiences, and not just in the case of music. Is Pop Art art? Are canvases with a few stripes or chevrons on art? Are the novels of Raymond Roussel or Alain Robbe-Grillet? Are art movies? A familiar answer is that time will tell. But my question is: What will time tell? That certain departures in art-like pursuits have become established (among certain audiences, in textbooks, on walls, in college courses); that someone is treating them with the respect due, we feel, to art; that one no longer has the right to question their status? But in waiting for time to tell that, we miss what the present tells – that the dangers of fraudulence, and of trust, are essential to the experience of art.[75]

It is only poetic justice that by the end of the decade Stockhausen, who, at the time, was still writing music that at least contained notes – was creating pieces that were little more than sets of instructions for doing the same thing as the fictitious Piotr Zak.

Epilogue

From Handel to Hendrix

For the last thirty-six years of his life, George Frederick Handel lived in the fashionable neighbourhood of Mayfair, at number 25 Brook Street, where he died in 1759, aged seventy-four. Next door at number 23, two centuries and ten years later, lived the rock guitarist Jimi Hendrix, soon to die of a drugs overdose at the age of twenty-seven. In 1995, when fans of Hendrix announced a campaign for a blue plaque on the house to remember him, the Handel Trust dismissed the idea as inappropriate. Not so the committee which decides these things. When the plaque went up two years later, unveiled by another rock guitarist, Pete Townshend, the Handel camp called it 'dumbing down' the street. Townshend dismissed the complaint: 'There's been a lot of talk about whether or not a pop performer, a rock performer, a blues performer, whatever Jimi was, deserves to be on the building next door to George Frederic Handel, and I think he does.' Hendrix, he said, was extremely special as a musician and as a performer, 'he's up there for me with Miles Davis and Charlie Parker as somebody who was a virtuoso, an innovator. He was different, extraordinary and new.'[1]

The incident, and Townshend's comment, throw the history we have been considering in these pages into a stark perspective. Hendrix appears here symbolically as the negation of the tradition of musical composition at whose head stands his dead neighbour. From a position at the centre of musical life, transforming the aristocratic culture of the *ancien régime* into the new culture of the ascendant bourgeoisie, the classic figure of the composer has not only been banished to the margins but is now displaced by a new kind of musical hero. (A year later, as if to confirm this dethronement, a plan to turn both 25 and 23 Brook Street into a Handel Museum was abandoned after the Handel House Trust failed to raise sufficient funds to buy the house. A *Daily Telegraph* columnist piously lamented that the owners had now leased

the ground floor to a fashion shop, and 'a once-in-a-century opportunity' had fallen between the cracks of the system. 'We employ a
Minister for Heritage to allow history to slip through the fingers of
unanswerable quangos . . . A nation that prided itself on tradition has
fallen victim to the whims of fashion.')[2]

The affair stands in here for a massive sea-change in musical culture
which hard-boiled members of the traditional establishment still
resisted. Let us call it the transformation of Tin Pan Alley over more
than half a century by the culture industry (and often in spite of it)
into a popular musical domain replete with its own complex divisions
and distinctions of taste, its own hierarchy of musical endeavour, and,
by the 1960s, its own progressive artists. Coming on top of everything
else that threatened the public status of the traditional (and professional) composer, all this becomes a parallel musical domain on a
scale dwarfing the musical lifeworld of the days before electro-magnetic
mechanical reproduction, a domain which hugely outstripped the
social reach of traditional modes of music-making and relegated the
classical tradition to minority and elitist status. In this modern sphere
of popular music, a figure like Hendrix stands among the peaks, an
exceptional name not because of his outrageousness, the macho smash-
ing of guitars, the drug-taking, in short the persona which his public
image symbolized in the mass media – or in the projective identification
of his fans – but after and despite all this, for musical reasons: because
what he did for the electric guitar was like what Paganini did for the
violin. He thus came to represent the pinnacle of virtuoso performance,
the luminary by which all other rock guitarists would be judged. And
in the process, his playing took off, abandoning the formulaic limits of
rock music convention in favour of a free-flowing, spiritually liberating
instrumental virtuosity more readily associated with the modern jazz
club – or with that other performer at the Woodstock Festival of 1969,
the Indian sitar player Ravi Shankar.

What then is the real distance between Handel and Hendrix? Hendrix on Handel: 'I like Handel and Bach. Handel and Bach is like a
homework type of thing. You can't hear it with friends all the time. You
have to hear some things by yourself.'[3] Handel for Hendrix has become
a private experience, equally far removed from the public ceremony,
ritual, or conviviality, of the social environment for which Handel was
writing, as well as the public spaces, the clubs and open-air festivals, of
Hendrix's own music. Hendrix for the Handelians is anathema, and
probably not music at all, but noise.

For the French economist Jacques Attali, writing a book called *Noise*
in 1985, Hendrix is one of those who exemplifies the latest stage of

development in the political economy of music, the moment of rupture with the past in which 'composition can only emerge from the destruction of the preceding codes'. In Attali's scheme, this is not just the prerogative of a Boulez or a Cage, but also of popular figures like Hendrix or, for instance, Frank Zappa. (Indeed Zappa is an interesting example, since he ended up both composing electronically and also turning himself into a traditional composer, writing avant-garde scores which were then performed by Boulez with his ensemble in Paris.) If Attali would not deny Jimi Hendrix the terminology of composer, even though the blue plaque is content to call him a guitarist and songwriter, then this is because he sees precisely in figures like Davis, Parker, Hendrix and Zappa the disappearance of composition as a specialism, and the emergence not so much of a new music but a new way of making music, 'the advent of a radically new form of insertion of music into communication'.[4]

Attali's account is highly speculative and sometimes historically inaccurate, but nevertheless possesses a curious logic, with a certain relation to the version of the transformation of the musical public sphere presented in these pages. Attali proposes a sweeping view of musical history, and the relations between music and society, divided into four stages. The first he calls the stage of sacrifice, where the codes in music simulate the establishment of social order, as in the remarks of the ancient Chinese authority Ssu-ma Ch'ien: 'The sacrifices and music, the rites and the laws, have a single aim: it is through them that the hearts of the people are united, and it is from them that the method of good government arises.'[5] Hence also the association of music with religion. The second stage is that of representation, where music becomes a spectacle to be found in specific places – opera house and concert-hall – which belong to the emergence of bourgeois society and the rise of capitalism. The third stage is that of repetition, which appears at the end of the nineteenth century with the advent of recording. (There is a play on words here in French, in which *représentation* means performance as well as representation, and *répétition* also means rehearsal.) In this new stage, the network of music 'is no longer a form of sociality, an opportunity for spectators to meet and communicate', but rather a means of stockpiling music on a huge scale, which reflects 'a new stage in the organisation of capitalism, that of the repetitive mass production of all social relations'.[6]

The fourth stage, which we are currently entering, is what he calls, bizarrely, composition. As Susan McClary puts it in her afterword to Attali's text, his use of the term is somewhat strange, but then the word has become mystified, summoning up 'the figure of a semidivine being, struck by holy inspiration, and delivering forth ineffable delphic utterances'.[7] Historically this figure is a specialist in the notes on the page, who first emerges, as we saw at very outset of our inquiry, on the eve of the Renaissance. Against this, Attali counterposes the performer, who speaks through their instrument, and discovers in it a realm of freedom and unfinalized possibilities which is 'the negation of the division of roles and labour as constructed by the old codes'. He seems to be speaking of what is normally called improvisation, or in classical terminology extemporization; an art which in the past, indeed as recently as Mozart and Beethoven, the composer also often possessed to the highest degree. Notwithstanding, this is what Attali calls composing, or 'doing solely for the sake of doing', free from the compulsion 'to re-create the old codes in order to reinsert communication into them'. It consists in 'inventing new codes, inventing the message at the same time as the language. Playing for one's own pleasure, which alone can create the conditions for new communication.' And through what Attali calls a kind of 'innovative cognitive practice', this may also free the composing musician from the commodity relation imposed by recording. At least, attempts to break away from economic dependence on the record industry are condemned to failure unless the musicians are able to transcend themselves in this way.[8]

This description fits the figure of Hendrix remarkably well (except for the problem of the record companies). The model for the kind of musical hero which Hendrix embodied comes not from the traditional musical lifeworld, nor does it spring from the milieu of commercial popular music unaided, but – as indicated by Townshend's hesitation over what to call him: 'a pop . . . rock . . . blues performer, whatever Jimi was' – issues from the cross-fertilization of blues, rock and jazz within the heady milieu of 1960s counter-culture. In none of these domains is the composer any longer a central or special figure. In rock and blues, the composer is merely the person whose notes on the page entitle him to a royalty; what matters more is the way the notes are rendered by the personality of the performer. In jazz, the ambitions of a Duke Ellington had come to represent a false lead; jazz would not become a privileged site of musical innovation by emulating the traditional composer and the formal quasi-codification of the score, but by placing the sonic creativity of the performer at the centre; the composition is emphatically not the notes on the page, but in the sound of the instrument. The evolution of jazz after Ellington thus discovers, again precisely in figures like Charlie Parker and Miles Davis, its own avant-garde, firmly rooted in an art of improvisation and the moment of performance. These musicians, by the 1960s, have acquired an influence that spills over into neighbouring musical domains. Indeed Davis himself, from the side of jazz, was one of the first to experiment in the crossover between jazz and rock, at the same time as Hendrix; and was also one of Hendrix's strongest admirers.

Over the course of this process, an effect which had been noticed by Adorno before the war took on a new significance. In his earliest piece of writing on jazz, dating from 1933, Adorno referred to traces in jazz of the dissonant harmonies of the new music of the 'classical' avant-garde, which functioned like echoes of the gruesome dissonances which popular music normally avoided 'but which it seemed one could mingle here without danger'.[9] By the 1960s the jazz avant-garde had inverted this relation to create a radical idiom every bit as abrasive – harmonically, melodically, rhythmically – as their classical counterparts. Whether those who supported the Darmstadt tendency ever listened to them or not, jazz players like Ornette Coleman, John Coltrane or Archie Shepp were no less uncompromising in the demands they made on their listeners to enter new musical territory. This was the model, taken over into the realm of rock music, which Hendrix emulated on the electric guitar, in a style that incorporated a series of experimental effects and techniques which he variously borrowed and invented, and which hugely extended the range of sounds the instrument could produce; especially at full volume, when every touch of the instrument, from a sleeve brushing the strings to the performer's body bumping against the body of the guitar, affects what is heard. (The list of techniques is extensive: tremolo effects using the 'wang' bar on the Stratocaster, which he specially adapted for the purpose; wrist vibrato, use of the thumb and the little finger for chording and runs; a wide range of slide effects; changes of tuning to achieve off-pitch wobbles and inflections; alteration of the instrument's tone and volume controls; playing the neck of the instrument; and assorted electronic effects; plus, of course, his two most famous traits – plucking the strings with his teeth, and destroying the instrument to produce aggressive and destructive noises, gimmicks which he largely gave up.)[10]

The songs that he wrote (and delivered in a vocal style much influenced by Bob Dylan) became the musical material for extended improvised performance. As Townshend commented, unveiling the blue plaque, 'If you've only heard his recordings, you're only hearing a very small part of what Jimi's genius was about.' What he means can still be seen in the film of the 1969 Woodstock Festival, where, in an account dating from 1974, you can observe Hendrix's 'astonishing version of "The Star-Spangled Banner" complete with screams and wails and machine-gun bursts and diving, exploding bombs – all produced by one man . . . with nothing but his electric guitar. Mr Hendrix gave us the best vision not only of what an electric guitar can do, but of the almost mystical way in which electric guitarists relate to their instruments.'[11] The act of composition is here subsumed, through rehearsal, into the process of performance. (According to one of the musicians in the band at Woodstock, the conga player Juma Sultan, they played on that day with 'freedom of spirit', well rehearsed but without any plan.)[12] In any previous age, this type of music-making would have brought the performer great renown but only limited influence. In the age of recording, however, with its multiplier effect, the physical preservation of the performance gives it a life extended through space and time in which the innovations of a virtuoso performer can become as powerful a paradigm as a written score. Even better, the film brings back to life the scene and thus the moment of performance-composition itself (although, to follow Walter Benjamin, without its aura).

Hendrix's version of 'The Star-Spangled Banner' was both extremely controversial and highly paradoxical, an obviously political statement whose meaning was subject to different, not always compatible interpretations; at the same time an anthem of antiwar protest and a hymn of solidarity with the soldiers fighting the war. Here we can treat it as emblematic of the position which this new kind of musical creator occupies in the public sphere of the popular musical domain, or, in plain words, of the artist who speaks in a voice of their own about things that matter to the public that receives them. When Hendrix performed the piece in Los Angeles a few months before Woodstock, the *Los Angeles Times* accused him of cheap sensationalism; three years later, after his death, a Canadian writer called it 'a vision of cultural crisis . . . breakdown and chaos'.[13] The paradox can be located in the very space of performance. Woodstock has been described as 'the counter-culture's great white Bacchanalia', and 'a cosy affirmation of affluent, white middle-class angst about Vietnam as a metaphor for the moral bankruptcy of the state'.[14] If Hendrix, by some accounts, did not entirely share this position, his politics were those of a boy from a black working-class neighbourhood in Seattle, who escaped from his dead-end life by volunteering for the military, serving as a paratrooper until a broken ankle rendered him unfit. He may well have changed his views, but as late as 1967 he made remarks to British and Dutch music magazines which supported American action in Vietnam, although after that, in Sweden, he dedicated concerts to American draft-dodgers. Be that as it may, his musical development was in stark contrast to the ideological acquiescence of his lumpen origins; as a self-taught musician, he found what the authors of a book on 'Music and Social

Movements' call a 'nurturing community' in urban blues and folk circles, located within an expanded bohemian class that was found in Chicago, New York, and London.[15] Here, say Ron Eyerman and Andrew Jamison, Hendrix, in common with others like Janis Joplin, reinvented the blues tradition within the social and cultural context of the 1960s, reaching a youthful audience which, although predominantly middle class, white and suburban, was open to the transgression of national, cultural and ethnic boundaries. It was also politically sophisticated. The counterculture, they say, which embraced musicians like Hendrix, constituted 'an alternative public sphere' in which this music functioned 'as another kind of social theory', translating the political radicalism of relatively small coteries of political activists and critical intellectuals into a different and more accessible idiom. The best popular music of the time, they say, identified social problems, gave names to vague feelings of alienation and spiritual oppression, even offered poetic explanations; the music catered to a sense of need to belong, a sharing of a collective vision, which for a period linked the musical and the political. 'It worked only briefly, when the conditions allowed it; when the contextual factors that shaped it disappeared, the music was "incorporated" into more established channels.' The forces of commercialism reasserted themselves, at more or less same time that a reactionary ideology regained control of the political arena, and the delicate balance between culture and politics dissolved. This account may well be true. At any rate, to search the internet for his name almost thirty years later, for example, is to discover that in this new virtual public space, 'Jimi Hendrix' is just one more fetish object of pop culture.

'The Star-Spangled Banner' at Woodstock in 1969 was an exemplary moment. The black music scholar Samuel Floyd has called it one of the most significant events in American music history:

> The consecutive descending thirds that open the introduction, followed by Hendrix's unaccompanied 'talking' guitar passage, immediately identify this performance as ring based. As the performance progresses, Hendrix inserts 'calls' at 'the rocket's red glare' and 'comments' appropriately at 'the bombs bursting in air' and other 'telling' points. Here, Hendrix is a musical teller of the narrative, using his instrument in a manner similar to that of [both] African callers and the tone painters of the European classical tradition.[16]

It is part and parcel of this form of narration that Hendrix is not the composer of the tune but appropriates it in order to re-compose its public meaning. This explains why it becomes ambiguous – because the significance it acquires in the process originates and remains entirely in the public domain; it is an icon into which everyone reads their own presuppositions, apprehensions, dreams, desires and fantasies.

It is exemplary also because here, very clearly, some, at least, of the functions ascribed to the composer are evidently not a property of the notes, or of whether the notes are written down, but belong to the form of rapport which the musician who is recognized as their creator establishes with a public. This figure, it turns out, does not have to be a fully fledged composer in the old sense at all. Nevertheless, in appropriating the individual musical voice, music ratifies itself as an affirmation of society, community, fellowship, and association, a free realm where the imagination escapes the contingency of the everyday and the psyche is restored to itself. In this situation, the figure of the musical creator is not an instance of rarefied genius but a social creation, the embodiment of a social need, and, in a crucial sense, a product of the public sphere itself, indeed a testimony to the fact that, in spite of the subjugation of music to the commodity function, a public sphere in the realm of music still exists. In short, it serves more than inarticulate emotive needs and desires and becomes a rallying point, a focus of identification, a mediator of opinions and attitudes.

Perhaps, in this perspective, the distance from Handel to Hendrix is not so impossible to traverse, but only requires a step into a different symbolic order – in either direction.

Notes

1. Composer and Public: Shaping the Question

1. Isaiah Berlin, 'The Naïveté of Verdi', in *Against the Current: Essays in the History of Ideas*, ed. H. Hardy, Pimlico, 1997, p. 291.
2. See Max Weber, *The Rational and Social Foundations of Music*, Southern Illinois University Press/Feiffer & Simons, 1977. For a discussion, see my earlier book *Musica Practica*, Verso, 1994, pp. 59 ff.
3. See Chanan, *Musica Practica*, pp. 123–4.
4. Quoted in Lorenzo Bianconi, *Music in the Seventeenth Century*, Cambridge University Press, 1987, p. 39.
5. Ibid., p. 21.
6. Ibid., p. 65.
7. Jürgen Habermas, *The Structural Transformation of the Public Sphere*, Polity Press, 1989, p. 39.
8. Quoted in Michael Foss, *The Age of Patronage: The Arts in Society 1660–1750*, Hamish Hamilton, 1971, p. 77.
9. Habermas, *Structural Transformation*, p. 40.
10. Ibid., p. 25.
11. Richard Sennett, *The Fall of Public Man*, Faber & Faber, 1986, p. 17.
12. Ibid., pp. 81–2.
13. Habermas, *Structural Transformation*, p. 59.
14. Terry Eagleton, *The Ideology of the Aesthetic*, Blackwell, 1990, p. 19.
15. Habermas, *Structural Transformation*, p. 41.
16. *Grove's Dictionary of Music and Musicians*, 5th edn, Macmillan, 1966, vol. 2, p. 521.
17. Quoted in Paul Henry Láng, *George Frideric Handel*, Norton, 1966, p. 195.
18. George S. Rousseau, 'Love and Antiquities: Walpole and Gray on the Grand Tour', in *Perilous Enlightenment*, pp. 176–7. Quoted in Gary C. Thomas, 'Was George Frideric Handel Gay?', in Philip Brett, Elizabeth Wood and Gary Thomas, *Queering the Pitch: The New Gay and Lesbian Musicology*, Routledge, 1994, pp. 173–4.
19. Thomas, 'Was Handel Gay?' p. 174.
20. Ibid., p. 143.
21. Quoted in ibid., p. 144.
22. John Rosselli, *Singers of Italian Opera: The History of a Profession*, Cambridge University Press, 1992, pp. 105–6.
23. Quoted in ibid., p. 233.
24. Thomas, 'Was Handel Gay?', pp. 158–60.

25. Ibid., p. 177.
26. Ibid., pp. 177–8.
27. Quoted in ibid., p. 178.
28. Ibid., p. 182.
29. See Rosselli, *Singers of Italian Opera*, p. 58.
30. Stanley Cavell, 'Music Discomposed', in *Must We Mean What We Say?*, Cambridge University Press, 1976, p. 188.
31. Quoted in Max Graf, *Composer and Critic*, Kennikat, 1969, p. 80.
32. See Hans David and Arthur Mendel, eds, *The Bach Reader: A Life of Johann Sebastian Back in Letters and Documents*, Norton, 1966, p. 52.
33. T.W. Adorno, *Introduction to the Sociology of Music*, Seabury Press, 1976, p. 158.
34. Quoted in David and Mendel, eds, *The Bach Reader*, p. 249.
35. Paul Henry Láng, *Music in Western Civilisation*, Dent, 1942, p. 505.
36. Ibid., p. 507.
37. J.J. Rousseau, *Confessions*, Penguin, 1953, p. 358.
38. See Giorgio Pestelli, *The Age of Mozart and Beethoven*, Cambridge University Press, 1984, p. 47.
39. Quoted in Maurice Cranston, *Jean-Jacques: The Early Life and Work of Jean-Jacques Rousseau*, Penguin, 1987, p. 278.
40. Ibid., p. 263.
41. Jean-Philippe Rameau, *Treatise on Harmony*, New York, 1971, p. xxxv.
42. Ibid., p. xxxiii.
43. Rousseau, 'Lettre sur la musique française', in Oliver Strunk, ed., *Source Readings in Music History*, Norton, 1950, p. 647.
44. Cranston, *Jean-Jacques*, pp. 288–9.

2. Subjectivity and the Space of Music

1. Alejo Carpentier, 'Música y emoción', in *Ese musico que llevo dentro*, Editorial Letras Cubana, 1980, vol. 3, pp. 301–2. English translation, 'A Feeling for Music', *Times Literary Supplement*, 22 September 1972.
2. See Michael Chanan, *Musica Practica*, Verso, 1994, ch. 4; John Shepherd and Peter Wicke, *Music and Cultural Theory*, Polity Press, 1997, ch. 3.
3. Arthur Schopenhauer, 'The World as Will and Idea', in F. Tillman and S. Kahn, eds, *Philosophy of Art and Aesthetic*, Harper & Row, 1969, p. 288.
4. Terry Eagleton, *The Ideology of the Aesthetic*, Blackwell, 1990, p. 76. (This is almost the only time Eagleton mentions music, which seems to me odd in a study of a group of philosophers for whom music was supremely important.)
5. Ibid., p. 28.
6. Ibid., pp. 43, 42.
7. See Henri Lefebvre, *The Production of Space*, Blackwell, 1991.
8. For a detailed and illuminating account of the nature of the concert hall, see Christopher Small, *Musicking: The Meanings of Performing and Listening*, Wesleyan University Press, 1998.
9. Arthur Loesser, *Men, Women and Pianos*, Simon & Schuster, 1954, p. 386.
10. See Geoff Eley, 'Nations, Publics, and Political Cultures: Placing Habermas in the Nineteenth Century', in Craig Calhoun, ed., *Habermas and the Public Sphere*, MIT Press, 1992, p. 309; Joan Landes, *Women and the Public Sphere in the Age of the French Revolution*, Cornell, 1988, p. 46.
11. Eagleton, *Ideology*, p. 32.
12. Lawrence Kramer, *Franz Schubert: Sexuality, Subjectivity, Song*, Cambridge University Press, 1998, p. 28.

13. Quoted in Derek Watson, *Liszt*, Dent, 1989, p. 41.
14. See William Weber, *Music and the Middle Classes*, Croom Helm, 1975, p. 30.
15. Eley, 'Nations, Publics, and Political Cultures', pp. 299–301.
16. Joan Landes, 'The Public and the Private Sphere: A Feminist Reconsideration', in Johanna Meehan, ed., *Feminists Read Habermas*, Routledge, 1995, p. 95.
17. Habermas, *The Structural Transformation of the Public Sphere*, p. 29.
18. Quoted in Siegfried Kracauer, *Orpheus in Paris: Offenbach and the Paris of His Time*, Vienna House, 1972, p. 47.
19. Carl Dahlhaus, *Esthetics of Music*, Cambridge University Press, 1982, p. 24.
20. Ibid., p. 27.
21. All quoted in Lydia Goehr, *The Imaginary Museum of Musical Works: An Essay in the Philosophy of Music*, Oxford University Press, 1992, pp. 154–5.
22. Eric Blom, ed., *Mozart's Letters*, Penguin, 1956, pp. 181–2.
23. See Goehr, *The Imaginary Museum*, p. 209 and E. Forbes, ed., *Thayer's Life of Beethoven*, Princeton, 1970, p. 456.
24. See Jeffrey Kallberg, *Chopin at the Boundaries: Sex, History and Musical Genre*, Harvard University Press, 1996, pp. 4f.
25. Mikhail Bakhtin, *The Formal Method in Literary Scholarship*, Harvard University Press, 1985, ch. 7, pp. 131, 140.
26. Mikhail Bakhtin, *The Dialogic Imagination*, ed. Michael Holquist, University of Texas Press, 1981, p. 84.
27. Suzanne Langer, *Feeling and Form*, Routledge & Kegan Paul, 1953, p. 109.
28. Thomas Mann, *The Magic Mountain*, Penguin, 1960, p. 541.
29. Ibid., p. 114.
30. Karl Marx, *A Contribution to the Critique of Political Economy*, Lawrence & Wishart, 1971, p. 216.
31. Lorenzo Bianconi, *Music in the Seventeenth Century*, Cambridge University Press, 1987, pp. 98–9.
32. David Harvey, *The Condition of Postmodernity*, Blackwell, 1990.
33. Eagleton, *Ideology*, p. 73.
34. Marx to Engels, 28 January 1863.
35. For a detailed account, see Chanan, *Musica Practica*.
36. See Charles Rosen, *The Romantic Generation*, HarperCollins, 1996, pp. 73–4.
37. Christopher Small, *Music, Society, Education*, John Calder, 1980, pp. 88, 22.
38. Edward Said, *Musical Elaborations*, Chatto & Windus, 1991, p. 66.
39. Christopher Small, *Musicking: The Meanings of Performing and Listening*, Wesleyan University Press, 1998, pp. 28–9, 43.
40. Richard Sennett, *The Fall of Public Man*, Faber & Faber, 1986, p. 209.
41. T.W. Adorno, *Introduction to the Sociology of Music*, Seabury Press, 1976, pp. 104–5.
42. Quoted in William Weber, *Music and the Middle Classes*, Croom Helm, 1975, p. 98.
43. Ibid., p. 125.
44. Ibid., p. 102.
45. Walter Benjamin, 'The Work of Art in the Age of Mechanical Reproduction', in *Illuminations*, ed. Hannah Arendt, Schocken, 1969.
46. A.K. Holland, *Henry Purcell*, Penguin, 1948, p. 57.
47. See A.L. Lloyd, *Folk Song in England*, Paladin, 1967, pp. 329–32.

3. The First Viennese School

1. Ernst Roth, *The Business of Music: Reflections of a Music Publisher*, Cassell, 1969, p. 62.

2. Eric Blom, ed., *Mozart's Letters*, Penguin, 1956, p. 73.
3. Ibid., p. 88.
4. Ibid., p. 139.
5. See Volkmar Braunbehrens, *Mozart in Vienna 1781–1791*, Oxford University Press, 1991.
6. Giorgio Pestelli, *The Age of Mozart and Beethoven*, Cambridge University Press, 1984, pp. 142–3.
7. Braunbehrens, *Mozart in Vienna*, pp. 138–9. Mozart's alleged poverty is only one of the myths which Braunbehrens manages to refute. Another is the allegation that he died of poisoning, probably administered by the composer Antonio Salieri – a rumour enshrined by Pushkin in a play written in 1830, which was later turned into a short opera by Rimsky-Korsakov. First, he not only traces the sources of the rumour, but pointedly quotes the ageing Salieri's denial, reported by the pianist Moscheles, that it was he who was responsible. Secondly, by carefully sifting the evidence, Braunbehrens shows that Mozart must have died from an attack of rheumatic fever – which he had also suffered several times in his youth – and the treatment prescribed. As for Peter Shaffer's play *Amadeus*, and the film version of it by Milos Forman, 'not a single word, scene, or location, to say nothing of the behaviour and appearance displayed by the film's characters, has anything at all to do with historical reality', however brilliantly they exploit the dramatic possibilities of the material.

The includes the notion that Mozart was buried in a pauper's grave. Reviewing the reforms in burial practices enacted by the Emperor in 1784, Braunbehrens concludes: 'it was no longer common practice to accompany the body to the gravesite after the relocation of cemeteries outside city limits. Moreover . . . communal graves were the rule, individual graves the exception.' The nobility and wealthy bourgeoisie might be buried in family vaults; otherwise gravestones were permitted only along cemetery walls, for reasons of space, and the tending of individual graves was unknown. The reforms were motivated partly by the latest ideas about hygiene, partly by theological considerations: by discouraging unnecesssary expenditure, 'in the burial ceremony the outward appearance of equality was reestablished'. He traces the idea of the 'pauper's burial' to the biography of Mozart published in 1828 by Constanze's second husband, who wrote: 'the coffin was deposited in a common grave and every other expense avoided'. This description, says Braunbehrens, gives no clue that the same applied to the vast majority of the population. But since these were among the least popular of Joseph's reforms and were eventually dropped, by the time this account was written, a 'common' grave had become a rare form of interment and was naturally misunderstood as a sign of callousness or extreme poverty (pp. 409–22).
8. Walter Benjamin, 'Goethe: The Reluctant Bourgeois', *New Left Review*, 133, May–June 1982.
9. Blom, ed., *Mozart's Letters*, p. 204.
10. Charles Rosen, *The Classical Style*, Faber & Faber, 1971, pp. 196–7.
11. Kurt Weill, 'Commitment to Opera' in Kim Kowalke, *Kurt Weill in Europe*, UMI Research Press, 1979, p. 458.
12. Edward J. Dent, *Mozart's Operas*, Oxford Paperbacks, 1960, p. 102.
13. Braunbehrens, *Mozart in Vienna*, p. 84.
14. Ibid., pp. 75–6.
15. Ibid., p. 80.
16. Ibid., p. 76.
17. April Fitzlyon, *Lorenzo da Ponte*, John Calder, 1982.

32. T.W. Adorno, *In Search of Wagner*, Verso, 1984, p. 46.
33. See the intricate analysis in the chapter 'Liszt, Goethe, and Gender', in Lawrence Kramer, *Music as Cultural Practice, 1800–1900*, University of California Press, 1990, pp. 102–34.
34. Ibid., pp. 107–8.
35. Thomas Mann, *Pro and Contra Wagner*, Faber, 1985, pp. 96ff.
36. Lévi-Strausss, *The Raw and the Cooked*, p. 15.
37. Adorno, *In Search of Wagner*, p. 31.
38. Robert Donnington, *Wagner's Ring and Its Symbols*, Faber, 1963.
39. Mann, *Pro and Contra Wagner*, p. 108.
40. Adorno, *In Search of Wagner*, p. 40.
41. Roman Jakobson, *The Framework of Language*, Michigan Studies in the Humanities, University of Michigan, 1980, p. 91.
42. Lévi-Strauss, *The Raw and the Cooked*, p. 30.
43. T.W. Adorno, *Philosophy of Modern Music*, Sheed & Ward, 1973, p. 183.
44. Bernstein, *The Unanswered Question*, p. 365.
45. Adorno, *Philosophy of Modern Music*, p. 183.

6. Nationalism and the Market

1. T.W. Adorno, *Introduction to the Sociology of Music*, Seabury Press, 1976, p. 167.
2. Ibid., p. 159.
3. Béla Bartók, 'Nationalism and the Study of Popular Song' ('El estudio de los cantos populares y el nacionalismo') in *Escritos sobre música popular*, siglo xxi editores, Mexico, 1979, p. 76.
4. Michael Beckerman, 'The Master's Little Joke: Antonin Dvořák and the Mask of Nation', in Beckerman, ed., *Dvořák and His World*, Princeton, 1993, p. 140.
5. Ibid.
6. Ibid., p. 145.
7. Quoted in ibid., p. 146.
8. Leon Botstein in ibid., p. 26.
9. Quoted in M.D. Calvocoressi, *Mussorgsky*, Dent, 1974, p. 21.
10. Beckerman, ed., *Dvorak and His World*.
11. Joseph Horowitz in ibid., p. 96.
12. Quoted in ibid., p. 141.
13. Quoted in Botstein in ibid. p. 31.
14. Ibid., p. 36.
15. Ibid., p. 39.
16. Ibid., p. 19.
17. Joseph Horowitz, *Understanding Toscanini*, Knopf, 1987, p. 24.
18. Norman Lebrecht, *When the Music Stops: Managers, Maestros and the Corporate Murder of Classical Music*, Simon & Schuster, 1997, p. 41.
19. Quoted by Jacques Attali in *Noise*, Manchester University Press, 1985, p. 39.
20. See Michael Chanan, *Musica Practica*, Verso, 1994, p. 160.
21. Lebrecht, *When the Music Stops*, p. 64.
22. Carl Flesch, *Memoirs*, London 1957, quoted in Lebrecht, *When the Music Stops*, p. 65.
23. Karl Marx, *Capital*, vol. III, Lawrence & Wishart, 1972, pp. 386–7.
24. Attali, *Noise*, p. 40.
25. Mark Rose, *Authors and Owners: The Invention of Copyright*, Harvard University Press, 1993, p. 28.
26. Ibid., p. 32.

27. Quoted in ibid., p. 39.
28. Quoted in ibid., pp. 76, 77.
29. Ernst Roth, *The Business of Music: Reflections of a Music Publisher,* Cassell, 1969, p. 63.
30. Pierre-Michel Menger, *Le Paradoxe du Musicien. Le compositeur, le mélomane et l'état dans la société contemporaine,* Harmoniques Flammarion, 1983.
31. Alan Peacock and Ronald Weir, *The Composer in the Market Place,* Faber Music, 1975. Performance rights were instigated in Britain in 1833, and extended to cover musical composition in general in the Copyright Act 1842, but the system acquired a bad reputation through 'unscrupulous' operators who bought up copyrights in successful music 'for the sole purpose of enforcing penalties against . . . unwitting performers'. This practice led to new legislation in the 1880s (the Copyright Acts 1882 and 1888), which suspended performance rights unless they were specifically claimed by a notice on the title page. In fact many British publishers encouraged sale by printing a disclaimer, such as 'This song may be sung in public without fee or licence'.
32. Roth, *The Business of Music,* p. 55.
33. Jürgen Habermas, *The Structural Transformation of the Public Sphere,* Polity Press, 1989, p. 165.
34. Ibid., p. 172.
35. Hans Gal, ed., *The Musician's World,* Thames and Hudson, 1978, p. 372.
36. Habermas, *Structural Transformation,* p. 174.
37. Quoted in Renato Poggioli, *The Theory of the Avant-Garde,* Harvard University Press, 1968, p. 191.
38. Arnold Hauser, *The Social History of Art,* vol. 4, *Naturalism, Impressionism, the Film Age,* Vintage (undated), pp. 190–91.
39. Roth, *The Business of Music,* p. 55.
40. Walter Benjamin, *Baudelaire,* New Left Books, 1973, p. 165.
41. See Max Raphael, *Proudhon, Marx, Picasso,* Lawrence & Wishart, 1980, pp. 130, 132.
42. Arthur Loesser, *Men, Women and Pianos,* Simon & Schuster, 1954, p. 512.
43. Quoted in David Frisby, *Fragments of Modernity,* Polity Press, 1988, p. 42.
44. David Harvey, *Condition of Postmodernity,* Blackwell, 1990, p. 216.
45. Quoted in Stefan Jarocinski, *Debussy: Impressionism and Symbolism,* Euelenburg, 1976, p. 172.
46. Benjamin, *Baudelaire,* p. 119.
47. Poggioli, *Theory of the Avant-Garde,* p. 31.
48. Hauser, *The Social History of Art,* p. 167.
49. Benjamin, *Baudelaire,* pp. 174–5.
50. Jarocinski, *Debussy,* p. 31.
51. Poggioli, *Theory of the Avant-Garde,* p. 96.
52. Ibid., p. 75.
53. Jarocinski, *Debussy,* p. 94.
54. Quoted in ibid., p. 89.
55. Eric Hobsbawm, *The Age of Empire 1875–1914,* Abacus, 1994, p. 232.
56. Quoted in Poggioli, *Theory of the Avant-Garde,* p. 92.
57. Stéphane Mallarmé, 'Music and Literature', in O.B. Hardison, ed., *Modern Continental Literary Criticism,* Peter Owen, 1964, p. 178.
58. Quoted in Frisby, *Fragments of Modernity,* p. 45.
59. Quoted in Jarocinski, *Debussy,* p. 11.
60. Arnold Schoenberg, 'Composition with Twelve Tones', in *Style and Idea,* Faber & Faber, 1975; translation from the 1950 edition, p. 104, as quoted in Jarocinski, *Debussy,* p. 19.

61. Richard Hamann, *Impressionismus in Leben und Kunst*, cited in Jarocinski, *Debussy*, p. 17.
62. Ibid., p. 67.

7. Modernism, or *Nervenkunst*

1. See Franz Kuna, 'Vienna and Prague 1890–1928', in Malcolm Bradbury and James McFarlane, eds, *Modernism, 1890–1930*, Penguin, 1976, p. 122.
2. Carl Schorske, *Fin-de-siècle Vienna*, Weidenfeld & Nicolson, 1980.
3. Allan Janik and Stephen Toulmin, *Wittgenstein's Vienna*, Simon & Schuster, 1973, p. 53.
4. Ibid., pp. 30, 37.
5. Robert Musil, *The Man without Qualities*, vol. 1, Capricorn, 1965, p. 33.
6. Cited in Janik and Toulmin, *Wittgenstein's Vienna*, p. 46.
7. Eric Hobsbawm, *The Age of Empire: 1875–1914*, Abacus, 1994, p. 235.
8. T.W. Adorno, *Mahler, une physionomie musicale*, Les Éditions de Minuit, 1976, p. 41.
9. Natalie Bauer-Lechner, *Recollections of Gustav Mahler*, Faber & Faber, 1980, pp. 155–6.
10. Adorno, *Mahler*, p. 118; Deryck Cooke, 'Mahler's Melodic Thinking', in *Vindications*, Faber & Faber, 1982, p. 97.
11. Cooke, *Vindications*, pp. 102, 107.
12. Adorno, *Mahler*, p. 38.
13. Nicholas Slonimsky, *Lexicon of Musical Invective*, University of Washington Press, 1969, p. 121.
14. Alma Mahler, *Memoirs and Letters*, John Murray, 1968, p. 101.
15. Theodor Reik, *The Haunting Melody, Psychoanalytic Experiences in Life and Music*, Spanish edn, *Variaciones psicoanalíticas sobre un tema de Mahler*, Taurus, 1975, p. 76.
16. Adorno, *Mahler*, p. 217.
17. See Isaac Deutscher, *The Non-Jewish Jew and Other Essays*, Merlin, 1968.
18. E.P. Thompson, *The Making of the English Working Class*, Penguin 1968.
19. Adorno, *Mahler*, p. 75.
20. Ibid., pp. 58–9.
21. Friedrich Nietzsche, *The Birth of Tragedy*, Doubleday Anchor, 1956, p. 106 and *passim*.
22. Quoted by Donald Mitchell in *Gustav Mahler: The Early Years*, Rockliff, 1958, p. 115.
23. Adorno, *Mahler*, p. 95.
24. Michael Chanan, *Musica Practica*, Verso, 1994, p. 89.
25. Schorske, *Fin-de-siècle Vienna*, p. 195.
26. Frank J. Sulloway, *Freud, Biologist of the Mind*, Fontana, 1980, p. 468.
27. Alma Mahler, *Memoirs*, p. 82.
28. Nietzsche, *The Birth of Tragedy*, p. 43.
29. Knut Martner, ed., *Selected Letters of Gustav Mahler*, Faber, 1979, p. 197.
30. Alma Mahler, *Memoirs*, p. 19.
31. Henry-Louis de la Grange, *Mahler*, Gollancz, 1976, p. 686.
32. Ernest Jones, *Freud*, Penguin, 1964, pp. 358–9.
33. See, in addition to Reik, especially Jack Diether, 'Mahler and Psychoanalysis', *Psychoanalysis and the Psychoanalytical Review*, Winter 1958; David Holbrook, *Gustav Mahler and the Courage to be*, Vision, 1975; Robert Still, 'Gustav Mahler and Psychoanalysis', *American Imago*, Fall 1960.

34. Adorno, *Mahler*, p. 109.

35. Schorske, *Fin-de-siècle Vienna*, p. 126.

36. Ibid., p. 43.

37. Pierre Boulez, 'Mahler Now', *New York Review of Books*, 28 October 1976, pp. 37–40.

38. T.W. Adorno, *Philosophy of Modern Music*, Sheed & Ward, 1973, p. 39.

39. H.H. Stuckenschmidt, *Arnold Schoenberg: His Life, World and Work*, John Calder, 1977, p. 183.

40. Willi Reich, *Alban Berg*, Thames & Hudson, 1965, p. 118.

41. Quoted in Thomas Szasz, *Karl and the Soul-Doctors*, Routledge & Kegan Paul, 1977, p. 24.

42. Arnold Schoenberg, *Harmonielehre*, Faber & Faber, 1978, pp. 416–17.

43. Ibid., p. 325.

44. Stuckenschmidt, *Schoenberg*, p. 187.

45. Quoted by Frank Whitford in a radio talk on BBC Radio 3, November 1988.

46. Letter of 14 January 1911, in Miesel, ed., *Voices of German Expressionism*, Prentice-Hall, 1970, pp. 67–8; see also Stuckenschmidt, *Schoenberg*, pp. 141–2.

47. See the reproductions in Josef Rufer, *The Works of Arnold Schoenberg: A Catalogue of His Compositions, Writings and Paintings*, Faber, 1962.

48. Stuckenschmidt, *Schoenberg*, p. 189.

49. Alma Mahler, *Memoirs*, p. 182.

50. Miesel, ed., *Voices of German Expressionism*, p. 67.

51. Quoted by Whitford on Radio 3.

52. Ibid.

53. Programme note by Schoenberg in Ursula V. Rauchhaupt, ed., *Schoenberg, Berg, Webern, The String Quartets, A Documentary Study*, booklet accompanying the recordings by La Salle Quartet, DGG 2561 050–054.

54. Translation by Carl Engel in ibid.

55. Quoted in ibid., p. 81.

56. Walter Benjamin, 'Karl Kraus', in *One-Way Street*, New Left Books, 1979, p. 260.

57. See Ernst Krenek, 'Karl Kraus and Arnold Schoenberg' in *Exploring Music*, Calder & Boyars, 1966.

58. Quoted in Szasz, *Karl Kraus and the Soul-Doctors*, p. 33.

59. Quoted in Janik and Toulmin, *Wittgenstein's Vienna*, p. 89.

60. Benjamin, 'Karl Kraus', p. 269.

61. Pierre Boulez, *Orientations*, Faber, 1986, p. 331.

62. Ibid., p. 335.

63. Stuckenschmidt, *Schoenberg*, p. 204.

64. Peter Heyworth, *Klemperer*, vol. 1, Cambridge University Press, 1983, p. 74.

65. Igor Stravinsky and Robert Craft, *Dialogues and a Diary*, Faber, 1968, pp. 104–6.

66. According to Henri Quittard in a review in *Le Figaro*, quoted in Richard Buckle, *Nijinsky*, Weidenfeld & Nicolson, 1971, p. 289.

67. Letter to Robert Godet, 9 June 1913, quoted in Buckle, *Nijinsky*, p. 290.

68. Igor Stravinsky and Robert Craft, *Memories and Commentaries*, Faber, 1981, p. 31.

69. André Boucourechliev, *Stravinsky*, Gollancz, 1987, p. 44.

70. Quoted in Buckle, *Nijinsky*, p. 158.

71. Ibid., p. 159.

72. Quoted in ibid., p. 198.

73. Ibid., p. 159.

74. Igor Stravinsky, *An Autobiography*, Steuer, 1958, p. 31.

75. Igor Stravinsky and Robert Craft, *Expositions and Developments*, Faber, 1981, pp. 147–8.

76. Boucourechliev, *Stravinsky*, pp. 65, 71.

77. Quoted in Buckle, *Nijinsky*, p. 300.
78. Igor Stravinsky and Robert Craft, *Conversations with Igor Stravinsky*, Faber, 1959, p. 46.
79. Quoted in Buckle, *Nijinksky*, pp. 300–301.
80. Ibid., p. 301.
81. Adorno, *Philosophy of Modern Music*, p. 147.
82. Ibid.
83. Ibid., p. 148.
84. Ibid., pp. 35–6.
85. Hamish Milne, *Bartók*, Omnibus, 1987, p. 55.
86. Georg Lukács, *Record of a Life*, Verso, 1983, p. 60.
87. Quoted in Milne, *Bartók*, p. 56.
88. Lukács, *Record of a Life*, p. 40.
89. György Lukács, 'El Mandarin Milagroso contra la alienacion' ('The Miraculous Mandarin against Alienation'), in Béla Bartók, *Escritos sobre música popular*, Siglo Veintiuno, 1979, pp. 240f.
90. See Chanan, *Musica Practica*, pp. 210ff.
91. Schoenberg, *Harmonielehre*, p. 419.
92. Quoted in Milne, *Bartók*, p. 32.
93. Slonimsky, *Lexicon*, p. 40.
94. Yehudi Menuhin, *Unfinished Journey*, Macdonald & Jane's, 1977, pp. 166–7.

8. The Jazz Age

1. Eric Hobsbawm, *The Age of Empire, 1875–1914*, Abacus, 1994, p. 235.
2. On the record industry, see Michael Chanan, *Repeated Takes*, Verso, 1995; on the cinema, see Chanan, *The Dream that Kicks: The Prehistory and Early Years of Cinema in Britain*, 2nd edn, Routledge, 1996.
3. Hobsbawm, *The Age of Empire*, p. 232.
4. Darius Milhaud, *Notes without Music*, Calder & Boyars, 1967, p. 69.
5. Ibid., p. 161.
6. Alejo Carpentier, *Ese músico que llevo dentro*, Editorial Letras Cubana, 1980, vol. 1, pp. 47–8.
7. Ibid., p. 44.
8. Glenn Watkins, *Pyramids at the Louvre: Music, Culture and Collage from Stravinsky to the Postmodernists*, Belknap Press of Harvard University Press, 1994, p. 115.
9. Milhaud, *Notes without Music*, p. 102.
10. Ibid., pp. 117–18.
11. Watkins, *Pyramids at the Louvre*, p. 117.
12. Ibid., p. 101.
13. Hamish Milne, *Bartók*, Omnibus, 1987, p. 73.
14. Quoted in John Willett, *The New Sobriety: Art and Politics in the Weimar Period, 1917–1933*, Thames & Hudson, 1978, p. 99.
15. Kurt Weill, 'Opera – Where To?', in Kim Kowalke, *Kurt Weill in Europe*, UMI Research Press, 1979, p. 507. Originally published in the *Berliner Tageblatt*, 31 October 1929.
16. Quoted in Ian Kemp, *Paul Hindemith*, Oxford University Press, 1970.
17. Hanns Eisler, *A Rebel in Music*, Seven Seas, 1978, p. 59.
18. See Willett, *The New Sobriety*; other details in this paragraph are drawn from Stephen Hinton, 'Weill: *Neue Sachlichkeit*, Surrealism, and *Gebrauchsmusik*', in Kim Kowalke, ed., *A New Orpheus: Essays on Kurt Weill*, Yale University Press, 1986, pp. 61ff.

19. Emil Utitz, writing in 1929, quoted in Hinton, 'Weill, *Neue Sachlichkeit*, Surrealism, and *Gebrauchsmusik*', p. 62.

20. David Drew in the accompanying booklet to the recording by the London Sinfonietta, DGG 2563 584.

21. Kurt Weill, 'Concerning the Gestic Character of Music', in Kowalke, ed., *Kurt Weill in Europe*, pp. 491f.

22. Kurt Weill, 'The Stylization of Opera', in ibid., ch. IX, Section 4.

23. Martin Esslin, *Brecht: A Choice of Evils*, Eyre Methuen, 1980, p. 124.

24. Kurt Weill in Kowalke, *Kurt Weill in Europe*, pp. 486–8.

25. Both letters, ibid., pp. 486–7; translation revised.

26. Quoted by Christopher Hailey, 'Creating a Public, Addressing a Market: Kurt Weill and Universal Edition', in Kowalke, ed., *Kurt Weill in Europe*, p. 25.

27. Ibid., p. 35.

28. Ernst Roth, *The Business of Music: Reflections of a Music Publisher*, Cassell, 1969, pp. 57–8.

29. Hans Heinsheimer, *Give My Regards to Aïda*, Knopf, 1968, pp. 122–3.

30. Hailey, 'Creating a Public', p. 29.

31. Kurt Weill, 'Shifts in Musical Composition', in Kowalke, ed., *Kurt Weill in Europe*, pp. 478–80.

32. Kurt Weill, 'Opera – Where To?', in Kowalke, ed., *Kurt Weill in Europe*, p. 506.

33. Hinton, 'Weill: *Neue Sachlichkeit*, Surrealism, and *Gebrauchsmusik*', p. 68.

34. Quoted in ibid.

35. Quoted in ibid.

36. David Drew, entry on Weill in *New Grove Dictionary of Music and Musicians*, quoted in Kowalke, ed., *A New Orpheus*, p. 7.

37. Kowalke in Kowalke, ed., *A New Orpheus*, p. 8.

38. Ibid., pp. 8–9.

39. Frederick Jacobi, in Edward Jablonski, *Gershwin Remembered*, Faber & Faber, 1992, pp. 125–6.

40. Olin Downes, in ibid., p. 127.

41. Paul Rosenfeld, in ibid., p. 120.

42. Zora Neale Hurston, writing in Nancy Cunard's *Negro* (1935), quoted in Watkins, *Pyramids at the Louvre*, p. 175.

43. Watkins, *Pyramids at the Louvre*, p. 197.

44. Quoted in ibid., pp. 199–200.

45. Virgil Thomson in Jablonski, *Gershwin Remembered*, p. 124.

46. Rudi Blesh in ibid., p. 130.

47. Edward Morrow, in Mark Tucker, ed., *The Duke Ellington Reader*, Oxford University Press, 1993, pp. 114–17.

48. Watkins, *Pyramids at the Louvre*, p. 198, citing Gunther Schuller and Graham Collier.

49. Ibid., p. 195.

50. John Edward Hasse, *Beyond Category: The Life and Genius of Duke Ellington*, Omnibus, 1995, p. 89.

51. Igor Stravinsky and Robert Craft, *Dialogues and a Diary*, Faber, 1968, p. 54.

52. Mike Hobart, 'The Political Economy of Bop', in *Media, Culture and Society*, vol. 3, no. 3, July 1981, p. 265.

53. Quoted in Samuel A. Floyd, 'Music in the Harlem Renaissance: An Overview', in Floyd, ed., *Black Music in the Harlem Renaissance*, University of Tennessee Press, 1993, pp. 18–19.

54. Ibid.

55. Ron Eyerman and Andrew Jamison, *Music and Social Movements*, Cambridge

University Press, 1998, p. 83. See also Ellington's own account in Tucker, ed., *The Ellington Reader*, p. 49.

56. Paul Gilroy, *The Black Atlantic: Modernity and Double Consciousness*, Verso, 1993, p. 88.
57. Quoted in ibid., p. 92.
58. Floyd, 'Music in the Harlem Renaissance', p. 3.
59. David Levering Lewis, ed., *The Portable Harlem Renaissance Reader*, Penguin, 1994, p. xv.
60. Ibid.
61. Mark Tucker in Floyd, ed., *Black Music in the Harlem Renaissance*, p. 112.
62. Ibid., p. 120.
63. Quoted in ibid., p. 121; for Villa-Lobos, see above, pp. 240–41.
64. Watkins, *Pyramids at the Louvre*, p. 188.
65. Tucker, ed., *The Ellington Reader*, p. 43.
66. H.A. Overstreet in ibid., pp. 98–102.
67. Ellington in ibid., pp. 46–50.
68. R.D. Darrell in ibid., pp. 59–61.

9. Towards Postmodernism

1. I have traced the history of recording in my book *Repeated Takes: A Short History of Recording and Its Effects on Music*, Verso, 1995.
2. *Queen of Fruit*, dir. Dominic Scherrer, 1992.
3. Jürgen Habermas, *The Structural Transformation of the Public Sphere*, Polity Press, 1989, p. 171.
4. 'Contemporary Music and the Public', in Lawrence Kritzman, ed., *Michel Foucault: Interviews and Other Writings 1977–1984*, Routledge, 1990, p. 317.
5. Walter Benjamin, 'The Work of Art in the Age of Mechanical Reproduction', in *Illuminations*, Schocken, 1969.
6. R.D. Darrell in Mark Tucker, ed., *The Duke Ellington Reader*, Oxford University Press, 1993, p. 61.
7. See Chanan, *Repeated Takes*, p. 63.
8. Kurt Weill, 'A Note Concerning *Das Berliner Requiem*', in Kim Kowalke, *Kurt Weill in Europe*, UMI Research Press, 1979, pp. 503–5.
9. Kurt Weill, 'Criticism of Contemporary Creative Works', in ibid., pp. 499f.
10. T.W. Adorno, *Introduction to the Sociology of Music*, Seabury Press, 1976, p. 148.
11. Quoted in Nicholas Slonimsky, *Lexicon of Musical Invective*, University of Washington Press, 1969, p. 152.
12. Quoted in H.H. Stuckenschmidt, *Arnold Schoenberg: His Life, World and Work*, John Calder, 1977, pp. 177–8.
13. Benjamin Britten, 'Variations on a Critical Theme', *Opera*, March 1952.
14. *The Times*, 26 September 1936.
15. *The Times*, 9 April 1934.
16. *The Times*, 19 October 1935.
17. *The Times*, 19 August 1938.
18. Andrew Lumsden, *New Statesman*, 11 April 1986.
19. Adorno, *Sociology of Music*, p. 134.
20. Christopher Small, *Musicking: The Meanings of Performing and Listening*, Wesleyan University Press, 1998, p. 19.
21. Ibid., p. 25.
22. Alan Durant, *The Condition of Music*, Macmillan, 1984, p. 34.
23. Small, *Musicking*, p. 27.

24. Adorno, *Introduction to the Sociology of Music*.

25. Quoted in Max Graft, *Composer and Critic*, Kennikat, 1969, p. 212.

26. Foucault, 'Contemporary Music and the Public', p. 316.

27. See, for example, the writings of Dick Hebdidge and Simon Frith.

28. Quoted in Jonathan Rée, *I See a Voice: A Philosophical History of Language, Deafness and the Senses*, HarperCollins, 1999, p. 36.

29. Adorno, *Sociology of Music*, p. 14.

30. Evelyn Wilcock, '"Über Jazz" and the 1934–7 British Jazz Debate', *Telos* 107, 1996, pp. 63–80.

31. Thomas Mann, *The Genesis of a Novel*, Secker & Warburg, 1961, p. 18.

32. Ibid., p. 38.

33. Ibid., pp. 40–41.

34. Quoted in Patrick Carnegy, *Faust as Musician: A Study of Thomas Mann's Novel Doctor Faustus*, Chatto & Windus, 1973, pp. 168–70.

35. Jean-François Lyotard, 'Adorno as the Devil', *Telos* 19, Spring 1974.

36. Ibid., original emphasis.

37. Ernst Roth, *The Business of Music: Reflections of a Music Publisher*, Cassell, 1969, p. 67.

38. Umberto Eco, *The Open Work*, Hutchinson Radius, 1989, p. 143.

39. Luciano Berio, *Two Conversations*, Marion Boyars, 1985, p. 61.

40. Andrea Lanza, *Historia de la Musica*, vol. 12, 'El siglo XX', Third Part, Turner Musica, 1980, pp. 96–8.

41. Quoted in Paul Griffiths, *Modern Music: The Avant-Garde since 1945*, Dent, 1981, p. 61.

42. As far as the debate about Strauss's politics is concerned, I agree with the Italian musicologist Andrea Lanza: 'The void created by Nazism, not least in cultural matters, allows no excuses: nothing remains of the culture of the Nazi epoch, and even its most prestigious exponents, like Richard Strauss, Wilhelm Furtwängler, Martin Heidegger and others, sympathisers before the establishment of the regime, came to feel the heavy shadow of tragic complicity.' Lanza, *Historia de la Musica*, p. 58.

43. Quoted in Reginald Smith Brindle, *The New Music*, Oxford University Press, 1975, p. 41.

44. Fredric Jameson, *Postmodernism, or, The Cultural Logic of Late Capitalism*, Verso, 1991.

45. Ibid.

46. Pierre Boulez, *Orientations*, Faber, 1986, p. 73.

47. Quoted in Joan Peyser, *Boulez*, Cassell, 1977, p. 67.

48. Roland Barthes, *Selected Writings*, ed. Susan Sontag, Fontana, 1983, p. 51.

49. Umberto Eco, *The Open Work*, Hutchinson Radius, 1989, pp. 1–23.

50. H.H. Stuckenschmidt, *Twentieth Century Music*, Weidenfeld & Nicolson, 1969, p. 214.

51. H. Eimert, 'The Composer's Freedom of Choice', *Die Reihe* 3, Universal Edition, 1960.

52. Quoted in Michael Nyman, *Experimental Music: Cage and Beyond*, Studio Vista, 1974, p. 23.

53. David Drew, 'Modern French Music', in Howard Hartog, ed., *European Music in the Twentieth Century*, Penguin, 1961, p. 309.

54. Quoted in Nyman, *Experimental Music*, p. 23.

55. Eco, *The Open Work*, p. 18.

56. John Cage speaking at the Almeida Festival in London, July 1990, on his last visit to England before his death.

57. Quoted in Wim Mertens, *American Minimal Music*, Kahn & Averill, 1988, p. 106.

58. See Pierre Boulez, 'Alea', in *Relevés d'Apprenti*, Seuil, 1966.

59. Quoted in Nyman, *Experimental Music*, p. 2.
60. John Cage, *A Year from Monday, Lectures and Writings*, Marion Boyars, 1976, p.53.
61. 'The Politics of Music', dir. Michael Chanan, BBC2 *Arena*, 1972.
62. Interview with Boulez in 'Pierre Boulez: A Life in Seven Chapters', BBC2, 3 February 1999.
63. Georgina Born, *Rationalizing Culture: IRCAM, Boulez and the Institutionalization of the Avant-Garde*, University of California Press, 1995, p. 95.
64. Pierre-Michel Menger, *Le Paradoxe du Musicien: Le compositeur, le mélomane et l'état dans la société contemporaine*, Flammarion, 1983, p. 223.
65. Born, *Rationalizing Culture*, p. 79.
66. Quoted in Menger, *Le Paradoxe du Musicien*, p. 225.
67. Foucault, 'Contemporary Music and the Public', pp. 316–17. Translation slightly amended.
68. Boulez in 'The Politics of Music', dir. Michael Chanan, BBC2 *Arena*, 1972.
69. 'I am for invasion': Pierre Boulez interviewed by Malcolm Griffiths, *Time Out*, 14–20 January 1972.
70. Norman Lebrecht, *The Maestro Myth*, Simon & Schuster Pocket Books, 1997, p. 183.
71. Quoted in Joan Peyser, *Leonard Bernstein*, Bantam, 1987, p. 136.
72. Ibid., p. 138.
73. The columnist was Tom Wolfe. See Lebrecht, *The Maestro Myth*, p. 186.
74. Quotations from this programme are taken from a transcript of the broadcast.
75. Stanley Cavell, *Must We Mean What We Say?*, Cambridge University Press, 1976, p. 189.

Epilogue: From Handel to Hendrix

1. Stuart Millar, 'Hendrix joins the Handel blue plaque band', *Guardian*, 15 September 1997.
2. Norman Lebrecht, 'Is this how to treat England's greatest ever musician?', *Daily Telegraph*, 13 May 1998.
3. Quoted in Caesar Glebbeek, 'Too Hot to Handel?', *UniVibes* 18, May 1995.
4. Jacques Attali, *Noise: The Political Economy of Music*, Manchester University Press, 1985, pp. 134, 135.
5. Quoted in ibid., p. 29.
6. Ibid., p. 32.
7. Ibid. p. 156.
8. Ibid., ch. 5 *passim*.
9. Quoted in Evelyn Wilcock, ' "Uber Jazz" and the 1934–7 British Jazz Debate', *Telos* 107, 1996, p. 75.
10. See Don Menn, 'Jimi's Favorite Guitar Techniques', in Chris Potash, ed., *The Jimi Hendrix Companion: Three Decades of Commentary*, Omnibus, 1996, pp. 83–7.
11. John Roxwell, 'How the Electric Guitar Became a Way of Music', *New York Times*, 15 July 1974, in ibid.
12. Harry Shapiro and Caesar Glebbeek, *Jimi Hendrix, Electric Gypsy*, Mandarin, 1990, p. 385.
13. Bob Hicks, 'Jimi Hendrix: A Memorial', in Potash, *The Jimi Hendrix Companion*, p. 209.
14. See ibid., and Shapiro and Glebbeek, *Jimi Hendrix, Electric Gypsy*, p. 385.
15. See Ron Eyerman and Andrew Jamison, *Music and Social Movements*, Cambridge University Press, 1998, pp. 130–39.
16. Samuel A. Floyd, 'From the Power of Black Music', in Potash, *The Jimi Hendrix Companion*, pp. 131–2.

Index